Irene E. Bliss

Hazel Henry Litterick

Vera Bonner

CHILCOTIN:
PRESERVING PIONEER MEMORIES

VEERA BONNER
IRENE E. BLISS
HAZEL HENRY LITTERICK

The authors' mother, Hattie Witte, with their six-horse freight wagon on the "road" through Bull Canyon in the 1920s. Although Mrs. Witte was a feminine woman who loved rings and pretty things, she took a man's place beside her husband when he needed help with ranch work.

PHOTO CREDITS

Most of the photos are from pioneer families, but the photographers in many cases are unknown. The authors have given credit to all photos which they can identify. For those that were missed, they would appreciate being informed so that credit can be given in a future edition.

Bayliff, T.: 100, 144, 276, 278, 281; Blenkinsop, N.: 54, 58, 181, 193, 219, 220, 224, 272; Bonner, Veera: OFC, 1, 103, 108, 149, 151, 176, 228, 269, 309, 313, 317, 363; Bracewell, Gerry: 352, 353, 354; Clemson, Donovan: 239, 242, 305, 308, 322, 406; Durrell, F.: 64; Fosbery, Bob: 222; Fosbery, Tex: 48; Glenbow-Alberta Institute: 364; Harrington, Richard: 125, 140, 142, 313, 381, 417, OBC; Heritage House: 42, 215, 269, 298; Hodgson, W. and C.: 81, 163, 268; James, Lise: 6; Lee family: 12, 35, 36, 123, 134, 135, 136, 143; Meldrum, B.: 38; Moon, Charlie: 48; Provincial Archives of B.C.: 9, 17, 19, 21, 32, 115, 145, 148, 201, 358, 391, 416; Public Archives of Canada: 125; Roberts, Dr. John: 29; Robertson, Phil: 295; Scallon, Kevin: 258; Stangoe, Irene: 36; Telford, V.: 301; Tourism B.C.: 137, 148; Wilson, Isabel: 381; Witte family: 85, 120, 127, 130, 146, 154, 171-173, 182, 213, 243, 244, 249, 250, 252, 253, 407, 408; Vancouver City Archives: 33, 35, 239; Vancouver Public Library: 27, 162; Vancouver Sun: 204. The drawing on page 106 is by Tom Hunter, all others by Hazel H. Litterick.

Copyright © 1995 Veera Bonner, Irene E. Bliss, Hazel H. Litterick

Canadian Cataloguing in Publication Data

Bonner, Veera.
  Chilcotin

  ISBN 1-895811-34-1

  1. Frontier and pioneer life – British Columbia – Chilcotin
River Region. 2. Chilcotin River Region (B.C.) – Biography.
3. Chilcotin River Region (B.C.) – History. I. Bliss, Irene.
II. Litterick, Hazel. III. Title.
FC3845.C48Z48 1995   971.1'75'0922   C95-910044-X
F1089.C48B66 1995

First Edition – 1995

HERITAGE HOUSE PUBLISHING COMPANY LTD.
#8, 17921 – 55 Avenue, Surrey, B.C.   V3S 6C4

Printed in Canada

THAT'S CHILCOTIN
Veera Witte

When you've gazed on a country
That's timbered and green
And you've kind of a hunch
It's the best you have seen:
That's Chilcotin, my friend, that's Chilcotin!

When you've travelled 'way back
Where the mountains are steep;
And you've camped 'neath the stars
In the hush of the deep;
And you've learned of the spell
That the wilderness holds
When the winds blow at night
As the darkness unfolds
O'er the silent blue hills of Chilcotin.

Then wherever you go
And whatever you do
They say these lone trails
Will keep calling you.
'Till some day once again
All your bundles you'll pack
And I'll bet my last cent
You'll be headin' right back
To Chilcotin, my friend, to Chilcotin!

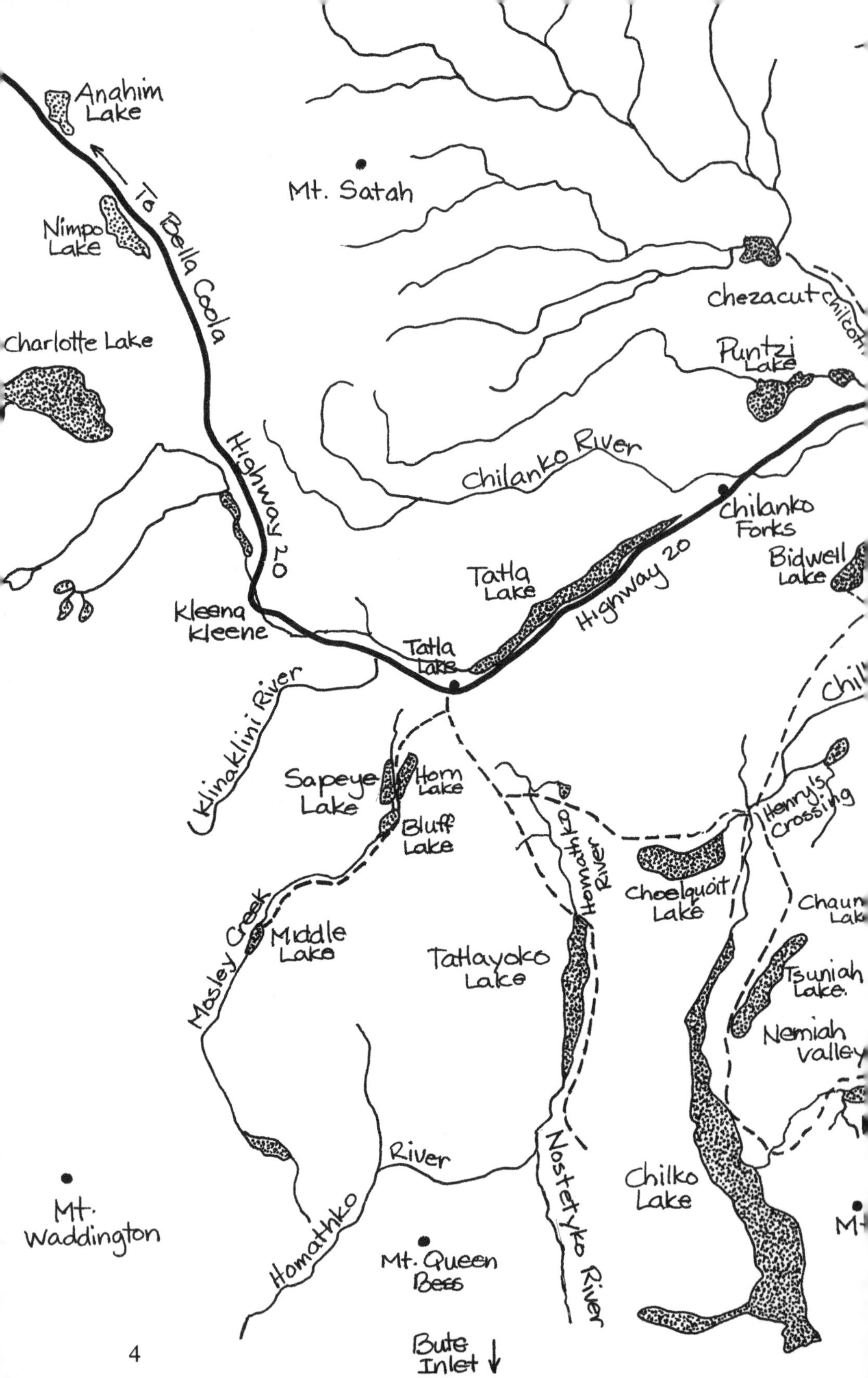

Anahim Lake

Mt. Satah

Chezacut

Nimpo Lake

To Bella Coola

Charlotte Lake

Puntzi Lake

Chilcotin

Highway 20

Chilanko River

Chilanko Forks

Bidwell Lake

Tatla Lake

Highway 20

Kleena Kleene

Tatla Lake

Chil

Klinaklini River

Sapeye Lake

Horn Lake

Homathko River

Henry's Crossing

Bluff Lake

Choelquoit Lake

Chaun Lake

Mosley Creek

Middle Lake

Tatlayoko Lake

Tsuniah Lake

Nemiah Valley

Mt. Waddington

River

Chilko Lake

M

Homathko

Nostetyko River

Mt. Queen Bess

Bute Inlet ↓

4

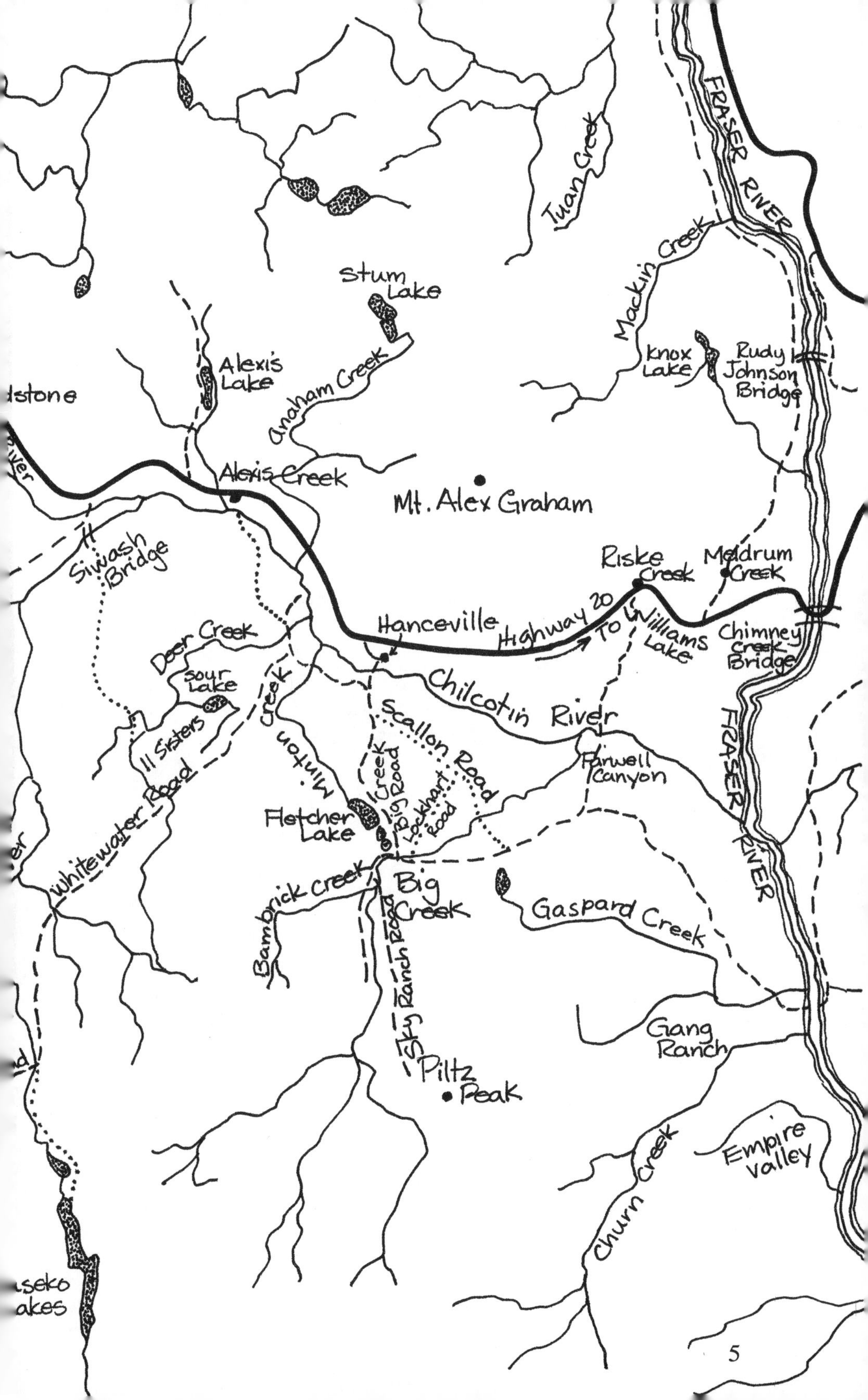

FRASER RIVER

Tuan Creek

Mackin Creek

Stum Lake

Alexis Lake

Graham Creek

Knox Lake

Rudy Johnson Bridge

dstone

River

Alexis Creek

Mt. Alex Graham

Siwash Bridge

Riske Creek

Meldrum Creek

Deer Creek

Hanceville

Highway 20

To Williams Lake

Chimney Creek Bridge

Sour Lake

Chilcotin River

11 Sisters

Minton Creek

Scallon Road

Big Creek

Lockhart Road

Farwell Canyon

Whitewater Road

Fletcher Lake

FRASER RIVER

Bambrick creek

Big Creek

Gaspard Creek

Sky Ranch Road

Gang Ranch

Piltz Peak

Empire Valley

Churn Creek

seko akes

THE AUTHORS

The Witte sisters, granddaughters of pioneers Tom Hance and Nellie Verdier Hance, were born in the Chilcotin, grew up, married and raised their families there. Home was at Big Creek where they were educated in a little country school.

Irene E. Bliss and husband, Bill, live in the Chilcotin on the Bliss family ranch at Redstone. Veera Bonner still lives at Big Creek where she has a resort on Fletcher Lake. Hazel Henry Litterick now makes her home in Williams Lake. Hazel is a well known artist, specializing in Chilcotin landscapes, using oils, acrylics, and water colours.

The Witte sisters, from left: Irene E. Bliss, Hazel Henry Litterick and Veera Bonner.

CONTENTS

INTRODUCTION

There is a vast storehouse of romantic history connected with the opening and settlement of the Chilcotin country of British Columbia. Yet much will be lost if it is not preserved in writing.

This book had its beginnings in the little gold-colored *History and Legends of the Chilcotin* (now out of print) put together as a Centennial project in 1958 by the communities of Riske Creek, Meldrum Creek, Hanceville, Big Creek, and Alexis Creek. Credit goes to the late Joyce MacDonald of Riske Creek for initiating this worthwhile undertaking and prodding it on to completion.

This new book is dedicated to preserving the memory of the early pioneers whose courage and spirit of adventure brought them into this country. With these writings, we hope to bring some of these hardy characters to life to share with the reader the unique magic of the Chilcotin we love. If errors have crept in please inform and forgive us and these will be righted in any future editions.

We are deeply indebted to Dave Falconer of Likely, and Marie Elliot of Victoria, for generously sharing with us their research of historical data relating to the Chilcotin. Their knowledgeable help has broadened and enriched this book immeasurably and we are very grateful. Thank you, Dave and Marie.

Our sincere thanks to all those who contributed their own stories or family histories. Also to Paul St. Pierre and John G. Woods for their encouragement, and to all the others who helped and cheered us on. Thank you.

Chilcotin wives performed remarkable feats under challenging conditions. Their first home was usually a hastily built log cabin, a bucket for water and a scrubbing board for a washing machine. The nearest neighbour was often several miles away and a doctor 100 or more. In addition to housework and raising a family, most helped with ranch chores. Mrs. Gertrude Bayliff, above, despite the awkward sidesaddle, chased cattle over fences and any-where else they ran. Chilcotin's first white woman, Mrs. Nellie Hance, in1887 rode sidesaddle over 300 miles to Hanceville.

EARLY RECORDS OF THE
CHILCOTIN INDIANS

There appears to be evidence to support the belief that in very early times, and as late as 1862, the Shuswap Indians occupied an area west of the Fraser along Riske Creek and the lower Chilcotin River. According to James Tait, who made a study of the Shuswap for the Jessup North Pacific Expedition in the late 1880s and early 1890s, the Shuswap had four settlements on the west side of the Fraser River: One on Riske Creek; one on the north side of the Chilcotin at the foot of the canyon — where, Tait claims, they had bridged the river; and another just opposite on the south side. These two villages were about 10 miles from the mouth of the river, where a fourth village was situated — also on the south side. The settlements were in choice hunting and fishing grounds.

These people were nearly exterminated by smallpox in 1862. The survivors joined either their own tribe at Alkali Lake or the Chilcotins at Anaham near Alexis Creek. (Farther west, spelling becomes Anahim.) One or two Shuswap families continued to live on the south side of the Chilcotin River. In 1905 their chief was Joe Kala'llst and this last name is still familiar around the Gang Ranch. Gradually the Chilcotins took over the deserted Shuswap territory.

Tait records a history of warfare, retaliation, and primitive brutality between the tribes and even within their own bands. It was, perhaps, to be expected that when settlement of the Chilcotin country was beginning in the 1860s and 1870s that there would be instances of trouble with the wild Chilcotin Indians. Massacre, murder, and robbery did occur, and some would-be settlers were threatened and run out. Others lived in fear of the natives. But there were good chiefs among the bands, and traders and settlers who came with respect and fair dealings were accepted.

As well as the murders and executions in connection with the Chilcotin Uprising in 1864, other incidents had also taken place. Around 1880, two Chilcotins were hanged for murder and others

10

imprisoned for robbery and cattle stealing, and it was felt that the chiefs needed support from higher authority to help them influence their people to obey the law. It also seemed necessary to set aside land for the native people before white settlement crowded in. Even after this was done there were, not surprisingly, other outbreaks of violence.

Nemiah, a strong chief with powerful influence among his people, was wanted for murdering a Chinaman, but for nearly ten years his band protected him from the law. Then in March 1891, in a fit of anger, he stabbed another Indian, cutting a gash from breast to thigh, almost disemboweling the man. The band then turned against him, tied him up and sent a rider to bring the police. During the night his klootch cut him loose and he fled. A special constable was put on the case and finally arrested Nemiah on another reserve. He was taken to jail at 150 Mile, but his trial was put off indefinitely as two key witnesses had escaped. These men, Cokex and Cushen, were wanted in connection with the rebellion more than twenty-five years before. When they heard they were needed as witnesses against Nemiah they gathered together fourteen other Indian men with good horses and deserted the settlement. Two police officers went after them but were too badly outnumbered to bring them back.

In 1898, Lewis Elkins, a white man who ran a store at what was called Gootzine (or Quitsin) Lake, fifteen miles from Tatla Lake, was shot by an Indian named Sam'hi'u. The Indian paid for the murder with a jail sentence. Two Chilcotins, Moses Paul and Paul Spintlum, were arrested in 1912 after being sought by the law for nearly a year for the murder of a Chinese miner. Both Indians were found guilty and hanged. Mike Farwell was on that jury and remembered that the judge, who was handling his first murder case, wept when he handed down the death sentence. The two Indians remained outwardly calm and appeared surprised at the judge's tears.

The first attempt by the government to organize the scattered Chilcotin tribes came in 1883 when the Indian Superintendent for B.C., J. W. Powell, stationed in Victoria, made a trip through the interior of the province to inspect principal reserves and make contact with Indians where no land had as yet been laid aside. On September 8, Powell crossed to the west side of the Fraser River at Soda Creek and rode through the unorganized Chilcotin country on horseback, escorted by two Chilcotin chiefs, Toosey and Anaham, who met him there. Also on the trip was the newly appointed resi-

Indians in the early days in front of Lee's store.

dent Indian Agent for Cariboo and Chilcotin, Captain William Lang-Meason, a retired Army Officer. (Meason held this post for about ten years and was apparently trusted and well liked.)

The first day out, the party rode thirty-six miles to camp at Deer Park above the Fraser where about forty of Toosey's band had gathered to meet them. The Indians' main camp was another twelve or fifteen miles farther on. To Mr. Powell's friendly greeting, Toosey replied:

"Chief: My people have a bad name, but you are the first Queen's man to visit us, except for police who have come to arrest us. You do not come among us to arrest and punish us, but to help and advise us. You must remember that our people are yet wild. They are like the deer which sleeps and starts suddenly at the first sound of alarm...."

Toosey promised that the Indians still hiding in the mountains would come in to see the "Big Chief" and "...hear his kind words," and the entire tribe would meet him next day.

Powell spent a week among the Chilcotin Indians. He found the Chiefs to be co-operative and friendly. They all earnestly requested that land be set aside for their people. Anaham complained that the money (about $800) promised his band for helping apprehend two murderers had not been paid. Powell assured the Chief that this would be taken care of as soon as he returned to Victoria. He kept his word. The Chief had refused a personal reward, saying that he did not wish to be paid for the blood of his children.

The Superintendent noted their need for more agricultural implements with which to cultivate the land, and made a list for each band: Toosey's tribe, Anaham's tribe, and the Stone tribe under Chief Quilt. A request for these supplies was sent to Ottawa on his return to headquarters "...they are too poor to buy these for themselves...and such a gift would do much to satisfy them and ensure their attachment." Powell reported that he re-crossed the Fraser on September 14 and arrived at Alkali Lake the same evening. He visited Canoe Creek and Dog Creek and arrived at Clinton by the River Trail on September 18. From there he continued on to Victoria.

Having seen the ill effects of liquor on the Clinton, Canoe Creek, Dog Creek, Alkali Lake and Soda Creek natives, all of whom were close to licenced premises, Powell concluded that the Chilcotin Indians were fortunate to have no licenced houses to sell liquor in their country. "If it is possible to prevent their introduction it should be done," he wrote to his superiors in Ottawa.

History has proven that this could not be done in spite of genuine and continuing concern of all those responsible for the well-being of the native people. By the 1890s there were saloons at Riske Creek and on the Chilcotin River below Hanceville. A law against retailing intoxicants on Sunday was passed in the Provincial Parliament of B.C. in 1892 and, according to Government Agent Meason, "...proved of great use in restricting the accustomed scenes of rowdy drunkenness which were witnessed at most bar-rooms on every Sunday."

Land for the Stone Band on the south side of the Chilcotin River was chosen in 1887 by P.O. Riley, Indian Reserve Commissioner for B.C., and surveyed in the summer of 1891. In his annual report in 1888, Agent M.L. Meason commends the Indians for the amount of fencing and farming done since their land was set aside the previous year. He mentions that these people had previously spent their time trapping and hunting, and judging by the amount of work done on the land in one year predicts that "from being the wildest of the Chilcotin bands" they would "soon be steady and prosperous farmers". Subsequent reports by the agents indicate that the Stoneys tired of farming and did go back to their old ways, making little progress about the reserve. But in 1891 they were growing good gardens and producing a big crop of potatoes as well as wheat for flour.

Mike Minton, who owned land next to the reserve, and a man

named Shuby, apparently helped the Stoney people learn to build log and rail fences and till the soil, and even harvested some of the Indians' grain with their self-binder. Grain was commonly cradled by hand. Only five miles away, across the river, Tom Hance had a good grist mill which he was able to run in the winter as well as summer since it was powered by spring water that never froze, and here the Indians took their wheat to be ground into flour. Any surplus grain was sold to Hance.

The Stone Reserve was surveyed in July, 1891 by O. Fletcher, District Land Surveyor for the Indian Commission. The rivers were high, and as there was no bridge over the Chilcotin, crossing his outfit to reach the Stoney on the south side was dangerous and difficult. Fletcher also surveyed for Stone a small plot of wild hay land – Reserve No.2 – in the Big Creek area (Siwash Meadow). Since Fletcher Lake lies only three miles from Siwash Meadow, it is likely that this body of water was named after the early surveyor.

By 1901 the people of Stone, still under Chief Quilt, a hereditary chief who held the position for life – his son, Louis, who died in the 1950s was the last hereditary chief – had ample water from a diversion ditch from Minton Creek to irrigate their fields. This year, too, they built a small log church. The present little church was built in 1904 and christened St. John the Baptiste Catholic Church. It is of frame construction covered with clapboard, and features windows with an odd combination of rectangular trim and arched sashes which is unique to the Chilcotin area, according to John Veillette and Gary White – experts on early Indian village churches. This church was restored by members of the Stone Band in 1983 with help from the B.C. Heritage Trust.

The reserve at Riske Creek was surveyed in 1891 by O. Fletcher, and named after the Chief. Land for the largest band of Indians in the Chilcotin, the Anaham Band, led by Chiefs Anaham and Alexis, was set aside at this time, too. This tribe ranged mainly along the north side of the upper Chilcotin River and its tributaries, and was allotted a large tract of arable land between Alexis Creek and Hanceville, Anaham Flats, and expansive wild hay meadows beyond. Roomy tableland jutting above Anaham Flats made an ideal site for their village.

By the fall of 1891, the allotment of reserves for Indians on the entire coasts of the Mainland and Vancouver Island was finished; and a good number in the north, central, and southern interior were laid out and surveyed. The Reserve Commissioner sent in a detailed account of the year's work to the Superintendent General of Indian Affairs in Canada, and in closing his report he summed up as follows:

"While a few of the Indians objected to reserves being made at all, on the ground that the whole country was virtually theirs, by far the greater number appeared glad that the land question was about to be finally settled, and expressed themselves well satisfied with the extent of the reserves I defined for them."

By 1912 Indian land reserves had been set up at Redstone, Nemiah Valley (this valley was interestingly described by Indian Agent Bell as being one hundred miles from Hanceville and two hundred miles from salt water); Anahim Lake (Ulkatcho); Kluskus Lake; and Nazko River.

The first missionary to visit the Chilcotin Indians was Roman Catholic Father Modette Demers. In 1842, he travelled with Peter Skene Ogden from Fort Alexandria to Fort Chilcotin and spent sixteen days there. This fort was a small compound on the Chilcotin River among a hostile people in a wild unforgiving land. Father John Nobili was next. He was sent by his superior, Father De Smet, from Fort Alexandria, probably over the Hudson's Bay Trail, in 1845. Father Nobili rode on through Nemiah Valley to the mouth of the Chilko River where, in October, near what is now called Canoe Crossing, he erected a wooden cross. (A new cross to commemorate the proclamation of the Good News for the first time to the Chilcotin natives was put up at the site in 1993 by the people of Nemiah Valley, Father John Brioux, and Bishop Sabatini. Called the Brittany Gathering, the day included many festivities and was attended by a large gathering of Indian people.)

Later, around 1871, Father Le Jacq, Father McGuckin, and Father A. G. Morice, all of the Oblates of Mary Immaculate order, made several trips through the country but met with little success with the natives. In his notes, Father Morice mentions staying at Hanceville in 1894.

It was Francois Marie Thomas, also of the O.M.I. who persevered in bringing the Catholic faith to the Chilcotin Indians. He came in 1897 and ministered in the country for sixty years – a legend in his own time. He travelled on foot and on horseback for the first twenty years and then had a one-horse buggy or sleigh. During his last years a car and driver were provided. A big hearty man – with white hair and beard as he grew older – he was a familiar figure throughout the Chilcotin. Bundled up in his sleigh in long fur coat and hat, he was never deterred by the weather but would stomp in out of the snow, red-cheeked from the cold in buoyant good humour, visiting non-Catholics on occasion, as well as his own flock. In 1935, Father John Hennessy came to help out in the wide-spread district that Father Thomas served. Although Hennessy was a big man, the Indian people called him "Little Father Thomas." Father Thomas died in 1957 and was buried at St. Joseph's Mission, where he wanted to be.

The Chilcotins were gradually learning a new way of life. By 1891 Toosey's band had three good wagons and harness, two mowing machines and two rakes, as well as a threshing machine. They were building ditches in 1900 and were interested in cultivating the land. A few had cattle by 1901. In this year they moved their buildings to a more convenient place on the reserve — where they are today. It seemed that the native people were healthier when they lived in their underground keegly holes. (Keegly, or keek'willy, holes were dug-outs covered with poles and hides or brush, used by the Indians for protection in the winter before the coming of the white man.) In their log homes they became susceptible to colds, pneumonia, and tuberculosis, blamed in part on the excessive heat of their houses and the sudden chill when going outside.

At Anaham the people were raising grain, cattle, horses, and pigs; and taking their wheat ten miles to Hanceville to be ground into flour. As early as 1900 some of the Anaham Indians were freighting on the Cariboo Road with their own teams and wagons. By 1907 they had their own self-binder and steam sawmill. Lilacs were planted and vegetable gardens sown. Members of all bands worked now and then for the white settlers as ranch hands, cowboys, packers, and later as guides. In the early reports on the Chilcotin Indians, the agents wrote that they seldom heard of a case of intemperance among them.

The Williams Lake Industrial School had opened at St. Joseph's Mission in 1891, but it was 1907 before Indian children from Chilcotin received any education. Then it was only a few boys and girls from Anaham and Toosey, and well past that time before any from the Stoney or other more distant reserves were sent that far from home. Much later, day schools, funded like the Mission School by the federal government, were established on most reserves. In 1944 the Sisters of Christ the King, from Gaspe, established a school and nursing station at Anaham Reserve which is still serving the Indian people. This, too, is funded by the government. Indian women from all over the Chilcotin made and sold moccasins and gloves, using hand-tanned deer and caribou hides, and fashioned baskets from spruce roots (a laborious task) and

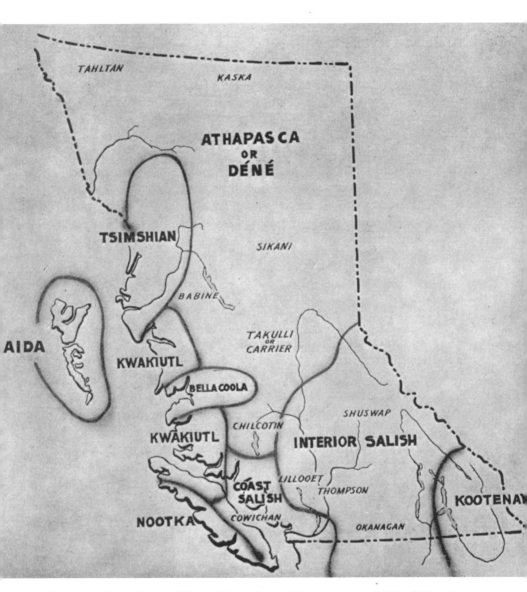

Language boundaries of the Indians when white men arrived. The Chilcotin are the southernmost of the Athapascan people.

birch bark. These water-tight baskets from spruce roots were of attractive and original designs. The Stoney people, and perhaps others, made robes from the skins of the marmot, a small gopher-like animal that they hunted in the high mountain valleys. These robes were very warm and handsome and sold for a good price. In those early days many of the Stone tribe trekked with horses up into the headwaters of Big Creek every summer. They camped in

17

the mountains for two or three weeks, hunting marmots in the alpine valleys and crossing the divide to pick berries on the western slopes. These they dried in the sun for winter use, bringing them out on pack horses.

At the head of Big Creek there is an old burial ground in a beautiful alpine valley, flanked by glistening glaciers and alive with whistling marmots. In it lie the graves of a group of Indians said to have been stricken with smallpox while camping in the mountains and who died there many years ago. The shallow graves were once covered with spruce logs and marked with crosses but these have now all rotted away. Only the name, Graveyard Valley, endures.

The population on the Chilcotin Indian Reserves in 1913, according to early Indian Agent reports, was:

Anaham: 274   Ulkatcho: 90 Redstone: 59
Toosey: 50   Stone: 49   Nemiah Valley: 57

By 1970 the count had risen sharply. Anaham now had a population of 606; Redstone, 311; Stone, 146; Toosey, 93; and Nemiah, 193.

In 1985 the combined population of these five reserves totalled 1,864:

Anaham: 829   Stone: 209   Redstone: 441
Toosey: 128   Nemiah: 257

Doctor, health, and dental clinics are held on the reserves, as well as treatment programs for drug and alcohol abuse when requested. Ambulance service is available. More and more young people are graduating from the Provincial Secondary School in Williams Lake and some going on to enter the professions and other aspects of community service. The Stone Reserve is the first in the Chilcotin to have a Band-operated School. This means that funds allocated by the government for education are distributed by the Chief and members of council who determine and pay the teachers' salaries.

The colossal undertaking of converting the Chilcotin Indian tongue into a written language, with a goal of translating the Scriptures, was started in the 1960s. Mr. and Mrs. Allan Franz and Quindel King of the Northern Canadian Evangelical Mission began the task at Alexis Creek with the help of the native people. This meant first determining the phonetic symbols used in their speech to work out an alphabet, then forming the written words. Mr. and Mrs. Franz were soon after transferred to Ontario, but Quindel King carried on. According to King, the Chilcotin – a sister language of the Navajo in the U.S. – is of complicated structure with each verb carrying the subject and object.

This phase is completed and the Chilcotin Indian language is now offered in School District 27 as a choice in second language requirements. Ed Cook, a linguist from the University of Alberta, helped prepare the course for the schools.

King has now finished the arduous task of translating the Gospel of Mark into Chilcotin. Many Indian people have assisted the translators over the years. Danny Case of Redstone, and William Myers of Stone, helped Quindel King check and revise the completed translation.

Roman Catholic Church at Stone Reserve, 1923.

THE RAILWAY SURVEY – 1872

By 1871 the Federal Government was committed to extending the Canadian Pacific Railway through British Columbia and monies were allotted to begin the necessary surveys, starting with the mountain passes.

Engineer Marcus Smith was in charge of the Pacific Coast Division of the survey. Four routes to the Pacific were to be explored: Chilcotin Plains to Bute Inlet, Peace River and Giscombe Portage to North Bentinck Arm, Lillooet to Howe Sound, and the Thompson and Fraser Canyons to Burrard Inlet.

On July 29, 1872, Marcus Smith set out from Fort Alexandria to lay out a rail line through the Chilcotin and establish a depot and survey camps. He had a train of 20 mules laden with provisions and was accompanied by three Indians and an axeman. In the fifth day out from Alexandria he met Chief Alexis. The Indian chief had expected to first meet up with a Mr. O'Reilly who was coming through from Bella Coola, but O'Reilly had been detained by high water and wild fires and the two did not rendezvous until reaching "Tatlah" (Tatla) Lake. Replenishing his provisions from Smith's stock, O'Reilly continued on to Alexandria. Smith and his party, joined at Tatla Lake by three more men, moved out to Middle Lake where a depot was formed and exploring done. "The Engineers' camp" was set up about 25 miles from the depot, and "Camp W" in the vicinity.

Leaving men in charge of these camps, Smith retraced his route to Tatla Lake, then explored along the Chilanko River (Marcus Smith's survey stakes could be seen in the Bayliff fields for many years) and down the Chilcotin River to its mouth. After investigating the country in this area, Smith returned up the west side of the Fraser River to Soda Creek. Here he left instructions for the various survey parties and pack trains that would complete the work. These instructions included routes to survey in order to meet the coast party coming in from the head of Bute Inlet. Pack loads of warm clothing, boots, blankets and food were sent out in August and September from Alexandria to stock the depot and "secure the comfort and safety" of the survey crews. Other parties were coming in from the North Thompson and Lac La Hache to join up with the Chilcotin survey.

This locomotive is said to be the first one over the Rockies. This photo was taken in Ashcroft in 1885.

Having finished his explorations west of the Fraser, Marcus Smith moved on to Tete Jaune Cache to explore the Clearwater, Thompson, and Fraser Rivers, terminating at Burrard lnlet. Smith would voice no opinion on the merits of the various routes until all the information had been studied. It was near the end of 1876 before the final reports of the Chilcotin-Bute Inlet survey were in. Included in the report was the discouraging news that a terminus at Bute Inlet would require eight miles of rock tunnelling.

In December 1877, Prime Minister Alexander Mackenzie announced that the Fraser River-Burrard Inlet route for the C.P.R. would be adopted and dreams of a Chilcotin railway died. The decision, upheld by Prime Minister Sir John A. MacDonald a year later, was influenced in part by Major General R. C. Moody of the Royal Engineers who strongly advised the Fraser River route for "strategic reasons."

Construction of the rail line through B.C. began in May, 1880 when 128 miles between Emory's Bar on the Fraser River and Savona at the west end of Kamloops Lake was let out on contract. Five and a half years later, November 7, 1885, work on the C.P.R. track through B.C. was completed. On July 4, 1886, the first passenger train from Montreal chugged through the Rockies and the southern Interior and pulled into the Port Moody terminus on the Pacific. Ashcroft instead of Yale was now the depot for Chilcotin-Cariboo.

BEFORE THE BRIDGES – AND AFTER

Before there were any bridges in the country the Chilcotin ranchers who, from Hanceville westward, ranged their cattle towards Big Creek on the open grasslands that are now Chilco Ranch pastures, had to swim their stock across the Chilcotin River in spring and fall. Kathleen Telford, daughter of pioneer rancher Alex Graham, gives a colorful description in her article, "Pioneer Days in the Chilcotin":

"In spring it (crossing) wasn't too difficult since the men would rope the calves and take them across in a boat. The calves would bawl and their mothers would eventually plunge into the river to be with them. But the October crossing was different.

"The men shovelled a trail down the river bank to the water's edge, then ran up and down the bank, banging coal-oil cans loaded with rocks and yelling until they were hoarse. To escape the din, some old cow eventually plunged into the river, then the men closed in and forced the rest into the water.

"Sometimes it was below zero weather and the cattle and horses emerged on the home side covered in icicles which jingled like sleigh bells. Once the local constable, Robert Pyper, decided to participate. It was well below zero with ice forming on the rocks in the river bed, a very treacherous condition. Both Pyper and his horse were inexperienced and in midstream the horse slipped and both went under. Dad (Alex Graham) threw Pyper his lariat and was able to drag him and his horse ashore. By the time they reached the ranch, Pyper's clothes were frozen into a suit of armor. But after a change and a hot rum he was little the worse for his dunking. Our Chinese helper, Kin Nauie, later laughingly described how he lassoed Pyper's stetson as it bobbed downstream in the swift current.

"Far more difficult than crossing cattle over the Chilcotin, however, was the beef drive to Ashcroft, which entailed crossing the Fraser River. These drives started before there were bridges or even ferries across any of the rivers – including the Fraser."

Alex Graham, Archie Macauley, and Hugh Bayliff took the first long drive to Ashcroft, the nearest shipping point, taking their three and four year old steers and any beef cattle their neighbours wanted to throw in with them. Bayliff was the most experienced man in crossing these dangerous rivers.

"The 220-mile, month-long trail drive proved a hard grind," Mrs. Telford wrote. "The men set out in early autumn with Dad's dog, some 300 head of cattle, a few packhorses and spare saddle horses to replace those which went lame or drowned on the way. Because cattle lose too much weight if pushed, they travelled about ten miles a day, and not at all on Sunday. Their route was across the Chilcotin River to Big Creek and the Gang Ranch, across the Fraser River to Clinton and down the Cariboo Wagon Road to Ashcroft. Fording the creeks and rivers took the most time because the cattle were extremely difficult to get into the water. On the month-long trip the men's food was mostly bannock, beans, and deer meat; their shelter a piece of canvas; their bed a blanket used during the day to cover packs. There were no corrals or stopping places on the route. When they halted for the day one or two men rode night herd while the others slept. By the time they were ready with their second beef drive a ferry had been installed on the Fraser River at the mouth of Churn Creek near the Gang Ranch. This ferry proved a great asset to the entire district as it eliminated the most dangerous crossing."

In 1890, $1,000 was allotted for a bridge over the Chilcotin River at Hanceville, the estimated total cost being $5,000. After pressure from Chilcotin residents the additional funding was allocated by the government and the bridge was built in the winter of 1892-93. Unfortunately, it was swept away in high water in June that same year but was rebuilt a little farther upstream as soon as conditions permitted. Extensive repairs were made to the Hanceville Bridge in 1901. In the summer of 1906 a portion of the bridge was again swept away. It was repaired the following winter. High water in April 1956 took out a span on the south side of the river. An army Bailey bridge was tacked on in November to repair it.

CHILCOTIN SURVEY – 1890

Victoria Colonist, January 1, 1891

"It was decided by the Commissioner of Lands and Works in the spring of 1890 to have an exploration of the Chilcotin Valley and the region north of it made; Mr. A. L. Poudrier D.L.S. was charged with the execution of the work. The instructions given by the Surveyor General were: to map the country as correct as possible with a track-survey, obtain all possible information as to the quality of the soil, the timber, the geology and the flora of the country; to make a study of the possibilities of communication, by roads, trails or rivers. It was also arranged that the exploration should start from Bute Inlet and reach the central plateau by way of the Homathko River.

"On the 13 of May Mr. Poudrier left Victoria with a party of three men, besides a volunteer, Lieut. J. Martin, R.N. They reached Bute Inlet on the 18. After taking a day to engage Indians and canoes the party left Waddington Harbor on their trip. Ten men and two good canoes formed the expedition to begin with, with a complete outfit of provisions: ropes, tents, instruments, etc.

"It will be remembered that during the first gold excitement there had been an attempt made to strike a trail to the Interior by way of Bute Inlet and the Homathko. After cutting thirty miles of trail fourteen members of Waddington's survey party were massacred. Few traces of that old trail can now be seen, an old crumbling bridge here and there, a few rock cuttings, some old tools scattered about are all that is left of that work, besides the evil name that has since clung to the Chilcotin Indians.

"The first part of the trip from Bute Inlet to the first canyon was performed with difficulty. The Homathko, like other mountain streams, reaches its flood in the hottest days of summer, but even at this date, the numerous glacial streams falling into it rendered it a wild rushing torrent of muddy water covered with drift wood. The only way of getting ahead was to leave two men in the canoe to steer and track-line the canoe from the shore with a long rope. After severe work the party camped at the foot of the canyon. Canoes could not be taken any farther.

"It was understood that the Indians would proceed with the party about half way, to pack provisions, but the hard work of the last few days, the fear of the Chilcotin Indians and last but not least, the mysterious appearance of a wild "Chilcotin" whose naked foot marks could be found every morning by the river, proved to be too much and they all left and did their best to induce the party to give up the job; so it was decided to proceed with the few men who could be depended on – four besides the volunteer, Lieut. Martin.

"The outfit was reduced to the smallest company: a tent, some ropes, flour, bacon, tea and coffee, guns and ammunition and instruments formed the whole baggage, even then the loads were heavy. This was the commencement of four weeks of hardship. Two or three miles a day was all that could be made. It was a continual climb. Baggage had to be taken down by ropes over great heights almost every day. The greatest obstacle proved to be the glacial streams. When in the heart of the Cascades a series of immense glaciers, some of which are superior in size and height to the renowned glaciers of the Alps, pour continual torrents of ice and snow into the river. Some of these streams are easily bridged, others, too wide, had to be crossed over the glaciers, thus increasing the distance to be walked by more than half. In making the trip more unpleasant the rain was continual. During the first part of the trip on the western slope of the range, game proved to be plentiful. A black bear and two mountain goats were shot. Grouse and duck were plentiful, some delicious trout were caught, but once in the heart of the mountains every form of animal life seems to have disappeared. Nothing whatever could be seen but 'mountain country.'

"The daily increase of the difficulties, the worthlessness of the information obtained, the continual and sure decrease of the provisions, the complete absence of game and fish, gave the leader more than one sleepless night, and it had been decided that on a certain day the rations would be reduced one third, when at noon of the succeeding day the welcome sight of the first lake, called Twist Lake, gave the party an assurance that the eastern slope was attained and by the general lay of the land that the worst of the trip was over.

"The last part of the trip proved to be very pleasant. The mountains were farther apart, the river much smaller and with very little current, the ground more level and traces of human travelling, old Indian camps and traps, were found in increasing quantity. At last on a fine evening the party emerged on the Chilcotin Plateau.

"The source of the Homathko which was then but a small creek was found, the cut in the snow clad mountains, followed for so many weary days, was left behind, like a great gate of a very uninviting appearance. Another day brought us to Tatla Lake, where Lieut. Martin has a fine ranch. Everyone felt light hearted, contented and pleased to have crossed the mountains without any accidents.

"At Tatla Lake the party was arranged on a new and better footing, horses were bought to do the packing and even to ride for one or two of the party, provisions became of much better quality and some men were known to have as many as two shirts which was a novelty. After that the regular survey began.

"Chilcotin is the southern part of that great central plateau discovered by Sir Alexander McKenzie a century ago – which he called New Caledonia. It is watered by the Chilcotin River, of which one of the principal branches takes its source in Tatla Lake, the name of this source is Chilanko. Tatla Lake is a lovely sheet of water, very narrow but over 10 miles in length. Its shores, especially the northern, like the rest of the course of the Chilcotin River, are generally covered with bunchgrass, sage brush and several rich forage plants. The shores are principally made in terraces very well developed, especially along the Chilcotin River. The upper terraces are generally covered with short growth of pine and small aspen poplars. The sidehills are often covered with service berry, rich with fruit later in the season. The view towards the southwest is very grand. The coast range, elevated four or five thousand feet above the plateau, makes a large snow-clad barrier, with only the gates formed by the cuts of the two branches of the Homathko River. The whole Chilcotin Valley, from Tatla Lake to the point where the river falls in the Fraser River and nearly all the tributaries, form a very rich pastoral ground. In the lower part of the river much land can be used for agriculture. There are several ranchers established who seem to do very well. Besides raising cattle they also do much regular farming. Their wheat, which is of the very best quality and in abundance, is reduced into flour on the spot with ingenious little grist mills of which there are several. The Indians themselves, under the guidance of Chief Anaham, of Waddington's massacre fame, do some very good farming.

"Between the mouth of the Chilcotin and the Fraser at Riske Creek messers Drummond and Beumont have one of the finest cattle ranches in the province. They have abundance of hay meadows and their pasture on the high level is of the richest. The flora of

26

The Bute Inlet route for the Canadian Pacific Railway across the Chilcotin would have required eight miles of tunneling to get through the Coast Mountains.

those elevated prairies is truly wonderful and large collections of the plants were made by the expedition.

"Though there are several ranches in the Chilcotin Valley there are still room for others. A large tract could be employed for culture in the lower lands. The climate is delicious but very dry in summer and irrigation is needed everywhere. Water is plentiful from creeks and springs. As a hunting ground few places in America could surpass it. Deer are common in the fall, mountain sheep come down from the Cascade Range and the lower part of the Chilcotin River is covered with their tracks. Grouse of different kinds — blue, ruffed, willow, and prairie chickens are very numerous and the streams are full of salmon and trout of several varieties.

"After surveying the Chilcotin, the Chilko, the Chilanko, Alexis Creek, and several other feeders of the principal river, the party proceeded to survey the Blackwater River, or West Road."

EARLY ROADS

ASHCROFT-HANCEVILLE — 1891-92

In 1891, Government Agent John Bowron and other government members proposed the construction of a road from Hanceville to Empire Valley. They had the road superintendent in Quesnel, Joseph St. Laurent, conduct an examination of the proposed 50-mile route and provide a cost estimate. St. Laurent reported that to build a road "of any material use" would be very difficult due to the nature of the country and would cost at least $25,000. He estimated the cost of a bridge over Big Creek at $600. St. Laurent reported that very few local residents were in favour of this proposed road to Empire Valley. Ranchers Hugh Bayliff, Tommy Young, Norman Lee, Fred Nightingale, Fred Copeland, Dan Nordberg, Ian and Frank Johnson, Archie McCauley, Tom Hance, and J. Haines requested that the money be spent instead on improving and extending the road from Hanceville up the north side of Chilcotin River where more settlers lived.

In 1892-93 a bridge was built over the Chilcotin River at Hanceville and in 1894 the first bridge over Big Creek was put in. A road was then constructed between Hanceville and Clinton via Big Creek and the Gang Ranch. It became known as the Ashcroft – Hanceville Road.

ON CROSSING RIVERS

The loss of a bridge or a ferry could cause tremendous hardship on the road in the early years, but a crisis of this kind was usually accepted by the frontiersmen with patience and fortitude. Often a heroic deed was accepted in the same quiet way. Such was the case in 1903 when the Gang Ranch ferry and its passengers were swept down the booming Fraser River and a daring unknown cowboy made a wild dash to save them.

It was early June and the Fraser was unusually high when an English settler, H. E. Church, coming from Ashcroft, pulled his team and wagon in to the scow ferry, anxious to cross over to the Chilcotin and be on his way to his new pre-emption on Big Creek. But when he arrived at the Fraser, minor repairs were being made to the wire stretched across the river and there was nothing to do

Scow ferry across the Fraser River at the mouth of Churn Creek.

but wait. Making camp, he waited there for 24 hours during which time another team and wagon showed up. On the Gang Ranch side of the river, cowboys and a drive of beef cattle waited to cross.

When the repairs were completed Church drove his outfit onto the ferry. As the force of the exceptionally high water struck the scow (which was held at an angle to the current by rope tackles at each end attached to pulleys travelling on the wire cable) they were hurled across the angry water at a frightening pace, with the tail end of the scow almost under water. It was with intense relief that they reached the quiet eddy on the far side and slid gently up the bank. As the team and wagon moved off the scow and slowly up the steep grade from the ferry landing, some of the cowboys rode past to board the scow and so be on the other side to hold the cattle as they were crossed on the ferry, 10 at a time.

The ferryman had set his tackles for the return trip, reversing the angle of the scow, but had failed to anchor securely to the shore and they started off before all the men and horses were on board. And here the ferryman made another fatal mistake: instead of continuing across he tried to alter the tackles in the middle of that powerful current and come back. He let the forward tackle out until the scow was hanging squarely across the river, but he and the two men on board were not strong enough to pull up on the other tackle against that tremendous volume of rushing water and so get started back. The furious current began to tilt the scow and they were in danger every second of being swamped and losing their lives in the raging river. Suddenly, there was a report like a rifle shot as the steel cable broke. The sudden lurch threw both men and horses off their feet and the scow and its passengers whirled off downstream to almost certain destruction. But, with instant and courageous reaction, a cowboy on the near side spurred his mount into a gallop and raced to the rescue.

H. E. Church was an eye witness to this drama but he records it in a few short paragraphs in his memoirs. Of the unknown cowboy's valiant ride he writes: "A cowboy on my side of the river galloped off downstream, and two miles below was able to catch a rope from them and by making fast to a tree brought the scow to the bank." The man's name was not recorded.

Their modesty was typical of the frontier. Three men and two horses being swept down the perilous angry waters of the Fraser and a rider going full tilt for two miles over rough and dangerous terrain to their rescue! Then daringly using with skill and precision his tools of the range to somehow catch a rope from his friends on the runaway raft, take his dallies [a wrap] on a tree growing near enough to the water and against the force of the current bring the men and horses to safety at the bank. What relief and gratitude must have been in the hearts of the rescued as they set foot on dry land again. But likely little was said as they turned to the tasks at hand and made their way back to solve the other problems caused by the accident.

Mr. Church tells us that it was not possible to get a new cable stretched and the scow back in place until low water in the fall. As a result, freight had to be taken around some 50 miles farther, near where the Chimney Creek Bridge is today, and crossed on a boat ferry. Since neither livestock nor wagons could cross on this ferry, an extra eight days was added to the trip with team and wagon to Big Creek.

During the winter months, when the river was frozen over and the ferries were laid up, it was the ferryman's job to locate a safe crossing on the ice and pilot people over.

In 1906, the Hanceville Bridge across the Chilcotin River was washed out by high water and crossing the river that summer entailed the hazardous procedure of rowing across in a boat which would be swept by the powerful current a good distance downstream before coming in to the opposite bank. The boat then had to be towed back up to the starting point for the next comer. In early winter a crew staying at Hanceville worked several weeks repairing the bridge and, during this time, crossing could be made in a boat attached to a block and cables, pulled across by an endless rope.

This same system, rigged up by John Wade of Chilco Ranch, was used by stranded residents on the south side of the Chilcotin when the middle span of the Hanceville Bridge was washed out by high water in April 1956. The Farwell Canyon Road was not passable for cars at that time and the only alternate route was a rough road of sorts another 50 miles farther around via Stoney and Deer Creek, crossing the Chilcotin River on the bridge below Alexis Creek. A trip to Williams Lake from Big Creek took the best part of a day, eating your lunch along the way. The gap was fixed with a Bailey bridge in November 1956.

The Bailey span was removed and the present bridge built in the 1960s.

THE CHIMNEY CREEK BRIDGE — 1902

Chilcotin residents had been lobbying the government for many years for a bridge over the Fraser River. Crossing the Fraser thus far was by an inconvenient and slow boat ferry at the mouth of Chimney Creek and at Soda Creek, and a scow ferry at the mouth of Churn Creek near the Gang Ranch. In 1898 a petition containing 42 signatures of Chilcotin ranchers was sent to the Lieutenant -Governor in Victoria stating several reasons why such a crossing was needed. One of the most convincing arguments was that the mail contract running from Soda Creek to Alexis Creek might soon be changed to 150 Mile House to Alexis Creek via Chimney Creek. Their voices were finally heard. In 1901, 1 1/2 miles of road was built approaching the river on the west side of the bridge site. Work on the first Chimney Creek Bridge across the Fraser River leading into the Chilcotin was started in 1902 at an estimated cost of $40,000. Due to many "unavoidable causes" the actual cost increased to $65,000 by the time it was completed in 1904.

The structure was designed by T. A. L. Waddell, an engineer with the firm of Waddell and Hedrick in Vancouver. Known as the Waddell-Hedrick Suspension Bridge, it was the first bridge of its type ever constructed. It was claimed to be the cheapest legitimate structure that could be erected at this crossing and was so designed that all perishable parts could be replaced without the use of false work and without interrupting traffic. The bridge was designed to

Chimney Creek Bridge with original wooden towers.

carry a total live weight of 700 lbs. per lineal foot and 80 lbs. per square foot live weight. Owing to its peculiarity of design, the lower cable and counter weights provided stiffening and rigidity even "with the crossing of heavy freight wagons and bands of livestock." A hundred feet above the water, the center span was 325 feet with an 80-foot Howe truss span and 130 feet of trestle connecting the bridge to the high plank roadway. On the west side, the bridge was connected to the plank roadway by 130 feet of trestle. On both sides of the river stock corrals were built to regulate the number of cattle crossed at a time: 25 head.

This marvel of engineering and design was supervised throughout by a man with the unassuming name of Sam Smith. A reporter writing for the *Ashcroft Journal* noted that great credit was due Mr. Smith as there were many problems involved such as "the difficulty of securing suitable rock for masonry towers, haul-

Chimney Creek Bridge with steel towers which replaced wooden ones in 1912.

ing timber from long distances and working where it was impossible to bring in machinery usually employed in such works." There was also the added expense of bringing in skilled labour from the Coast.

It was a great day for the Chilcotin when the new bridge across the Fraser River opened for traffic in September 1904. It served the country well for nearly 60 years.

In 1912 the wooden towers were replaced with steel towers.

With new decking when needed and occasional repairs, the first Chimney Creek Bridge took travellers and commerce in and out of the Chilcotin for 57 years. But, built for a different era, the loaded logging trucks, cattle trucks, and all manner of heavy traffic of the 1950s and 1960s took their toll on the old bridge, including breaking a cable. The bridge was replaced with a new structure in 1961 and the historic old Waddell-Hedrick Suspension Bridge was blasted into the river.

The tale is told that when Jack Skinner drove the Chilcotin Stage he made his passengers understand that they must walk up the steep hills to lighten the load for his team on the long journey. Leaving Hanceville, headed east, he had passengers start ahead of him on foot so that they would have reached the top of Hance's Hill – which climbs sharply for about a mile and is no longer in use for vehicles – by the time he and his team and wagon or sleigh arrived there. Heading west, Skinner would stop on Chimney Creek Bridge and order his passengers to bundle out and start the steep three-mile climb up Sheep Creek Hill. One hefty lady protested that her heart would not stand the long climb but the driver was unimpressed. "Get out, get out," he insisted. He would wait at the top and rest his team until the climbers caught up.

No doubt this was practiced to some degree by most stage drivers of those days – teamsters who were concerned about the welfare of their horses. Dorothy Bayliff remembers having to walk up the long hill at the 100 Mile when travelling on the stage as a young girl with her family after a visit to the Chilcotin. As she trudged along uphill, the stage with her parents on board moved farther and farther ahead. She recalls being terrified that they would continue on without her and she would be left behind in this wild country.

Chilcotin stage pulling in towards Hanceville Post Office from 150 Mile House, below, the transfer point on the Cariboo Wagon Road.

A tall fir tree beyond the east end of Becher's Prairie was known as "Skinner's Tree." In winter when the road was drifted in across the prairie, Skinner used this tree with its distinctive bent top to guide his team and sleigh across the trackless snow.

Becher's Prairie is named after Fred Becher, shown with his wife, Florence, and their Cadillac, first car in the Chilcotin. (See page 53.)

MELDRUM CREEK

Allan Jeffery researched and wrote the original Meldrum Creek history and we are indebted to him. Some of the stories remain as he wrote them. We wish to thank Orville Stowell for cheerfully giving of his time and sharing his knowledge of Meldrum Creek to enlarge and update this section. Thanks also to Betty Meldrum, Agnes Moon, Joan Huston, Jennie Warde, and Mary MacLeod.

Meldrum Creek is on the west side of the Fraser River, 20 miles south of the Soda Creek Ferry. This ferry, linked to the old trail through Meldrum Creek, was the first gateway to the Chilcotin country. Many of the first settlers came in this way. In the very early days mail for the Chilcotin was picked up at Soda Creek Post Office on the eastern bank of the Fraser and carried by packhorse across the river and up the mountain on the Meldrum Creek trail, leading south into the Chilcotin. The Meldrum Creek Road now joins Highway 20 at the top of Sheep Creek Hill and it,via Chimney Creek Bridge, is the usual route to Williams Lake and beyond. In November 1968, Rudy Johnson's Bridge across the Fraser below the ferry gave people on the west side another route to Highway 97. The well-travelled road from Rudy's Bridge to Meldrum Creek passes scenic places with interesting names, including Copeland Flat, Dead Horse Bluff, Blue Rock, and Sunflower Hill. Meldrum Creek is noted for ranching, trapping, fishing, and hunting and, more recently, lumbering. Three-phase Hydro power and the telephone came to Meldrum Creek in 1973.

THOMAS MELDRUM was one of the earliest settlers in this part of British Columbia. There is no record of the correct date of his arrival but as he came into the country with William Pinchbeck it must have been in the late 1850s or early 1860s.

Meldrum was born on board ship in 1828 en route from Scotland. His people settled in Barrie, Ontario. Young Meldrum came west and after looking around he decided to settle in a little valley on the west side of the Fraser River which today carries his name. He was the first Justice of the Peace in the area.

With his wife, Betty Kevah, Meldrum raised three sons and three daughters. Thomas Meldrum died on October 7, 1889. He

Thomas Meldrum and his wife, Betty Kevah, at their Meldrum home.

knew that he was suffering from a terminal illness and had his casket and headstone at the ranch before he died. He and his wife, their three sons: Thomas Jr., Thrift, and Jack, daughters Margaret and Catherine, are all buried on a knoll overlooking the original homestead. Daughter Ellen married Fred Copeland and is the only one not buried in the family cemetery.

Thomas Jr. married and lived at Meldrum Creek all his life. He died in 1955 at age 77. One son, Arthur, took over his father's place, married and raised a family. Art Meldrum died in 1989, 100 years after his grandfather. His widow, Betty, son Willy and family still live there.

Thrift Meldrum bought out the Frank English place on Sheep Creek and later sold to Charlie Moon. He had a photographic business and many of his excellent photos still survive. He was blind for a number of years and it was thought that exposure to developing fluid may have been the cause. Thrift was living in Meldrum Creek when he died in 1946. Jack was accidently killed in November 1916 at 32. His head was crushed when his horse ran with him into a leaning tree.

Thomas Meldrum's original pre-emption is owned by the Moon family. The log house built by Meldrum in 1888 is still in use, forming part of the Mel Moons' family home. Still in use and of the same age are a log building originally used as a store by

Meldrum and a small log cabin that housed Chinese help. Meldrum's log barn is also still in use, and he is commemorated by Meldrum Creek.

CARY GIBSON took up land in 1886 on what is known as Copeland Flat. FRED COPELAND also had holdings on Copeland Flat in 1890. (He married Ellen Meldrum.)

CHARLIE ROSS came in from Nova Scotia around 1890. He had several places and lived at his brother's place at Ross Gulch for awhile. He was ferryman at Soda Creek for many years. Mrs. Eric Collier was a daughter.

MURDOCK ROSS, Charlie's brother, took up land in Ross Gulch on the Fraser (now owned by Riske Creek Ranching) and built a house there in 1895. His first wife, Jennie, died on July 2, 1896, and is buried there. She left a family of six children ranging in ages from 12 to 10 months: Millie, Fannie, Maggie, Charlie, Wallace, and Jeanet.

Murdock then moved to the mouth of Chimney Creek and ran the ferry across the Fraser from 1897 to the opening of the Chimney Creek Bridge in 1903. This was a boat ferry – all livestock had to swim. With his second wife, Florence Hunt from England, he lived at the Milk Ranch at Riske Creek, later owned by Jaspers and now belonging to Gilbert and Joan MacDonald. From there he went to Meldrum Creek, taking up land in what became known as Ross Valley. Jennie Warde, Flora Schoonover, and Blanche Barlow are daughters; Harvey, Murdock, Allen, and Sam Ross, sons, all from the second marriage.

ALLEN and SAM ROSS lived on the family ranch on Meldrum Creek. Sam was quite crippled from childhood yet he managed to do a lot of work on the family ranch. They sold it in 1971 to Eric Reay, an Englishman working at the Circle S Ranch. Reay also bought the joining Dick Stowell place from Alfie McKnight of Merritt who had owned the Stowell Ranch for about four years. The four men got together and with a handshake settled their deal of buying and selling the two ranches. Lawyer Lee Skipp who drew up the papers said he had never seen a deal like it. No quibbling, no arguments, just hands across the table. Eric Reay, wife Diane, and family make their home there.

E. C. CASSIDY had a place at the head of Sword (Sheep) Creek in 1893. He sold out to F. N. Sutton in 1908 and moved to Bailey

Flats across from the mouth of Chimney Creek. Cassidy sold to Jerry Buckley who sold to Moons. It is still called the Cassidy Place. E. C. Cassidy made a cattle drive to Telegraph Creek with Cornell and Henri. He died in Williams Lake in 1930.

BILL YORSTON came from the Orkney Islands in 1904. In 1907 he, with his brother, took up a homestead at Leech Lake on the Meldrum Creek Road and started the YB Ranch — Yorston Brothers. He bought Kenny MacKenzie's place on Meldrum Creek below Mel Moon's in 1920, and also Adams Meadow on Mackin Creek. Yorston sold out to Graham Kinlock in 1936 and the Adams Meadow is now called Kinlock Meadow. Yorstons had two daughters: Nellie, who married Billy Muir, and Mary (Spalding) who lived in Victoria.

KENNIE MACKENZIE eventually settled at Quesnel Forks east of Williams Lake where he died in 1937.

JOHN MALONE was born in Cornwall, Connecticut. He took up land on Buckskin Creek in 1909. He was well known as a dance-hall caller. Malone also had a place at the mouth of Meldrum Creek that he sold to Moons. His wife was killed on a narrow grade going in to this place when her team ran away and the buggy upset on top of her. Malone then moved to a 20-acre homesite on Richards Creek purchased from Wes Jasper. He sold this place to Dick Stowell in the 1930s. Stowell's son, Orville, sold it to Harold Burns. Burns makes his home there with his wife, Susy, and family. The old cabin that Malone built still stands.

The land on Buckskin Creek that became the Buckskin Ranch went to JIM KEEFE (son of Mrs. John Malone) in 1921. JOE DEMAR, from France, was his partner. He ranched there for many years, selling the Buckskin Ranch to Jorgenson and Wells Logging Company in 1955. Lloyd Beaman was ranch manager for J. W. Logging. They sold to RUDY JOHNSON, who with his wife, Helen, and family enlarged and improved it. In 1968 Rudy bought a bridge in Alaska, 300 feet long and weighing 200 tons, and with the help of engineer Howard Elder of Victoria, accomplished the incredible feat of spanning the Fraser for less than $200,000 and completing the job within six months. This chopped off more than 30 miles from Johnsons' Buckskin Ranch in to Williams Lake. Two cattle trucks rumbling across it in late November 1968 marked the unofficial opening of Rudy's Bridge. The trucks were owned by Elton Elliot and driven by Ken Boychuk and Jim Pigeon. Rudy sold the Buckskin Ranch in 1991.

The Salmon Ranch (later the Soda Creek Ranch and now the Fraser River Ranch) was named after the JOHN SALMON family. They lived there more than 100 years ago but did not apply for a crown grant. The ranch changed hands several times. The CROW-STON family grew a lot of wheat there in the early 1920s. They owned the mill at Soda Creek and ground their wheat into flour.

WALTER COULTHARD came from North Dakota. He worked at various ranches and then took up land above the Soda Creek Ferry on top of the mountain on the west side. Coulthard married Susie Crowston. They had three sons. Billy married Fay Knoll and lives at Chezacut. John Valentine (Val) married Gerry Frizzy. Jimmy still lives on the Coulthard place, called the T Hanging O Ranch after his T Hanging O brand – registered originally by his father, Walter Coulthard. A daughter, Grace, was Gordon Woods first wife. She is now Mrs. Bob Nore and lives near Williams Lake.

C. E. RICHARDS came from England in 1910. He owned several places. He rented to Sutton for five years and sold to Charlie Moon in 1923. Then he pre-empted Copeland Flat. Sold to E. R. Bobbs. Richards owned the first car in Meldrum Creek. Richards Lake is named after him. He moved to Enderby in 1924.

ERNIE MADDEN came to the country about 1912 and stayed at the old MacIntyre Place near the bridge. He and his partner, NOR-TON JOHNSON, took up land near Fish Lake and raised horses. They sold to R. C. Cotton. These 320 acres now belong to Niel MacDonald and are still known as the MJ Meadows.

Madden and Johnson were musical, with Madden an excellent violinist and Johnson playing the piano. They carried their small portable piano around in a buckboard and played at dances and other functions. At a time when entertainment was scarce they were welcome and popular. Ernie Madden ended up with a leather shop at Cache Creek and lived out his life there.

EDWARD RUBEN BOBBS came to Copeland Flat in 1924. He ran sheep for awhile. The hay shed he built on Copeland Flat is still standing and in good shape. No nails were used in the superstructure, it was all pegged and mortised. He moved to a trapline north of Mackin Creek. His line was a long one, running all the way to Twan Creek. Bobbs built a small log cabin and barn every 8 or 10 miles along his trapline, each with a shake roof. A skilled crafts-

Rudy's bridge at Soda Creek is a well-used testimonial that the pioneer spirit still flourishes in the Chilcotin.

man and rock mason, he built in each cabin a brick chimney on the outside wall which extended inside the building to form a stove for cooking and heating. Since there were no roads of any kind, the bricks and shakes were made at the site from materials at hand. Some 50 years later the shake roofs are still intact and the bricks still sound and solid. During the summer he filled the hay lofts on his barns with swamp hay, cut with a scythe and hauled in with a small homemade sleigh. Bobbs did well on his line – he was an expert muskrat trapper.

Bobbs' wife was from Kentucky and claimed she was raised on gun smoke and black coffee. "Where I came from," she used to say, "you shot first and asked questions later." She came by train and stage to be Edward Ruben's bride and he declared that she was "the prettiest thing that ever got off the stage at Soda Creek." She had the reputation of making top-notch moonshine at Meldrum Creek. Bobbs lived in Quesnel for a time and died in the Old Men's Home in Kamloops in 1989.

Bobb's cabin and barn, built over 70 years ago. Because there was no road, he made all building material at the site, including bricks for his chimney.

I. J. PURKEYPILE came to Meldrum Creek in 1912 from Oregon where he was a telegrapher. He took up land at Stack Valley and later bought the Milo Emily meadows. His brand was US. He worked for Becher, driving Becher's Cadillac as the first taxi in Chilcotin, making trips to Ashcroft in 1913. For five years he drove between 150 Mile House and Hances. Purkeypile died in 1935, but his wife carried on the cattle ranch until 1957 when she sold to Mel Moon. Mrs. Purkeypile was the first school teacher at Meldrum Creek. After selling the ranch at Meldrum Creek she lived in Chilliwack and Williams Lake and then went back to Oregon.

GENE AND SARA STOWELL with family – Richard, Jess, Emogene and Geneva – came from Oregon in 1912. Gene ran Becher's sawmill before taking up land on Meldrum Creek. The cabin he built there in 1914 is still standing. Gene Stowell played the violin. He took his responsibilities lightly and after some years returned to Oregon, leaving his wife and family behind at Meldrum Creek. Orville Mackay, who married daughter Emogene Stowell, bought the Gene Stowell property. He sold it to Charlie Woods in 1940 and Woods sold the 160 acres to Gene's grandson, Orville Stowell, in 1968. Orville and wife, Susan, lived there until June 1992 when they sold and moved to Vancouver Island.

DICK AND EMMA STOWELL had a cattle ranch on Meldrum Creek where their two sons, Orville and William, were raised. They sold the ranch and it now belongs to Eric and Diane Reay. Dick's brother, Jess, went back to Oregon where he died in 1935. Geneva married Phil McRae of Riske Creek in 1927 and had one daughter, Willena Hodgson. After McRae's death, Geneva married Mickey Martin.

ORVILLE ALBERT McKAY was born in Wascada, Manitoba, in 1896. When he was 11 the family moved to land at Redcliff, Alberta, where he and his 10 brothers and sisters helped develop the farm. In 1918, at 18, Orville joined the Army. His picture and medals are on display in the Canadian Legion in Williams Lake. After the war he came to the Cariboo and at Meldrum Creek met and married Emogene Stowell. On the original Stowell homestead their family – Richard, Hazel, and Joan – were born and raised. In 1941-42 McKays ran the Becher Place at Riske Creek. The next year McKay sold the old homestead at Meldrum Creek to Charley Woods and bought a bigger place at Bear Lake above Soda Creek. Here they ranched until Orville's death in 1957. Richard, Hazel and Joan now all live north of Williams Lake.

BEN GARY, a relative of Sara Stowell, came into the country in 1912. He worked for various ranches in the Chilcotin, leaving in 1917.

WILLIAM JOHN (BILLY) MUIR, a World War One veteran, came from Scotland and located on Meldrum Creek above Mel Moon in 1912. He drove the first pure bred bulls some 225 miles on foot from Ashcroft to the Australian Ranch near Quesnel for the Yorston bothers. Three of these animals came to Meldrum Creek.

Muir married Nellie Yorston and the couple had a daughter

and a son, Margaret and Reginald. Margaret married Wesley Jasper of Riske Creek. After his untimely death she moved to Vancouver Island. Reg lived in Quesnel. Billy and Nellie Muir sold out to JOE CLUCK in 1953 and moved to Quesnel and then to Vancouver Island to be near their daughter. Billy Muir died there in 1987 at 95. His wife, Nellie, predeceased him in 1967.

WILL ROBBINS came to Soda Creek in 1913 to build a river boat. He took up land above the Fraser River on the west side a mile north of Buckskin Creek. His cabin, the dirt roof caving in, still can be seen from the road.

MILO EMILY, a construction worker on the railway, came to the country in 1915 and worked for various ranches. He was a very tall man and was nicknamed "Long Shorty." The wild hayland he pre-empted is called the Long Shorty Meadow.

ERIC COLLIER took up meadows at Madden Lake in 1929 and established a trapline on the Meldrum Creek watershed. Here he brought back the beaver, importing a pair or two to start. Eric was a clever mink trapper – few could elude him. Eventually, beaver was his most important pelt. Eric sold his 38-mile trapline to Orville Stowell and Val Coulthard for $2,500 on March 26, 1964. Eric drew up a detailed agreement of sale, fixing three, 5-cent stamps (the letter postage of the day) to the document over which the three men put their signatures. Helen McCue was their witness. Eric and Lily Collier's log home still stands at Madden Lake. (See also page 95.)

GEORGE WATT came to Mackin Creek in 1918. He and Jim Kennedy came from Vancouver by horse and wagon. George was road foreman for a long time.

JIM KENNEDY came from Scotland in 1912. He and his wife had a small orchard on the west side of the Fraser in an area called Glencoe. It was serviced by the Soda Creek Post Office. Kennedy experimented grafting and crossing various fruits and he also kept bees. Two of the Kennedy girls married the two eldest Moon brothers: Agnes married Mel Moon and Lizzy married Jack Moon.

JOE MURRAY, a sailor, had a cabin below Malone in 1920 on the banks of the Fraser. He raised a big garden and prospected all around the country, as well as working for various ranches in the district.

Most of the land along the river was surveyed in 1921. Quite a number of men took up pre-emptions about that time. To mention a few:

ANDREW JOHNSON, from Sweden.

GUS STEARN, from Germany.

TOM THORENSON, from Norway.

CHARLIE DAY from England.

MALCOM MacLEOD came from Scotland in 1924. He married Mary Meldrum in 1927. They had four sons – Norman and Don of Meldrum Creek, Alvin of Quesnel and Neil of Merritt. Malcom had a meadow and trapline on Maken Creek and also ran a sawmill at Meldrum Creek. He died in 1984 after a lengthy illness. His widow, Mary, lives in Williams Lake.

ALLAN JEFFERY left England in 1923 and came to Meldrum Creek in 1926. He and Will Robbins bought meadows north of Meldrum Creek and raised sheep. Later, Jeffery bought out Robbins and Ed Bobbs. Allen Jeffery went back to England and married his childhood sweetheart, Minnie, who was then widowed, and brought her to Meldrum Creek. They lived happily at Copeland Flat for more than 10 years before moving to White Rock. Allan Jeffery died in Vancouver on January 31, 1987, at 87.

GRAHAM KINLOCK arrived in 1936. He bought out Billy Yorston. Sold to Mel Moon and moved to Kamloops. Kinlock Meadow is named after him. He had two children, Mickie and Pidgie.

SONG OF AN OLD SADDLE
Veera Witte

My tree is broke so I'm hung aside
To rest on the stable wall,
While a brand new saddle now takes my place
On that pony in yonder stall.

And I'll hear the cattle bawl no more
On the range at set of sun,
Or thrill to a bronco's twisting leap –
For the last of my days are done.

But in dreams I ride o'er the lonely hills
That never again I'll see
As I hang on the wall of an old log barn
Living in memory.

When winter comes with its deepening snows,
And the wild mustangs grow thin,
I race with a phantom rider and
In fancy chase them in.

And in spring again at the log corral
I hold the lasso tight
As the cowhorse braces his noble strength
To the downed steer's useless fight.

While the smell of smoke and of burning hair
And the sound of laughter gay,
And the bawl of cows and a cowboy's yell
Mingle and fade away.

Oh, no more I'll carry the hunter's gun
Or the cowboy's lariat,
But I camp in dreams with my rider still
When the fading sun has set.

I can see him now as he rolls a smoke
From his well-worn leather sack,
As he turns his face from the blazing fire
And pushes his stetson back.

Hush! ... for I hear his boyish voice
Swell to a phantom tune,
And the echoes stir as a phantom wolf
Howls to a phantom moon.

And far away o'er the lonely trails
That never again I'll see
My spirit roves as it lives the days
That forever are gone from me.

For I'm hung inside on the stable wall
And those carefree days are gone –
But in memory till I rot and fall
They will still be living on.

After a day of spring branding at Stack Valley in 1942. At top are Jack Moon, Joe McLaughlin and Tom Rafferty. Standing are Jerry ....., Tex Fosbery and Willy Kennedy. At bottom are Leonard English, Pudge Moon, Ed Garland and Mel Moon.

RISKE CREEK

We owe George Terry a great debt for the work he did in 1958 on the Riske Creek section of the original *History and Legends of the Chilcotin.* Terry spent many weeks interviewing old-timers and talking to people from one end of Riske Creek to the other, often travelling on foot. Much of the historical information he obtained would now be impossible to unearth.

Parts of the Riske Creek history have been rewritten for this new publication. Corrections have been made and, wherever possible, more details added. But the names and times of many of the Riske Creek pioneers appear here as researched and written by George Terry.

Thanks to Lillian Moon Fletcher, June Jasper Bliss, Wilfred Hodgson, the Durrell family, Carol Cotton Hutchinson, Willena McRae Hodgson, Joan Farwell Buckmaster, and all others who provided help with their family histories and other details in this revised history of Riske Creek.

Travelling west from Williams Lake, you cross the Fraser River on the Chimney Creek bridge and after climbing 1,400 feet are on a rolling rocky plateau that extends 35 miles to the Chilcotin River. This is the Riske Creek area. Settlement began in the 1860s with L. W. Riske and Sam and Ed Withrow. Many followed. Open bunchgrass rangeland dotted with numerous lakes and scattered poplar thickets and fir-covered ridges made cattle raising the principal industry. Harper of the Gang Ranch took up land, too, and ran cattle at Riske Creek. Large herds fattened on the hard bunchgrass feed. In the early days the range was divided into three parts: Gang Ranch Range in the south, Withrow Range to the west, and Riske Range in the east. Withrow became Raven Lake and Bald Mountain Ranges; while Riske became Bechers Prairie. In the 1950s and 1960s logging contributed to the economics of the area and still plays a part, although ranching remains the prime industry.

The first post office in the Chilcotin, named "Chilcoten," opened at Riske Creek on May 1, 1886. Fifteen years later, on May 1, 1911, the spelling of Chilcoten post office was changed to Chilcotin, as it is spelled today. On November 1, 1912, the post office again had its name changed, this time to Riske Creek. It was rumored that this change was due to confusion in the mails with Chilecothe, Ohio.

L. W. RISKE and HERMAN OTTO BOWE came to the country from Alsace-Lorraine about 1859. Bowe settled at Alkali Lake and Riske in 1868 took up land in the Chilcotin on the creek that bears his name, the place that became the Cotton Ranch. His wife, Freda, was Bowe's sister. The first cattle and pigs were brought into the country by Riske and Sam and Ed Withrow. Withrows took up land on the Chilcotin River below O. T. Hance and started the River Ranch.

They had a flour mill and a lumber mill and shipped flour, bacon, ham and butter to the mines at Barkerville. Riske also had a lumber mill and shipped ranch produce to the gold mines. He was offered the office of Justice of the Peace in 1883 but declined. L. W. Riske was the first postmaster for the newly opened Chilcoten Post Office in 1886, serving from May 1 until September 19. The name of the post office was changed to honor him 26 years later, becoming Riske Creek Post Office on November 1, 1912. Riske and Withrows sold out to Mortimer Drummond and Fred Beaumont in 1880. In 1918, Mrs. Sam Withrow and a daughter hired a horse and buggy from BX stage line to come up from Vancouver to visit the old ranch.

In August 1868, DONALD McINTYRE pre-empted 160 acres near the mouth of Riske Creek. This claim was Crown granted to L. W. Riske in 1896. McIntyre moved to the foot of Sheep Creek Hill in 1880 and developed a small place. He cut hay on Moon's Point near McIntyre Lake, east of the Meldrum Creek Road above Chimney Creek Bridge.

THE 1870s ERA
JACK SIMISTER, a prospector and trapper, ran the sawmill on Withrow Creek for Withrows. Mrs. Jim Keefe of Soda Creek was a niece.

PATTERSON ran a mill above a meadow on Withrow Creek (called Sawmill Creek then) and O. T. Hance operated a mill below the present road on Sawmill Creek.

MOSES WYLIE and his partner were from Kentucky, the latter known only as "Old Kentucky." They were, apparently, gold rush miners, coming to the country about 1870. Wylie lived first at St. Joseph's Mission and Sugar Cane Reserve. They located north of Farwell Canyon on land that now belongs to Riske Creek Ranching. A hill nearby is named Wylie Mountain. Old Kentucky died in 1890 and is buried above where Wylie's cabin stood. Wylie's wife,

Mary, and daughter are buried at nearby Mary's Gulch. Wylie went to the Old Men's Home in Kamloops in 1907. He had lived in filth and on his arrival at the home was forced to take a bath. He died shortly after on October 13, 1907.

DANIEL NORDBERG from Finland was an independent fur trader who left his ship in Bella Coola and crossed the mountains to start a post at Ulkatcho in 1866. He left that site and started trading with the Indians on the south side of the Chilcotin River at what became Stone Reserve. About 1871 he moved above Tom Hance. He was naturalized in 1889, Thomas Meldrum J.P. signing his oath of allegiance. Nordberg sold to Norman Lee in 1891 and took up a small holding at Strouse Springs. He operated a little horse ranch there which he sold to French Henri in 1910. He continued to live at Strouse Springs until his death in 1917. He is buried there on property that is now part of Durrells' Wine Glass Ranch.

His grave, as well as that of Bill Strouse (1896) and two Strouse children, can be seen above Strouse Springs. The graves were fast becoming obliterated but were restored by Dave Falconer in the 1980s. In 1909, Einer Nordberg came out from Finland to live with his uncle. Einer died at Alexis Creek in 1955. Dan Nordberg claimed to have seen his first and last train at the age of 10 when the boat on which he was cabin boy was loading in Boston, Mass. (These Nordbergs were no relation to the Norbergs of Williams Lake.)

After gold was discovered on the Fraser, prospectors and traders started coming in from this direction. Among them were O. T. Hance and Benjamin Franklin "Doc" English. Hance became a permanent settler in the Chilcotin Valley. English left to take up a pre-emption at Deer Park, but later moved to Ashcroft where he bred race horses.

By his first wife he had three boys: Frank, who started a ranch half way down Sheep Creek Hill which he later sold to Thrift Meldrum. He died at Williams Lake in 1953. Chris was killed by a horse at Hazelton in 1920, and Fred died at Alexis Creek in the 1920s. By his second wife, English had three daughters and one son: Mrs. Nellie Baker, Dragon Lake; Mrs. Alice Cornelison, Phoenix, Arizona; Mrs. Lily Smith, Vancouver; and Ben, West Quesnel. Mrs. John Hutch is a granddaughter.

JOE MYERS rented Riske's place and ran a store. He was postmaster of the Chilcoten Post Office for nearly two years, 1889 to 1891, and then left the country with his wife and family to go north.

TOM McLEOD took up holdings below Hances. Sold to Archie Macauley in 1890. Macauley sold the land to Phil McRae in 1929.

HENRY LOVE had a cabin and irrigation system on Chilcotin Flats south of Bald Mountain. This property was later surveyed by the Gang Ranch and is now part of Durrell's home ranch. One daughter, Madeline Strumm, lived at Alkali Lake.

HENRY CARGILE started a trading post on Cargile Gulch above Farwell Canyon. He also built a second post on the south side of the Chilcotin, down towards the mouth of the river. A creek there bears his name. At one time he owned the Hat Creek Ranch north of Ashcroft and built Cargile House in Ashcroft about 1890.

GEORGE DESTER, an English sea captain, started a trading post on Riske Creek on what is now part of the reservation. He was later in partnership with Fred Becher and sold to him after a few years. Dester was postmaster of the Chilcoten Post Office from March 1892 to July 1894. About this time he left his Indian wife, Jessie, and returned to England, taking their eldest daughter, Isabel, with him. Another daughter, Lottie, and son, Baptiste, stayed with their mother and grew up and lived in the Chilcotin. Lottie married Johnny Chell of Anaham.

BILL SWANSON came out from his ranch near the site of the present city of Williams Lake and started a place across the river from the mouth of Chimney Creek where he grew grain and potatoes and other produce. He went to the Similkameen rush in 1886 and returned the next year. He had two daughters, Jessie Swanson and Anna McKill.

JIM CORNELL from Tennessee took up holdings on Fraser Flats above the Chilcotin River. He later built a cabin half a mile above the post office and took up meadows on the north fork of Riske Creek. He left his place and, taking his herd of a 100 head of cattle, went north with French Henri. That was the first cattle drive from the Chilcotin to reach Telegraph Creek. Cornell took over Dominic Burns' butcher shop there and sold the cattle at 75¢ a pound. The next spring he went north again and started the first hotel at Discovery near today's Atlin. After the rush he returned to the Chilcotin and took his horses south. He was last heard of running a hotel in Seattle. He had one daughter, Katie Liddell.

Although hundreds of Chinese swarmed up the Fraser and its tributaries, very few names are remembered on this side of the river. One notable exception is JEW YE TONG, better known as "China Tom." He was brought out from China by his uncle in Barkerville at the age of 14 and worked on the river boats and for various ranchers throughout the Chilcotin. In later years he made his home at Wes Jasper's. He was found dead on the road near Williams Lake.

BOB GRAHAM started a sheep ranch one mile above the present Meldrum Creak Road, hence the name "Sheep Creek" where he settled. He also built the road from Meldrum Creek to Soda Creek. (See Tatla Lake.)

MORTIMER DRUMMOND and FREDRICK M. BEAUMONT bought out Riske and Withrow but they split up. Drummond kept the Riske Ranch and Beaumont kept the Withrow Ranch. Drummond sold to Cotton and returned to England in 1898. He died in 1937 and his wife in 1938. Beaumont sold to McRae and died in Victoria.

W. J. "YOUNG" DRUMMOND bought Deer Park from Doc English. His wife died on the way out from England. He sold out to Young Davis in 1890.

FRED BECHER was a big, good-looking man with brown hair and eyes. He stood, in his prime, 6' 2" inches tall and weighed 220 pounds. He ran a saloon, stopping house and post office at Riske Creek for many years, and in full black beard, mustache and Stetson hat, he fitted most people's image of a typical western saloon keeper. If a fight broke out Becher could handle the toughest frontiersmen, but he was good-natured and optimistic in disposition and easy going to a fault in his business deals.

Frederick Metheun Becher was born in India in 1862. His father was a colonel in the British Army and was transferred from India to Northern Ireland where Fred grew up and was educated. After finishing school, he came to Canada as a young man in 1880 and at 18 joined the Hudson's Bay Co. and served as a clerk at Fort St. John. Later he came to Soda Creek and, through Peter Dunlevy, got a job packing freight to Hanceville. He then went in partner-

Becher House after renovations in the 1940s.

ship with George Dester who had a trading post on Riske Creek. When this piece of land was included in the Indian reserve in 1891, Becher moved a half mile farther up the creek to the site of the present Becher Place, pre-empting 160 acres on August 9, 1893. He bought Dester's share of the ranch and trading post and began building the first big hotel, including a saloon. He kept Dester's brand, the letter "D," and used that iron throughout his career.

Becher became postmaster of the Chilcoten Post Office on August 1, 1894. (As already noted, Chilcotin was spelled with an "e" in those days. This post office opened on May 1, 1886, with L. W. Riske as postmaster. It was the first post office in the Chilcotin. Riske ran the new office for only four and a half months, then rancher Fred Beaumont took over for a four-month stint. A. Provis was the next in charge but he also lasted only four and a half months. Then it was Joe Myers. He did a little better, keeping the job for nearly two years before leaving the country with his wife and family for the "Northwest." George Dester took over on March 1, 1892, and resigned in July 1894.) Fred Becher brought stability to the little office. He was postmaster for better than 30 years.

In 1912, a telephone line was strung through the Chilcotin and Becher had the first phone installed in his hotel. In 1913, he brought a Cadillac to the country. He hired I. J. Purkeypile as a chauffeur and for several years ran it as a taxi between 150 Mile and Hanceville. Becher's hotel and saloon, strategically located in this big country with long miles, winding dirt roads, and horse travel, did a good business. It soon earned a reputation as a stopping place for rest and refreshment. Race meets were held once a year on Becher's Prairie where the entire Chilcotin converged for a week to test their horses and enjoy horse racing.

Whiskey was brought in to the saloon in kegs by freight wagons from Ashcroft and sold for 15 cents for one drink or 25 cents for two. A pint of whiskey was $1.00, but only 75 cents if you brought your own bottle. Dan Nordberg often tended bar in the very early days. A round gambling table covered with a red cloth sat in one corner and saw many a rowdy poker game drag on into the night. Women were not admitted to bars in those days.

The store was well stocked and served the community for miles around. Becher had an easy credit policy which resulted in many bad debts. On the plus side he is credited with acquiring Ross Gulch and Becher Meadow on a $600 debt and three years later sold Ross Gulch to R. C. Cotton for $3,000. By 1914 Becher was doing well. He had 200 head of cattle, a big flock of sheep, good horses, and several meadows, in addition to his home place. Then in 1915 disaster struck. The famous Becher House burned to the ground. Becher optimistically rebuilt in larger and grander style. With his water-driven sawmill, he cut lumber for the frame building, which held 22 rooms. But he carried a debt load from which he never recovered.

In 1917 Becher married Florence Cole, a clergyman's daughter from England, and the couple kept up a genteel lifestyle for a time. Mrs. Becher enjoyed entertaining in her garden with lace tablecloth and elegant silver tea service. Becher House remained a celebrated and popular stopping place, catering to those travelling through the country as well as ranchers, cowboys and Indians. The stage stayed over at Bechers, and those who came a distance for their mail, travelling with horses, usually stayed all night. Special lady guests were shown into Mrs. Becher's private sitting room, while other women and children relaxed in a different parlour. Men had separate quarters, commonly called the "smoking room." Upstairs there were two bedchambers a little fancier than the rest – the "Blue Room" and the "Pink Room." At the far back, stark little sleeping rooms were reserved for rougher clientele.

Dances at the big house were elaborate affairs, with Mrs. Becher regally dressed. The annual Becher Ball became famous and brought people from as far away as Soda Creek, 150 Mile, and later, Williams Lake, as well as all parts of the Chilcotin. Most of the guests stayed over, filling the hotel to capacity and some camping in the yard. In an effort to raise a few dollars, the Becher Ball was revived in the 1930s. It was advertised as "The Last Dance at Becher House." Bert and Tissie Spencer supplied good music, but the crowd was small. Though Mrs. Becher swept about in a long flowing gown overseeing the event, the dance lacked the grandeur of the early days. It marked the end of the famous Becher Ball.

Sadly, the common use of the automobile and the coming of prohibition contributed to Becher's decline, and as his health and eyesight began to fail, debts piled higher. When he died in 1936, almost blind but still courageously cheerful, his finances were in dire straits. With the help of a girl named Isabel Goebel, Mrs. Becher continued to operate the business. Later she moved to Vancouver, leasing the place to Goebel, and then to Bert Roberts.

Bert Roberts organized and put on the first Riske Creek stampede during his time at the Becher Place. This meant building corrals and chutes and holding dances once more in Becher House.

Florence Becher finally sold the place, including Becher Meadow, to Geneva (McRae) Martin of River Ranch in 1941, and returned to England where she died in 1957. Fred Becher is buried at Riske Creek on a hillside overlooking the valley where he made and lost a fortune. He left no heirs but his name lives on in Becher's Prairie and Becher Dam. Also buried in the Becher plot are Billy Arthur, Tom Sward, Sherwell, Johnnie Wall, and Earl D. Myers.

Geneva Martin made extensive repairs and renovations to Becher House, a place she had always loved, completely remodeling the roof over the main quarters. She and her husband, Micky, made their home there for a time but this arrangement proved inconvenient and they eventually went back to living at River Ranch.

In 1943, the Riske Creek Post Office was moved from Bechers, its home for 48 years, and transferred to Tom Rafferty at Chilcotin Lodge where Rafferty also kept a store. (A nearby incline on Highway 20 is named Rafferty's Hill.)

When ill health forced Mr. Rafferty to move away the post office went to Red and Dionne Allison at the Riske Creek Store and Cafe. It remained in the Riske Creek Store (John Rose was postmaster for 18 years) until 1991. When John Rose retired the post office went to the Big B Store and Garage where mail boxes are set up under a contract arrangement.

Willena Hodgson inherited the Becher Place from her mother, Geneva Martin. In the interests of safety, Willena had the historic old house demolished in 1981. The big log barn with stalls for 20 horses, built for freight teams and saddle horses before the turn of the century, is still standing, sound and solid.

Once a hive of activity, the Becher Place sat quietly for many years, aloof from the mainstream of life, wrapped in memories of a by-gone era. Life returned in 1989 when Marcus Nairn, bought the Becher Place from Willena. His nephew, Mark Nairn with his wife, Sally, and family, built a log home and took up residence and began ranching. Nairn later purchased Ross, Davis and Moose Meadows from Neil MacDonald.

BILL McTAGGART built and operated a sawmill for Becher. He built the Alex Harris cabin and had a meadow five miles north of Meldrum Creek.

TOM SWORD, an old packer and harness maker, bought out Bob Graham, started raising horses and opened a harness shop on the north fork of Riske Creek. Before coming to the Chilcotin he had a cabin at Four Mile Creek. He sold out to Billy Till. Sword died at Riske Creek and is buried in the Becher plot.

CHARLIE MOON, who was born and raised in England, came to the Cariboo on foot when he was 16, walking in from Ashcroft in 1888. He was actually bound for the goldfields at Barkerville, but on reaching Soda Creek changed his mind and crossed the Fraser to a ranch on the other side owned by Thomas Meldrum.

Here, deciding he had had enough walking, he bought a saddle horse and proceeded into the Chilcotin – a casual decision that shaped his life. The Chilcotin became his home and that of his three sons. He acquired much land and finally even owned Tom Meldrum's Ranch where he had bought his first saddle horse and decided that land was better than gold. Moon worked for W. J. Drummond at Deer Park and Fred Beaumont on the River Ranch for several years. He was employed by Mortimer Drummond in 1892, at what is now the Cotton Ranch, when his childhood sweetheart came out from England to be his bride. He met his wife to be, Jessie Collard, with team and buggy at Ashcroft and they were married in the bustling little town.

Moons were still working for Mortimer Drummond and had two children, Melville and Violet, when they decided in 1901 to return to England for a holiday. Son Rexford was born there in 1902. His parents nicknamed him "Pudge" and this name stayed with him throughout his life. The family returned to the Chilcotin that same year and Charlie Moon invested in his first piece of

Charlie and Jessie Moon at Deer Park in 1932.

Canadian real estate: fertile benchland on the west side of the Fraser River called "Deer Park." This name goes back a long way. In his report on a trip through the Chilcotin in 1883, J. W. Powell, Superintendent of Indian Affairs in Victoria, refers to the area as Deer Park.

This piece of land was originally taken up by Benjamin Franklin (Doc) English. He applied for 320 acres on November 24, 1873. Doc English Gulch where the first steep narrow road went in carries his name. English sold Deer Park to W. J. Drummond, and Drummond sold to "Young" Davis in 1890.

In 1902, Charlie Moon paid Davis $1200 – with only $40 down – for 88 deeded acres at Deer Park and a 200-acre swamp north of Riske Creek, still known as Davis Meadow.

Moons planted ornamental trees, shrubs, and fruit trees (still growing and bearing fruit today) and worked hard making a home. By 1914 two more children were born: Jack and Dorothy. That year a nine-bedroom house was started, framed by logs and built mainly of rough lumber from Becher's sawmill. "Trapper" Tom Evans, who did most of the carpentry work, planed the lumber by hand for the finishing inside. This building housed the Moon family through adulthood and son Jack's family for a number of years before burning down in 1956. Jack rebuilt in the same spot.

Through hard work, frugal living, and thrifty management, Charlie Moon bought up land until he owned thousands of acres, including Hillcrest, Till Place, Cassidy Place, Meldrum Ranch, Sheep Creek, Kinlock Ranch, and Kinlock, Davis McRae, and Ross Meadows. The family worked long hours on the ranch operation and were paid in cattle, not cash, until each owned a small herd. Working cattle with seven different brands was quite a challenge.

With help from the Conservative government a lower road to Deer Park, following the Fraser, was started in 1918. It was finally finished in 1923 after the Conservatives had regained power. It was a narrow, precipitous wagon trail teetering above the river in many places but an improvement on the old road through Doc English Gulch. Improved some through the years, it is now officially named Moon Road.

As years advanced Charlie Moon divided his property among his sons. The Meldrum Creek Ranch went to Mel, Jack had Deer Park, and Pudge took over Hillcrest where Charlie and his wife had been living. The Senior Moons then moved to Sheep Creek, where they had a comfortable home, planted with apple trees and lilacs. The old gravel road winding down Sheep Creek Hill went through their property.

The two girls had married and left home: Dorothy Peterson lived in Vancouver and Violet Sharp in Quesnel. Tragically, Violet and her husband were both killed in a car accident in the 1970s.

Jessie Moon died in 1938. Charlie married her sister, Bertha Collard, who had come from England in 1902 and lived at Meldrum Creek for many years. During their last years the Charlie

Moons lived in Williams Lake. Charlie Moon died in 1956 and Bertha some years later.

Melville Moon married Agnes Kennedy and lived his life on his Meldrum Creek Ranch. There were four children: Francis, Charles, Alex, and John. Their father died on November 10, 1968, but his widow and sons, Alex and John, have carried on ranching at Meldrum Creek. Francis is a registered nurse working in Cariboo Memorial Hospital in Williams Lake, near enough to spend time on the ranch.

Pudge married Georgina Copley and had a family of four: Norah, Rexford, Lillian and Gerald. Pudge sold the Hillcrest Ranch (the "Top of the Hill" as Georgina called it), the Sheep Creek place and the Riske Creek Meadows to the Lee Thomson family from Wyoming in 1954. It now belongs to Neil MacDonald, husband of the late Joyce Thomson, and their daughter, Karry. Ray Thomson and his wife, Mary, ranch at Big Creek.

Pudge and Georgina Moon moved to Williams Lake, living first on South Lakeside and later on the north shore side. Beautiful rolling pasture land lying on the west side of the city of Williams Lake was purchased by Pudge from his father's estate, permitting this successful and well respected man to keep his hand in the ranching game even though living in town. Pudge Moon died on April 16, 1981, and the land has been sold to developers. Part of it is now known as the Moon West Hills Estates.

This area has an interesting background. Charlie Moon bought the rolling 400 acres of timber and grassland from Jerry Buckley, owner of the Sunnyside Motel and one time rancher. Earlier, the pasture belonged to Frank Goodrich, with a small field at the bottom once farmed by the Weetmans of Chimney Valley. Pudge Moon farmed the fields as well. He kept a few cattle and horses, fenced off the arable land to raise alfalfa hay, and put in a dam to store water.

The first settler on this west hills property was Henry Curtis who build a home near the timbered hillside about 1920 and lived there with his wife and family for 10-12 years. Curtis had a sawmill and cut ties for the new Pacific Great Eastern Railway. The children walked, according to Ray Curtis who was one of the youngsters, via the roundhouse and the graveyard to attend school in the village of Williams Lake. Part of Curtis's abandoned dwelling was later used as a ski cabin. It eventually burned down.

Pudge Moon's widow, the bright, witty Georgina Moon, now spends time in Victoria as well as her home on North Lakeside in

Williams Lake. Rex and Lillian (Fletcher) live in Williams Lake, and Nora (Cobbin) in Vancouver. Gerald was tragically killed in a car accident in 1963.

Jack Moon ranched at Deer Park throughout his lifetime. He married Elizabeth Kennedy (Agnes Moon's older sister) and the couple had three children: Robert, Shirley, and Dale. Jack Moon passed away in April 1963, and his wife Lizzy three months later. Rob took over the family ranch; Dale is fire chief in Williams Lake, and Shirley (Redden) lives in Kamloops.

Rob and his wife, Lynne, were instrumental in bringing three-phase power to the Chilcotin. Rob then installed a sophisticated irrigation system at Deer Park which lifts water to productive fields 650 feet above the Fraser. Rob sold the Deer Park Ranch, now consisting of 3,100 deeded and leased acres, in November 1981 to Riske Creek Ranching Ltd. and now lives in Williams Lake. Partners in the Riske Creek Ranching Company, Lynn and Myrna Bonner and family, make their home at Deer Park.

California bighorn sheep, protected from hunting, can be seen on the ranch almost every day, grazing on pasture land and in the alfalfa fields. This band, now numbered in the hundreds, was started by two ewes and a ram that wandered to Deer Park in 1924 from the band at the junction of the Chilcotin and Fraser Rivers. The Moons protected and cared for the wild sheep as they increased over the years and the present owners of Deer Park carry on that tradition. Mule deer are plentiful as well, and the two species are often seen together feeding in the fields, and sometimes in the haystacks. The river breaks and fir-clad hills provide cover and natural habitat. (See page 269.)

BILL and HOMER STROUSE came from Oregon and located at the spring, now part of Wineglass Ranch, which was named after them. They used Strouse Meadows on Riske Creek and the Chilcotin River range. They built the cabin above Farwell Canyon which became Gang Ranch Company Cabin. Homer left the country. Bill died in 1896 and is buried with two of his children, who predeceased him, at Strouse Springs.

KATHLEEN SEEMAN, as a young girl of 10, came from Eagle Lake to Riske Creek. She was still living in 1958.

PETER MURDOCK "YOUNG" ROSS, a cousin of Murdock and Charlie, took over Jim Cornell's holdings on the north fork of Riske Creek, later named Ross Meadows, when Cornell went north in '98. At the time of his death Ross had between 3-400 head of cattle.

THE 1890s ERA
FRED "OLD" DAVIS and HERBERT "YOUNG" DAVIS bought Deer Park from W. J. Drummond. They took up the Davis Meadows and bought out Pinchbeck in 1907. Herbert Drummond sold to Charlie Moon in the early 1900s and returned to England where he taught school. He died in 1955. Prior to her death, his wife lived in a nursing home on the Isle of Man where their son, Eric, worked for the Colonial Office. Another son, Jack, was a pilot and was killed in the World War One.

A part of the social life of the country was spring branding and fall roundup. Every family would bring their chuckwagon and spend a week or two working in the daytime with sing-songs and story telling in the evening. The women did not always confine themselves to the cook fire, either. Some of the local girls like the Swansons could out-ride almost any man on the range. But what always astonished the Americans was to see some of the English girls riding down steep banks and turning racing cattle while using a side saddle. Some even rode bucking horses on a side saddle.

Another form of community life much practiced in the early days was the wild horse roundups. Several families would gather at a neighbour's place with their best saddle horses and spend from up to a week or more running bands of wild horses. In addition, there were the professionals who made a living rounding up wild horses and selling them to the freighters and jackers on the Cariboo Road.

WILL and ED OAKLYN had a cabin on the Milk Ranch. They left in 1894. Their departure may have had something to do with the fact that Oaklyns were charged in February 1894 with shooting a cow belonging to Gerald Dester and stealing her calf.

VARISH "FRENCH" HENRI was born in Clarence Creek, Ontario, in 1867. He spent two years on the Ottawa River and six years in Michigan before travelling west. In the Chilcotin he worked for Billy Pinchbeck, Billy Adams and Bill Robinson. In 1898 he bought 25 head of cattle and went north with Jim Cornell, the second cattle drive to reach Telegraph Creek in northwest B.C. Vieth and Borland with 200 head of mules were the first train to reach there. Beef was selling for $3 a pound in Dawson and 75 cents a pound in Telegraph Creek. French Henri sold his beef in

Telegraph Creek and went on to the Yukon where he worked for several years.

In 1906, he returned to the Chilcotin and bought out Dan Nordberg, also acquiring Ross Gulch for winter range. He sold horses throughout B.C. and Alberta, making three trips to Telegraph Creek, a number of treks to Prince George and Hazelton and to Edmonton and Athabasca. He sold his ranch and outfit to Harry Durrell in 1938 and retired to a small cabin near the railway tracks in Williams Lake. He died in 1958.

BILLY PINCHBECK came out from his father's ranch at Williams Lake and started a blacksmith shop and store on the north fork of Riske Creek and raised cattle. In 1895 he married Nellie Isnardy from Chimney Creek. In the bad winter of 1906-07 he lost most of his cattle and in 1907 sold out to Young Davis. He moved to Chimney Creek and was Brand Inspector until his death. His widow lived on at Chimney Creek with son, Wilfred, who ran the old Chimney Creek Ranch for many years. One son, Fred, was blacksmith for the Gang Ranch. He was killed in an automobile accident in 1953 near Williams Lake. Son, Tom, was a cat operator; Percy Pinchbeck, a carpenter.

DAVE and BILLY ARTHUR, born in California, came from Ladner and settled on Riske Creek near the forks. They cut hay on Bechers Prairie. Dave moved to Vancouver but Billy stayed. He died in 1933 and is buried in the Becher plot.

ED HART and JEP, MURDOCK and FLORENCE ROSS took up the Milk Ranch, milked cows and shipped butter, thus giving this place its name. Remains of the old vat were still visible in the creek in 1958. Jep, who was a brother to Murdock and Charlie, went to live in Alberta.

HENRY DURRELL — by Jack Durrell
My father, Henry Durrell, always called "Harry" in the West, was born in Pembroke, Ontario, in 1870 on a farm near the Ottawa River. He had seven or eight brothers and sisters. The family were United Empire Loyalists who came from the United States at the time of the 1776 Revolution. They arrived in the American Colonies about 1714 from the Channel Islands – Huguenots who had fled France and religious persecution. I joke that we got run out of Europe and the United States and I believe my father found Ontario too conservative and square, so here we are in the Far West, no more room to run.

Harry and Kay Durrell with baby, Jack, in 1920.

In 1891, Dad headed west to Manitoba and worked in the grain harvest. He said he worked two days stooking bundles then said to himself, "This is why I left Ontario!" So he sneaked away and didn't even ask for the two days' wages owing him. From there he worked his way to Calgary on a C.P.R. telegraph line job and wound up in Vancouver that fall. He then worked a few months on the West Coast of Vancouver Island on a survey job and learned a little about surveying. Apparently, the wet climate didn't agree with him because he had fits of bronchitis the rest of his life. On a doctor's advice to go to a dry climate he went to the Nicola country and worked several years at Douglas Lake. His job there was as a store and time-keeper, fetching the weekly mail from Quilchena, and at times put to work on a saddle horse. So that is really how he got started in the cow business.

In the spring of 1894 Dad got bucked off his horse and broke his leg. After recovery he wandered into the Cariboo, going first to Barkerville. Finding no work in Barkerville, he heard there was work haying in the Chilcotin and he and a young Englishman walked over here. He said he decided that the Riske Creek Valley was the prettiest place he'd ever seen.

His first job was haying at the Beaumont Meadow. A fellow hay hand was Charlie Moon. He said he felt sorry for Mrs. Moon having to cook over a campfire with smoke and ashes blowing around, and she was then not long out of England.

I cannot now recall what he did in chronological order for the next 10 years. Among other things, he settled on a flat just across the Chilcotin River from Beaumont's Ranch (River Ranch). There is a nice spring on this flat, and I believe he was not the first to try his luck there. Being still a farmer at heart, he planted grain. Threshed it with a flail, winnowed it by tossing shovelfuls up in the wind, and for all I know, had cut it with a scythe. Then it had to be horse-packed to the river beach, ferried across in a canoe, packed once again to the nearby Beaumont Ranch, from where it was hauled by wagon to the customers. One customer was "Young Davis" at the Davis meadow and he never paid up!

Sometime early in the century, Dad got a few cattle of his own. Once he went to Lone Cabin Creek on the Fraser to buy a few stock cows or heifers.

He had formed a loose association with Louie Vedan, who was ranching at the Pothole in Farwell Canyon. At least they made hay in partnership. I remember he told me that whereas he was satisfied with what could be cut with a horse mower at the Jameson Meadow, Louie had to go after the small recesses in the willows with a scythe.

In the 1890s, Norman Lee had cut some small meadows in the vicinity of Raven Lake. He also did some drainage work on the main Raven Lake Meadow, and then quit the area. About 1905-06, he took up Raven Lake Meadow as he built his first cabin on the margin of the meadow, which was not a good building site, but was on the surveyed lot. Later he moved his buildings further up the water course.

Dad worked awhile on the first bridge across the Fraser at Sheep Creek. As he had a somewhat better education than many in those days, his job was to sort out the timbers as the teamsters arrived. The original towers were of long timbers, perhaps 12" x 12" and 30' x 40' bolted together. He said the cables, weighing more than 5 – or was it 10? – tons apiece, were rolled on several spools as the sleighs or wagons from Ashcroft could not take them in one large spool. He left this job before completion to go haying for himself. He bought a second hand mower at Springhouse and drove it home across the new bridge.

Dad's first winter at Raven Lake Meadow was a tough one due to deep early snow. In the beginning the ranchers almost totally relied on wintering cattle "out." That is, relying on winter chinooks to clear enough grass along the river valleys. But after the tough winter of 1906-07, changes were made. For example, although the Gang Ranch had taken up Harper Meadow about 1884, and may have hayed it now and then, it was not until 1906 or so that it was fenced for protection from stock grazing. He cut the rails and I believe put up the original fence on a contract. Also, after this bad winter the Gang Ranch got split pine rails and strung them out 5-6 miles to the head of Ross Gulch to preserve the grass for winter and early spring use.

In 1910 Dad made his first trip back to his home range around Pembroke, Ontario and went again in 1914. In those years the nearest shipping point was Ashcroft. The small ranchers, either threw in with a big outfit like Gang Ranch or Cotton, or a few would join together: H. Durrell, Arthur Bros. and McRae, and perhaps Murdock Ross as well.

About 1915 Dad bought some 20 draught horses (mares) to raise work horses.

In those days there were many wild horses at large. Some branded that couldn't be easily corralled, and their unbranded offspring. Both Indians and whites made wild horse corrals to catch them. My father said there really wasn't much profit in it but some sport. Louie Vedan and French Henri were often partnered with him in these ventures. It was illegal to brand a cow or horse not the brand owners stock, but if the real owner was unknown then it belonged to the Crown. These unbranded animals were known as "slicks."

He said that the partners were fairly successful at catching and branding slicks and some less lucky people were jealous and bad mouthed them as horse thieves. That accusation later appeared in print. The story began when a man known as "One Arm Phillips" – he had a hook on one arm – joined Dad, Henri and Vedan in horse chasing one spring. Phillips was always practicing with his six-shooter and could roll a tin can along the ground with it. It turned out that he was wanted in Washington State for murder. He had feuded with a neighbor and promised to kill him – which he did. He was later captured at Quesnel. At the time my father took a Vancouver newspaper, in which there was a write-up about the capture of this desperado. It noted: "The wanted man had spent the previous summer consorting with Chilcotin horse-thieves."

About 1916 my father went to Chilco Ranch, where he met Katherine MacPhail who was to become my mother. They were married in Vancouver in November 1917 and went to Ontario on a honeymoon. My father had left a saddle horse at Ashcroft. On their return he bought a cutter and with the saddle horse hitched to it arrived back in the Chilcotin about Christmas.

He had left Sherwell in charge of his place in his absence. Sherwell was a remittance man who had a little place on the south side of the Chilcotin River, just west of the Dry Farm. Sherwell had got behind on rounding up my father's stock for feeding. In consequence some were never found.

By 1919, the Pacific Great Eastern Railroad (now B.C. Rail) had reached Williams Lake and the long cattle drives to Ashcroft were no more. My mother said Williams Lake was a tent town when she arrived there with her new baby (I was born in Vancouver).

About 1921 Dad decided to try sheep raising. That only lasted two summers and one winter. He had never gone completely out of cattle and was soon back in the cow business again. At that time he could not have had many more than 150 to 175 head as his only hay supply was Raven Lake and a small irrigated acreage at the old place where the family lived in those years.

To help with the feed problem around 1923-24 he bought the Eno, or Einer, Place.

In the early 1920s the government began to take an interest in the use, or misuse, of the Crown range. By that time it was grossly overstocked, not only with cattle but also with horses, many unbranded and wild. In the fall of 1925 people were notified to remove their horses from Crown range onto their fenced properties. The ones remaining outside were shot by the hundreds. Dan Wier, later a Provincial policeman and Dave Chesney, who later spent years on the road crew, did most of the shooting. Dad lost four or five good mares he hadn't found. As well, the Forest Service instituted a charge for grazing: 5¢ a month per head, at which it remained for many years. In addition, the season of use was restricted from about April 15 to late October or even November. So from the middle 1920s ranchers began leasing and fencing like never before.

In 1927 Dad and Henri went partners on a lease on about half of Ross Gulch, extending west to near the old road to the Farwell, about 3,000 acres. Several years later they divided, Henri taking the eastern third and fencing it off separately.

The 1920s saw more changes than any other decade from the first settlement till the present. In 1920, with the exception of winter pastures fenced off along the rivers and quarter-section or so homesteads, the country was unfenced. The beef drives and wagon freighting from Ashcroft had just ended, and motor vehicles were uncommon. By the end of the decade horse-drawn vehicles were out of date except in the winter. Although the roads were not much by 1930, they were much superior to roads of 1920, although not much snow plowing was done till the 1940s. Also in the 1920s purebred bulls replaced bulls selected from the current calf crop, and the cattle no longer lived and died with horns but had them cut off as yearlings. The meat packers objected to the damage and bruising caused by horns in shipment.

My brother, Don was born in 1921, then a daughter about December in 1922 or 1923. She was premature and only survived hours and is buried at the Old Place. I can just recall my mother appearing quite ill, I and my small brother being locked up in a bedroom and left to ourselves. My father raced off to Henri's, about 2 1/2 miles away, and returned. Henri raced off to Becher House and phoned Dr. Wright at Alexis Creek. He arrived I suppose within the day (about 40 miles by cutter).

My sister, June, was born in 1926. She was also a "preemie" but was born in Vancouver General Hospital and even so had a narrow squeak. I believe the last, a boy, was a still-born in 1929 in Vancouver.

In the fall of 1929, Phil McRae sold the River Ranch. The new owner, having just a small herd of cattle, rented the Beaumont Meadow to my father for three years. So my father's hay problem was over for awhile.

In 1932 he traded his Ross Gulch lease and some cash for Lots 45, 771 and 772 and several leases along the Chilcotin River that the Gang Ranch had. Dad pre-empted the S.E. quarter of 15, but to get the deed meant to do so many dollars worth of improvements, and actually live on it so many months a year. To prove up on S.E. 15 he made a ditch from Mary's Gulch to a little flat. To reach the flat, the ditch had to run a little uphill, but no matter, there was never any water in the gulch anyway. He plowed a few acres under the ditch, and built a dinky log cabin. Also dug a shallow well in the dry sand and gravel. Geoff Brown who worked on it, got in the spirit of the scam. He told me that on the day the Inspector came to look, he put a pail of water in the bottom of the well so that the Inspector could see the gleam of water if he peeked through the cover. As soon as the pre-emption was approved, the cabin was torn down for fence posts.

Having acquired the Gang Ranch property my father set about building a ditch out of the river, and seeding the hayfields below the ditch. The first small cabin was built about half a mile east of the present buildings. Not a good spot because the water supply was a channel, well removed from the main river, which only flowed a few months a year. The next cabin was built in the fall of 1933.

In the spring of 1933 a camp was established on the "Camp Flat" and cultivation and seeding began. By the fall of 1934 a fair amount of hay was put up, and by 1937 most land below the ditch was producing heavily. Because there was no wagon road in, all supplies were packed on horses, and machinery was hauled straight down the mountain with a tree tied behind for a brake. Lumber for fluming, the same way, on a stone-boat, or a travois-like affair, the front end of which was mounted on the front wheels of a wagon.

At this time the family lived at the Old Place and my father often was only home weekends. He was in his early sixties then but worked hard at his new project. He said that, like Brigham Young, he would make the desert bloom like a rose. And so he did. It was a great treat to have products such as corn and tomatoes and later fruit that could only be grown in the river valleys. The first fruit trees were planted in 1936. Two crabapples, a transparent and a hybrid plum are surviving yet.

By 1936 he had more than enough hay and increased the cow herd. He bought about 40 cows, calves, and yearlings when Butch Helewig (from Nazko) sold out; about the same number when Bob Pyper (from Chilanko Forks) died, and around 60 from Leonard Palmantier.

In 1938, French Henri claimed to be 76 and decided to retire in Williams Lake. (He lived another 20 years in pretty good health, taking care of himself and his little cabin near the railway tracks.) My father bought his ranch at Riske Creek: a half section deeded, about 800 acres leased, 105 head of cattle and 7 horses, plus a little machinery and harness. He paid $8,500 for the whole package. The only time I ever saw my father showing the effects of liquor was one summer evening when he returned from Henri's where he was dealing with Henri for the place. He tried hard not to let it show. I never saw my father drink but the odd brandy at Christmas or a rare glass of beer. Although I did see an old account book he had kept and in it was the item: "One bottle of rye, $1.00."

Henri had a still and made a little moonshine. Once he nearly got in trouble over it, as he shared the proceeds with his old friend, Billy Pinchbeck. Billy must have given a bottle of it to someone who fell afoul of the law, and the cops were sniffing around. Early one summer morning I saw Billy's old car pass our place and I wondered why he was abroad so early. We learned later that he was out to warn Henri.

For all I know, stills had been around here since the beginning but the first I heard of them was about 1929 when Clarence Slee, a brother of Jim Slee, spent awhile with Jim. Clarence had just got out of a Washington State jail for a liquor offence. He showed the locals how to make a still out of a copper wash boiler.

About 1931 my mother noticed her left arm was becoming numb. By 1934 she was largely incapacitated with Parkinson's disease. So from then on there was a string of hired girls or older women on the ranch.

In 1940 Dad bought the Slee Ranch from Slee's widow. (Jim had died of a heart attack in 1933.) In 1941 he bought the Brown Place at the mouth of Big Creek. There was only about 12-15 acres of irrigated hayland, and poor land at that. My father had a new ambition: to divert water from Big Creek above the Scallon Ranch and bring the ditch across the top country and then down to the middle benches on the south side on the Brown property. The middle benches were, and are, good land and only needed water. That is when he got the idea to buy a tractor and bulldozer to do the job. Wartime shortages prevented the purchase till 1948. By that time the Brown Place had been sold to my cousin, Gordon Durrell. However, Dad always had some project on hand. During the 1940s he made improvements to the swamp meadows at Slee's, especially after the crawler was bought.

He was fairly active till his late seventies. Riding, fencing, a little haying, and other jobs filled his day. All the more remarkable as he was a diabetic and took insulin after the age of 69. Then, insulin had to be injected three times a day. He would have a tin cup tied to a saddle string so that wherever he might be he could sterilize his needle and take a dose. As I recall, he made his last beef drive in 1946 or 1947. He and I took a small drive of dry cows in about early August. We had a packhorse and camped out four or five days.

My sister, June, got her grade schooling partly by boarding out and high school the same way. She married in 1946, and moved out, although she and her husband, Bert Buckle, worked again on the ranch at times.

My brother, Don, joined the R.C.A.F. in 1941. His last visit, only visit home in fact, was a 10 day or so leave at Christmas in 1941. He later went overseas and transferred to the R.A.F. because he did not have enough schooling to qualify as Air-Crew in the R.C.A.F. The R.A.F. was not so fussy. He became an air-gunner in a bomber and was killed near Kassel, Germany, in 1943.

By 1949 my father was suffering from prostatitis, and had to go to Vancouver for an operation. I think he was a little nervous about it. He came back much improved and in a good humor. I met him in Williams Lake and as we passed Clark, the old undertaker who was loafing on the bench by the Log Cabin Hotel, he clapped Clark on the shoulder and said, "You didn't get me this time!"

But Clark did get him just about a year later. He suffered a heart attack at Slees, in September 1950. My mother's sister and her husband were visiting at the time and his brother-in-law rushed him to the hospital. He had a second and fatal attack a few days later and is buried in Williams Lake cemetery.

My mother was almost a total invalid by this time, and about a year later we placed her in a nursing home in Vancouver. She survived there about a month. She died in November 1951.

In closing this history, Dad was not what today would be looked upon as a typical Chilcotin rancher the way the media and TV look at it. He couldn't rope worth a darn, was no fancy bronco rider, never dressed "Western" in my memory, except for chaps now and then. He wore work boots and a battered old fedora hat. But he did know how the mind of a horse or a cow worked, and knew how to handle cattle with a minimum of hardship to stock or hard work for the riders.

As to his employees, they were expected to do an honest day's work, and get up early enough to wrangle the horse herd, or what -ever chore had been assigned to them. As well, he usually paid the going wage or generally a little better. Board and bed were provided in those days and he was never stingy with the grub. Lots of beef or bacon, bread, butter, Rogers Golden Syrup (he considered jam somewhat of a luxury), dried fruit, etc. He liked vegetables but balked at buying canned stuff. It was home grown or do without. Canned milk was provided when there was no milk cow on hand, and I think he looked on milk cows and chickens as a perhaps necessary but bothersome frill.

1895 — JOE DAN SMITH was a Negro carpenter who worked for Fred Becher in 1895. His cabin on the south bank of the Chilcotin River below Farwell Canyon can still be seen. Known as Nigger Dan, he was well liked in the country but got into trouble when his Indian wife was drinking at Bechers. Nigger Dan was arrested on a shooting charge and sentenced at the Spring Assizes in Clinton in 1908 to 5 years in jail. He did not return to the Chilcotin.

1895 — GEORGE HALLER came as a boy of twelve from his father's place at Jesmond to work for Joe Truen at Harper Meadow. He was still riding for the Gang Ranch and others in the 1960s. Joe, Bill and Frank Haller were relatives.

THE 1890s ERA – continued
ROBERT CECIL COTTON came by stage to Soda Creek and made his way to Riske Creek in 1897. He was a 19-year-old "mud pup," or paying pupil, on M. G. Drummond's ranch which later became the Cotton. When his first year was up he stayed for one more summer without pay and a winter at $25 a month. Cotton then returned home to England. When he came back to Canada in 1907 he bought the ranch from Drummond.

R. C. Cotton was a tall, fine looking man and came from a royal, wealthy family of Hampton Court, England. His brother, Lord Combermere, once came out from England to spend some time with Robert on his Chilcotin ranch.

Cotton married Maud Waller from Tasmania who was working as a governess for Yolland at the 150 Mile House. The Cottons had one daughter, Sylvia. Carol Stoner (Mrs. Gary Hutchinson) of Williams Lake, and Pat Murphy (Mrs. Jack Hodgson) of Vancouver, are granddaughters. Carol was raised by her grandparents on the ranch – a lonely life for an only child.

Mrs. Cotton was a very talented woman. She was a gifted pianist and singer, an excellent gardener and ran her own herd of purebred Shorthorns in which she took great pride. In later times she drove a big Packard car but her husband refused to ride in it with her. The Cottons had Chinese help in the person of Chow Gatt

Mr. and Mrs. R. C. Cotton.

who stayed with them for 30 years.

Cotton acquired more land and ran about 1,500 head of cattle. His brand was "W." Water for irrigation was brought from Riske Creek and stored behind what is still known as Cotton Dam. He built a spacious two-story log house on the ranch with private sitting room and fireplace. Years later, in 1966, this house was used by the CBC in producing "The Strong People," a play written by Paul St. Pierre for the TV series, "Cariboo Country." Leila Worthington and Bobby Allison were among the local people acting before the cameras in front of the grand old house. It burned down in the 1970s.

While still ranching in 1935, Cotton was asked if he yearned for the "good old days" when merchandise and wages were cheap. His answer was a definite "No! Drifting into Williams Lake in a closed sedan," he said, "is preferable to pounding the saddle in all kinds of weather; and roads are far better now than when I bought my first auto."

In those days he would sometimes sleep all night in his car at the foot of Sheep Creek Hill, "Waiting for the slippery trail to dry up." But in spite of the hardships of pioneer living, this man from wealth and royalty loved his ranch and the frontier country he adopted permanently in 1907. "There are no Elysian Fields (a place of paradise in Greek mythology) comparable," he declared, "to the wide flung and sun drenched Chilcotin rangelands." Cotton raised pheasants on the ranch and friends joined him for weekend hunts.

Cotton sold out to John Wade of Chilco Ranch in 1945, and he and his wife made their home on the west end of Williams Lake. He kept about 75 head of cattle that he ran on land where Lignum Ltd. and Jacobson Forest Products now stand. Here he fed and finished his beef for sale at the Williams Lake stockyards.

They also had their own milk and eggs. Chow Gatt stayed on to help with the work. When Mrs. Cotton passed away in Williams Lake Hospital in 1954, Gatt looked after R. C. until his death in 1956.

Neil Harvie of Cochrane Alberta, bought the Cotton Ranch from Chilco in 1964. Norman Worthington had managed the ranch for John Wade and was there again for Harvie until 1968. Ernie Cyr was in charge until 1973. The Cotton Ranch is now part of the Riske Creek Ranching spread, the home of partner Grant Huffman, his wife, Susanne, and family.

In 1900, a Race Track was started on Becher Prairie at what was called "Racetrack Lake," a few miles north of the present Loran C. installation. A three-day meet was held every year and people came from Redstone to Soda Creek. They camped out on the prairie. After the meet it was usually a week before all the horses were rounded up and the people able to return home. One year Doc English brought in two horses from San Francisco and let his old partner, Tom Hance, in on a good thing. Between them they covered all bets, but the local horses proved too fast and they found themselves without their proverbial shirts. Another time Doc English heard that his jockey had been bought so at the last minute he substituted 12-year-old Jimmy Isnardy. His opponents claimed Jimmy was too light so Doc fastened weights on the saddle. While the horses were lining up he went to calm his horse and brought back the weights. His horse won!

BILLY TILL bought out Tom Sword and later F. N. Sutton. After Till's death in 1930, Charlie Moon bought the property.

JACK MORRISON, a retired coal miner, had a cabin and orchard at the foot of Sheep Creek Hill. He was watchman for the bridge for several years. While irrigating his orchard he once forgot to turn the water off at night and the ditch overflowed, covering his orchard and half burying his cabin.

JIM STEWART, foreman for the Gang. Later partner with Shorty Sherringham. He died in Vancouver.

PHIL D. McRAE came from Nova Scotia and in the Riske Creek country bought out Billy Pinchbeck. In 1927 he married Geneva Stowell from Meldrum Creek. McRae bought the River Ranch from Beaumont in 1928 and a year later sold it to Tom Campbell, who immediately resold the place to Frank Humphries. But Humphries failed to meet his payment and McRae repossessed the River Ranch in 1930. Phil McRae died in 1936. Mrs. McRae stayed on the ranch with their only daughter, Willena.

Geneva McRae married Micky Martin and enlarged the ranch, buying the Renner place in 1938 and the Becher place in 1941. Geneva moved into Williams Lake in 1953, leaving Willena and her husband, Cookie Hodgson to live and work on the ranch. Geneva held the reins. In 1964 she sold to George McMorris of Milo, Alberta, but kept the Becher Place. She died in 1971. McMorris also bought the Sawmill Creek Meadow from Gerry Amsden who purchased this property on Withrow Creek from the Hance brothers. McMorris sold to Bob Lee. The River Ranch is now owned by Tommy and Donna Rae Ilnicki who still use the old BC brand.

1908

F. N. SUTTON came from 150 Mile House. He bought E. C. Cassidy's place at the head of Sward (Sheep) Creek and later sold to Billy Till. Sutton married Ethel Paxton. They moved back across the river and took up property on Williams Lake.

JACK McINTYRE, who came from the McIntyre Ranch near Calgary, worked for Young Ross when he first came to the country. He was head rider for the Gang Ranch for 20 years and then ranch foreman, a quiet, capable well-liked man. He left the Gang headquarters to manage the Perry Ranch. During his last years he had a trailer camp at Kamloops.

EAGLE LAKE JOHNNY moved to Riske Creek from Eagle Lake. He worked for various ranches in the district.

1910

BILL HARMON, an old buffalo hunter and trapper, had a cabin on what became the Slee place. Harry Durrell wanted him to pre-empt but he never bothered. When Jim Slee came to the country in 1912 he gave Harmon a horse for his rights to the place and Harmon then took up a place above Harper Meadow. He suffered from cancer, so his sister came from Montana to take him home. He died on the way at Kamloops in 1929.

HANK SWEENEY homesteaded Moon Point. Left in 1927.

MARION "BUTCH" HELWIG came from California. He acquired his nickname while working as a butcher for Pat Burns during the beef drives north. He married Aggie Boyle. Helwig returned to California in 1940 and died in 1945.

WES JASPER — by June Jasper Bliss
The Jasper family came to America in Colonial Times and were of Scotch-Irish origin. They settled in Kentucky and were granted the land they now call "Churchill Downs."

The Jaspers left Kentucky and crossed the plains in covered wagons. Some settled in California and Oregon. Wes' parents settled in Dayton, Washington, where all their nine children were born. John "Wesley," the eighth child was born August 5, 1894.

In 1910 young Wes came to Canada and worked at Douglas Lake where his older brother, Bill, was foreman. When in Kamloops, Bill heard that Pat Burns was taking an experimental drive of cattle from the Chilcotin to Hazelton to supply beef for the construction crews building the Grand Trunk Pacific Railway to Prince Rupert. Pat signed them both on, along with cowboys Ezra Knapp, Butch Helwig, Bill Owens, Alva Shaffer, and Frank English, to name a few. They made successful drives for four years. Later, Wes wrote the story "Twelve Thousand Head North," an account of their trips.

A cowboy at heart, which his sons and grandsons have inherited, the Jasper name is still well known at all the rodeos.

Wes was a Jack-of-all-trades – building houses, braiding rawhide lariats and making horsehair cinches. He was also instrumental in getting the first school at Riske Creek in 1935. He was trustee for several years. At that time the trustee hired the teachers – which was quite an undertaking. The first year he had to choose one teacher out of 200 applications.

Wes was a good cook and was hired many times for construction crews. As well as serving good food, he kept the crews happy with his good humour and stories of the early days.

He also did good log work and with his oldest son, Wesley, built the house for Eric and Lily Collier at Meldrum Lake.

One of Wes' biggest undertakings was a trip into Chezacut to buy sheep. He was told by many it was impossible for one man to drive a flock of sheep 75 miles through timber and swamp. He took his saddle horse and a collie dog named Harry. Wes bought sheep from Knoll and, as he travelled home, he bought from Bayliff, Bliss, Newton and Lee – his flock totalling around 300 head. Wes gave his dog the credit for the success of the drive, saying that the dog did more work than six men.

Wes married Mabel Mackin in 1918 at Chilco Ranch.

She was born in Quesnel in 1888. Her father, John Mackin, came from Scotland and settled at Alexandria. Mackin Creek is named after him. Mackin married Minnie Moffitt, daughter of Tom Moffitt and Mary Manning of Lac La Hache. Moffitt came from Williamsport, Indiana, and with partners Dunlevy and Sellars took up mining and were the first to find gold on the Horsefly River.

Mabel, a versatile lady, excelled in all her endeavours, but like all the pioneer ladies, she suffered many hardships. Raising their family of five children and two nephews, Clifford Lyons and Willie Johnson, during the depression years were trying times. Mabel was a courageous person. As a young woman she had to paddle a canoe across the Fraser River at Alexandria to go to work – a feat few men would attempt. Her family's health and well-being came first, but she was kind and generous to everyone, and acted as midwife many times.

Wesley, their oldest son, married Margaret Muir and they had one son and three daughters. Wesley died October 10, 1947.

Mary married Bert Roberts and they had one son. Bert died April 7, 1976. Gordon married Betty Sanford and they had two sons and one daughter. Gordon died June 12, 1982. June married Jack Bliss and they have one son and one daughter. Delmer married Irene Muir and they have four sons and four daughters.

Mabel died April 24, 1947, and Wes on November 9, 1966.

BILL JASPER, brother to Wes, was foreman for Burns beef drives. He went overseas to war in 1915 and returned in 1919 to work for various ranchers around Riske Creek. Bill Jasper was head cowboy for Guichon at Quelchena Ranch near Merritt at the time of his death in 1932.

1912

CHARLIE BRISTON pre-empted Hillcrest at the top of Sheep Creek Hill which he sold to Charlie Moon in 1930.

DAVID "SCOTTIE" LIDDELL was born in Berwick-on-Tweed, England. He came out to Ontario and worked his way west on railroad construction. In B.C. he worked for the Public Works and various ranches in the Chilcotin. He got his place at Riske Creek, just east of Bechers Dam, in 1940. He married Katie Cornell. Scottie Liddell was still living in 1958.

T.E. BARNETT worked for R. C. Cotton and Charlie Moon.

TOM BOYLE worked for Becher. He had a cabin at Palmantiers.

MARSHALL STONE worked for Public Works and various ranches in the Chilcotin.

ANDY STEEMAN came to Riske Creek from Anaham.

JIM SLEE, from Washington, pre-empted Harmon's place. Slee gave Harmon a horse and the right to remain on the place as long as he wished. Jim Slee married Addie Bristol's sister from Oregon. He partnered with George Renner in 1916. The partnership dissolved in 1928. Slee died of heart failure in 1933.

1913

GEORGE RENNER was best known as owner-editor of the *Williams Lake Tribune* but he had ranched at Riske Creek for 21 years before that. He came to the country in 1916 from New Bedford, Oregon, and ranched in partnership with Jim Slee at Riske Creek for 13 years. In 1912 he established a place of his own above Harper Meadow. He bought the hometown newspaper in 1937 and moved to Williams Lake, selling the ranch to Geneva McRae in 1938.

George Washington Renner was born in 1896 near Walnut, Illinois. That he came into the world on George Washington's birthday was a happy coincidence since it was ordained that this first born baby boy would be named after the famous president. This family custom was established seven generations before when a John Renner was an aide to President George Washington.

Renner married Geraldine Troeh of Portland, Oregon, in 1931 and she was a great help to him in his publishing business. She had had some experience in writing and in setting type, the latter all being done by hand in those days. Renner was an independent and colorful editor and once landed in the Supreme Court, acting in his own defence, after advertising in his newspaper for an "honest lawyer to deal with honest people in the Cariboo." The town's only practicing lawyer, Henry Greenfield Lockwood, sued him. Lockwood was awarded $1 in damages. Lawyer J. A. V. Cade answered the ad for an honest lawyer and in 1947 set up practice in Williams Lake.

Renner was active in many aspects of community life. In 1939, along with George Mayfield, Gabe Luyat, R. C. Cotton, Lord Martin Cecil and Charlie Moon, he helped organize the Cariboo Cattlemen's Association.

He sold the *Tribune* to Clive Stangoe in 1950 and pursued his hobby of rock hounding and lapidary work. He died in 1972, predeceased by a stepson, Jack, in 1949. Renner Road on South Lakeside is named after him. Mrs. Renner (Gerry), who was also active in community work, continued living in Williams Lake until her death. The Renners had two daughters, Hattie Patricia and Dora.

BARNEY BARRON homesteaded on Moon's Point. Sold to Charlie Moon.

BILL OWENS from Riverside, Washington, freighted north for Brewster for six years. Worked for Pat Burns. Worked at the Gang Ranch and other ranches.

Bill Owens saw no reason to change with the times. When he visited Eric and Lily Collier at their new little house at Riske Creek in 1964, Eric had just finished putting up a knotty pine wall of which he was justifiably proud. Owens studied the boards for a moment and then asked: "What are you going to do about all the knots in that lumber, paper over it?"

1965

BILL OWENS — by Paul St. Pierre

Old Bill Owens retired at Riske Creek eight or nine years ago after a long career during which he lived mostly under his hat. He got what is usually known as the "Cowboy's Pension" — a roof over his head and a saddle horse to ride. The owners of Becher House, the old hotel near Bechers Prairie, gave him a home in the abandoned hotel. He had cowboyed for their predecessor, Fred Becher himself.

The Gang, for whom he also cowboyed in the years just before retirement, gave him a saddle horse named Two Bits. Two Bits was a straight bay, without a blaze, a stocking or a star or anything else white upon him, and although he was somewhat shrunk out of shape, like Old Bill, he was still a good horse.

In winter, Old Bill moved 100 yards up the hill to a smaller cabin at Red Allison's place, and Two Bits wintered with the Indians on Toosey Reserve a couple of miles distant. On December 20, 1994, when the big blast of Arctic air came down and froze almost all this province, there was no smoke from Old Bill's cabin, so Red went there to stoke a fire. Bill Owens, born Riverside, Washington, immigrated to B.C. in 1913 on a freight wagon, one time wild horse hunter, was dead at 83 or 84.

On December 30, 10 days after Old Bill's death, Donald Grambush came from the Toosey Reserve to Red's store. "Sure funny thing," said Donald. "I go out this morning to see Two Bits, he's lyin' down in the snow. When I come up to him he lifts his head just a little bit. Then he lies down and he's dead" ...all of which is a matter of small importance, I suppose, merely a report that the year has made another cycle in the Chilcotin country. This time, however, Old Bill Owens and Two Bits did not winter.

TOM EVANS, carpenter, built Deer Park house for Moons in 1914 and the Becher House in 1915.

TOMMY HODGSON, the man and his sons and the name on the trucks that brought mail and freight to the Chilcotin on a regular basis, week after week, month after month, for 30 years.

Tommy Hodgson was born in Yorkshire, England, in 1885 and came to Canada with his parents when 12. A job at Cherry Creek Ranch breaking horses for the Inland Express Company which was operating stages and freight lines in the Cariboo, led him to his destiny. Hodgson had been put on as a spare driver and in 1914, after he had been turned down by the army because of varicose veins, Inland offered him the contract on their 150 Mile to Alexis Creek mail run. He took it. And kept it, with the exception of 1929 and 1930 when Captain D. A. Foster underbid him and attempted to run the Chilcotin line but was unable to cope with the rugged conditions. Tommy Hodgson continued to haul mail and freight to the Chilcotin against formidable odds for the rest of his life.

Irene Stangoe, writing in the *Williams Lake Tribune,* has given a good description of this hardy entrepreneur: "A big man, power-

Tommy Hodgson.

fully built, well over six feet in height, Tommy Hodgson was well suited to the rough life he led. Son Wilf admits that his father had a terrible temper but was genial and outgoing too, and made good friends all over the Chilcotin, particularly at his overnight stops." These were at Bechers at Riske Creek, Hances at Hanceville, Grahams at Tatla Lake and, in the early days, Bob Pyper at Chilanko Forks. When the mail run was extended to Kleena Kleene he stayed with the Jim McKills. The Hodgson trucks eventually went all the way to Anahim Lake, Bella Coola and Tatlayoko.

Hodgson wore high-topped leather boots or leather-topped rubbers laced up over his pants and these became the trademark of the Hodgson truck drivers. In addition to the Hodgson family, Claud Huston, Harold Mainguy, Roy Haines, Don (Squeak) Widdis, Red McCue and Vernon James were among those who took

Tommy Hodgson, left, with 150 Mile government agent Fred McLeod in a right-hand drive Cadillac on Sheep Creek Hill in 1916.

their turn at the wheel of the Hodgson trucks.

They battled road conditions that today's traveler couldn't even imagine – potholes, rocks, ruts, dust in dry weather and in wet spells, mud that could bog a vehicle down to the fenders. Narrow winding grades that dropped steeply to the rivers without benefit in winter of plough or sand – and in most places no room to pass. For many years, Hodgson continued to use horses when the snow got deep, and battled the cold and the wind and the drifted snow across Becher's Prairie. Drifts on the prairie could take hours to plod through, sometimes tipping the sleigh pulled by a tired four-horse team. Bechers was his first overnight stop. In 1916 during 50 below zero weather George Renner and Wes Jasper put up a barn on the Slee place where Hodgson kept eight head of relay horses. The mail always got through, and in many places along the road was left on the rancher's gate in a mail sack.

Tommy Hodgson married Edyth Paxton in 1915 and they had a family of six: sons Jack, Wilfred, and Patrick (Cookie); and three daughters: Phyllis, Marjorie and Betty Jean. Hodgson's sons drove truck for him as soon as they were big enough to reach the gas pedals. Later Marj's husband, Joe Gillis, was a valuable member of the team.

Tommy Hodgson died in 1945. His son, Wilf, and Joe Gillis carried on. They sold the Hodgson Mail and Freight Lines in 1962. As well as the trucks which still carry his name, Tommy Hodgson is commemorated by Hodgson Place and Hodgson Road in Williams Lake. Sons, grandsons, and great-grandsons carry on the family name.

1915

CHARLIE STEEMAN came to Riske Creek from Anaham.

J. J. BARKER was a ranchhand.

E. J. STRANGER, mudpup.

T. P. REED, came from Lillooet in summers to run the store for Becher.

MISS M. BURT, governess for Cottons.

DAVE CHESNEY, employee of the Public Works and also worked on ranches.

E. J. WINKLER, Swede. He had a cabin near Becher Place.

EARL D. MYERS took up pre-emption above Riske Creek. He died in 1919. Mel Moon noticed his horse was dead and on investigating found him asphyxiated in his cellar where he had gone to get out of the cold.

L. WARD BRISTOL took up pre-emption near Charlie Bristol at Hillcrest. Sold to Charlie Moon.

JOHNNY SPENCER, ranchhand.

OSCAR PETERSON homesteaded Stack Valley. Sold to Wes Jasper in 1927. He was a construction worker.

JOHNNY WALL came from Victoria. Took up holdings east of Riske Creek. His cabin can still be seen alongside Highway 20. He was a saddle and harness maker who married an Indian girl and had a family. He died in 1940 and was buried in the Becher plot.

NICHOLAS CHATRAND CARTER, known as Nick, took up land in the open Riske Creek country, now part of the Cotton Ranch. Lived in a cabin at Becher's Meadow and worked out in the district.

JACK TRESIERRA was born at Four Mile Creek and came to work for C. Moon. He was foreman for Cotton for seven years and then foreman for Jack Moon at Deer Park.

HAROLD JAMES MacKAY came to work for George Renner. Took up Cold Spring Ranch in 1920. He ran a sawmill and worked for the Public Works. He played the violin and making violins was his hobby. MacKay married Ruth Bliss and they had a family of eight children: Jimmy, Russell, Inez, Catherine, Mike, John, Kay, and Marjorie. Jim and Ruth MacKay sold to C. L. Todd in 1955 and moved to Williams Lake.

ALEX HARRIS came from Cirencester, England, to Manitoba in 1906 and worked his way west. He was employed by Public Works and various ranchers around Riske Creek. He lived in a cabin on land belonging to the Becher place near the Chilcotin Road. He lost his life in the 1960s when the cabin burned down.

JERRY BUCKLEY started a grasshopper field on Bechers Prairie to study grasshopper control. Indian Jack said he was crazy, "dipping for salmon on prairie." Later Spencer took over the work. After leaving Riske Creek, Jerry Buckley with brother, Dan, started the Sunnyside Motel in Williams Lake.

EDDIE HALLER came to cook for the Public Works. Later became foreman, then moved to Kamloops.

GUSSIE HALLER worked for Public Works.

ROBERT HOLLOWAY came from Lac La Hache. He bought out Sweeney and raised sheep. He sold to Charlie Moon in 1933 and moved to Horsefly.

WALTER TYLER worked for George Renner and Billy Till. He took up a place below Harper Meadow which he sold to Wes Jasper. The Tyler place now belongs to June Durrell Klassen. Tyler died in 1939.

DAN and JERRY BUCKLEY operated the Slee place until it was sold to Harry Durrell. The Buckley brothers bought the A & P ranch (Chimney Creek) in 1940 and sold it to Avery and Pidgeon in 1948. They owned and operated the Sunnyside Motel in Williams Lake through the 1960s and then moved to Vancouver. In 1940 Jerry Buckley married Barbara Reid who came to teach school at Riske Creek in 1938.

BERT ROBERTS operated the Becher place. He married Mary Jasper. In 1943 he started the store and auto camp which was sold to Bob and Joan Scott. Bert and Mary Roberts lived in Williams

Lake. They had one son, Jimmy. Bert also had a daughter, Patricia, from a previous marriage.

GEORGE CHRISTIANSEN started the Chilcotin Lodge and Store. Sold out to Tom Rafferty in 1941. Rafferty took over the Riske Creek Post Office in 1943.

Louis Vedan and Frank Witte with the first moose taken in the Big Creek country in 1927.

Mule deer and caribou were the only big-game species besides furbearing animals seen in the country by the early explorers and traders. Many years before that, elk were present in large numbers but that was beyond the memory of the oldest Indians. The elk perished, presumably in a hard winter. Their antlers can still be found occasionally, buried in swamps and lakes.

The first moose seen in the Riske Creek area was reported to have been in 1914. Homer Renner and Ernie Damon shot one at Harper Meadow. Then an Indian named Moleese killed a moose at Indian Meadow in the fall of 1916. He didn't know what this huge beast was but figured it might be good to eat. Afraid to taste the meat, he cut out the tongue and lips and galloped off to the reservation to talk to his friends. The rest of the tribe were excited, too, and a dozen men accompanied him with pack horses back to the kill to bring in the meat, head and horns. But no one knew what the big mowich was, not even the Old One who had lived for over a hundred years.

It was the trader, Fred Becher, who identified the animal as a

moose when Moleese brought hide and horns to him at the store. Becher had worked in the north with the Hudson's Bay Company and was familiar with this ungulate. The first moose killed in the Big Creek country was by Frank Witte and Louis Vedan in 1927. By 1930 there were moose everywhere and the country became overrun with them. Many died off in hard winters in the 1950s.

TWELVE THOUSAND HEAD NORTH
– by Wes Jasper
courtesy *Canadian Cattlemen* magazine.

There have been many articles written on the early day cattle drives from Texas and the Southern States, but nothing has ever been
printed about one of the biggest and most successful cattle drives
in Canada, when Burns and Co. contracted to supply beef for all
the construction camps of the Grand Trunk Pacific and the Pacific
Great Eastern (now B.C.R.) railways through B.C.

When the steel got to the Fraser River in the Rocky Mountain
Trench, the beef was transported down the river by boats or scows
to the camps along the route; but when the line left the river and
started across central B.C., all supplies, including cattle, had to go
overland through rough country. Construction had started on the
west end of the line about 1908, and by 1910 had come to the end
of the river transportation on the Skeena at Hazelton. Then all beef
had to be driven in overland from the Chilcotin, one of the largest
cattle raising areas of B.C., and this is where I, Wes Jasper, entered
the picture.

I had come from Washington across the line as a lad and was
working at the Douglas Lake Ranch in 1910 when I heard about
Burns taking an experimental drive of cattle from Chilcotin to
Hazelton, which was evidently a success. About this time, I
received a letter from my brother, Bill, in Kamloops, telling me to
come at once as he had signed us both on for the next beef drive to
Hazelton – wonderful news for a young fellow my age who had big
ideas of becoming a top cow-hand. We were to leave Ashcroft on
April 20 for the Chilcotin to start rounding up beef for the drive.

Joe Paine, foreman on the experimental drive, was in ill health
now, so Ulysses Campbell, who had been on the previous drive
with Paine, took his place. Most of the crew were recruited at Kamloops. They were: Campbell, Antoine Allen, Johnny Cannon, Gus
McGregor, Ezra Knapp, Abe Spooner, Alva Shaffer, Jack Lidlaw,
Pete Duncan, my brother Bill Jasper and myself. At Ashcroft we
got our horses when we met up with Cy Hymen, Burns' cattle
buyer for the Interior of B.C., who had bought up a bunch of sad-

dle and packhorses for us. Everything had to go by packhorse after we left the Chilcotin. It was an eight-day trail drive to Quesnel on the west side of the Fraser, and 500 miles of trail from there, the end of the wagon road, to Hazelton. Most of the horses Cy had bought were very poor due to the previous hard winter, so we were glad to hit Canoe Creek where the horses from the first beef drive were wintered. Now we were pretty well mounted for our trip through the Chilcotin to Chezacut where we started gathering the beef that Hymen had contracted for at the price of $50 a head for three-year-old steers; $60 for anything older, and $35 for cows. The cattle were pretty thin this time of year so we handled them slow and easy to get all the fat on them we could before they reached the construction camps. Burns received 25 cents a pound delivered to the camp.

From Chezacut, on the upper Chilcotin, we started south, receiving cattle at various ranches along the way, till by the time we reached Riske Creek we had nearly 800 head. Riske Creek was to be our main camp and receiving point for the beef that were to go north, as there was plenty of grass on the rolling prairie country and lots of good water.

On our arrival at Riske Creek with our beef, we were pleased to find Archie McLean and Jim McDonald there with 60 head of fresh, fat saddle horses, sent over from Alberta. We spent several days shoeing the horses – all the saddle horses and 15 head of pack horses – and branding all of them with a 10 on the left hip. We also branded all the beef with Burns' N L for a trail brand. There was no brand inspection in those days, and in all the thousands of cattle we drove out of the Interior there was never a complaint of P. Burns taking an animal he hadn't paid for.

We weren't planning to leave Riske Creek till May 10, but when Blake Wilson, Burns' superintendent from B.C., arrived unexpectedly by horse and buggy from Ashcroft, he said the camps in the north were out of meat. We were to pick out 500 head of steers and make a fast drive to Hazelton. So we loaded enough supplies – mostly bacon, beans, flour, sugar, syrup, dried fruit, coffee and tea, Klondyke vinegar, and rice – to last till we got to Quesnel, our last store till we reached the Bulkley Valley. There were seven cowboys, a cook, and a packer, who would act as horse wrangler as well, and about 45 horses.

The first night out, we night-herded the cattle as they were restless so soon off their range. We held them on the flats north of Meldrum Creek, which is now Allen Jeffery's ranch. Two riders

88

were on duty, changing one at a time every two hours. One man would go to camp, unsaddle his mount, wake up his relief and usually get a cussing for doing so; and so on till daylight. At daybreak we could count scores of deer coming up from the river, heading for the mountains.

At Riske Creek we left about 300 head of beef which was to become the nucleus of another drive; Harry Curtis was to start out with this drive 30 days after us. During this 30 days he was to enlarge the corrals and build a branding chute – we had had to rope and stretch out every head we rebranded.

Our route followed the west side of the Fraser River, and the trip was uneventful until we reached what is known as the China Ranch, owned by Sing Lees. Here we took a vote on a new cook: our present one we figured would make a better packer. We voted in my brother, Bill, who was a first class cook as well as a top cowhand. He wrangled the horses as well. Eight days passed before we reached Quesnel. Here we stayed a couple of days to rest the cattle and stock up on provisions to last the entire trip; bacon and beans were the staple articles.

At Quesnel we met Jean Cataline, the famous old packer. He had two pack trains, 60 mules and 60 horses, loading up for the trip to Hazelton and north to the Ninth Cabin on the old Telegraph Trail. From him we got information regarding the camping places along the trail, as there were only certain places where there was enough feed and room to night-herd the cattle, as well as good water. Some of these spots were only three or four miles apart; others 12 to 15. We were always on the move by 6 o'clock in the morning, so sometimes we would be in camp by 9 or 10 for the day.

As this northern country is all covered with brush, mostly red willow, and the trail narrow, the cattle had to be strung out single file. We counted 15 head to start out, and a rider swinging in behind every 50 head. That way, they were soon all in single file. You never saw the cowboy in front or behind you all day unless you were in the lead and got stuck at some mud-hole or boggy creek and couldn't get the cattle across. The foreman always counted out in the morning and the lead man counted in at night. Sometimes it took about two hours before the last of them were in.

When we reached Mud River we decided to rest the cattle in this big open, grassy country for a couple of days while the cowboys cleaned up and had a good sleep. A swim and change of clothes sure felt good, as we had taken off nothing but our boots at night since we started. From Mud River on it was the usual routine: count the cattle out in the morning, ride all day, count them in at night – bacon, beans, bannock, and coffee – until we came to the Nechako River at Fort Fraser. Here we had to swim the cattle across the big river. We let the herd rest and fill up for a couple of days, during which time we built a pole corral and chute or runway into the water where the river was about 150 yards wide and very sluggish. We found an old flat-bottom scow at this point, which we used to ferry two cowboys and their horses across to hold the cattle as they came out of the water. The boss had hired two Indians with their canoes to point the leaders across. We had to wait two hours for the sun to get around so it would not shine in the cattle's eyes when they were swimming, as they were apt to turn back if it did.

After getting the first bunch about a quarter of the way across, and seeing that they had made up their minds to keep going, we started stringing the rest of the herd in. It was only a half hour before the whole bunch was on dry ground on the other side of the river. Then came the job of loading all our camp outfit on the scow and ferrying it across. After that we swam our horses, but that took but a short time as horses swim much faster than cows.

It was about two miles to the Hudson's Bay post of Fort Fraser from the crossing, and we decided to camp there and do some trading. The factor at the post hadn't had any fresh beef since the fall before, so the boss ordered a steer butchered for trade. After the tallying up was finished we had a balance to our credit, which was adjusted with a gallon of Hudson's Bay rum, much appreciated.

Up to this time we had very good weather. But after we left Fraser Lake it started to rain, and we had rain and drizzle every day for 30 days. Some of the cattle got mud fever, or foot rot – the foot swells to three times the normal size and then breaks between the toes. These animals had to be watched very closely during the day, as they would sneak off the trail into the thick underbrush and lie down. We often passed them by, not missing any till the count was made at night. Next morning someone had to back track to find the lost ones, which were generally following along at a very slow pace.

We were getting into the vicinity of Burns Lake by now, and had been warned by packers and Indians to watch for poison weeds in this area. Having had so much rain the wild parsnip, which is deadly to cattle, was easily pulled up by the roots. We were lucky to lose only three head going through this stretch of country.

When we finally came to the Bulkley Valley, it looked like the promised land to us, after fighting the underbrush and mud holes of the last 400 miles. We travelled down this valley of large open sidehills till we came to what is known as the Government Ranch, about 56 miles from Hazelton. Here we decided to hold the cattle for the summer and drive out from this main herd whatever was needed every week for the camps.

Burns and Co. had built a slaughterhouse at Hazelton by now, and wanted meat right away, so we took a 100 head of the best steers there, killing a few along the way at the construction camps that were just getting started east of Hazelton. Two men were left to range herd the 400 head left in Bulkley Valley.

Because there was such a demand for horses, the boss at Hazelton, Bog Grant, decided to sell all the surplus saddle stock and send the outfit around by Prince Rupert and Vancouver to Ashcroft. There he would get a fresh bunch of horses and start out again for Chilcotin to round up another drive for the north. A butcher and I were sent back to the herd camp for another drive to supply the slaughterhouse and camps for a week. We worked at this job for three summers. We would take the camp orders on the way out, and that way knew how many head to bring each week. If a camp wanted four beef or one, it was killed right at the camp on the ground, and I would continue on to the next camp and wait for the butcher to overtake me. Again, he would shoot as many as they required, and I would travel on with the rest of the beef, until none was left.

During the course of the summer three more drives of 500 head each arrived at the herd camp, making a total of about 2,000 head that summer. Cattle fatten very quickly in that north country on the lush peavine and vetch but they also lose their fat just as fast when the frost hits the peavine. So about the tenth of September we started making larger drives to the slaughterhouse at Hazelton. There they froze 1,000 carcasses to last till fresh beef could arrive from Chilcotin the following year.

The last of the cattle were brought in the first of November. As there was a good demand for horses we sold all our saddle stock at $150 a head and loaded our camp outfit and gear in a forty-foot Indian canoe and started down the Skeena River to Kitselas, about 80 miles from the end of the steel. Track laying had been tied up here, waiting for completion of the Skeena bridge at Kitselas Canyon. At Prince Rupert we took passage on an old coast steamer, the *Camosun 2*. It was my first boat ride and I got very sick crossing the windy Queen Charlotte Sound.

After a few days on the town, the crew split up in Vancouver. I was sent to Ashcroft by Burns and Co. to drive a meat wagon delivering beef to the Grand Trunk construction camps along the Thompson River. I worked at this till it was time to start north, about April 20. Some of the old hands were in the new crew and we had a fresh bunch of horses from the Okanagan. We started gathering beef from Canoe Creek, Dog Creek, and Alkali Lake ranches.

We arrived at Chimney Creek Bridge on the Fraser River with 350 head in 1912, just when they were taking out the old wooden towers and putting in the present steel towers. During this construction they allowed only three head on the bridge at one time, so it was a slow job crossing our cattle. The cattle were wild, never having become gentle on the feed ground as ranchers seldom fed cattle in winter in those days. It took us three days to cross, and we had to rope the last few and drag them over the bridge.

As the grass had become pretty well eaten out along the old Telegraph Trail north of Quesnel, it was decided to try a new route through the Nazko River where we found large open bunch-grass sidehills and splendid fishing in the river. Frank English and I each staked a homestead here on these sidehills, 70 miles north of Alexis Creek. They were the first stakes in this locality – but we never went back.

From the Nazko we followed an old Indian trail, crossing the Blackwater River and Mud River about 30 miles up-stream from the Telegraph Trail crossing. We came onto the Telegraph Trail again at what was then known as the Government Meadow, about three days travel from Fraser Lake. After a short rest at the Nechako River we swam the cattle across and encountered a lot of poison weed between Burns Lake and the north Bulkley River. After a very dry summer the country was just blue with wild larkspur, which at a certain time of flowering is poisonous to cattle. We had to camp one night where the growth was very heavy.

In the morning we found nine of them dead and nearly 40 head unable to get off the bed ground. After more than two hours work, such as bleeding by cutting the tail or ear, and keeping them rolled up on their stomachs to prevent bloating, I was left to get the poisoned ones along as best I could. As one recovered a bit it would get up and follow the trail for a mile or two, then fall down in a fit. After a short rest it would get up and continue slowly on.

92

In handling these animals you had to stay well away from them for when they got excited they would fall down in a fit and that caused another delay. After three days slow work the poisoned animals were all back in the herd, quite a few minus their tails or ears, but we only lost about nine head.

By this time the railway contractors had built a good many miles of wagon road from Burns Lake west and driving cattle was much easier than the previous year through this part of the country. We were told by road gangs that the road would be finished by late fall.

The cattle were herded at the Government Ranch as before, and butchered at the camps. By now the camps had built corrals and a windlass to hoist the carcasses, which was a great help to the butchers.

After killing off the last of the cattle – and selling the poorer horses to the Indians, who were by now beginning to appreciate a horse for packing but seldom ever rode one, – we loaded 25 head of horses on the train at New Hazelton, now the end of steel, and travelled to Prince Rupert. From here we took our horses on the *S.S. Prince Rupert* to Vancouver. We encountered some very rough water which made most of the horses miserably sick. They were a sorry looking bunch when we unloaded at Vancouver, and still were not at the end of their journey. They were loaded again on the C.P.R. and shipped to Ashcroft where they wintered on a ranch in Highland Valley.

Burns and Co. got all their beef in the winter from Calgary, and there were two train loads a week to be unloaded at Kamloops and fed and watered. I was sent to Kamloops to look after this stock. I stayed till spring, then went to the Perry Ranch at Ashcroft to take care of the saddle horses that had wintered at Highland Valley. The horses were really poor and had to be fed oats as well as hay. As they had tons and tons of potatoes on the ranch for which there was no market, the foreman suggested feeding them to the horses. This was finally successful after mixing the spuds with cut up carrots and oats. After 30 days you wouldn't have known they were the same horses. When the time came to start north on the beef drive three cowboys were bucked off the first morning.

In 1913, the cattle drive started out earlier than before as there was a greater demand than ever for beef on the Grand Trunk Railway. We had close to 1,100 head gathered at Riske Creek to be divided into two drives – one going by the Nazko route and the other by Quesnel and the Telegraph Trail, starting at the same time. The herds had been sorted and corralled for the night, ready to start early next morning. Sometime during the night something gave them a scare and they stampeded. They tore down the fence and, as there was only one wrangle horse in camp, there was nothing we could do till daylight. It took us three days to round them up again. For several days the steers would spook and run at the least unusual sound.

I had been working with Harry Curtis' outfit during the beef roundup in the Chilcotin and had gone with his drive via the Nazko route as far as the Blackwater Crossing on the Telegraph Trail. I then joined my brother's drive on north. Curtis' drive went into Prince George where Burns had built corrals and a slaughterhouse. The main herd was left at Six Mile Flats and a bunch was driven in every week to the slaughterhouse. This was the boom year for Prince George which had, with all the construction workers and land seekers, an estimated 10,000 people in the area.

When we got to the Nechako River the water was very high, too high for cattle to land at their usual place. After waiting 10 days for the water to recede we attempted a crossing, but the river was still high and the cattle got to milling around in the middle of the stream and about 10 head were trampled under and drowned.

I worked at my job of driving beef to the camp all summer. We slaughtered about the same number of beef on our end of the line and about 1,500 head went to Prince George, making 3,500 head of beef for the railroad in 1913.

On November 10 I had a wire from my brother at Riske Creek. He was gathering cattle for the last drive to Prince George and he wanted me to meet him at Quesnel as soon as possible as he was short of men and horses. After butchering the last of the beef, Ezra Knapp, Jim Pratt, and I headed south with a bunch of tired, weary horses – and 10 inches of snow on the ground. Our horses were thin. There had been a lot of swamp fever that summer and we had lost three head on the way to Quesnel, shortening our saddle string. We were glad to see the boys feeding their horses oats when we met up with the last big drive at Quesnel. There were 10 packhorses loaded with oats as well as a four-horse team for the chuck wagon. Fifteen cowboys handled the 860 head of cattle in this final big drive north.

About the fifth of December we arrived at Prince George with the last beef drive for the construction camps on the building of the Grand Trunk Pacific Railroad. In the course of four years this had been a profitable market for close to 12,000 head of Chilcotin cattle.

Eric Collier, author and conservationist, whose book about life in the Chilcotin wilderness became an international best seller.

The classic Canadian wilderness tale . . .

THREE AGAINST THE WILDERNESS

Eric Collier

ERIC COLLIER, a tall lean Englishman with a rare gift of public speaking, came to the country as a young lad of 19, new to the ways of the frontier. He died on March 15, 1966, at 62, a renowned author, conservationist and public speaker. He was the first non-resident of the United States to win the *Outdoor Life* Magazine Conservation Award; and his book, *Three Against the Wilderness* published in 1959, was condensed in *Reader's Digest* and translated around the world, even behind the Iron Curtain.

After arriving in the Chilcotin in 1915, Collier worked first for Fred Becher in the store at Riske Creek. Then with his wife, Lilian, whom he married in 1928 at Riske Creek, moved to an isolated place on Mackin Creek where he trapped, reinstated the beaver population and began writing. He also perfected the humanitarian

Conibear trap which is now widely used. Collier was, as well, a big-game guide: the first to take non-resident hunters into Yohetta Valley for sheep and goat.

Collier's obituary, published in the *Williams Lake Tribune,* noted: "To watch Eric Collier stride through the woods was a joy to behold. He strode confidently along, brushing branches aside as he went and observing the growth of every tree and the movement of every animal and bird. Gun crooked comfortably in his arm he moved along as easily as the city dweller would stroll down Granville Street."

Eric and Lily worked side by side on the trapline and in the home. Petite, attractive and out-going, Lily took her place beside her husband in any situation. Their only son, Veasy, was raised in the wilderness and received an excellent education there by correspondence. Those years are chronicled in Collier's best-selling book, *Three Against the Wilderness.*

Eric also wrote short stories for *Outdoor Life Magazine,* his theme always conservation. He was a man of strong opinions and was often at variance with the Game Branch. In verbal or written debate Collier was a formidable opponent, highly respected by members of the Game Department to whom he never took a back seat.

"And yet," wrote his biographers, "there was a quietness about him that is the hallmark of the outdoorsman. He was in every respect a gentleman."

In later years, Eric and Lily moved to Riske Creek. After Eric's death in 1966, Lily made her home in Williams Lake.

Veasy Collier served in the Korean War and was decorated for valour. He married Judy Borkowski and the couple and family live in Williams Lake.

CHARLIE WOODS died on September 24, 1985, just after his 85th birthday. He was driving his truck towards Williams Lake, a favorite pastime in later years, when he was stricken with a fatal heart attack. His vehicle just went quietly across the road and into the ditch, causing no injury or harm to anyone.

Just four years before that he had been honoured with a surprise party in the Riske Creek Community Hall to celebrate his 81st birthday. It was a gala potluck dinner and dance affair. Long tables centered with exotic flowers from Joan Huston's garden were laden with an assortment of delicious home-cooked food. Led by the guest of honour, over 150 people loaded their plates in single file and crowded into seats around the hall.

Charlie's family were all there: his half-brother and sister, Bob Davis from McLeese Lake and Nellie Needles from Kamloops; his sons: Gordon of Meldrum Creek and Jack of Prince George; his daughter, Dorothy Nicholson of Williams Lake; and their children and their children's children. There were nieces, nephews, in-laws, and numerous distant relatives and friends. Familiar names were there: Mulvahill, Collier, Jasper, Stowell, and Hodgson – people Charlie Woods had known all his life.

Following dinner, Jack Woods acted as MC to extend good wishes on behalf of the crowd and to lead the singing of "Happy Birthday." Gifts were then presented and Charlie, visibly moved, expressed his appreciation before carefully opening each package, while a circle of young people watched eagerly. Last gift to be presented was the big one: a .243 rifle and scope – a gun Charlie Woods had always wanted. The birthday cake was made and decorated in the shape of a rifle by Gordon Woods' daughter, Connie Frost.

Tables were cleared away and dancing began with lively western music by Gordon and Jack Woods on accordion and guitar. Charlie and his sister, Nellie, led the first dance. The Woods (including Charlie) are a musical family and there was always someone ready to take a turn on accordion, guitar, saxophone, or drums. At one time the old hall fairly rocked with rhythm when Jack Woods and Paul Hoyer tuned up together like old times. Dancing went on into the early morning and Charlie, who said he'd never had a birthday like it, stayed to the end dancing and visiting.

Credit went to Joan Huston and Gordon's eldest daughter, Eileen Boyde, for planning and piloting the happy event that brought together so many original Chilcotin families — once a common occurrence when country roads restricted travel and these small communities celebrated festive occasions only with each other.

Charlie Woods was born at Clinton and took his early schooling there, completing his education in Vancouver. He came to the Chilcotin when he was 22 years of age and went to work for Jim Stewart who was managing Beaumont's River Ranch. Woods had been working around Clinton and Empire Valley but once he had seen the Riske Creek country he kept coming back. In 1925 he took up land on Riske Creek where the Chilcotin Lodge now stands, and two years later married Pearl Boyle of Meldrum Creek. They raised a family of three: Gordon, Jack and Dorothy. Woods worked at a variety of jobs, including the Department of Agriculture's grasshopper control program on Bechers Prairie, and haying contracts on the Cotton Ranch for 12 years in a row. When his family was ready for an education and there was no school at Riske Creek, he sold out to a man named Christiansen and went into ranching at Meldrum Creek. (Christiansen built the Chilcotin Lodge and soon after sold to Tom Rafferty.)

Pearl Woods died in 1970 and Charlie moved back to Riske Creek where he rented a house from Delmer Jasper. He worked for the Forestry for awhile, looking after campgrounds, but for the last few years was retired. He drove a new pickup and was always on the go. You could spot him anywhere – tall, slim, and straight at 85. The free life of the Chilcotin had been good to Charlie Woods.

A brother, Bill Woods, passed away in 1972; a half-sister, Goldie Mulvahill, in 1961; and a half-brother, Johnnie Davis, was lost in World War Two in May 1945, just before the conflict was over.

It was all in the day's work for ED GARLAND – if roping a fugitive instead of a cow can be considered part of the day's work. Roundup was underway and ranchers at Riske Creek were gathering cows and calves for the spring branding. The sun was shining and out on the prairie the grass was green and dotted with bright wild flowers, nodding and bowing to the spring wind. A beautiful day. But nobody seemed to notice, none could get their mind off the shocking story that had spread like wildfire across the range.

A few days before a young mother, alone, going quietly about her work, had been the victim of a savage attack by a demented youth. He had knocked her to the ground with a club, then hit her again, inflicting deep wounds to her head. Her screams sent him streaking for cover. Though an R.C.M.P. officer from Kamloops with his tracking dog, Klia, had been searching for him for two days, the dangerous offender was still at large.

Ed Garland was riding for River Ranch, gathering cows and calves in a big open pasture. It was May 25, 1966. Suddenly, ahead of him in the distance he spotted a slight figure on the run, heading west across the pasture. Without hesitating to consider "whys" or "ifs," the fast-acting cowboy spurred his cowhorse into a gallop and raced after him across the prairie. "I knew this lady had been beaten by a boy," he said later, "and police were looking for him around here, so I took after this guy. My dog was a good cowdog and he was right behind him too."

Garland quickly overtook the fleeing figure. "The boy went up a tree," Ed said, "so I took down my lariat and roped him. I pulled him out of the tree and my horse tightened the rope and held him while I got off and took his knife away from him."

Garland then asked a question: "What are you doing here?" When the fugitive admitted that the police were after him, Garland knew he had the right man on the end of his lassrope [lasso] and started leading the wildly fighting captive out towards the highway. He hadn't gone far when he met the Corporal with his tracking dog and turned the suspect over to him. The 17-year-old Indian youth later confessed and was convicted and sentenced in court at Williams Lake.

It was a bold and colorful capture – but it was all in the day's work for Ed Garland. When a news reporter interviewed him at the Riske Creek Rodeo a few days later, he was noncommittal about the incident and much more interested in keeping his turn in the team-roping event.

Ed Gartland – who changed his name to Garland because that's what everybody called him anyway – was part Cree and came to the Chilcotin from Alberta in the 1930s to work for Chilco Ranch. He worked on various ranches throughout the country, more or less settling at Riske Creek after marrying MaryJane Grambush of the Toosey Indian Band. They had three daughters: Hazel, who died of pneumonia as a young girl, Judy and Sadie, and an adopted son, Albert.

The Garlands moved to the Gang Ranch in the late 1960s where Ed worked for awhile; and then to Douglas Lake. Ed Garland never returned to the Chilcotin. He was drowned in September 1976 when his pickup truck left the highway between Merritt and Kamloops and disappeared in the deep waters of Trap Lake.

MaryJane was at Toosey in the Chilcotin at the time looking after her mother and she has made her home there with her people. One daughter, Sadie, works in Merritt, and Judy works for the Toosey Band. But MaryJane is not alone: she has adopted a grandson, Jason, and a nephew, Tyler, and raised them from babyhood.

She still has Ed's saddle and spurs – and his lariat in its rope can.

LEONARD PALMANTIER came from Riverside, Washington. Always a horseman, he brought a number of horses with him when he came to the Cariboo in 1914. He sold them and returned to Washington. In 1919 he was back to break horses for Alkali Lake. In 1921 he fed cattle for the Gang Ranch and went on to cowboy for all the big ranches, including Douglas Lake, Gang Ranch, and Alkali Lake.

Above is the first Siwash Bridge about 1880. It consisted of a few big logs across the Chilko River about 10 miles above its confluence with the Chilcotin. Pioneer rancher Hugh Bayliff claimed that before attempting this makeshift crossing, you uncoiled your lassrope (lasso) and tied the logs firmly together, then led your saddle horse across.

Palmantier was unsurpassed as a bronc rider and won and re-won the bronc riding title of the Cariboo. One year he earned the honor of being the Best All-Around Cowboy of B.C. and caused a stir in Williams Lake by riding his horse into the Stampede Hall to receive his prize. He was said to be the only man in Washington State to stay on the famous rodeo mare, Red Pepper.

In 1935 Palmantier married Josephine Grambush and settled at Riske Creek. He took up Tommy Boyle's place and McTaggart Meadow. Leonard and Josephine raised seven children: Fred, George, Jack, Julia, Joan, Susan and Lillian. Leonard's three sons took after their father and are all good horsemen. George and Jack are exceptional bronc riders. George has won many trophies and buckles and over 20 saddles and has consistently qualified for the North America Rodeo Championship Finals. Jack has rodeoed all over North America and is always in the money. In 1976 he won the saddle bronc event at the National Finals in Oklahoma City. Joan went on from being Williams Lake Stampede Queen in 1966 to British Columbia Indian Princess in 1967. In competition across Canada she then became the Canadian National Indian Princess. Joan competes in barrel racing. She became a teacher and is involved in Native Education.

When Leonard Palmantier passed away in the fall of 1963, Eric Collier penned these memorable words: "Although almost 75 years of age and in failing health, Palmantier was riding for Mel Moon on fall roundup. On Monday, October 21st, he herded a bunch of yearling steers in off the range and put them into a pas-

100

Leonard Palmantier.

ture two miles from Allison's Store at Riske Creek. He then dropped in on us for a bite of lunch. A cold wind was keening in from the south east, bringing with it a mixture of sleet and rain. There was a deathly pallor on his face as he crouched over the stove, coaxing some warmth into his bones. He ate lunch with us, rolled a cigarette, sat around for a spell, discoursing on that one subject to which his entire mature life had been dedicated – range cattle. And listening to him I could not help but think: 'He's no business being out punching cattle on a day like this.' Then he thanked us for the meal, went outside, led his horse to a block of wood and hoisted stiffly into the saddle. And watching him ride away I thought: 'But that's the way he wants it to be. He'll be riding and working cattle as long as he's sufficient strength to climb on a horse. Because it's the only life he knows, the only life he cares for, the only one at which he's really happy.'

"Twenty-four hours later, at his home at Riske Creek, Palmantier suffered a severe hemorrhage and was rushed to War Memorial Hospital, Williams Lake, where the combined efforts of Dr. Atwood and the hospital staff were unable to renew his lease on life. He passed serenely away on the forenoon of Thursday, October 24th."

Leonard Palmantier is buried in Williams Lake Cemetery.

GANG RANCH AND AREA

JEROME and THADDEUS HARPER founded the famous Gang Ranch and brought the first sheep into the country in 1863. They came from Harper's Ferry, Virginia, to the western states and at the outbreak of the Civil War moved to Victoria. They were accused of plotting raids on the northern states and the Union brought pressure in Victoria to have them move farther from the border.

The Harpers first sighted the country which was to become the Gang Ranch from the Dog Creek side of the Fraser. They rode to a point on the river opposite the mouth of the Chilcotin and sent a smoke signal to Indians on the other side who came across and picked them up in a spruce log canoe. The place known as Home Ranch in the valley on top and River Camp above the mouth of the Chilcotin were the areas first developed.

Sheep are not good swimmers and Harpers decided that rowing them across the river was too arduous and costly. They moved the sheep to Big Bar Mountain and brought in horses and cattle. Harpers branded their stock with Jerome's initials: JH, and this brand is still used by the Gang Ranch.

Harpers had already been involved in mining and sawmill operations at Yale and Horsefly (Horsefly went by the name of Harpers' Camp for some years) and eventually had title to ranch land at Canoe Creek, Clinton, Kamloops, and the Perry Ranch at Cache Creek, as well as the main Gang Ranch. Tragically, in 1870 Jerome was kicked in the head by a horse and never fully recovered. He died in California in 1873.

In May 1876, Thaddeus undertook the famous beef drive to Ogden, Utah – some reports say Salt Lake City – and thence on to Chicago by rail. This trip of about 1,200 miles is the longest drive ever made from Canada. He wintered the herd in Washington, trailed them slowly through Idaho and, with a change in plans dictated by market prices, shipped the beef out of Utah by train to San Francisco. Sadly, the long, hard venture was a financial failure. Coupled with a severe winter in 1878-79, it almost broke Harper – but he forged ahead.

Harper Meadow and the open pastures on the north side of the

Gang Ranch as it looks today.

Chilcotin, including Lot 44 which comprised 8,900 acres and was said to be the largest lot in B.C., was purchased from the government by Thaddeus Harper in 1883 for $1 an acre. This open bunch grass pasture land was Crown Granted in 1884. The Gang Ranch ran their steers on the north side of the river and built a cabin and barn for the range rider beside a big spring on top overlooking the canyon. This became known as the Company Cabin. Harper Meadow and the Canyon pastures, including Company Cabin, now belong to Riske Creek Ranching. In 1973, after Neil Harvie of Cochrane, Alberta, bought this land, 928 acres on the west end of Lot 44 were set aside for California big horn sheep range, leaving 7,972 acres in the old lot.

The Chinese miners had flumed water on to the river benches above Gaspard Creek, and a route was finally found to bring the water down a side-draw in large volume to irrigate Harper's Ranch. Large gangs of men were employed building ditches and breaking the sod with gang plows, and cowboys began calling the ranch "The Gang." The Gang Ranch Crown range took in most of the open grassland on the south side of the lower Chilcotin River below the mouth of Big Creek, still called the "Summer Range." Their range extended to the mountains and Hungry Valley, taking in the Big Meadows around Gaspard Lake and open country on Churn Creek.

In 1884, Thaddeus suffered an accident similar to his brother's. He was riding the range alone when he was thrown from his horse and kicked in the face. He was found, unconscious, a day later and spent six weeks in hospital in Victoria. Financial troubles multiplied and, in 1891, the Western Canadian Ranching Company headed by a London publisher, Thomas Galpin, bought the Gang and all its holdings. Galpin's sons-in-law, Jim Prentice, Cuyler Holland, and Stobbart were involved in the company. Prentice managed the ranch.

Thaddeus Harper died in Victoria on December 10, 1898.

There was a store and a post office at the Gang and a big cookhouse, usually with a Chinese cook, to feed the gangs of workmen and any traveller who happened by. During the 1960s a school was opened on the ranch and ran for about ten years.

An early name connected with the Gang was Cy Hymens, who became a well known buyer for Burns. He was a familiar sight in the early days, driving his buggy from ranch to range, often driving cattle and even at times getting down and turning some ornery critter on foot. Others were Antoine Allen, Charlie Conners, Jim Reynolds, Newman Squires, Angus Stobie, Jim Stewart, Quinn Able, Tommy Morgan, Shell Gillespie, Ulysses Campbell, Tommy Cooney, Harry Roper who gave his name to a flat above Farwell Canyon, Jim Ragan and a host of other riders. Wallace McMorran was ranch manager for many years. Jack McIntire was head rider and then ranch foreman. Rosette has been a long standing name at the Gang. Walter Keeble managed the store for many years. Eddie Bambrick was head rider in later times.

In 1948 two Americans, Bill Studdert and Floyd Skelton, bought the Gang Ranch. Studdert lived on the place and managed it — but not too well. Through the years the big ranch went through many changes and turbulent times. But in 1993, under the able management of Larry Ramstad, the Gang Ranch is once again a well-run, productive operation.

WILLIAM W. WYCOTTE in June 1868 pre-empted 160 acres at the mouth of the Chilcotin River. He also had a place on Churn Creek above the Gang, called Wycotte Flat. He died in 1910 and Gang Ranch bought the estate. A lot of his cattle had to be shot because, left for years on the open range, they were too wild to be rounded up. Daring and capable cowboys tried. Ranging on the good bunchgrass hillsides these cattle grew to immense proportions. One old steer that was rounded up and said to have been in poor shape, weighed on arrival at Ashcroft 2,260 pounds.

Wycotte's sons, Fred and Cal, worked on various ranches throughout the Chilcotin.

DAVIE BURNS built a cabin two miles below Farwell Canyon in 1914. He inherited his uncle's estate in Australia and returned there in 1922.

JOHNNY and EFFIE DAMON and daughter, Ruth, lived below Farwell Canyon on the banks of the Chilcotin, settling there about 1916. A brother, Ernie Damon, lived with them.

JEFF BROWN, who came from London, England, took up a preemption at the mouth of Big Creek in 1919. He sold to his brother, Dan, in 1930 and went into raising and running race horses in Vancouver. Dan Brown disappeared in 1933. Dick Church bought the Brown place in the early 1950s. It is now owned by John Weetman.

ALEX KALA'LLST, now spelled Kalelest, (in the early days the T was silent) a Shuswap Indian, had a small ranch on Gaspard Creek next to the Gang's Home Ranch Valley. He was related to Joe Kala'llist, chief of the small Shuswap Indian Band who once lived on the west side of the Fraser River. A few of the last big cows Alex shipped in Williams Lake were so fat they could no longer get in calf. He put his cows in with a Big Creek beef drive in 1940 (Blenkinsops, Bambricks, and Wittes) and rode with the cowboys on the long drive to the stockyards via Farwell Canyon. His daughter, Cellina, with her family of small children brought his camp outfit along with team and buggy. Cellina gave birth to a baby one night on the trip. Next day she was out gathering firewood as usual.

Kala'llst's place was sold to the Gang Ranch. Long ago, Alex built a cabin in the Big Creek country on what is now part of the Teepee Heart Ranch. Aging in the 1930s, it stood for many years, always known as Alex's Cabin.

E. M. T. SHERWELL, an Englishman, settled on a fir-covered bench above the Chilcotin River near Cargile Creek in 1914. A wild horse hunter and dealer, he built a sturdy log house which still stands. He died at Bechers in 1923 and is buried there.

CHARLES MANUAL CASTELLAIN, a handsome Englishman, married a Chilcotin Indian girl and in 1913 took up 160 acres of land on the south side of the Lower Chilcotin River near Poison Lake, beside a spring that is named after him. The land was Crown granted in 1917 and a further 180 acres applied for. The home he built there was a cellar-like construction and can still be seen. Castellain was broken hearted when his wife contracted tuberculosis and died in a hospital in Vancouver. He soon after left the country and was killed while working on construction in Vancouver.

Cowboy's Christmas Star. (See page 366.)

HANCEVILLE

"Hanceville is the leading settlement in the Chilcotin Valley in the District of Cariboo about 75 miles from Soda Creek and 45 miles from the mouth of the Chilcotin River. It is the furthest inland settlement of the northwest in the Province of British Columbia." – *from the British Columbia Directory 1893*

Hanceville is named after ORLANDO THOMAS "TOM" HANCE, first permanent settler in the valley.

He was born in Illinois into an aristocratic Eastern family. Although he left home at an early age and spent most of his life in wild unsettled country on the other side of the continent, this influence never left him. In primitive surroundings on a far inland plateau where a frontier post office was to bear his name, he sought to establish a gracious way of life. Through hardships, dangers, and difficulties, Hance never lost his polite gentle manners, his quiet sense of humour, his love for good music. In the massive home he built in the Chilcotin and furnished by mail order from the East, he was never known to sit down to dinner without wearing a jacket.

The call to adventure came early to Tom Hance. He enlisted as a young lad to fight for the Union in the Civil War. When the conflict was over he joined a covered wagon brigade and crossed the plains to California. There he was caught up in the gold fever and got in on the rush to the Cariboo.

Hance was a musician and played in a brass band in California. He was, however, first a violinist and carried that precious instrument with him across the plains and then north into the wilderness of British Columbia.

As well as classical music, he liked to play and sing Stephen Foster's darky songs for his own and his family's enjoyment. In later years he played for dances when the scattered ranchers gathered for a social evening. When Hances' lavishly furnished home burned with most of their possessions in a tragic fire in the early 1900s, it was the loss of his violin that grieved Tom Hance the most.

When Hance reached the Cariboo in the late 1860s the excite-

Tom and Nellie Hance.

ment of the gold rush was diminishing, and he took a job as a herder for Harper brothers at the Gang Ranch. It was while there that he first glimpsed the Chilcotin Plateau from the south side of the river and a new dream took shape.

He worked that winter as a bookkeeper for the general store in Clinton and in the spring set off to explore the virgin country west of the Fraser. He had heard tales of this promising land of plains and forests with its abundance of wild game and fur, and the idea of locating a trading post there had taken hold in his mind. There was one draw-back, apparently – the wild Chilcotin Indians were not to be trusted. But he brushed this warning aside.

Taking the horses he had wintered at Clinton, he rode up the river trail to the mouth of Chimney Creek, camping along the way. With the help of friendly Indians he crossed the Fraser in a dug-out canoe, his saddle and packhorses swimming behind. His saddle horse became so accustomed to this procedure that he wouldn't even tighten the lead rope.

Following old trails, Hance made his way to the Chilcotin River. Continuing on for 45 miles, he found an ideal homesite where two big springs gushed from the hillside, babbling over pebbles in the spring sun. Grass was greening below the fir-clad ridges and birds sang in the willows. His mind raced with plans and dreams as he unsaddled and camped there between the two springs. He loosed his horses to graze, leaving his dependable sorrel free but hobbling the other two before building a small fire and preparing his supper.

When Hance learned that the Indians valued this camping place and were suspicious of his presence there he bought the land from them for $500 dollars. He then staked 270 acres and began to build. He became the first permanent, independent fur trader to settle among the warlike Chilcotin Indians. Later, in partnership with Benjamin Franklin English, a famous Ashcroft pioneer, he established a base trading post which is the site of the present TH Ranch.

There had been some trading with the Chilcotin Indians prior to Hance's arrival. The first excursion into the country to look for trade was made in 1822 by three Hudson's Bay men accompanied from Alexandria by three Indian guides. The prospects of fur trade with the natives appeared favourable. In 1825, and again in 1829, the Chief Factor of Alexandria, William Connolly, headed a reconnaissance into the valley which led, in 1834, to the construction of a Hudson's Bay fort and trading post near the confluence of the

Chilko and Chilcotin Rivers. Factor William Fletcher Lane was in charge for the first few years, transporting fur and trade goods with pack animals to and from Alexandria over what became known as the Hudson's Bay Trail.

Some domestic stock was brought in as there is a record of "obtaining 372 bundles of hay from Petite Pond" to feed two milk cows, one calf and a bull. This hay would have been cut with a scythe, tied in bundles and carried to the fort on packhorses from the unknown location of "Petite Pond." The Company did business at Fort Chilcotin for 11 years under various Hudson's Bay men. But the Chilcotins remained treacherous and hostile, and trouble erupted in 1839. By 1845, the Hudson's Bay Company had abandoned Fort Chilcotin and moved their operation to Kluskus in the Blackwater. This trading post had been forsaken as well by the time Tom Hance arrived in the 1860s. Dan Nordberg, an independent ex-sailor who came in through Bella Coola, ran a post for a short time across the river among the Stone Band about 1871.

Because of their fair dealings, Hance and English won the respect of the Indian people and their trading post flourished. Once a year their pack train would leave for Yale loaded with the year's take in furs. Yale was the head of navigation at that time and as the trip to the outside took about two months, the men took turns taking their pack train over the rough trails and the newly constructed Cariboo Wagon Road to sell their pelts and bring back trade goods and supplies. This trip often included a visit to Victoria.

Hance's partner, B. F. (Doc) English, was a racehorse fancier and was always well mounted. On one of his early trips he was riding a fast quarterhorse and won $500 dollars from some Oregon traders he met. On his next journey to Yale two years later, they were waiting for him and won all the money he had taken in from the sale of fur, some $3,000. On his return to the Chilcotin he turned his share of the TH over to Tom Hance to square the debt. English then went to live at Deer Park where, in 1870, he preempted 320 acres.

It appears that Hance must have continued fur trading on a large scale for some time. He branched out for a farthest northwest trading post at Kluskus Lake, maintaining communication with horse and mule train via Puntzi Lake, about 150 miles from his headquarters in the Chilcotin Valley. Since there were no roads in the upper country, packing jobs were available in the off season. Hance's pack train of 30 horses and 30 mules was busy all summer in 1890, packing H.B.C. supplies from Quesnel to Stuart Lake. It took 25 days to make a round trip. Any surplus supplies from the ranch such as flour and potatoes, were loaded on pack mules and horses and taken to Soda Creek on the Fraser River. Here the supplies were crossed in a boat, the animals swam, and the journey continued to the mines at Barkerville.

On one of Hance's trips to Victoria he fell in love with Ellen Verdier, a petite vivacious girl with hazel eyes and dark curly hair. Although he was twice her age, Miss Verdier was swept off her feet by the charming, soft spoken frontiersman and they were married in Victoria on July 7, 1887.

Ellen Verdier, known to family and friends as Nellie, was one of a family of eight born to Ettiene and Honorah Verdier in Saanichton on Vancouver Island. Her father, Ettiene, was a big husky Frenchman who came from France with his brother, Alfonse, and settled on Vancouver Island in 1852. He married a small Irish lass, Honorah Kilroy, overcoming in courtship a difficult language barrier since she spoke Gaelic and he knew only French. Their youngest son, "Big Frank," a tall husky man like his father, made a name for himself and a modest fortune logging with oxen on the Saanich Peninsula. He also blazed out the original route for today's Malahat Highway. The engineers who came later followed almost entirely the route he recommended. The wood and stone home Frank built in 1912 still stands, overlooking Brentwood Bay near the avenue named for him where he once skidded logs with oxen into the bay.

Nellie Verdier Hance was only in her teens when she rode with her husband on the long saddle horse journey accompanying the pack string to his isolated trading post in the Interior and the log cabin that would be her first home. The cookstove that she used throughout her lifetime was brought in on packhorses. On her arrival in the Chilcotin she was the only white woman in the country, with visits to family and friends in Victoria few and far apart.

What a trip that nearly 300-mile journey from Yale to Hanceville must have been for a young woman unaccustomed to riding – and using a sidesaddle. Each long adventurous day took them deeper into a wilderness she knew little about, fording rivers, braving rough trails, depending only on the capable frontiersman who led the way. At last the home stretch, the 75-mile ride down the narrow canyon trail to the Chilcotin Valley and Hance's pre-emption where neat buildings and fences nestled below the hill. Juniper, fir, and willow clothed the hillsides, while open fields, with clumps of aspen, dropped away to the turquoise river and blue hills rising in the distance.

As the young bride took in the beauty of the wild unsettled land, her husband's words came back to her: "There are no white women, only the natives and they speak little or no English. No doctors, no mail delivery, only rough wagon trails and no bridges. But we are working to change these things. It's a good country, Nellie. I'll build you a fine home there."

Nellie Hance was quick and industrious and took on the task of homemaking cheerfully. As she matured she responded to the challenge of pioneer living with courage and dedication: feeding the hungry, ministering to the sick and injured and, when necessary, laying out the dead. During the years when there was no medical aid in the country, her family remembered that she always kept a bag packed and ready in case she should be called away in a hurry.

As settlement progressed, she delivered many of the babies born in the Chilcotin. When Mike Minton, who homesteaded on the south side of the Chilcotin River, was hurt in an accident, she rode over every day to take care of him, her infant daughter tied on her back in a shawl. This visit meant overcoming her fear of water because she had to ford the river as there was no bridge. On one occasion while in the middle of the ford she felt the bundle on her back slipping. Terror gripped her as she struggled to hold the baby at her back and at the same time keep a grip on the bridle reins as her horse plunged through the deep, swift water. Once safely across she slid from her mount, collapsed on the grassy bank and, hugging her baby to her breast, burst into tears. By the time she had collected herself and proceeded up the steep hill and across the flat to the Irishman's cabin, the anxiety was gone and she could smile again. She entered the room in her usual quick, competent way and Minton never guessed that anything had gone wrong.

Although she never learned their language, her association with the Indians was amiable. In the early years, both in spring and in fall, it was a familiar sight to see a long line of old Indians, the halt and the blind, walking along the dusty road to Hanceville, some coming all the way from Nemiah Valley on foot. On arrival, they sat on the steps of Nellie's house where she affably communicated with them across the language barrier while the natives drank tea and ate a meal. When they left in a day or so these "blind creatures," as the Hance youngsters dubbed them, were loaded with gifts of food and other essentials packed into their big baskets which they carried on their heads. Always generous, Nellie gave to Indians and whites alike wherever there was a need – a fortune in flour, jam, vegetables, butter, cloth, and meals.

112

At Nellie's funeral a lengthy column of natives followed the crowd of mourners winding their way up the hill to the burial ground to silently show their regard for this small woman who had held the respect and loyalty of the Chilcotin people for nearly 50 years.

As more and more people settled, Tom Hance's application for a post office was granted on October 1, 1889. The post office was located on his TH Ranch and named "Hanceville." The Hanceville Post Office remained on Hances' TH Ranch for 83 years and was manned by the Hance family for 77 consecutive years. Tom Hance was appointed postmaster in 1889 and Robert Graham took the contract to carry the mail to and from Soda Creek once a week. The *Daily World* newspaper, published in Vancouver, reported on March 11, 1890: "Mr. Graham's remuneration is very meagre and the service accordingly is not as complete as it should be...." Three months later, in June, 1890, Graham resigned in favour of O. T. Hance, "the energetic and enterprising trader and postmaster at Hanceville," according to the *Daily World.*

Hance carried the mail for many years, first by packhorse over the old Bald Mountain Trail and then with a team. In the fall of 1890 he cut out a sleigh road, by-passing the bleak and exposed Bald Mountain trail. He finished the "Hance Timber Road," as it was called, the next year. This route was straightened, widened, and ditched in 1922 when the Conservative government was in power and Roderick Mackenzie was member for Cariboo. It was eventually gravelled and is now paved.

Tom Hance was appointed a Provincial Police Constable on August 16, 1895, one of six men so appointed by Superintendent F. S. Hussey in Victoria. He had, however, been acting constable for some time before that as evidenced by letters dated February 21, 1894, empowering him to seize and hold a stolen calf. A log jail, erected on the TH Ranch in 1898, was described by Government Agent Wm. Stephenson of Quesnel Forks as a "good strong place with two good cells in the back, and a room 10' x 14' in front." Hance was jailer as well. The Government Agent suggested to Superintendent Hussey that two pairs of leg irons be sent to Constable Hance for use in the "Lockup." When an Indian had broken the law and was brought in to the jail, he was usually allowed out to do little tasks about the place during the day and only locked up at night. On cold nights the prisoners slept on the floor in Hance's warm kitchen.

After the murder of Lewis Elkins in December 1897, the set-

Provincial Police Department,

Superintendent's Office,

Victoria, B. C., August 16 , 1895.

Sir,

    I have the honour to notify you that, in accordance with the ' Provincial Police Act, 1895,'' I have appointed you a Constable upon the force under my jurisdiction to take effect July 1st last.

    You will receive for your services as Constable a monthly salary of $ 50 which sum has been fixed by Order in Council.

    A copy of the Regulations framed under the above Act is being sent to you. Your attention is especially directed to such Regulations, as complete familiarity and a strict compliance therewith will be expected.

    Unless already provided you will also receive copies of "The Criminal Code 1892," 'The Indian Act" and amendments, a badge and other supplies.

    Kindly acknowledge receipt.

I have the honour to be,

Sir,

Your obedient servant,

F. S. HUSSEY,

Superintendent.

To Mr Thos A. Hance

Provincial Constable,

Chilcotin

Letter appointing Thomas Hance a B.C. Provincial Policeman. The letter was the only "training" the newly-appointed officers received.

tlers in the upper reaches of the Chilcotin sent a petition to Victoria, asking for a mounted constable to patrol the frontier. Robert Pyper of the North-West Mounted Police was dispatched in January 1898 as a full time Provincial Constable. In December of that

Until completion of the Canadian Pacific Railway in 1886, access to the Chilcotin was mainly by sternwheel steamer from Victoria to Yale, above, then some 300 miles up the Cariboo Wagon Road to Soda Creek, below. Travellers then crossed the Fraser River by boat and, finally, headed westward into the Chilcotin.

year Hance, who had been criticized by Edmund Elkins, brother of the murdered man, for not being aggressive enough with the law-breaking Indians, was suspended from the Police Force. A year later Norman Lee, Charles Crowhurst, and Bidwell (JP) were complaining to the Superintendent of Police that Constable Pyper was too aggressive with both whites and natives. Pyper was, however, generally well liked and credited with doing a good job. Two years later Pyper was transferred to Soda Creek and Hance again appointed Constable for Chilcotin.

On May 2, 1899, papers were sent by the Provincial Secretary in Victoria to O. T. Hance appointing him Coroner for the Province of British Columbia. Hance returned the papers stating: "...I do not feel that I would like to hold a position of that kind...."

In July, 1905, the Chilcotin Stage was robbed somewhere between Hanceville and 150 Mile House. When the stage arrived at the 150 Mile it was discovered that a large hole was torn in the Hanceville mail sack which had contained a "considerable amount of registered mail," and the sack was empty. It was thought that the robbery took place at one of the stopping places along the way. The *Ashcroft Journal* reported on August 12, 1905, that "Constable Hance (who was also the postmaster), immediately on receipt of the information, camped on the trail of the thief and has now under arrest an employee on a ranch near Riske Creek. A second party is suspected of being an accomplice and is probably in the hands of the law by now.

"Hanceville has always been considered a post office of importance as the ranchers and other residents of that locality do most of their business through the registered mail, and reliable information is to the effect that this particular week the consignment was a valuable one."

Hance had always maintained fair and honourable dealings with the native people and had no trouble with them. He kept a well stocked store with reasonable prices and carried on a brisk trade with the local bands. Their high regard for him was reflected in the Chief's actions when a crisis arose after an Englishman named Hewer moved in and applied for the Anaham Meadows, land considered Indian property. This encroachment touched off a council of war among the Indians. They decided to run the intruder out, with a massacre if necessary. Chief Anaham quickly rode down the river to warn Hance to be ready to leave the country in a hurry.

With his lathered horse standing at the hitching rail, Anaham entered the Hanceville Store and in a few words of broken English and Chinook delivered the warning: "My boys start, maybe go crazy," he warned. "Kill 'em all whiteman. Can't help it, me. You go quick." The Chief explained that he would send a runner ahead to tell the trader when to leave. Hance thanked him. They shook hands and the Chief departed.

Realizing the danger, Hance immediately sent a message to Hewer to impress upon him the seriousness of the situation. He then got together a light camp outfit and for many uneasy days and nights kept a team standing harnessed in the stable. Fortunately, Hewer was frightened by the threat of an uprising. He dropped his application and violence was averted.

Tom and Nellie Hance had a family of four sons and one daughter: Grover, Percy, Hattie, Judd, and Rene. Grover Orlando was the first white baby to arrive in the Chilcotin. He was born at 150 Mile House on April 19, 1888, under a doctor's care. The next son, Percy Royal, was the first white child born in the Chilcotin. He, Hattie, Judd and Rene were all born at Hanceville with an Indian mid-wife in attendance. When the older children were small, their playmates were Indians, children of natives employed on the ranch or those who came to trade at the store. The Hance youngsters sometimes wondered why they were the only kids with white skin while all the rest were brown.

Many natives worked for Hance, living with their families on the place. An Indian named Silpat helped him plant his crops each spring. Another, Sklam, was there for many years and when he died, was buried on the TH. Though Hance hired help for the heavy field work, he liked to put in the vegetable garden himself and always planted his onions on Easter Sunday. Chinese people were also part of Hances' lives. One of their Chinese helpers was named Hang. He did chores around the house, helping with cooking, gardening, and milking. Hang was good-natured and dependable, and would readily interrupt his work to run to the youngsters' aid if one of them needed help. As a little girl, Hattie took full advantage of this. When frightened she would yell at the top her voice: "MAMA, PAPA, HANG!" confident that at least one of them would hear her and come to her rescue. The children learned early to be considerate, courteous, and respectful to those around them regardless of colour or race, and these became lifelong attributes of the Hance family.

A few Chinese men would winter east of the Hanceville Bridge overlooking the river in what was called a China House.

This cavelike dwelling was built into the sidehill near the top of the first bench. Tom and Nellie Hance and their family were regularly invited there for Chinese New Year, and the children remembered it as warm and pleasant. The family would share a meal with their Chinese hosts and then be laden with gifts to take home: China nuts, ginger in earthenware jars, China tea and fascinating Chinese matches that fizzled and spit, smelling of sulfur, before bursting into flame. Sometimes there would be a special gift of a small ring or bamboo bracelet for Hattie.

The Hance children were tutored at home through the winter months by an Englishman named Jefferson. The front, or office section of the jail, was used for a classroom. As soon as the weather turned warm in the spring, Jefferson went off prospecting, leaving the youngsters free again. There was a playroom upstairs where Judd spent happy hours carving and painting realistic horses and cows which the children used in their games. But the great outdoors was their favourite place to play. The eldest four would sometimes all scramble onto their gentle old horse named Tommy and ride over the hillside trails, their dogs, Wozzle and Zena, frolicking beside them. But life wasn't all play; there were chores to do, too. One was bringing in the sheep in the evening. If the flock was hard to find and the children were gone too long, they would see their father's tall form walking out to look for them. He was always anxious for their safety.

A school ran for a short time on the flat beside the Hanceville Bridge, but the four eldest Hance children were finished with studies by that time. It was housed in the old saloon, a hexagon-shaped log building built by a German named Schultz. Remembered as a kindly man, Schultz ran the saloon by the river for a number of years in the late 1880s and early 1900s and called his place "San So See." When a nephew of Davey Allen named Willy came to stay, he found it lonely and renamed the place "Dewdrop Inn." Schultz was a prospector and although he was a good swimmer, he was drowned in the Homathko River on one of his prospecting trips. Attending school in the old saloon building were the Jameson children, Rene Hance, and Irna Trethewey. The teacher, Jan McPhail, boarded at Chilco Ranch with Joe and Rita Trethewey. (Dan Lee later owned this river flat and moved one of the odd shaped buildings to Lee's Corner.)

Another German, Feuhreller, lived in a cabin near the bluffs below Hanceville in the late 1800s, and had a limekiln at the foot of a 500-foot cliff where, in the canyon wall, there was an outcropping of almost pure limestone. The kiln fire died out for the last time before the turn of the century.

Tom Hance had packed in a saw and mill stones from the coast in the early years and set up a connected flour and sawmill on his ranch, powered by a waterwheel in the big spring behind the barn. This massive wheel had 12-foot spokes making it 24 feet across. The sawmill was first set up on Withrow Creek, or Sawmill Creek as it was aptly called then, where lumber was cut in Hance's Timber to finish Hance's log stable and other out-buildings as well as a two-story 12-room log house. This grand house was beautifully decorated with fur rugs and fine furnishings.

Inside a picket fence the spacious yard was planted with lilac bushes and hardy yellow roses and many other kinds of flowers. In the back garden, crabapple trees and red, white and black currants flourished, while through the length of the yard and into the hay-field went a sparkling spring that never froze. Water for the house was carried from this spring just a few feet from the kitchen door. Watercress thrived and made a tasty green in April and May.

Hanceville was a popular stopping place. A man named Brown, travelling through the Chilcotin in February 1892, mentions the place having a post office, store, gristmill and blacksmith shop and describes the "Hanceville Hotel" as "a pleasant place of resort." After his visit he publicly extended thanks to Mr. and Mrs. Hance for "kindness, courtesy and help."

The big house at Hanceville burned sometime in the early 1900s. Chinese help had built up the fire in the big heating stove very early on a cold winter morning and neglected to close down the damper. Over-heated pipes resulted. In the kitchen at the far end of the house a fire in the cookstove had not yet been kindled and this stove was saved. It was the range that Nellie Hance cooked on throughout her life.

The family lived temporarily in the old store across the road while Hance started immediately to rebuild. During this time, Mr. and Mrs. Hance and the three youngest children slept in the meat house while the two elder boys set up make-shift beds in the cellar.

The next house was a big two-story building with 16 rooms and a huge veranda, but it was never finished or furnished like the first one. The rooms were big and bare, and after the days of Chinese help were over must have been a nightmare to look after. Only Mrs. Hance's private sitting room with its flowered wallpaper, high white ceiling, bay windows and fur rugs reflected some of the

The Hances' house.

grandeur of the first house. Much of the lumber for this second home came from Becher's sawmill. This house, too, burned down some 30 years later.

An account of the opening of the new house appeared in the November 21, 1908, edition of the *Ashcroft Journal*: "Last Friday evening, October 6th, at the home of Mr. and Mrs. O. T. Hance, Hanceville, was held a most enjoyable party, on the occasion of the opening of their new and very handsome residence. Some fifty guests partook of an excellent supper, after which dancing was enjoyed to the full with the assistance of Mr. Harry Durrell and other accomplished musicians.

"It would take too long to describe the many beautiful costumes worn by the ladies, but among the most noticeable might well be mentioned that of our very genial hostess, which was a handsome gown of black relieved with touches of white, and her charming daughter was becomingly gowned in light blue.

"Both Mr. and Mrs. Hance are well known through the country for their very bountiful hospitality. It is the wish of all those present that they may be enabled to spend many such happy evenings.

"The dance was concluded by Mr. Tom Lee expressing the thanks of all present and calling for 'Three Cheers' which were heartily responded to."

Hance grew grain and hay and raised sheep, pigs, horses, and a few cattle. His branding iron was a combination of his initials, TH. The original site of Hanceville still goes by that name: TH Ranch.

After harvest each fall the wheat was ground into flour, middlings, shorts and bran. Hance ground for his neighbours as well as for his own household, some bringing grain from as far away as Chimney Creek. The Indians were learning to farm and they, too, brought their wheat to be ground into flour. The mill ran through the winter as well, being powered by the amazing spring that never froze. The source of this large volume of water was not more than a 100 yards from the mill and was termed a wonder, or freak of nature, by an early writer in the Vancouver *Daily World*.

Once the job of grinding the grain started the mill ran day and night. The two oldest boys, Grover and Percy, took turns with their father as soon as they were old enough. Daughter Hattie learned while only a little girl to make flour sacks on the sewing machine and stitch up the filled bags with needle and thread. There was always an abundance of by-products to feed to chickens, pigs and milk cows. This was a time of great activity at Hanceville, with the stable full of horses and a tableful of men to be fed as they waited to take home their year's supply of flour. It was a happy time and the Hance family carried with them into adulthood warm memories of the good sounds of the flour mill running – the roar of water as it poured from the big wheel, the hum and slap of moving belts, and the grinding clatter of the mill stones.

A miller, A. F. Haertl, came every winter to help Hance keep the millstones in shape. He worked for Borland in Williams Lake in the summertime. When Haertl became ill Mrs. Hance looked after him for a long time. He finally died of cancer in Vancouver.

About this same time Tom Hance suffered a stroke and was confined to bed. For Hance, leaving home was unthinkable and his wife cared for him there. He died at Hanceville on August 6, 1910, and was buried on the ranch above the canyon trail that led him to his dream.

At his funeral along with family, friends and settlers from far and wide were, reported the August 20, 1910, edition of the *Ashcroft Journal,* "about 100 Indians to whom the deceased had always been a good friend." A permanent monument to this intrepid pioneer is the Post Office and District named for him in 1889.

Each afternoon for many days after Hance's death, when the family was gathered in the big house for four o'clock tea, an unexplained shadow would pass across a southern window. Tom's old dog, Wozzle, would suddenly lift his head and look up. In the hush that followed Nellie would say gently: "That's Pappa...."

Tom Hance's Violin
Pearle Beale

It hangs in silence on the wall,
Its tones are hushed and still.
The fingers that once pressed the strings
Lie sleeping on the hill.

Could it but speak in language known
To us that here remain
It would tell of happy days
Ne'er to return again.

Of days where youth and pleasure met
As part of Life's young riddle.
Now none calls back so many things
As dreams of this old fiddle.

THE HANCE FAMILY

It could have been the influence of the free unrestricted way of life in the early years, but whatever, the fact remained that Tom Hance had been negligent about some aspects of his business. Although his home Lot 377, which includes the two springs, was recorded as "Pre-emption No. 1" in the Chilcotin, these 270 acres were not Crown granted until some years after Hance's death. And there is no record of his brand, the TH, being legally registered in his lifetime. Neither was he compensated for building the Hance Timber Road in the late 1800s. These oversights placed a costly burden on his heirs.

At the time of Tom Hance's death, land taxes were in arrears on Lot 377 but Mrs. Hance refused to settle this bill until the government acknowledged their responsibility to pay for building of the road through Hance's Timber years before. Time dragged on while interest accumulated on the land debt. It took reams of correspondence, 15 years of frustration battling government officials and a trip to Victoria before the matter was finally settled. Interest had by that time eaten up the profit there should have been from the early road work.

In the 1920s Rene Hance, armed with a briefcase bulging with correspondence and letters of support from local politicians, made the journey to Victoria on his mother's behalf, intending to meet with the Minister of Public Works. He was turned down – the Min-

Grover Hance's wife, Mary. Like most Chilcotin women, she could ride as well as any cowboy. Only the first generation used the awkward European sidesaddle. Thereafter, they used the much more practical Western saddle.

BX stage at Hanceville, with passengers Queenie Wheeler and Hattie Hance.

ister had no time to see him. Young Hance then got in touch with the Leader of the Opposition, Harry Pooley, who was acquainted with his mother. Pooley arranged a meeting with Premier John Oliver and accompanied Rene to the Premier's office next day. Here an agreement was reached that would put in motion the government process wherein one debt would cancel out the other. A Crown Grant on Lot 377 was then processed.

After their father's death, the Hance boys discontinued growing wheat for the grist mill, sold the sheep and increased the cow herd, turning the TH into a cattle ranch. They increased the alfalfa crop and bought a meadow in the Whitewater from Mac McDiarmid. They also owned a meadow on Sawmill Creek adjacent to their range. The ranch remained a popular stopping place, remembered for the cheery hospitality and Mrs. Hance's good cooking, especially her baked beans and raisin buns.

As soon as they were old enough, Percy and Judd joined the Canadian Army and went overseas to fight in World War One. Grover had lost an eye from a fragment of hot steel while working in the blacksmith shop and was not accepted. Rene was too young to be involved in the conflict. (He joined up in World War Two and served six years in the Postal Corps in Ottawa.)

Percy and Judd served in France and Germany but both returned safely. Neither ever married. Judd died as a young man from pneumonia. Already suffering from a bad cold, he was riding on the fall roundup in wet and bitter weather when pneumonia developed. Percy took him home from the range and two doctors were summoned but it was, sadly, too late.

After being widowed for a number of years, Nellie Hance married Jim Ragan, an American cowboy from Oakland, California. He had cowboyed for Quilchena and Douglas Lake Ranches and was at the time riding for Gang Ranch, in charge of steers on the north side of the Chilcotin River. He joined the family at Hanceville. To most people, Mrs. Jim Ragan was still Mrs. Hance.

Jim's customary dress was brown corduroy pants, cowboy boots, vest and a small kerchief knotted at his neck. Being an incurable practical joker made Ragan unpopular with some people. Ragan Lake on the Whitewater Road bears his name.

Nellie Hance Ragan died suddenly in 1935 in Williams Lake Hospital and is buried beside Tom Hance at Hanceville. Jim Ragan died some years later in Victoria where he had spent his last years with his wife's relatives, the Verdier family.

The TH became one of the Chilcotin's first guest ranches, attracting visitors from as far as New York and London.

For many years, beginning in 1904, Percy Hance was the Chilcotin's mailman. Winter and summer, with his four-horse team he met the B.C. Express Company's red and yellow stagecoaches at 150 Mile House to pick up mail, express and passengers.

GROVER ORLANDO HANCE, the oldest son, looked the part of the typical old-time cowboy. Good looking with dark curly hair, he liked big rowelled spurs that jingled, red neckerchief and always wore wooly chaps when riding. Grover was mannerly but outspoken. He was often glum and moody but was warm-hearted and generous. His reputation as a wild hell-raiser when drinking was well known. He rolled his smokes from Bullduram tobacco and called them "cigareets." Always in authentic western dress, Grover was a favorite subject for photographers and his picture appeared on the cover of various publications.

In 1917 Grover married Mary Wright, part Indian daughter of ferryman Bill Wright of Dog Creek. Mary was quick, slim, and pretty with big gray eyes and dark hair. Though a good rider, she was hurt when thrown from a horse into a rock pile which left her with a slight limp, most noticeable in the high-heeled slippers she loved to wear.

Grover and Mary lived for the most part away from the home ranch. He took up a flat on the south side of the Chilcotin River and a meadow on Minton Creek (still known as Grover's Meadow), which were both sold to Chilco Ranch. Mary died from tuberculosis in Kamloops in 1932. They had no children.

Much later Grover re-married and with his second wife, Francis, ran a guiding camp in the Big Creek country. He sold his share of the TH Ranch to his brothers, but he and his wife made their home there in a small house by the spring above the road. Francis, a rough-hewn woman with a big heart, died in 1958. In 1960 Grover sold his hunting business – horses, saddles, his OZ brand, and 40 acres with three cabins along the Big Creek Road – to Tom Smith.

Grover was handy in the blacksmith shop and at leather and silver work. He was pretty good at first aid though he had no training. "Grover's kind of a doctor," Percy used to say. His temper was close to the surface and one thing sure to trigger it was an impatient motorist honking the horn while making his way through Hance's drive of spooky steers en route to the fall sale in Williams Lake. Grover would quickly spur his cowhorse to the offending vehicle and giving the luckless driver a colorful tongue lashing. Once when one of his guides got out of hand at the hunting camp Grover dabbed a loop on him and tied him up to a jackpine tree. He left him there until the man had sobered up and promised good behaviour. Grover at the time was crowding his three score and ten.

He died in Cariboo Memorial Hospital in 1960 at 72, having

126

Rene Hance.

never fully recovered from a broken pelvis sustained while feeding grain to his saddle string at the hunting camp.

PERCY ROYAL HANCE was tall and easy going, with a quiet original sense of humour. He was policeman in the Chilcotin for awhile. Except for four years overseas during the World War One and a winter in California, he spent his life at Hanceville where he was born. At 15 he drove stage for his father with a four-horse team hitched to a "democrat" (a light wagon) in summer or a light sleigh called a "cutter" in winter. With the opening of the new Chimney Creek Bridge over the Fraser in 1904, the Chilcotin mail pick up was changed from Soda Creek to 150 Mile House and delivering the post to the Chilcotin was a full-time job. "On Saturday," Percy recounted, "I set out with the four-horse team from Hanceville and went as far as Bechers. It was a long day from there to the 150 Mile and I stayed over for two days to rest my team and make connections with the BX Stage." On Wednesday it was back to Riske Creek with the mail, Thursday to Hanceville, and Friday to the Alexis Creek Post Office and back home to Hanceville ready to start all over again on Saturday.

Percy Hance is best described in an article by Reverend Ed Wallace in the *Calgary Herald* following Percy's death:

"Percy was an ordinary type of person, a cowboy essentially but also a gentleman in the first and finest sense of that term. During the latter years when he and his brother, Rene, ran the TH Ranch together his true gentleness came to the fore. To quote Paul St. Pierre's column in the *Vancouver Sun*: 'Some men in such circumstances develop the contempt of familiarity. They converse in grunts and sign language. But of a family which gave high priority to courtesy, this never happened to these two men. In the most ordinary of day to day contact they addressed one another with the same grace which they showed to friends, acquaintances, and strangers....' Percy was a delight to know. His sense of humour, soft spoken voice and gentle manner belied the kind of life he had led, for being a cowboy in the Chilcotin was anything but a soft life at even the best of times. Hospitality was second nature to Percy and his brother, Rene, and the TH Ranch in the Chilcotin Valley is known all over Canada for just that old fashioned quality. People came back year after year — often times driving many miles out of their way across an impossible road — just to say hello to Percy and Rene. So many people have the idea that men who perform jobs like those that the ranching, lumbering, and fishing industries require are hard and calloused. Nothing could be farther from the truth. My experiences have taught me that the bigger the job the bigger the man required to do it. Percy Hance was a good example of this. He was big enough and strong enough to cope with all the problems, hardships and difficulties met with in the course of a cowboy's life but he was also big enough and strong enough to retain his essential nature as a gentleman in the highest sense of the term."

Percy Hance died in Cariboo Memorial Hospital in May 1967 and is buried in Williams Lake Cemetery.

EDWIN RENE, light-hearted and charming, was the youngest member of the Hance family. His accomplishments were extraordinary. Self-educated except for short stints in country schools, (the saloon building by the Hanceville Bridge over the Chilcotin River and Big Creek school), and a year or two at 150 Mile House, he became lawyer, coroner, notary public, marriage commissioner and in later years, Provincial Judge. He was postmaster for better than 30 years. A good rider and horseman, he loved the ranch and was the moving force in its progress. As well as a good cattle ranch, neatly kept, the TH expanded to become a guest ranch where visitors came from as far away as London and New York.

In 1927 Rene married Vera Graham, an English girl working at Lees. They built their own house on the edge of the alfalfa field below the big house. Their marriage ended after nine years but they remained friends. They had no children. As already noted, Rene joined up in the World War Two and served nearly six years in the Postal Corps in Ottawa.

Rene was interested in law. As a young boy he studied at home, using his father's old law books, Dally's *Criminal Procedure*, and a copy of the criminal Code. Then he apprenticed with Williams Lake lawyer Neil MacDiarmid, a friend of the Hance family. Money was scarce and MacDiarmid, struggling to support a wife and three children, could not afford a clerk. He offered Rene work in his office for experience gained and law lectures at night. This opportunity was just what Rene needed and he jumped at the chance. The bright, energetic young Hance was a boon to MacDiarmid and the two became lifelong friends.

Rene apprenticed with MacDiarmid for one and a half years and then successfully applied to become an Inferior Courts Practitioner. (A lawyer who, not having written the Bar examination, could only plead cases in the lower courts. Qualifications included a working knowledge of the law and an unblemished record as a good citizen.) Rene took cases throughout the Chilcotin, representing clients in Police, Magistrate, or Provincial Court. If the case went to higher court Rene worked up his brief and appointed a qualified lawyer to represent him in the courtroom. He seldom lost a case.

Rene was one of the original members of the Notaries Public

Judd Hance and, below, Percy and Grover Hance. Grover is also on the outside back cover.

TH Ranch Lodge.

of B.C., with much of his work done free of charge for neighbours. He was appointed Coroner when he was 29 years of age and held that position longer than any other coroner in the province. His first case was in 1930 and his last in 1976. Coroners in the early days went to the scene of the crime and this travel took Rene to isolated parts of the country where roads were nonexistent and travel was on horseback. Later, aircraft were sometimes hired. As marriage commissioner, Rene conducted numerous weddings and the occasional funeral.

After the sale of the historic TH Ranch in 1966, Rene and Percy moved to Williams Lake. Rene was made a Provincial Judge the following year. He retired in 1975.

With a good-natured love for all living things, especially his horses, Rene remained a country boy at heart. When interviewed by the newspaper in 1975 he affirmed that "without a doubt I like ranch life best. You have your freedom, you are your own boss – it's an open life. I'm not a house person. I'd have stayed with law if I had been."

Rene died from cancer in 1977, the last of Orlando Thomas Hance's immediate family. Hance's only descendants are the children of his daughter, Hattie Witte, and their families.

The TH Ranch at Hanceville has changed hands a number of times since it was first sold in 1966. The place has now been subdivided and will never again be an operating cattle ranch. Lot 377, with control of the two springs, is owned by the British Columbia

Ministry of Environment. The constant flow and temperature (11°C) of the spring water makes it an ideal site for their fish hatchery. Raising steelhead was their first project and now rainbow trout are being reared. The land is currently leased by John and Shirley Scagg.

The Hanceville Post Office was moved from its original site at the TH Ranch to Lee's Corner in 1972.

HATTIE HANCE, only daughter of Tom and Nellie Hance, was a beautiful but modest girl who could ride and shoot like her brothers. She was sent to Victoria to finish her education. She stayed in Victoria with her mother's sister, Anna Lacoursiere, and apprenticed with a hair dresser, Mrs. Billy Vann. Hattie married Frank Witte and their story is told in another section of this book.

VERA ELIZABETH GRAHAM (HANCE) was born at Alloa, Scotland, but spent most of her girlhood in England in the cities of Hull and London where her father was in the shipping business. After the family moved to London, Vera and her sister were put in boarding school. Vera was a confident girl and admits she was always a bit headstrong. Her family thought if she were going to emigrate, Australia would be the place to go. But Vera chose Canada. "I've never regretted it," she firmly states.

Vera Graham came to Canada in the early 1920s with an organization called the Overseas Settlement of British Gentlewomen. The girls stayed in Vancouver in Queen Mary's Coronation Hostel. Here the young women were taught how to cook, sew, shop, use Canadian money – and a wood burning cookstove. They were also assisted in finding work. Vera had voiced a preference to work in the country and after a few short jobs on Vancouver Island was given first chance at a position with Mrs. Norman Lee in the Chilcotin. She took it eagerly. "It was terribly exciting seeing real cowboys and Indians for the first time," she recalls. She was glad to find that Lees had a Chinese cook in the kitchen and her job was to help Mrs. Lee in the store or wherever she was needed. Her commitment to the country of cowboys and Indians was cemented when she met and married Rene Hance and moved four miles down the road to Hanceville.

After her marriage broke up in the mid 1930s, Vera worked in Vancouver and then at Fairbridge Farm School near Duncan on Vancouver Island. She was House Mother for boys there for a number of years. She spent her holidays in the Chilcotin at the TH Ranch at Hanceville with the Hance brothers and their guests.

Vera Hance with Rene at the TH Guest Ranch.

In 1952, Vera returned to the Chilcotin to work as a telephone operator under Nellie Kinkead at Alexis Creek. The telephone office was in Kinkead's home and at that time was the Government Telephone and Telegraph Service. This service was purchased by B.C. Tel in 1954 and the office and switchboard enlarged. Vera's voice became a familiar and welcome sound on the wire as she was always pleasant and helpful. Often when a call was put through to Alexis Creek she would help locate your party from the big window at the switchboard: "I just saw him enter the garage. I'll try there for you." Something was lost as well as gained when the little office at Alexis Creek was closed in 1968, with Vera the head operator by this time.

Vera Hance moved to an apartment in the Johnson Block on First Avenue in Williams Lake, where she still lives, and went to work in sales at Fields Store. Vera also worked for years as a faithful volunteer at the Williams Lake Library where she made many friends. She is now retired.

In April 1884, NORMAN LEE, accompanied by an Anglican minister, Reverend Henry Horlock, set sail from England for Canada via New York and San Francisco. They reached Kamloops, B.C., in the fall where a ministry in the Anglican Church awaited Horlock. Norman Lee got a job supervising Chinese labourers on C.P.R. construction. He later went to work as a bookkeeper for the Hudson's Bay Company. In 1884, Lee came to the Chilcotin with Hugh Bayliff and the two men went into partnership.

Pooling their resources to buy a team and wagon and a few goods to trade with the Indians, they settled in the Upper Chilcotin Valley where the Bayliff Ranch is today. When Bayliff got married in 1891 Norman sold his share to his partner and struck off on his own. A few miles up-river from the Hanceville Post Office he bought a trading post from a Finlander named Dan Nordberg. Nordberg had no faith in banks or paper money. He insisted on being paid in gold pieces and for years after Norman took over he kept finding gold coins in tea and coffee bins in the store.

Lee called his place the Beaver Ranch and developed it into a cattle ranch as well as a trading post. On May 17, 1898, Lee started out to take a drive of beef cattle to the Klondike. The party suffered many hardships as they pushed the 200 head northward, often through terrible weather conditions. Mud knee deep on the trail and lack of feed for the animals took a heavy toll. Finally, at Teslin Lake they butchered the cattle and tried to raft them down the lake, hoping to get the beef to Dawson City. But the rafts broke up

Norman and Agnes Lee and son, Daniel.

Travelling salesman at Lee's Store.

in a fierce storm and all the beef was lost. Making their way back on foot through extreme winter cold and storm where only the hardiest of men survived, they finally reached Wrangel, Alaska. Copeland caught a boat to Victoria next day and Lee finally landed in Vancouver with a dog, a dollar, and a blanket. He took the train to Ashcroft and from there started "footing" it back to his ranch in the Chilcotin, finally borrowing a horse to complete the journey. By 1902 he was well established ranching again. Norman Lee's diary of this ill-fated adventure was later published in book form. (See *Klondike Cattle Drive* by Heritage House.)

In October 1902 Lee made a trip back to England to see the coronation of Edward VII. He enjoyed, too, a visit with his relatives and after a whirlwind courtship married his cousin, Agnes Lee. The couple sailed for Canada in January and arrived back in the Chilcotin in February 1903. Norman and Agnes went back to England in 1905 and adopted a three-year-old boy, Daniel, son of a doctor friend.

Lee built up his cattle herd and further developed the fields. To enhance his crops, Norman attempted an ambitious project to bring water for irrigation from Big Creek through ditching and down Minton Creek and across the Chilcotin River by flume. He succeeded in completing this difficult undertaking but when the flume collapsed he gave it up.

Lee kept up an active fur trade with the Indians. Both he and his wife learned to speak the Chilcotin language and had many faithful friends among them. Their general store stocked with a great variety of goods served the country well for many years.

The ranch was sold to an Englishman named Jack Temple in 1913 and the Lees moved to Victoria where Dan went to school. They had to take the ranch back in 1919 and both Norman and Agnes lived happily there the rest of their lives.

Norman Lee died in March 1939 at 77 and was buried on his homestead.

His Beaver Ranch, with additions and improvements by son, Daniel, and his sons, Brud and Robin, is now known as Lee's Corner and was in the Lee name for 100 years.

AGNES (MRS. NORMAN) LEE: The Chilcotin had only four white women when Agnes Lee arrived in 1902 to begin a life startlingly different from the world she had left behind in England.

Agnes Lee, known to family and friends as Nessie, was born in Shropshire, England, in 1872. She was visiting friends in Ireland when she received a telegram from her brother that led to an adventurous turn in her life: "Please come and help entertain our cousin, Norman Lee, from Canada."

Her first reaction was to refuse. Her holiday had only just begun and the cousin would probably be boring, having spent 18

Agnes Lee in front of Norman's old store.

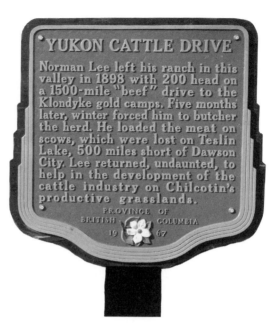

A Stop-of-Interest plaque near Lee's Ranch commemorates Norman Lee's ill-fated cattle drive. He arrived back in Vancouver with, as he noted, "...a dog, a dollar and a blanket." He spent the dollar on a drink so as to have "...a fresh start with a clean slate."

YUKON CATTLE DRIVE

Norman Lee left his ranch in this valley in 1898 with 200 head on a 1500-mile "beef" drive to the Klondyke gold camps. Five months later, winter forced him to butcher the herd. He loaded the meat on scows, which were lost on Teslin Lake, 500 miles short of Dawson City. Lee returned, undaunted, to help in the development of the cattle industry on Chilcotin's productive grasslands.

PROVINCE OF
BRITISH COLUMBIA
19 67

years in the Canadian wilderness. However, with the hope that he would not stay long, she returned to England.

Norman Lee proved to be anything but boring. He had unbelievable tales to tell of taking a drive of beef into the north, only to lose everything and start all over again. Norman proved, in fact, to be quite fascinating, and in a short time he and Nessie were engaged. They were married in December and in January 1903 left for Canada.

In was -30°F when their ship landed at Halifax, and even colder when the train pulled into Ashcroft, B.C. Norman's brother, Edward Penrose Lee, who ranched farther up the Chilcotin Valley at Redstone, met them there with team and sleigh. The 200-mile journey from Ashcroft to Hanceville took six days in extremely cold weather, and included crossing the Fraser River on the ice at the mouth of Chimney Creek.

Held in the grip of winter, the ranch lay silent and desolate when Norman's bride, chilled and cramped, climbed out of the sleigh on February 17, 1903, and surveyed the surroundings that were to be home for the rest of her life.

Her first home was a hand-hewn log house built for her husband by Steve and Tom Verdier, brothers of Mrs. Tom Hance, her nearest neighbour. It was frugally furnished when she arrived but warm with a big barrel heater burning day and night. To Agnes it seemed dreary when the short Canadian winter days gave way to early darkness. But when spring came, stirring the waking earth till it fairly burst with life, she knew she would find real happiness in this strange and lonely land.

"My husband jabbered pidjin English to the Chinese cook and Chilcotin to the natives," Mrs. Lee recalled. "I decided to learn the Indian tongue myself to help overcome my homesickness. Some words, such as baking powder and scissors, are very hard to pronounce but Norman helped me and I finally mastered them." Her determination was rewarded and, in the busy round of pioneer living, homesickness was forgotten.

In fact the rugged frontier life appealed to Agnes Lee. Chinese help in the kitchen allowed her time to work in the store, keep books, and help outdoors. Housework didn't interest her. The round-up was one event of the year that she always looked forward to. The majority of ranchers from Redstone to Big Creek ranged their cattle together on the unfenced grassy tableland lying on the south side of the Chilcotin River, southeast of Chilco Ranch and stretching for miles towards the mouth of Big Creek. Norman's wife enjoyed this annual get-together when the ranchers and their wives gathered to round up the cows and brand the calves. This was a happy time, spent on the grassy windblown plateau with hearty meals of brown beans, bannock and beef, and the sociability of stories, fiddle playing, and singing around the campfire at night. (The English and Irish ranchers built and used separate branding corrals. Years later, when this land became part of Chilco Ranch and was fenced and divided, two of the big pastures were named accordingly: "the Englishman Corral Pasture" and "the Irishman Corral Pasture.")

All life in those early days was free and informal. Agnes remembered trying on an imported hat before the owner had even seen it! The reason was that one of her neighbours to the west bought all her clothes from a mail order house in London. One mail day the old stage driver came into Lee's store with a torn and battered box in his hand and asked if she would like to try on a London hat. Pulling the thing from the half-opened box, he placed the English creation on her head. After an admiring glance in the mirror, Mrs. Lee placed the headpiece back in its wrappings and on it went to its rightful owner.

She recalled with amusement when the first telephones were installed in Chilcotin. One man with a yen for jesting would call up the ladies early in the morning and say: "Good morning, my dear, how pretty you look this morning...." And the lady would gasp, still not quite understanding all the possibilities of this modern contraption, and say: "You can't see me, can you?"

The Lees had no children, so on a trip to England in 1905 they adopted a three-year-old boy from a doctor friend who had seven children of his own and was planning to marry a widow with three more. Their adopted son, Daniel, from the beginning was a lad with definite personal opinions. Once while out driving with a young woman who was visiting Lees he found himself listening to an endless volume of praise for the Chilcotin. "Isn't it beautiful!" she enthused. "Don't you just love it?" Taking advantage of this first lull in the glowing recital, Dan looked at her coolly and replied: "No. I've been here three years and I'm sick of it."

Various young ladies acting as governess helped Dan with his early schooling as there was no public school near enough to attend. He was sent to boarding school in Victoria to complete his education but disliked it intensely. Then in 1913 Lees sold the ranch to Jack Temple and all moved to Victoria. After the war and a bout with the dreaded flu epidemic of 1918, Agnes and Norman went on a holiday to California, leaving son, Dan, at boarding school again. They had been away two months when he wrote to say: "If you don't come home soon I am leaving school and going to live with Uncle Pen (Ed Lee) in the Chilcotin."

They came back. Because payments on the ranch were long overdue they decided to foreclose and all return home to the Chilcotin. The Lees travelled to Williams Lake as guests of the Pacific Great Eastern Railway, then under construction. "We slept for awhile," Mrs. Lee recalled, "and then had to turn our bunks over to the work crews. I spent half the night making sandwiches for the men. We went off the tracks seven times between Squamish and Williams Lake." A pair of socks which she began knitting when they boarded the train were handed, completely finished, to the conductor in Williams Lake.

The ranch had deteriorated in the six years they'd been away, but they were happy to be back and, all working together, soon had the place in order again. The store particularly interested Nessie. When Norman passed away in 1939 she took over that responsibility entirely and did a thriving business — especially with the Indian people. She had great friends among them and could converse with them in their own language when they gathered to trade in the store. Mrs. Lee branched out to open a dry goods store in

"Gan Gan" and Rene Hance in 1956.

Williams Lake and stayed in town to run it for a time. But she missed the ranch and the family and soon give it up. By this time she was known to her four grandchildren – and to all the Chilcotin – affectionately as "Gan Gan."

When her eyesight began to fail and she had trouble reading the numbers on the old-fashioned weigh scale in the store, she would simply say to her customer as she scooped the desired commodity into the tray: "You fix it to the correct number of pounds." She kept a plate full of coins nearby where the customers could pick out their change. And because of her whole-hearted trust in them, no one ever cheated.

A highlight in Gan Gan's life came a few months before her death. She was officially presented to Princess Margaret in Williams Lake in the summer of 1958 during the town's centennial festivities. Mrs. Norman Lee died in November of that same year at 86.

She had spent her life happily in the land she adopted as an English bride. "I consider this God's good country," she once wrote, "and wouldn't change my home for any other place I know."

She was buried in the family plot on the land she loved with neighbour Rene Hance officiating, as she had requested.

DANIEL LELAND "DAN" LEE was six years old when he announced that he had been in the Chilcotin for three years and he was sick of it. But as he grew into adulthood, reaching 6'4" and straight as a rod, he grew to love the country. Looking back at 72, he reflected that working on his father's ranch on the frontier was a magnificent life for a young man.

Dan had a horse named Nigger when he was growing up and liked to go riding. But he was industrious by nature and when he was older spent most of his time working in the fields or mending fences and tending stock. Although his Dad had a trading post, Dan was more interested in the cow business. In 1929 that interest led him to a gamble that paid off old debts and financed his dream of getting started in purebred Hereford cattle.

It was July, and an Indian named Capoose rode in, anxious to make a deal to sell 100 head of mixed cattle at Anahim Lake to Cosens Spencer of Chilco Ranch. Spencer, however, quibbled over the price and finally refused the offer. Capoose sat in Lee's store, despondent. "If I had the money," Dan thought, "I'd buy those cattle, and more. I think I could make money on them." He decided to take a long chance.

Making a hasty trip to Williams Lake, he arranged a loan of $5,000 cash and authority to write cheques on the Bank of Montreal. He came home with his head in the clouds, though not without some trepidation. He was in debt, but financed to buy cattle wherever he could find them. He closed the deal with Capoose on the 100 head at Anahim Lake, giving him $200 to bind the deal. He then started getting ready for the long trip on horseback to bring them home – plus any other cattle that might be for sale at Anahim Lake. It took a week shoeing horses and getting a camp outfit in place for the long trek. To help, he hired two Indian cowboys, Joseph Bobby and Edward Johnny.

The cattle buying venture stretched to three months as word spread through the country that Dan Lee was paying cash on the spot. He was offered cattle in the Nazko Valley, down the Blackwater to Trout Lake, and many side trips, picking up a few head here and a few head there. The greatest compensation for the long hours in the saddle, roughing it day after day in all kinds of weather, was the honesty of the Indian people he was dealing with. One man rode for two days to give Lee back the deposit he had paid Capoose and forgotten to take off his account. "You make a mistake," the fellow grinned, handing Dan a roll of $200.

Dan and his cowboys got home in October, trail worn and weary, but bringing with them a herd of mixed cattle, including one massive old steer that tipped the scales at 1,760 pounds. He got nine cents a pound for him, the same price paid for smaller animals. The beef market had improved while Lee was away and he was surprised to find three cattle buyers waiting for him when he got the herd to the Williams Lake stockyards.

Dan's gamble proved even more successful than he had dared to hope. He paid off his bank loan, squared up an old debt of Norman Lee's, and had enough money left over for that coveted start in purebred Herefords. Dan eventually had a big herd of highly prized purebreds. His tall figure was a familiar sight at the sales in Williams Lake, showing and selling his Hereford bulls.

In 1931 Dan married Margaret Cousins, who came out from England in 1929. Margaret industriously took part in ranch life. She grew an exceptional vegetable and flower garden. Dan and

A snowy October cattle drive was a scene well known to Dan Lee, opposite. The cattle are being driven to market by the legendary Pan Phillips, third from left.

In the days of horse-power, Hugh Bailiff leveling his field. (See page 275.)

Margaret had a family of four: Wendy, Norman (Brud), Sheila, and Robin.

In the 1960s Dan reached out for one more gamble. He built a new store across the road from the old one and included a restaurant with full basement for living quarters, and named it "Lee's Corner Cafe." Included in the development were two separate motel units. Staff was hired to run the bright new stopping place, but in emergencies the family pitched in to help; Margaret or daughter Wendy cooking in the kitchen and Dan waiting on customers. Again the gamble paid off. The cafe quickly became popular with travelers on the gravel road that ran right by the Corner.

The Lees finally sold the cafe complex. A laundromat was added by the new owners. It is presently owned by Bill and Maurine Spill (1992). The Hanceville Post Office was moved from its original location at the TH Ranch to Lee's Corner in 1972.

Dan Lee died in 1979 and is buried at home in the family plot. His wife pre-deceased him in 1971. Their heirs, Brud and Anne Lee, Brian and Wendy Fletcher, and Robin and Cindy Lee, carried on the ranch and the trucking business. Sheila lives in Sorrento with husband, Tony Fosbery. In 1989 the Lee family sold much of the original Beaver Ranch to John Van Horlick. The Fletchers kept the Spring Meadow back of Alexis Creek; Robin and Cindy have part of the old place, including buildings and the trucking; and Brud and Anne now ranch at the Gables where they built a nice new home.

CHILCOTIN POLICEMEN

Orlando Thomas Hance was the first policeman in the Chilcotin, appointed constable under the Criminal Code of 1892, but was not sworn in until 1895 when the Provincial Police Act was passed in Victoria. He was then sent a police badge by Superintendent F. S. Hussey and received 50 dollars a month in wages. At the ranch a two-cell log jail was built across the spring from the stable. The doors were seldom locked except at night. Prisoners were escorted to Clinton for trial by Hance when "the grass turned green."

In 1891, H. C. Strause was sent up as a Special Constable to assist in the capture of a renegade Indian, Nemiah, who had recently killed another Indian with a knife, splitting him from breast to groin. After a chase of some 160 miles Nemiah was captured.

After the shooting of Lewis Elkins in December 1897 (Elkin's murderer was quickly captured by a posse of local men – see "Nemiah Valley"), Constable Robert Pyper of the B. C. Provincial

Constable Robert Pyper and his dappled grey at the Soda Creek jail. The Chilcotin's Pyper Lake is named after him.

Constable Frank Aiken at Hances.

Police was stationed in the district. Pyper rode a big grey horse named Duke and stayed at Grahams or at Hanceville. He was noted for his thoroughness and exactness in performing his duties. After two years, Pyper was transferred to Soda Creek and Hance again took over as Constable in Chilcotin. Five years later, in 1905, Robert Pyper was discharged from the police force for a number of unfortunate reasons. He returned to the Chilcotin and started a store and trading post five miles west of Hanceville. In 1924 he moved his store to Chilanko Forks where Pyper Lake is named after him. He died at his store and is buried in Alexis Creek Cemetery.

Tom Hance resigned in the fall of 1909 and died a year later. His second eldest son, Percy, acted as policeman until Frank Aiken was sent to Chilcotin, making his headquarters at Hanceville. Early in 1915 Constable Aiken was transferred to Clinton and Constable Cape replaced him, followed in a year or two by Constable Petentry. As a small boy, Bill Bliss remembers Constable Petentry stopping at their place for lunch, riding a black horse and leading another with a mounted man wearing handcuffs. The prisoner ate lunch, too, still wearing the handcuffs. Two trappers, MacDonald and Oscar Gustavesen, had gone up the Chilcotin River to the Icha Mountains to trap foxes. They quarrelled and Gustavesen came out to report that his partner had shot at him. Petentry made the long ride up to the mountains alone and brought MacDonald out.

The next officer was Harry Clark, very well liked by everyone, who could be found riding his big buckskin horse anywhere in the Chilcotin. He made a long ride, too, by himself to Tsuniah Lake and arrested Indian Bedel Jack and brought him out to appear before local J. P. Alex Graham on a charge of theft.

After Bob Pyper had moved his store to the Chilanko River, the Provincial Government acquired Pyper's good log buildings west of Norman Lees. They were renovated for a jail and living quarters for the new policeman, Ian McRae who had a wife and child. Bill Bliss Sr. and Walter Barlow were hired to pipe the spring water to the house, four feet underground below frost with water tap outside the door. Later Constables Dan Wier and Bill Broughten lived there before moving to Alexis Creek to be nearer to the school.

About 1937, Tom Lee built a rental house in Alexis Creek, living quarters and jail all in one building, first occupied by Constable Johnnie Blatchford and family. Blatchford left the police force four years later to start cattle ranching at Tsuniah Lake.

Constable Walter Bailey with wife, Verna, then came to Alexis Creek staying only a few years when Constable Bob Turnbull and wife, Rose, arrived. Constable Turnbull worked in the Chilcotin for 12 years and during this time, in 1950, the Provincial Police were replaced by the Royal Canadian Mounted Police. By the 1980s there were large office and jail buildings at Alexis Creek staffed by a sergeant, four corporals and office staff.

This classic photo of the Chilcotin – cowboys, rolling rangeland, narrow dirt road, Russell fence – was taken near Riske Creek in the 1950s. In the background is historic Becher House, now demolished. The dirt road is also gone, widened and paved to become Highway 20 from Williams Lake some 300 miles westward to Bella Coola.

Chilco Ranch.

CHILCO RANCH

The famed Chilco Ranch is picturesquely situated on the south side of the Chilcotin River near Hanceville. Present owners are John and Sharon DeBoer, but more than a dozen others have come and gone before them.

The first pre-emption on benchland above the river was in 1884 by Mike Minton, a big humorous Irishman whose name is remembered by the creek which provides irrigation for the big fields. He had a partner for a time, a Frenchman named Pete Bergault. They raised a few cattle, as well as pigs and grain, and eventually had their own self-binder. The *Inland Sentinel*, a Kamloops newspaper, reported Bergault marketing 100 hogs in Quesnel in the autumn of 1890 which, the reporter wrote, were "fattened on the range." There was no bridge over the Chilcotin River and crossing was made by canoe when the water was high. In low water they forded and in winter crossed on the ice.

The partners soon had a near neighbour when a Scots-Canadian from Toronto named Davy Allen, a jolly man remembered for his white beard, took up land down-river from them. This parcel of land is still known as the "Davy Allen."

In 1896 Mike Minton sold out to Claud Wilson, an Englishman who gave the Chilco its name. He bought out Davy Allen and purchased a swamp meadow on Upper Deer Creek from brothers Frank and Ira Johnson. Little is known about the Johnsons. They pre-empted this meadow in 1888 and must have lived there for some years as they built a multiple-roomed house on the middle lot on a rise of ground above the rocky creek. One of the brothers was married and his wife was one of the first white women in the country. Their meadow became known as the Wilson Meadow. It now belongs to Wayne and Trena Plummer.

Frank Johnson also took up a pre-emption on Lower Deer Creek, Lot 133, which became part of the Deer Creek place.

About this time a joint project was underway between Wilson and the Stoney Indians to divert water from Big Creek, some 20 miles away, to the Stone Reserve and on to Chilco Ranch. Norman Lee had at one time attempted to bring water from Big Creek to his Beaver Ranch via the same route, but the date is unknown. It would appear that this was later, or surely Wilson and the Indians would have made use of the beginnings of the deep ditch that Lee abandoned. Lee faced the problem of spanning the Chilcotin River with a flume. The flume collapsed from the weight and pressure of the water and was never rebuilt. Evidence of the beginnings of Lee's ditch by the old Church Ranch and remnants of flume along the Chilcotin River are still visible. The Chilco Ranch-Stoney irrigation system was a success and is still in use after more than 90 years – upgraded as time passed.

Mike Minton had built a small ditch in the early 1890s to bring water from Minton Creek (called Brigam Creek then) to his farm (Chilco Ranch). A short diversion from this ditch irrigated a 70-acre field at the reserve as well. But without storage there was not enough water for either enterprise to expand.

Wilson and the Indians used horse-drawn scrapers and shovels to channel water from a head-gate on Big Creek through Rush and Abrams Lakes into Fletcher Lake where it could be stored and regulated by a dam and head-gate at the foot of the lake. The

Part of the old flume that carried water to the Davy Allen.

increased volume of water flowing down Minton Creek was sufficient to irrigate not only the Stone Reserve and the home fields at
Chilco but the Davy Allen as well. To reach the Davy Allen, water
had to be flumed across rough places and over a gully known as
"Crazy Man's Gulch." (Flumes were narrow troughs built from
boards and mounted on a latticed wooden framework, commonly
used in those days where it would be impossible to put in a land
ditch. At Chilco this picturesque structure, spilling water from
moss-covered boards, was a familiar sight for many summers
viewed from the road between the Chilco calf sheds and Davy
Allen.)

In 1931 the land ditch to the Davy Allen and part of the flume
were replaced by more efficient 20-inch wooden pipe, purchased
from Springfield Ranch at Soda Creek where Hargraves were
changing their irrigation system. The used pipe was moved to
Chilco Ranch by truck (Bill Bliss Jr. hauled some of it). As part of
the deal, Ray Hargraves assembled and strung the pipe to the Davy
Allen where fields each year produced two heavy crops of alfalfa
hay. The wooden pipe was in time replaced by half round steel pipe
and then plastic. In the 1960s both hard and soft plastic were tried.
Using the soft plastic meant screening the intake as silt and sticks

settling in the low places created serious problems in the pliable tube.

Underground springs eventually caused the hillside above and in the path of the pipe to shift and slide until the system collapsed. Present owners irrigate the Davy Allen with Big Creek water from a co-operative Ducks Unlimited project in the big pastures above, where a drop of many hundred feet creates an awesome amount of pressure to handle any number of sprinkler heads.

Compared to later years, Claud Wilson's fields were small. He ran 300 head of cattle, branded with a Circle C. (Brands at that time were registered in Barkerville for fifty cents for life.)

After being a bachelor for a number of years, Wilson married and with his wife, Molly, entertained with many parties and dances in their long, low log house. He is commemorated by Wilson Mountain and Pasture above the home place, and Wilson Meadow on Upper Deer Creek.

JOSEPH OGLE TRETHEWEY registered the T2 brand after he became owner in 1909 and Chilco Ranch stock carried it for 60 years. The T2 became another name for Chilco and the easily recognized brand was known far and wide. Trethewey increased the deeded land to 23,000 acres, including the huge expanse of open pastures on top reaching as far as the Scallon Ranch. He is credited with having 90 miles of fencing. Under his management cattle numbers doubled, chief breeds being Hereford and Galloway, while horses went from 50 head to 400. The calf sheds still standing along the road leading to Big Creek were built at this time.

He also added a sawmill to the ranch equipment. An amusing anecdote is told about Joe Trethewey and his sawmill. Everything was going wrong one day as Joe and a crew were working. He suddenly lost his temper and fired the lot of them. "Take your partner and get out of here!" he roared at one surprised young man.

"I don't have a partner," the fellow replied.

"Well, I'll damned soon find you one," was Joe's reply.

Joe Trethewey was a prosperous man when he bought the Chilco Ranch in 1909. He started logging in his native province of Ontario at 16. Coming west in the fall of 1880, he got his start in British Columbia cutting ties for the C.P.R. By 1895 he had established logging at Harrison Lake and discovered the Providence Mine. Before buying Chilco, the largest cattle ranch in the Chilcotin owned by one man, he had farmed on Lulu Island and bought an interest in the rich Coniagas Mine in Cobalt, Ontario. In 1911 he founded the Abbotsford Timber and Trading Company in the Fraser Valley.

152

Wedding of Edgar Trethewey and Madge Church.

Joe Trethewey.

Trethewey sold out in 1922 and went to live in Abbotsford. He died there in 1929. His son, Edgar married Madge Church of Big Creek, and their sons, Richard, Allen, Bill and J. O. (named for his grandfather) carry on the Trethewey enterprises. There is one daughter, Phyllis Watt, now living in Vernon.

The door in the Deer Creek ranch house where Spencer shot Dave Stoddart in the back.
Below is Coroner Rene Hance's first car.

The man with the shortest tenure on the big ranch was M. S. Logan, former Parks Commissioner in Vancouver who bought from Trethewey in 1922 and sold to Cosens Spencer about a year later.

Cosens Spencer was an English-Canadian who made money in the motion picture industry in Australia. His surname was really Cosens and Spencer his Christian name but he switched them around to more effectively advertise his theatrical concerns.

Spencer was a middle-aged man when he bought the Chilco. He wore a small mustache and a goatee, was slightly paunchy and, usually dressed in suit and vest, took little part in manual ranch work. But he was a forceful business man and ran a good ranch operation. Among other things, he built the big store above the house, expanded the retail trade and coined the slogan "Everything from a needle to a wagon." His wife, Mary Stuart, was highly regarded throughout the country, while he himself had the reputation of being stingy, unneighbourly and unpredictable. Pressure of business proved too much for him finally and his life ended in a tragic mental breakdown.

By 1930 Spencer's behaviour had not been normal for some time. His wife and associates were fearful that his mind was slipping, but none suspected the violent outburst that shook the country on September 10, 1930. On that autumn day Spencer asked his foreman, Dave Stoddart, and bookkeeper, Ed Smith, to accompany him on business to the Deer Creek place, an isolated part of the ranch farther up the river. He took his shotgun "in case we see a grouse." The business at Deer Creek finished, Smith turned to lock the door of the unoccupied house. Spencer shot him in the back, then fired at his foreman, felling him with a blast that struck his right arm. Shotgun in hand, Spencer then left on foot.

Stoddart managed to get a tourniquet on his bleeding arm and went to help Smith. Though dying, Smith dictated his will to his friend before he succumbed. The wounded man started back to the ranch in the truck but ran off the edge of a culvert and was stuck. Suffering from pain and shock, and fearful that Spencer would return, he hid in the ditch until ranch carpenter, Christopher Vick, and Mrs. Spencer, who had become alarmed when the three men were overdue, came looking for them. Stoddart was taken to Williams Lake Hospital and the police were alerted.

A young policeman from Williams Lake and Rene Hance of Hanceville, on his first assignment as coroner, were sent to bring Smith's body in. It was dark and raining and the dead body lay in a pool of blood. And out there in the sinister night was the killer waiting with his gun? The two men sat for a moment surveying the grisly scene in the headlights. The policeman spoke first. "Well, you are the Coroner, what do you want to do?"

"I want to resign," Hance answered wryly. They brought the corpse in and a search was started for the killer.

An aura of suspense and tragedy hung over the countryside. Cosens Spencer was still at large and armed. The ranch hands at Chilco were put on guard with rifles and ordered to shoot if Spencer approached. The Stoney Reserve was deserted with houses locked and Indians sleeping in hay stacks at night and keeping hidden by day. Mrs. Spencer, convinced that her husband was dead – "If he were alive he would come to me," she said – posted a $500 reward for finding his body and kept doubling it as the months went by.

Two months later, Little Charlie from the Anaham Reserve, an excellent tracker who had followed a lead towards the river, saw what looked like a hand sticking out of a log jam in the Chilcotin River at the lower end of the Deer Creek place. Spencer wore a gold ring on his right hand and sunlight glinting on this small band of gold caught the tracker's eye. Upon investigation it proved to be Spencer's body and Little Charlie collected $2,000. He then went back and found the shotgun and received a $100 reward for it. The gun was in the water, upstream from the body. Supposition was that in trying to cross the river, Spencer was swept off his feet in the swift current, dropped his gun and was carried downstream to his death. $8,000 was paid from Spencer's estate to the mother of the man who was shot and killed to compensate for loss of support in the death of her son. Dave Stoddart lost his right arm, but what compensation, if any, was made to him is unknown. Spencer's body was taken to Vancouver for burial.

Spencer was a rich man at the time of his death in 1930, leaving his wife an estate worth $500,000 – a lot of money in 1930. As well as cash, there was Chilco Ranch, debt free; shares in Spencer's Pictures Ltd. in Australia; and property in Vancouver. After expenses were paid and personal bequests taken care of (his wife's mother received a generous legacy, as did his own parents and brother) monies were left to orphanages in Sydney, Australia.

Ranch carpenter, Christopher Vick, stayed on to run the Chilco. He married Spencer's widow, Mary Stuart, on October 8, 1932, in Vancouver. They gave the famous ranch the most stable management of its career. The fabulous big house was finished and expensively furnished. It had gothic-like columns at the front entrance, polished hardwood floors, and Australian walnut paneling throughout. There was a massive fireplace, built-in leaded glass china cabinets and bay windows. The wide staircase leading from the vestibule to roomy bedrooms on the second floor was a masterpiece of craftsmanship. The large master bedroom and bathroom were on the first floor.

Life for Mrs. Vick was luxurious, with Chinese cook and houseboy to take care of the work. The men ate in a large dining room off the kitchen but the Vicks had their own private dining room and were served by the houseboy. For many years the sprawling T2 under such able working cowmen as Walter and Ed Bambrick and Norman Worthington ran over 3,000 head of cattle and put up hay enough to feed them. Their Whitewater range took in a vast area stretching south-west to the Taseko, Onion Flats, Cheta Meadows Vedan Ranch, and back to Fletcher Lake, taking in miles of swamp.

Cecil Henry camped on the Chilco range all summer for eight years, watching the cattle and moving them about as required. In the winter, cowboys fed cows at distant swamp meadows with team, sleigh, and pitch forks, usually two men together. Other well known cowboys were Joe Desault, Alex Paxton, Donald and Jimmy Myers, and Virgil (Blondie) Blue. Virgil rode the Chilco ranges for 12 years, and when Ed Bambrick left in 1962, Virgil took over the job of head cowboy for awhile. Many others, including capable men from Stoney and Anaham, came and went as general ranch hands, contractors and riders. Irrigating in the earlier years was done by Chinese help. Large crews were hired for haying at the ranch, with meadow hay usually put up by contract.

The store was always a fascinating place to enter. Clean and tidy and smelling of oranges, new saddle leather and buckskin gloves, mingled in winter with the fragrance of fir wood burning in the long barrel heater. It was warm and pleasant in the coldest weather, cool in summer, and was a jovial gathering place for the bunkhouse crew on most evenings. You could find anything there, from riding gear and harness to needles and thread; from cooking utensils and stoves to clothing and food. Most decorative was the stack of yard-square silk handkerchiefs piled on the wide varnished counter. Every color of the rainbow was there, as well as black and white. Cowboys wound them around their necks and Indian women tied them on their heads. Almost every outdoors person wore one and considered it a treat to get a new silk handkerchief.

Mr. and Mrs. Vick by the big house at Chilco.

Some of the best known storekeepers were Tony Orford, Joyce Russell, and Charlie Barstow (Chilco Charlie). One of the earliest store-keepers, Bill Beck, is buried on the Chilco. He died in 1924 as a young man, stricken with an asthma attack. Alex Paxton and a man named Jack Steel dug his grave.

The store then was in a little building not far from the grave site. Three of Walter and Beulah Bambrick's infants are also buried there. Another unmarked grave is believed to be that of Bert Mathers who was drowned in 1935 while cowboying for Chilco on the Whitewater range.

Mathers was riding the range with Cecil Henry and they were camped at Dummy Swamp. Mathers shot a duck and swam his horse out in the muddy slough to retrieve it. Mathers was an experienced and capable horseman and no one is sure what happened, but in the melee that followed between horse and bog, he lost his life.

In 1937 the Vicks sold Chilco Ranch to brothers GEORGE and FRANK MAYFIELD of Klamath Falls, Oregon, for $155,620 and moved to Vancouver where they built another luxurious home. Unhappily, Mrs. Vick did not live long to enjoy it.

A short time after buying into Chilco Ranch, GEORGE MAYFIELD, his wife ELNA and three sons, MELVIN, MARVIN, and ROLAND, left the partnership and bought the 141 Mile Ranch on the Cariboo Road. Frank and Margaret Mayfield and son, Miles, kept the big Chilcotin ranch for eight years. Their reign at the Chilco was a tempestuous one. Maggie Mayfield was an interfering woman and scrapped with the ranch hands at the drop of a cowboy hat. A common saying at the time was that Chilco Ranch had three crews: one coming, one working and one going.

And then there was JOHN L. WADE, major shareholder in the firm that bought Chilco from Mayfields in 1945. His first exercise was to sue Mayfield for a short in the cattle count.

A slick businessman from Los Angeles with a Texas ranching background, Wade made his money in the distributional end of the publishing world. He ran the Chilco for 16 years, longer than any other one man. Husky, good looking, always impeccably dressed, John Wade could be charming and accommodating but he was also a hard bargainer whose personal interests came first. He mixed freely with his hired hands and the neighboring Stoney Indians – often nonchalantly instigating a poker game with cards dealt on a pair of bat-wing leather chaps spread out on the ground in front of the ranch store. He increased the acreage of Chilco Ranch by buying up many ranches, including the Bell and Scallon Ranches at Big Creek and the Cotton Ranch at Riske Creek.

Wade married during his last year at Chilco. He and his wife, Ruth, had one son, born in Hawaii where they made their home after leaving the Chilcotin. He also had a daughter, Rhona, from a previous marriage who often visited at Chilco.

The fortunes of Chilco began to slip when JOHN MINOR of Abby, Saskatchewan, who bought the ranch from John Wade in December 1961, was killed when his Comanche airplane crashed near Surrey in the Fraser Valley on November 19, 1962. Then the old store burned down on Christmas Day that same year. It was rebuilt in a new location: a large frame building that included living quarters adjoining the store and apartments upstairs. The store has now long since been closed. The frame building burned down in 1990.

John Minor's widow, GERTIE, with her family and other members of the syndicate – Hargrave Mitchell, Bryce Stringham, Neil Harvie, and Don Clark – decided to carry on at Chilco. Harvie became general manager, flying out once a month or oftener from his ranch at Cochrane, Alberta. Gertie Minor Hale has recorded the events of those troubled years in a book titled *Lady Rancher,* published in 1979.

When Minors made the difficult decision to return to their former ranch at Abby, the management of the Chilco was taken over by Tom Livingstone of Milk River, Alberta, and Johnnie Dodd, well known Chilcotin stockman. After Livingstone left, Dodd became general manager and young Lynn Bonner, of Big Creek, farm boss. Lynn also flew the company airplane and his wife, Myrna, kept the books.

The ranch was then put up for sale and buyers were soon attracted. The Alberta syndicate sold the vast acreage of freehold and leased land, stripped of machinery, cattle, horses, and equipment in the fall of 1966.

On November 10, a giant auction began on the place and everything but household goods and land went under the auctioneer's hammer, including the Piper Super Cub airplane and the well-stocked store. The land was bought in a separate deal by Jim Stewart of Kelowna, who also purchased the store goods and building in a package at the auction. The aircraft went to Harvie and Bonner.

In front of the spacious workshop where a cheery bonfire blazed, large crowds gathered for the three-day sale in spite of the raw, bitter weather. Shivering in the cold but caught up in the mania of an auction, they fought to buy everything that was offered, including broken pitchforks, worn-out screw drivers and boxes of scrap. One rancher even went home with seven aging grease guns!

The horses were sold in much the same fashion. Felix Bobby, ranch cowboy, rode the saddle stock around the ring formed by the eager crowd. When someone would yell: "How old is he?" his answer was always the same: "Oh, 'bout seven." It was good enough. They bought them just the same. The cattle were auctioned off at the corrals and loading chutes adjacent to the pastures, while big trucks and trailers waited to carry them away. Most of the breeding stock stayed at Chilco, bought by the new owner, Jim Stewart.

It was at this time, too, that the A1 Ranch near Alexis Creek, part of Chilco since Spencer's day, was sold to Wayne Robison, formerly of Gang Ranch and one-time manager of Chilco; and the Deer Creek place and Wilson Meadow to Neil Harvie. Harvie had previously purchased the Cotton place at Riske Creek as well.

JIM STEWART, well known rancher in the Kelowna region, never lived at Chilco. He was hurt in a car accident and ill health forced him to sell out to DICK and HILDA NEWSOME of Vancouver. Mrs. Newsome was alone in the big house with her twin boys during their latter years there while her husband looked after business

160

in Vancouver. The Whitewater range passed out of their control during this time.

RODGER and HARLEY HOOK of Kamloops bought the ranch from the Newsomes in 1975. Rodger with his wife, De De, and family lived at Chilco Ranch and ran the place until selling to DEBOERS a few years later. Hook, who got on well with the Stoney people, was told by their old medicine man, George Myers, that he had now removed the curse that he put on the Chilco Ranch in 1962.

During Newsomes' time under manager Marvin Guthrie the old T2 brand was dropped in favour of the Ladder brand, and new owners have since each used a different iron. DeBoers brand is a Double Circle.

A Ducks Unlimited project in the Chilco pastures, conceived in John Wade's time, carried on by Minors and finished in the 1970s and 1980s, now brings water from Lower Big Creek to provide habitat for waterfowl in the West Pasture block and irrigation to much of this fine grazing land, as well as to the Davy Allen fields below.

The sprawling ranch has shrunk further in size as the Bell Ranch, Duck Lake, Upper Nighthawk, and Bog Hole in the Big Creek area; the Vedan, Hance and Stoby Meadows in the Whitewater; and Birch Flat on the Whitewater Road, have also been sold.

The Bell Ranch and upper Nighthawk Meadow belong to Walt Mychaluk and Art Warner, Duck Lake to Mack and Beth Suter, Bog Hole to Twilight Ranch, Vedan to Pete Schuler, Hance and Stoby Meadows to Duncan Baynes, and Birch Flat to Wayne and Trena Plummer.

The Chilco Ranch is now a compact unit of productive land, stretching from the south side of the Chilcotin River at Hanceville to the Scallon place on Lower Big Creek. Owners JOHN and SHARON DEBOER and sons, Marvin, Jody, and Wayne, raise good Charolais-cross cattle, now ranged nearer home, and run a logging show.

In 1992 the ranch, including breeding stock and the Double Circle Brand, was sold to DEAN and LORRAINE MILLER. DeBoers bought the Semlin Ranch at Cache Creek and moved there.

Some years ago after author-columnist Paul St. Pierre wrote one of his popular pieces on the Chilcotin, he received a note from TOM CAROLAN: "Your column on Alex and Ann Paxton brought back many years. Forty-three of them. Just figured it out."

"Alex and I worked at Chilco Ranch. We were cowboys. Not the kind that fixed fences and hauled hay, the kind that walked slowly and stilted from the bunkhouse to the horse barn in the morning and at night.

"There were many range men on the ranches then. Their gear was almost identical. Different makes of saddles. Saddles always came in for a lot of small talk. There was no radio in those days. The names of the saddles are almost like music to me now: Visalia, Riesackers, Hamley, Riley, MacCormick. There

Freighting on the Cariboo Wagon Road. Mrs. J. Mulvahill, who arrived at Chezacut in 1908, recalled that their supply point was Ashcroft, over 200 miles away. "My husband made an annual spring trip with the wagon for supplies. If we forgot anything we could always get it in the fall when they went down with the beef. This drive took three weeks – one way."

Wedding picture of Thomas Paxton and Agnes Haggerty.

was Double Rig and Single Rig and Centre Fire.

"The Purjues of Nemiah Valley made us silver mounted bits and spurs, from $15 to $30 a pair. Most all carried .30-30 carbines in a scabbard. Coyotes worth $25 a skin.

"Anyhow I knew Alex. Knew his dad, old Tommy P. who lived a great long time. Told tales of the BX Stage days. Long ago Ann's mother married Pablo Tresierra, the son of a Mexican packer. I knew him in his 80s.

"What a store of history we have lost in these grand old-timers – names like Velenzuella, the first rancher in the Cariboo.

"I liked your column about Duane Witte. I knew Duane as a little boy. His mother (Hattie Hance) named him after the Duane in Zane Grey's 'Lone Star Ranger'."

DEER CREEK

TOMMY and AGNES PAXTON, formerly of the Onward Ranch at the 150 Mile House, came with their large family to live by the Chilcotin River at Deer Creek in 1904. This land, Lot 133, was granted by the Crown to Frank Johnson in April 1904, and in June was acquired from him by Agnes Paxton. It was valued at $1,000. The Paxtons lived here, growing a big vegetable garden, for a number of years and then moved back to the Williams Lake district. Taxes on Lot 133 were delinquent on December 31, 1919, and when they were not paid the land went up for tax sale. It was sold on October 12, 1920, for $76.97 at public auction.

DANIEL MACAULEY from County Antrim, Ireland, came to join his brother, Archie, at Alexis Creek in 1902 and later obtained the Deer Creek place. Dan, in contrast to his brother, Archie, was known to be a rather hard, mean-tempered man.

JOHN HAINES had pre-empted Lot 132 on Deer Creek in 1891. It was cancelled in January 1904, and a month later Dan Macauley bought this land from the government for $320. It was Crown granted in 1917. Macauley bought the adjoining Lot 133 which had been Paxtons' in February 1922 for $800 from a speculator, Casper Phair, of Lillooet. As noted above, Phair had picked up the land at public auction for the taxes: $76.97.

Macauley married Margaret Service from Ireland soon after moving to Deer Creek and the couple had four daughters. Macauleys' buildings were under the hill at the upper end of the flat where a spring comes down. Life was hard and Mrs. Macauley died in 1923. She was buried on the hill above the buildings.

Macauley was hard up and deeply in debt. He had probably borrowed from C. Spencer of Chilco Ranch or run up a store bill and on May 30, 1925, he turned the deeds to Lots 132 and 133 over to Spencer for $1.00 and left the country. He went back to Ireland with his four young daughters. Two years later he remarried and returned to Canada, settling at Grand Prairie in the Peace River. In 1979, two of the Macauley sisters, Sylvia and Myrtle, returned to Deer Creek to visit their mother's grave. The eldest, Sylvia, had vivid recollections of her mother's pretty flower garden.

Chilco Ranch sold the Deer Creek place, including the Witte place at the upper end, to Neil Harvie of Cochrane, Alberta, in the fall of 1966. In the spring of 1981 it was sold to Duncan Baynes of Vancouver.

ISABEL and LOTTIE were sisters raised in two cultures. Isabel was an educated English woman. It was evident in her manner of speech, her neat, stilted handwriting and in her dress and deportment.

Lottie was an Indian wife. Her skin was weathered from wind and sun and the smoke of many campfires. She wore a kerchief on her hair, wide skirt about her ample figure and moccasins on her feet. She spoke the Chilcotin tongue with ease, English haltingly. Lottie had no schooling.

Two women, worlds apart. But Isabel and Lottie were sisters, born to George Dester and his Indian wife, Jessie, at Riske Creek.

While George Dester made plans to return to England about 1900, he left his elder daughter, Isabel, with the Tom Hance family at Hanceville where she would have her first taste of school work, attending, with the Hance children, Mr. Jefferson's classes in the old jail at Hanceville. Dester had often left his little girl with Hances for a few days to play with Hattie, or at Englishes to play with Nellie English (Baker). His younger daughter, Lottie, and son, Baptiste, were now with their mother at Anaham Reserve but Dester was taking Isabel to England with him. Once

Lottie (Dester) Chell with granddaughter beside her home at Anaham Reserve.

165

settled in Bath in the south of England, Isabel would attend a regular school. Her father wanted only the best for his dark little daughter.

In Bath, Dester married an English woman and life changed for Isabel. She was well dressed, attending school regularly and learning the ways of aristocracy, but she missed her family and her playmates and the wild free life she had left behind. She was comforted when her father spoke of returning to British Columbia for her sister, Lottie Dester, who would soon be old enough to leave her mother. "Lottie must have an education too," he often said.

The day came for the well-planned trip back to the Chilcotin, and Dester set sail for Canada, leaving an excited Isabel at home with his English wife. But the mission to bring his younger daughter to England was never completed. At the 150 Mile House on his way into the Chilcotin by stage, Dester contracted pneumonia and died. As a consequence, Lottie remained to grow up with her mother's people in the wilderness of British Columbia.

Like the Indian girls around her, Lottie married young and raised a large family, content with the only life she knew. With her Indian husband, Johnny Chell (Blacknose Johnny he was called because of a prominent mole), she learned the trails of the hinterland, camping by lonely lakes to fish for trout and to hunt deer, and by the river to dip for salmon. Their log house in the village above Anaham flats was planted with vines, and Lottie grew a garden. From her mother she learned to make buckskin and sew gloves and moccasins. The well-tramped earth around her home spoke of many little feet of children and grandchildren playing there.

In England, after her father's death, Isabel was sad, lonely, and unwanted. Mrs. Dester looked with disfavor on her late husband's Chilcotin daughter. There was one bright spot in 1915 when Percy and Judd Hance, who were in the army enroute to the front lines in France, came to visit her. She was overjoyed to see again her childhood friends, to hear news and speak of loved ones far away.

In Britain after the war there was a popular movement to emigrate to Australia, and it was arranged for Isabel to go. She changed her name from Dester to Davis and set sail for Sydney, Australia. There she spent most of her working life. She moved to Adelaide in 1946 after she had suffered a stroke and lost the use of her left arm, but remained active and able to care for herself.

Isabel dreamed of returning for a visit to the land of her birth but time slipped away without her saving enough to realize this

Isabel Dester in Bath, England.

dream. She never married. "Good chances I had," she wrote, "to men with white collar jobs, as they say over here, but I thought I could get along by myself and left myself on the shelf. I often regret it."

Isabel Davis corresponded regularly over the years with her childhood friend, Hattie Hance Witte, of Big Creek, and Hattie's brother, Rene Hance, of Hanceville. In her letters Isabel always remembered to ask about her Chilcotin sister, Lottie Chell, and send love and greetings or a handkerchief, which Hattie always conscientiously delivered. Occasionally, Lottie would come to Wittes to seek news of Isabel and look with pride at her latest snapshot. Lottie never learned to read or write.

Isabel and Lottie – an English woman and a Chilcotin Indian. Sisters, separated for a lifetime by continents, cultures, and the wayward winds of chance.

GEORGE MYERS was a unique individual, born at Riske Creek on September 10, 1883. He lived to be 95, riding his racehorse in local competition well into his eighties and active and interested to the end of his life.

His mother was an Indian woman named Lucy and his father a white man named Myers. He was raised by his grandmother, Manny, at Toosey. When he was 21 he married Pauline Quilt from the Stone Reserve and from then on made his headquarters there. George and Pauline had two sons, Jimmy and Donald. Jimmy died from appendicitis after riding in a stampede at Riske Creek in the 1940s. Donald married Helena Williams of Nemiah Valley and raised a big family at Stoney Reserve, all well-respected members of the community.

George worked around the country on ranches, even as far from home as the Perry Ranch near Kamloops, and often trapped in the wintertime. He was well-known, honest and progressive, encouraging his family to make the reserve a better place to live. He was honoured as a medicine man among his people. Myers spoke good English and acted as interpreter when the need arose.

He had an enquiring mind and liked to discuss politics and world events with the ranchers across the river. He had an original and entertaining approach to these topics. He was keenly interested in prospecting for minerals and roamed the high country year after year, often alone, studying the lay of the land and formation of the

George Myers at Stoney.

rocks. Finally, failing eyesight forced him to give up this freedom and the joy of searching the peaks for silver and gold. Horse racing was another love and he kept on riding and racing even when he could barely see.

George's wife, Pauline, died in 1947 but George never remarried. When he died in hospital on February 13, 1978, he left one son, 16 grandchildren, 30 great grandchildren and one great, great grandchild. He was buried on the Stone Reserve.

WILLIAM FREDRICK "BILL" WOODS was well known from one end of the country to the other. He was a drifting cowboy who never settled in one place for any length of time. He was long and lean with a twisted hand, had a laconic manner, a slow drawl and dry wit and even his walk was a little bit different. Although he died in 1972 he is still imitated and quoted.

Woods was born in 1902 in Empire Valley. He grew up and started school around Clinton and with brother Charlie went to school for five years in Vancouver. While there he was involved in a bicycle-street car accident that left him with damaged cords in the left arm and his left hand bent backwards. He hurt that hand again later on when it was caught in his lassoo while roping a horse. But this permanent disability never slowed him down: he was a crack shot, a good roper, and played the violin. He learned to fiddle when he was in his early twenties, holding the violin in his right hand, the bow in his twisted left. While in his teens and twenties, Bill took part in rodeos, specializing in roping and riding in the Roman race. The latter involves standing on the backs of two race horses, one foot on each, while the horses gallop around the track.

Bill Woods came to the Chilcotin as a young man and left only for one winter during World War Two when he worked on a rock crusher during construction of the Kamloops Airport. "The pay was good," he admitted, "but I got tired of living like a ground hog and yearned to come back to the Chilcotin and smell the clean free air."

He married a girl from Chase, Unice Baker, nicknamed "Billy," who was working for Maxwells at Chezacut. Woods went into the guiding business, but his yen for drinking and drifting interfered with both his business and his marriage. Neither lasted too long.

Woods got a "license to occupy" at the foot of Whitewater (Taseko) Lake and there built his Whitewater Lodge and cabins, rustically finished inside with furnishings made of peeled poles.

His guiding area took in the surrounding country. The Whitewater Road, all the way from Chilco Ranch to the foot of the lake, was at that time narrow, winding, and rough – full of mud-holes and rocks – and Bill and Billy made their headquarters at Hanceville where Billy cooked at times for Hances and their guests.

Bill ran a good hunting show. He worked himself and hired veteran guides like Jimmy Bouillon, George Turner, Joe Haller, Vic Montgomery, and James Moore. Randolf Mulvahill took time from his Chezacut Ranch to guide on a few hunts, too. Once Woods was out with a "green" hunter who wounded a bull moose on an open swamp while Bill was out of sight checking a nearby slough. The moose charged and the frightened stranger managed to climb the only tree in the meadow. Bill heard the commotion and hurried back to see what was going on. He finished off the wounded animal and then, squinting up at the hunter still clinging in the tree, asked in his slow drawl: "Can you see any more moose from up there?" Woods was a good packer and used his outfit (mostly Mulvahill horses) at times to move goods to the Taylor Windfall Mine and later to the Pelaire. He sold the Whitewater Lodge to an American named Bill Gremmell in 1953.

Prospecting took up a lot of Woods' time. He staked a few claims and made many trips to the mountains with pack and saddle horse looking for various minerals. He had a knack with animals and always had a well-trained horse and dog.

Bill Woods died at Tatla Lake on July 25, 1972, at 70.

Gremmell sold the Whitewater Lodge to four partners from Washington and Oregon: Gun Solley, Bert Wassell, Boot Schell, and Roy Wynbrenner. The wildfire that scarred the hillside above the lodge swept through in the dry spring of 1958, during the time that Bert and Estelle Wassell were there.

JOHNNIE and DIXIE MURDOCK and CLIFF DILLABOUGH bought the lodge soon after and ran a good hunting business for a number of years, selling in the 1970s to DICK NEWHAUSEN. His was a short stay. He sold to SHERWOOD HENRY who, under the name of "Taseko Lake Outfitters," specializes in guiding hunters for bighorn sheep.

The old lodge Woods built burned down and Sherwood built a warm spacious log house nearer Swift Creek, with big windows looking out on Vic's Mountain.

HAYIN' TIME
Veera Witte

Hayin' time is coming -
I can tell 'cause men are out
Fixing up machinery
And wondering about
The way the crops are looking,
Which field needs cutting first,
And fretting 'bout the little patch
That kinda died o' thirst.

Hayin' time is coming -
They'll be driving broncs once more,
Familiar words'll be a drifting
'Bove the clatter of the mower.
And we won't be long a-waiting
For the weeks are slipping by
And the hay is standing ready
In the meadows, green and high.

Hayin' time is coming,
I can tell it's nearly here
By the rumbling of thunder
In the heavens far and near.
By the storm call of the robin
And the silver of the rain
A-fallin' swift and silent like
Upon the bending grain!

Mowing rye at the Circle A.

Raking hay at Stoney.

Hauling hay at the Bell Ranch, 1936.

The first load goes up on the Stoney fields.

Putting up swamp hay at the Circle A Meadow – Irene Witte stacking.

Topping off a high stack at Church's Ranch.

Lowering the derrick poles.

BIG CREEK

Big Creek heads in the remote and beautiful Coast Range, flowing out of Lorna Lake. Glacier fed and joined by many smaller tributaries, it flows in a north-easterly direction to empty into the Chilcotin River at the Brown Place, an old pre-emption a few miles above Farwell Canyon. This land of jackpine and poplar-covered hills with numerous valleys, meadows, lakes and streams has always been cattle ranching country. There is ample rangeland and an abundance of moose, deer, and other wild animals. Cattle ranching is still the main industry but logging, guiding, trail riding, sheep raising and tourism are now included in the way of life at Big Creek.

The Indians called this river "Gothlaneko" which meant creek of many rabbits. It was given its present name by Nels Haines of Empire Valley many years ago before the first settlers came in. Upon seeing it for the first time he was impressed by its size and called it "Big Creek."

Where the snow-capped mountains tower
High above the timber line,
And the groundhogs in the valleys
Whistle out so clear and fine,
Where the winds are always blowing
And the glaciers abound,
There where mountain springs are flowing
Big Creek waters can be found.

On down through the hills and valleys,
Growing bigger as it goes,
Through the stunted spruce and jackpine
And the meadowland it flows.
Down where cattle graze and wander
O'er its grassy banks at will,
And where moose and deer oft linger
When the land is hushed and still.

Down through ranches broad and fertile
Where the good folks work and play:
Through the Lazy HL Bar Ranch
And down through the Circle A;
'Neath the bridge it flows at Bambricks
And right through the CHE,
Past the grassy flats at Hutches
And down through the Lazy Z.

Down by Scallons — through deep canyons,
Growing swifter — flowing free -
Till it joins the broad Chilcotin
And goes onward to the sea.
Telling tales of lonely places
Where men yet but seldom go,
And the hunter and the cowboy
Only of its wonders know.

And wherever I may wander
Through the years that are to be
The cold waters of old Big Creek
Will keep calling back to me;
For to some it's just a river
Flowing where the cattle roam,
But to me its hills and valleys
Will be always "Home Sweet Home."
Veera Witte

GEORGE McDONALD was Big Creek's first settler. A talkative Scots-Canadian from the East, he staked the Bell Ranch, Lot 2224, on March 22, 1896, but had built a cabin and trapped on Lower Big Creek before that. To get a start he worked for Claud Wilson on the Chilco Ranch and later put up hay on his pre-emption on Big Creek to winter cattle for Norman Lee, taking cows in payment. After 10 or 12 years McDonald sold his wild hay ranch to an Englishman named Ted Willan and returned east where he bought a place near Embro, Ontario.

Ted Willan registered the Bell brand and named his new place the "Bell Ranch" after his former home in Arizona. He added another 160 acres in 1913 and took up a wild meadow as well on the south side of Big Creek near Mons Lake. Willan went to war in 1914, leaving his place under the management of Hubert Blenkinsop. After the war Willan settled in Bournemouth, England, and

Big Creek.

eventually sold out to Gerald Blenkinsop who was then managing the Bell Ranch. In later years Willan Meadow was sold to Ronnie Nelson. It is now owned by Randy and Gay Saugstad. Blenkinsop sold the Bell Ranch to John Wade of Chilco Ranch in 1948. It now belongs to Archie and Fran Warner and Walt and Elsie Mychaluk. The big log barn built in the early days has been straightened and reroofed by the new owners and is still being used, dominating the barnyard as it has done for over 70 years.

Bell Ranch buildings in 1929.

CHARLIE and VIC ERICKSON were among Big Creek's first settlers – and among the most successful. They were born in Finland
and came to the U.S.A. about 1901 and to Big Creek soon after.
Both brothers were of medium stature but their characters were
opposite. Vic was good-natured and easy going while Charlie was
caustic and critical and inclined to let Vic shoulder the heaviest
load. Another difference was that Charlie wore a shaggy mustache,
while Vic was clean shaven.

They staked a fertile piece of land along Big Creek and a
swamp meadow about five miles away. They also acquired a parcel of land above the mouth of the Chilcotin River which they
called the "Dry Farm" as there was no irrigation.

For the first eight years there was little income from their new
ranch so one brother worked out for wages, while the other worked
at home. They toiled long hours, tirelessly, to develop their place.
Their enterprise was a success and they became financially well
off, eventually running about 300 head of cattle, debt free. They
branded with a Lazy Z and at first ran their cattle on Scallon Creek.
Vic once said that he hadn't had a Sunday off in 40 years. Both
were excellent axemen and the log buildings they put up on their
ranch more than 80 years ago are still in use. They were kind-
hearted men and gave a helping hand to many another struggling
to get a start.

Ericksons had pre-emptions on both sides of Big Creek and
for a long time forded the creek – which can be a raging torrent
during high water – to work their land. Then in 1911 the Liberal
Member, Archie MacDonald, allotted $500 towards the building of
a bridge at their place. The crossing here provided a shorter, more
direct route to the settlement of Big Creek from the Ashcroft-

Hanceville Road. The Erickson brothers and Charlie Hutchinson took on the construction job – entirely done by axework. No lumber was used – timbers and decking were all hand-hewn from logs with broadaxe and pole axe.

Charlie and Vic both played the violin, but Charlie was a shy frontiersman and seldom played for company. He was, in fact, so shy of women that he would turn his back and look away over the back of his chair if forced to carry on a conversation with a member of the fairer sex. Occasionally, the Ericksons hosted a country dance in their home. On these occasions Charlie would be persuaded to tune up with the Scallon brothers and play for the dancers. Ericksons' front room with its smooth, well laid floor made an excellent place to dance.

Neither Charlie nor Vic ever married, though Vic fell in love with Dolly Church and hoped to marry her. Dolly was a petite, lively girl with a saucy tongue and a ready laugh. She and Vic could swing together on the dance floor with the best of them, particularly to the old-fashioned waltz and the Swedish polka. But Dolly's feelings for the loyal Finlander were platonic, and when she married Ken Moore of Tatlayoko, Vic gave up on matrimony and resigned himself to bachelorhood. "I vould even have vashed her clothes," Vic was known to have regretfully commented.

Vic Erickson died of cancer in Kamloops in 1949 and Charlie sold the ranch and cattle to Bruce and Phyllis Watt the following year. Five years later Charlie passed away. Ericksons left no known relatives here or in the old country.

Bruce and Phyllis named the Erickson place "Breckness Ranch," and four of their children – Roddy, Dee, Ryan, and Gay – were born while they lived here. The youngest, Kirby, arrived after the Watt family had moved to their "Dry Farm" at the mouth of the Chilcotin River where Watts and Tretheweys had set up a logging camp. From there Watts moved to Williams Lake to be close to schools. They sold Breckness Ranch in the 1970s.

Jim and Sharon Caddy bought the land with the buildings on the south side of Big Creek and moved there with daughter, Gwineth. Their two sons were born there. It now belongs to Tom and Colleen Hodgson with children, Michael and Taunis, and sheep now graze the pastures. Mary Thomson owns the field on the north side, while the meadow near Mons Lake belongs to Joan Fisher with son, Aaron and daughter, Angela. The property above the mouth of the Chilcotin went to Steve Andrus and then to Marcus Nairn of Vancouver who bought the Dry Farm in 1989.

Mary Thomson sold this field in 1993. It now belongs to Richard and Diane Dillabough.

CHARLES JOHN "CHARLIE" BAMBRICK was a tall lean man, bent in later years from hard work and arthritis. He was fearless and determined, with a wild, uncontrollable temper when crossed. A man of contradictions, he ruled his household with an iron hand but had a tender affection for his wife, Lilian, through their 40 plus years of marriage. He lived frugally, accepting the stark privations of pioneer living without question, at the same time nurturing a deep appreciation of grace and beauty. A grove of tall poplar trees were left growing in the middle of a productive hay field strictly for their aesthetic value, and lofty spreading Siberian willow and caragana planted on his homestead 80 years ago still stand, attesting to his artistry. In later years he and his wife retired to their meadow where they lived for awhile in a log cabin, leaving the ranch to the children. Here Bambrick worked to create a pleasing approach to their dwelling with a driveway through spaced trees and grassland, although there was a shorter route to the cabin. He put up a sign calling this roadway "Park Drive" and insisted that visitors use it.

Bambrick was born in 1869 and raised on a farm in Truro, N.S. He was 19 when he came to B.C. in 1888 and went to work for a building contractor in Vancouver – then just a shack town. He soon headed for new adventures up the Cariboo Road.

At the 150 Mile House he got a job with Veith and Borland taking care of BX stage horses. He liked the work but got into a fight over the horses with a man named Bill Parker who was a driver on the stage line. Bambrick proved a hard man to tangle with. After giving Parker a licking, he quit the job at the stable and went to work in the hay fields. When Bambrick took sick shortly after, Parker was the first man to offer his help and they were good friends thereafter.

In the early 1890s Charlie and two more men took a raft of lumber consigned to the Gang Ranch down the Fraser River from Soda Creek – a wild and dangerous ride! The river was rolling high and the men were unable to bring the raft ashore at the Gang but were swept on down the river. At Canoe Creek where the water was somewhat quieter – some 10 miles or so farther on – they managed to beach the heavy raft of boards and tie it up. As Canoe Creek Ranch was just beginning to build, they bought the lumber.

Charlie Bambrick as a young man.

Bambrick helped cut and hew the timbers for the first bridge over the Chilcotin River at Hanceville in 1902. In the Chilcotin he met and married Lilian Haines, a pretty girl born in Empire Valley, daughter of John Nelson Haines and his Indian wife, who then lived at Deer Creek on the Chilcotin River.

In 1898 Charlie joined the rush to the Klondike, packing for an outfit in Victoria. The venture failed when, on reaching Tele-

Lilian Bambrick.

graph Creek, he was turned back for want of the necessary grub stake and funds for the trip.

Bambrick had staked 160 acres on the Chilcotin River below Hanceville on November 20, 1893, now part of the River Ranch. When his cabin burned down he moved to Brigam Meadow below Fletcher Lake in the Big Creek area where there was plenty of feed for his horses. The eldest son, Walter, was born there in 1899. (This is now part of Hutch Meadow.) Rocks that formed the foundation of Bambrick's house can still be seen on the hillside above Minton Creek at the upper end of the meadow. Hutchinson was located on the lower end.

Bambrick had been told about good land farther on. Looking around, he staked a pre-emption at the confluence of Big Creek and the stream which was to be named after him, Bambrick Creek. He began to develop a homestead, the first man to break sod on the virgin Big Creek plateau.

There were no roads or bridges and times were hard developing the raw land while raising a big family which eventually num-

Alice Bambrick, Ruth Anderson and baby Ruth, Gertie and Doris Bambrick.

bered 12 children. Bambricks were good neighbours and along
with their own large family looked after a nephew, Roy Haines, and
a neighbour's son, Douglas Kinkead. They put in a big patch of red
and white currant bushes and rhubarb, grew a large garden and kept
milk cows and chickens, ducks and geese. Lilac bushes were
planted, and hardy perennial flowers. Provisions were brought in
once a year from Ashcroft. If a man couldn't find the time to make
the trip himself, someone else would bring his freight in for him at
a cost of 3 1/2 cents a pound.

In 1910 Bambrick decided to raise trotting horses and purchased a Hamiltonian stallion in Kamloops. He believed that with
the new Pacific Great Eastern Railway coming north from Squamish
there would be a market for carriage horses. Unfortunately, the tim-
ing was wrong as the advent of the gas-powered automobile soon
after killed the horse market. He went into raising cattle, then in the
fall of 1918 sold them all and tried his hand at sheep. After a few
years he went back to beef cattle again. His brand was the Window
Sash. His growing family was a great help in all these endeavours.

Charlie and his eldest son, Walter, built a log bridge by hand across Big Creek on their ranch which was a great asset to the community. The road to the country on the south side of Big Creek went through the Bambrick Ranch buildings for many years.

When Bambrick's eldest daughter, Alice, married, a house was built across the bridge in the pasture for her and her husband, Charlie Paxton, and they made their home there for a time. Their eldest son, Art, was born there. Paxton took over the mail contract between Big Creek and Hanceville from H. E. Church in 1920 and drove stage for a year or two. Cliff Kinkead and son, Douglas, later lived in Alice and Charlie's house for a short time.

Bambrick was keenly interested in mining. He had claims in the Whitewater and spent time in the mountains on horseback whenever possible searching for gold. At one time he had staked most of Red Mountain above Taseko Lake.

When Charlie was getting on in years the family bought a Model A Ford sedan. One of the boys, Arthur or Frank, usually drove it, but their father with some difficulty learned to handle the horseless carriage as well and liked to take the car on jaunts around Big Creek. One day he and his wife went to visit their neighbours, the Wittes, rolling along happily in the Model A. When they arrived, instead of slowing down and stopping at the kitchen door as usual, Wittes were surprised to see the car sail right on by, making two lively circles around the yard before coming to a halt. The couple got out laughing and the driver explained that he had momentarily forgotten how to stop it!

The first wedding in the Bambrick family was that of Alice, the eldest daughter. She married Charlie Paxton at the Bambrick Ranch at Big Creek in a formal Catholic ceremony with the bride and attendants in long white dresses and the men in dark suits and ties. Charlie and Alice lived on the ranch at Big Creek for a few years before moving to Horsefly and then to Prince George. They had five children.

GERTRUDE, always called Gertie, worked in Williams Lake for the Tommy Hodgsons for some time. She returned home and married her childhood sweetheart, Harold Wales. They lived at various places around B.C. Harold and Gertie had one daughter, Patricia.

DORIS married Gus Jakel, a widower with two young sons, Gordon and Norman. They lived at Hanceville briefly, then Alexis Creek. Here they established the first hotel, garage, beer parlour, dance hall and movie theatre. They had one daughter, Verna. Gus and Doris moved to Clinton when they sold out at Alexis Creek.

EMMA married George Stephens, a quiet young Englishman who was working for Gerald Blenkinsop at the Bell Ranch. For a few years they lived in a log cabin built for them by Emma's brothers, Frank and Arthur Bambrick. Their son, Wesley, was born there. A daughter, Jean (Bowe), was born after the Stephens left Big Creek and were working for Priscella Martin at the Gables, west of Hanceville. George and Emma worked and lived at Bralorne for most of their lives.

ARTHUR BAMBRICK married Trixie Fosbery – a cousin to Bob Fosbery. The marriage was short lived. After the Bambrick family left the ranch, Arthur went to work in Williams Lake. He always wore a buckskin coat.

EDDIE (EDWARD) BAMBRICK was a big raw-boned cowboy with light hair and eyes. His life's work was on horseback. He was a top hand and looked the part. Eddie was head rider at Alkali Lake Ranch, at Gang Ranch and, lastly, at Chilco Ranch. He was a renowned bronc rider, taking part in the Calgary Stampede and winning the trophy belt in the home town rodeo at Williams Lake. A showy rider, Eddie was popular with the crowd. In 1931 while working at Alkali he married a Swiss girl named Jean Herren who was governess for the Wyn Johnson children.

Eddie and Jean had two sons, John and Oliver. But life in the West with a free-wheeling cowboy was too much for the well educated city girl and she went back to Switzerland, taking the boys with her. Her sons returned to Canada, when grown, to live in Montreal. John Bambrick passed away in Geneva, Switzerland, where he had returned for medical care. Jean later accompanied her son, Oliver, west to visit the Bambrick relatives at Williams Lake and Big Creek.

Charles John Bambrick died at home from pneumonia in 1932, his eyes never leaving his wife's face as she moved about his room during the last hours of his life. His resting place on a tree-shaded knoll on the homestead is shared by two daughters who went before him. Lucy was drowned as a child in Bambrick Creek not far from the house, and May died from measles in early womanhood.

After her husband's death, Lilian Bambrick rented the ranch to Frank Witte and moved with her youngest son, Frank, and two youngest daughters, Evelyn and Ethel, to Williams Lake and then

Ed Bambrick.

to Vancouver. None of them returned to the Chilcotin. Mrs. Bambrick died in Vancouver in 1953.

The youngest three in the family, Frank, Evelyn, and Ethel, lived in Williams Lake and then in Vancouver after leaving the ranch. Frank never married. Ethel married Collin Curtis and Evelyn married in Vancouver. She became badly crippled with arthritis but did her own work from a wheelchair.

WALTER BAMBRICK was of medium height, broad shouldered and heavy set. He had shiny black hair, brown eyes and a ruddy complexion – his countenance was open and pleasant. He was conscientious and reliable, with a reputation of being one of the best cowmen in the country.

He was born at Hutch Meadow on Minton Creek but grew up on the Bambrick homestead on Big Creek. He left home early to make his own way but was the one to eventually buy the old home place and keep the family name on Big Creek.

Being the eldest in a large family, Walter learned to work hard at an early age. At 17 he left home to work for wages – first at the neighbouring Bell Ranch and then at Chilco Ranch, for both Joe Trethewey and C. Spencer. He soon proved a valuable ranch hand.

He then travelled to Alberta to see new country and work for a rancher named Ewing who had been at Chilco Ranch as manager when Walter was there. Walter spent six years in Alberta, working for Fred and Ambert Ewing and at the Kessler Ranch. He invested some of his wages in a car and in the summer of 1930, accompanied by a young Irishman named Cecil Henry, came back to the Chilcotin. Both men went to work haying at the Gang Ranch. They had been there a month when Cosens Spencer drove down to the Gang to offer Walter a steady job as cow-boss at Chilco Ranch. Walter accepted, urging Spencer to hire the young Irishman as well. Walter and Cecil had been at Chilco only two weeks when the fatal Spencer shooting took place. With a crew of men, he was responsible for the cattle winter and summer and most of the haying on one of the biggest ranches in the country; highly regarded by his employers. He stayed eight years. Walter married Beulah Birdsell in 1932 and they had their own little house at the Chilco, situated by a spring near the entrance to the ranch.

Walter and Beulah Bambrick.

186

In 1938, after Frank Mayfield had taken over Chilco, Walter bought the original Bambrick homestead from his mother who was then living in Vancouver, and moved back to Big Creek. A short time later Mayfield persuaded him to return to Chilco to look after the cattle. He stayed a year. Altogether he was 13 years at the big ranch.

Walter built up a 200-head cow ranch at his old home, registering the Bar OF brand. He re-registered the old Window Sash iron for his horses. He added to his income by riding through the country in the spring, buying cattle from the Indians then turning them out to fatten on the range and selling them in the fall. In those days beef cattle were moved to market on the hoof, usually in time for the annual Williams Lake fall fair and sale in October – although some ranchers liked to ship later in the year. Beef drives from Big Creek via Farwell Canyon took about a week. At Big Creek, if a man couldn't go on the drive himself he liked to put his beef in with Walter's where he knew they would be well taken care of.

In 1952, for the first time, cattle were trucked in for sale at the Williams Lake stockyards. The Williams Lake paper noted: "The whine of trucks marks the path of the modern beef drive ....This fall for the first time there will be no Big Creek cattle going to market on the hoof – no beef drive winding its leisurely way down the long dusty road to Williams Lake."

The cattle all went out on Hodgson trucks, signalling the beginning of a change in ranching methods: Gradually, ranchers went to shipping calves or yearlings instead of holding their steers over to two- and three-year-olds. Many old hands claimed that the animals lost more weight in a few hours on the trucks than they would in a week on the hoof.

When Walter and Beulah first moved to Big Creek they repaired the old original low log house to live in temporarily. Ten years later they built a modern two-story frame house with bathroom and fireplace and plenty of room for their growing family. The Bambricks raised six children. Walter served as rural representative on District 27 School Board while his family were in school at Big Creek.

After being in deteriorating health for some time, Walter died suddenly from a heart attack in the spring of 1966 at 67. He is buried on a hilltop in a registered family plot on the Bambrick Ranch.

In 1948, record breaking high water in the spring washed out the Bambrick Bridge built by Walter and his father over

Big Creek on their ranch in 1926. In the fall of 1948 the bridge was replaced by the government. But again in 1955 the Bambrick Bridge was undermined. This time high water changed the course of Big Creek, causing one span of the structure to collapse. Then in June the brown raging torrent swept around it, leaving the remains of the bridge on a bed of dry rocks.

A new site and a new design was then chosen for the Bambrick Bridge. It was built at its present location that fall when the water was low, using a pile driver and doing away with the piers.

This bridge stayed in place – with minor repairs and changes – to serve the community for 35 years. But on June 27, 1991, extreme high water swept it away, slick and clean. The Bambrick Bridge was replaced that fall in the same spot, high above the water with steel girders for support. This time it looks to be permanent.

BEULAH BAMBRICK was the daughter of William and Jean Birdsell of Kelly Lake and was raised in the Clinton country. She was a big outdoors girl, strong and capable. She had brown hair and pretty gray eyes, and was an interesting, forthright person, a loyal friend, cheerful and uncomplaining. It was very hard for her when, later in life, she developed asthma and thyroid problems which limited her activity, but she never gave in to her illness.

Beulah met Walter Bambrick in 1931 when he had a haying contract at the Gang Ranch and she was hired to cook for his crew. They were married in June, and cooking for this dark-haired cowboy became a lifetime occupation for the outdoor girl from Clinton. Walter fed cattle at Meadow Lake the winter of 1932 and rode all the way to Clinton by saddle horse to visit her. The first years of their married life were spent at their little home at Chilco Ranch and from then at the ranch at Big Creek.

Beulah gave birth to nine children. The first baby was stillborn. Twins, Gordon James and Stella May, born a few years later, died soon after birth. These babies are buried at Chilco Ranch. Beulah worked hard on the ranch at Big Creek with six children to look after – Phyllis, Charlie, Joyce, Collin, and twins Eleanor and Elaine – and in spite of ill health grew a big garden, milked cows, and raised chickens and turkeys. She sold eggs by the case to Mrs. Norman Lee for resale in the store. Beulah was also secretary of the Big Creek Livestock Association for ten years. Beulah was often in the hospital in Ashcroft or Kamloops, and with no medical plan in those days the doctor and hospital bills placed a critical strain on Bambrick's income.

188

After her husband's death Beulah and her sons carried on at Big Creek until 1973 when they sold the ranch to Hugh Redford of Fort St. John. Beulah and her granddaughter, Roxanne, then moved to Williams Lake. Beulah passed away in May 1980 after a long period of failing health. She is buried beside her husband in the family plot on the old home ranch, now owned by Ralph and Yvonne Sapp.

TOM "HUTCH" HUTCHINSON was born in Detroit, Michigan. He came to Canada as a young man, lured by the gold rush. At this time there was a demand in B.C. for packers to move freight to the Cariboo goldfields. Hutchinson got together an outfit of pack mules which eventually numbered about 300 and ran a pack train from Lytton to Barkerville. He had sold most of his pack string before he came to the Chilcotin to settle on Minton Creek below Fletcher Lake, pre-empting 120 acres, Lot 986, in 1894. This meadow, which still carries his name, provided an ideal place to winter his animals and he built a home there.

Hutch married Minnie Haines, a sister to Lilian Bambrick. They had a family of four: Charlie, Cynthia, Patrick, and William. (The Hutchinson family were also always called "Hutch.")

When Hutch died he was buried on his meadow on Minton Creek but the location of his grave is unknown. The Hutch Meadow was sold to Norman Lee, and Lee sold it to Chilco Ranch many years ago. Hutch Meadow is still part of Chilco Ranch and has recently been involved in a Ducks Unlimited project creating habitat and nesting sites for water fowl.

Hutch's widow married Jack Robison in 1907 and the younger boys went with her to Robison's place, now Twilight Ranch. Daughter Cynthia had married and left the country. The eldest son, Charlie, enlisted in the army and went overseas in World War One. Ironically, he was tragically killed under the wheels of a train on his way home after the war was over.

When Minnie and Jack Robison separated in 1916, Minnie and her sons made their home at the Gullikson Place on Big Creek below Churches. Hans Gullikson pre-empted the 171 acres in 1914 but had built a house and lived on the land before that. He had the reputation of being an excellent axeman and is credited with helping Ericksons on their log house with its well-fitted, dove-tail corners. He sold his land and buildings to Hutch and returned to Wisconsin.

Minnie Robison had also acquired a meadow on Upper Bambrick Creek where she and the boys wintered their cattle. Drifting cowboys often joined Hutches at their meadow in the winter time, and the late night musical parties there – Pat and Bill both played the violin, banjo and guitar – prompted Minnie to name the place "The Nighthawk." The meadow saw tragedy, too. Pat Hutch, suffering from a serious and painful brain tumor, took his life there in 1935 at the age of 33 and is buried on the Nighthawk.

"The Bluebird" was Hutches' name for the little place on the meandering creek below the Nighthawk where Pat and Bill had built a tiny cabin. Bill Maxted acquired the Bluebird sometime in the 1940s, and in the 1950s sold the property to Claude and Ella Bartley who catered to hunters. A few years later Bartleys sold to Robert and Jenny Scheres, a young couple just out from Holland. Taking the name of Hutches' meadow, Scheres called his place the "Nighthawk Guest Ranch." They made improvements and specialized in taking teenage boys and girls through the summer months. This place is now owned by Gary Miller of Vancouver.

Bill Hutch married a Scottish girl named Annie Bryce and they had a family of four daughters and a son: Norah, Eileen, Mary, Lou, and Billy, all born and raised at Big Creek. Minnie acted as midwife at most of these births. The Hutches were hospitable, and

Bluebird Cabin on Bambrick Creek. It was so small you could build a fire in the stove without getting out of bed.

Bill and Annie Hutch and family – Norah, Eileen, Mary, and Billy. Another daughter, Lucille, was born later.

Bill and Annie's family were musical like their father. Many a jolly evening was spent in their home. Young Billy was especially talented and later played with a band in Williams Lake.

Bill Hutch went out of cattle and sold the Nighthawk Meadow to Gerald Blenkinsop. Bill then took out hunters in the fall, and being handy, did carpentry work and odd jobs around the neighbourhood. His daughter and son-in-law, Norah and Tom Wilson, took over the guiding business after Bill's death. They built a log home for themselves on the home place and a hunting cabin on Coyote Lake.

Bill Hutch died in April 1953 early on the morning of his 53rd birthday and is buried in a hillside plot at the Bambrick place where his mother, Minnie Robison, who died in 1947, and grandfather, John Haines, also lie. Bill's widow, Annie, and most of the Hutch family now live in Kamloops.

The Hutch place on Big Creek passed out of the family name when it was sold in the 1960s to Jardy and Cameron. They sold to the Harold Nickasons a few years later. Steve Linger and Scott Fairless from California bought the place in 1976. A German woman, Andrea Huber, seeking a location to start a fish farm, purchased the old Hutch place in 1987.

JOHN ROBISON CUNINE was a tall, blue-eyed man with an angular face. Of Irish decent, he came from Quebec sometime in the 1800s. He worked around Kamloops and Savona, freighted on the Cariboo Road and finally worked his way to Big Creek, homesteading above the Bell Ranch on Bambrick Creek in 1902. The creek was then called Battle Creek. He dropped the last part of his name and was known simply as Jack Robison.

He married Minnie Hutchinson on June 17, 1907, but they separated nine years later and he lived most of his life as a bachelor. He left no heirs.

Although his place deteriorated as he grew old, Jack Robison in his prime had a well built and well kept cattle and horse ranch and raised many good horses. He told of selling one big work horse as many as three times, the animal always coming back to his home range again. The last time he was sold his new owner took him to the Prince George district but the next spring he was home again. Jack turned him out with his bunch, deciding that if the gelding liked it so well he would let him live out his life on his home range. Robison's brand was the FZ connected.

The range between his ranch and the Whitewater is still known as the Robison Range. Robison's ranch was at the end of the car road for many years. The old wagon road continued on, climbing steeply beyond Robison's fence line up the face of "Jack's Mountain" and straight down the other side to the creek

Bill Hutch with his winter fur catch.

192

Jack Robison on Prince in 1930. Robison had trouble pronouncing the letter "L" and always refered to his saddle horse affectionately as "nittle Prince."

bottom below and on into the Whitewater. Now a wide gravel highway, built as forestry access in 1969-70, sweeps by, skirting the side of Jack's timbered mountain where logging is underway.

Old Jack was proud of his mode of travel — a fancy high-topped buggy with padded leather seat and back, drawn by a good horse. In later years this was a lively sorrel gelding named Jerry who trotted briskly along, pulling at the bit and making the high, narrow buggy wheels hum like a top along the winding dirt road. Eventually he purchased a touring car and learned after a fashion to drive it, but like many another old teamster had problems with this gas-powered machine and frequently collided with a gate post or a jackpine. He managed to maneuver the car around Big Creek to the Bell Ranch, the Circle A, and Fosberys', and periodically even as far as Hanceville to visit the Hances for a week or so. His last saddle horse, a bay gelding named Prince, grew old along with his master and to the end lived fat and contented in the pasture below the house, his long black tail sweeping his fetlocks. Robison frequently went on a spree as he got older and over the years Hattie Witte nursed him through many a bout of D.T.s.

The middle finger on Old Jack's left hand was missing and the story went that it had to be removed after being badly chewed in a fight with Louis Vedan. The two men were enemies the rest of their lives and never spoke, even though Vedan passed only a few yards from Robison's gate when riding to and from his homestead in the Whitewater.

Jack Robison died in Vancouver in 1939. The ranch went to Hattie Witte and was Duane Witte's first home after he married Jacquie Shultz of Vancouver in 1944. He named it Twilight Ranch. Their three children, Arda (Ratcliff), Caroline (Palmantier) and Franklin were born and raised there. Ronnie Thomlinson, a hard working well-liked Englishman, bought the Twilight Ranch in the late 1960s. He built a new house and barn, improved the land and ran about 200 head of cattle. Sadly, he died there of a heart attack in 1983 at the age of 52. His ashes are buried on the ranch. Bill and Darlene Freding were the next owners, but they sold in 1990 to Dieter Kammernacht, just out from Germany. The place is still called Twilight Ranch.

HERBERT EDMOND CHURCH, a personable Englishman with a striking resemblance to King George the Fifth, first saw the Chilcotin in October 1902. In May 1903 he staked 320 acres of bottomland along Big Creek and recorded his pre-emption in the land office at Clinton. He returned with team and wagon and the first load of supplies three weeks later. By the first of October he had put up a 40-foot log building, built a half mile of fence, made a trip to the Gang Ranch ferry for a mowing machine, and raked and cut and stacked enough hay to winter his three horses. By the middle of October of that same year, 1903, he had moved his wife and family up from Vancouver.

Church had emigrated from England in 1886 at 18. While homesteading in Alberta he had heard about the Chilcotin district being good cattle raising country and hoped one day to see it. After moving to a farm at Comox, B.C., he found that working outdoors in the wet coastal climate brought on crippling attacks of rheumatism. A plan to find land in the dry Chilcotin country he had heard about began to take shape. In October 1902 he and a friend started out for the Interior to find out if that dream could become a reality. They travelled by C.P.R. to Ashcroft and on by stagecoach to Clinton where they bought saddle horses and headed towards the Chilcotin via Mountain House, Dog Creek, and Alkali Lake. Here his friend tired of the trip and turned back but Church continued on alone.

In his book: *An Emigrant in the Canadian Northwest,* now out of print, Church writes that he misunderstood the directions given him at Alkali Lake which were to keep straight over the mountain till he reached the Fraser, go down the river valley to the lowest bench, then follow upstream to the ferry which would take him into the Chilcotin. "And for the next ten miles," he wrote, "having gone down too near the water, had great difficulty getting along at all." However, he reached the spot safely and "The ferryman came over in a rowboat into which I got with my saddle, the horse swimming behind the boat."

He spent the night at the ferryman's cabin and the next four days looking the country over. Finding it to be already occupied he continued on to Hanceville. Here he stayed with Tom and Nellie Hance for three days while continuing his search.

He liked the Big Creek country 20 miles south of the Chilcotin River and returned the following spring to have a better look. Travelling this time from Ashcroft by one-horse buggy, he crossed the Fraser on the Gang Ranch scow ferry and again spent some time at Hanceville. After a week or two, assisted by Tom Hance, he found good land along Big Creek and staked 320 acres on May 18, 1903. There were only two others on the glacier-fed creek at the time: Charles Bambrick two miles above Church's pre-emption and Vic Erickson five miles below. George McDonald had a place as well but was working at Chilco Ranch.

The 200-mile trip from Ashcroft five months later to bring in the family was made in a wagon hired from the B.C. Express Company and took six days. There were nine in the party altogether: Herbert and his wife Gertrude, six children, including a month-old baby, and a girl of 17 who was to help Mrs. Church for the winter. It was well past the middle of October when the family reached their stark little home at Big Creek. Winter would soon be closing in and there was still a lot of work to do in the interior of the house (all partitions were made of logs hewn on both sides and caulked with moss). Church himself carried a heavy load, that winter building a log barn and getting out logs for fencing, in addition to all of the routine work.

The Clinton Hotel at Clinton was a familiar landmark to Chilcotin residents travelling to Ashcroft. The hotel, shown above on Christmas Day 1891, never closed its doors from 1861 until it burned down in 1958.

Opposite: H. E. Church.

Church was hardened and experienced by the time his Chilcotin adventure began. He had spent a year in Ontario as a farm pupil, or mudpup, and 12 years on a homestead in the Sheep Creek area of southern Alberta where there was plenty of hard work – fencing, farming, and breaking horses both to saddle and harness. In 1894 he married a girl he had become engaged to on a trip back to England in 1891. She came out to Calgary and they were married there. The couple had three children when Church moved his family to Vancouver Island to take over his aunt's farm at Comox, where he spent three years building and farming before moving to the Chilcotin.

In the spring of 1904 the most important task on the Big Creek homestead was to survey a ditch. Then with plough, scraper, and shovel bring water from Big Creek to the flats of natural grass below the house, thus ensuring enough hay for the horses and milk cows the following winter. Wild game and fish were plentiful and a big garden supplied vegetables. A small yard was fenced in at the side of the house for flowers and shrubs, land was ploughed and crops planted.

Church concentrated on bringing hay land under cultivation and getting started in beef cattle. By the spring of 1906 he had 25 head of cows and these had increased to 80 head by 1909. He had registered the HE (che) brand before the turn of the century when he was ranching in Alberta, and it is still in the family, kept up by the original owner's grandson, Johnnie Church.

The Churches had marketed some butter to mines around the country and it appeared that this venture promised a good return. For this reason the struggling rancher decided to sell some of his range cows and calves and invest in dairy stock. In the fall of 1910 he made a trip to the Fraser Valley and bought a few well bred yearling heifers and three or four older milk cows and had them shipped to Ashcroft by rail. He also invested $500 dollars in a big combined churn and butter worker, a gas motor to run it and a cream vat. The next year they sold $1,500 worth of butter.

Moving the milk stock from Ashcroft to Big Creek in winter conditions was beset with difficulties. It was late in the fall when Church started out with the drive and by the time he reached the Fraser River he found that the Gang Ranch scow ferry had been laid up for the winter the day before. He was obliged to leave the herd at the nearest ranch, 16 miles away until an ice bridge formed over the running water. To get home, he had to ride 60 miles farther to cross on the Chimney Creek Bridge. In January 1911 Church and his 12-year-old son, Dick, rode down through the cold and snow to drive the cattle across the ice bridge and on home. This was a three-day drive through bitter winter weather – and both father and son were stricken with flu during the trip. The coast cattle adjusted to the Chilcotin winter very well.

Up to 4,000 pounds of butter was sold in a year from the small herd of dairy cows – a unique venture in this part of the country.

The older children pitched in to help with the work involved. The butter was sold locally and to mining camps in the Cariboo; but in the fall of 1917 Church and his eldest daughter delivered 600 pounds of their butter by team and wagon to the new Pacific Great Eastern Railway near Clinton for shipment to Vancouver. The whole lot was sold at once to a big grocer in Vancouver for 50 cents a pound. In 1912 and 1913 the Churches showed butter at the New Westminster Fair. They won a second prize the first year and a first and second the next year. It was a distinct honour as their butter had to travel 200 miles by horse stage and as far by rail without refrigeration, and was in competition with that produced in the Fraser Valley.

By 1907 there was more settlement on the Creek and through Church's efforts a post office was opened on his ranch. Church was appointed postmaster at a salary of $60 a year. He also took the contract to carry the mail once a fortnight between Big Creek and Hanceville for $125 a year. The mail route lay via Scallons and Ericksons and using horses and buggy or sleigh the trip took two days. He gave up the contract in 1920 (by then there was a weekly mail service), but the Big Creek Post Office remained on the Church Ranch and in the Churches' name for 64 years. A Meteorological Station was also established there by the Dominion Government and manned faithfully by the Churches down through the years.

Records of weather observations at Big Creek go back over 100 years, starting in 1893. Mary Thomson, who now operates the Big Creek Meteorological Station, was told that the names of former recorders were not kept. Historical research suggests that George McDonald may have been the first Big Creek weather recorder. He staked the Bell Ranch in 1896 and before that had located for awhile on Lower Big Creek. Observations through the first years were somewhat erratic, perhaps because McDonald worked for wages away from home part of the time. In 1904, according to the records Mary has, the Big Creek temperatures were faithfully recorded and this was no doubt when Church took over.

In July 1993 the greatest total rainfall recorded in 24 hours was 139.8 mm. This downpour was only exceeded once in 100 years, in August 1954 when 149 mm was recorded in 24 hours.

In the autumn of 1907 Herbert Church and his neighbour, Charlie Bambrick, got out logs and built the first school on Big Creek, placing it between the two ranches where their properties met. Most of the lumber used was whipsawn by hand. The school opened in January 1908. It was called an "assisted school" because the Provincial Government paid the teacher's salary, while Church and Bambrick supplied not only the building but all other necessities as well. Teachers were chosen from letters of application – with an element of surprise on both sides at the beginning of term. One lady teacher, on being told that a large tub and water, heated on the stove, would be available when she wished to take a bath, decided she'd rather wait till she returned to Vancouver five months later. This school stayed open until most of the children were over 16, then the younger children continued studies at home and some were sent "outside" to finish their education.

Being so far from medical aid caused much hardship for pioneer families. In January 1907 when Church's three and a half-year-old son, Percy, broke his leg Church started out with team and sleigh to get the leg set. A neighbour had ridden 90 miles to Clinton to summon a doctor but none would come so far in the cold. The Hanceville Bridge was being repaired and Church could not get his team and sleigh across, but finally with help, he got to Hances and next day caught the stage for 150 Mile. A doctor met them at Bechers and set the limb, though Church had done a pretty good job of that himself. With lay-overs, this took a week. On June 26, 1911, Gertrude Church began a grueling drive to take her six-year-old daughter, Marian, who had broken her arm, to a doctor at the 150 Mile, 95 miles away via Hanceville. With a suffering child and a tired team, the long trip was a nightmare. It was July 2 before they were home again.

In August 1913 Church had his first experience with the automobile when Jack Temple, then owner of the Lee place at Hanceville, took him for a ride in his Cadillac. It almost ended in disaster. Coming home in the evening something jammed in the steering gear and the car ran over a low embankment and turned upside down on top of them. Church's left leg was pinned to the ground by the frame of the broken windshield. Badly bruised, he managed to free himself and crawl out. Temple was in worse shape; he couldn't move. Church then hobbled the quarter mile to Lees and sent two men with a horse and buggy to bring him in. Both men were covered with gasoline and Church wrote that because he could not strike a light he had never wanted a smoke so badly in his life. Temple was back to normal in a couple of weeks but Church claimed that his leg was never quite right after that. Six years later he bought one of the gas-eating contraptions himself.

After only a few driving lessons in Vancouver he had the car shipped to Ashcroft and, accompanied by his loyal wife, undertook to drive it home to Big Creek.

It was April and roads for the most part were either deep in mud, or snow and ice. For the first 100 miles beyond Clinton theirs was the first car over the road since the previous fall. Church admits in his book that if he had known more about a car he would probably never have attempted the journey so early in the year.

At one point the car slid sideways into a washout and tipped over on its side. Farther on, running a 30-yard mud slide, they broke a gasline and lost all their fuel. But this was nothing compared to the hair-raising trek down the steep, narrow grade to the Fraser River Bridge and up the other side to the Gang Ranch. The driver himself recorded: "We must have been on the very verge of going over the edge several times. At two or three spots where the road had been narrowed by washouts I clearly heard rocks which had been disturbed by the hind wheels rolling down the steep hillside behind me...."

"It's an awful long way to the bottom," appears to have been his plucky wife's only comment.

Church noted that the car never fully recovered from that trip and he got rid of it two years later. His wife was made of tougher stuff. Gertrude Church was a devoted and true helpmate. Despite hard times and the trials of raising seven children, she maintained the family's gracious English customs. A talented artist, she found pleasure in painting in water colors and oils the familiar scenes around her.

She was a devout Anglican and was instrumental in having a pretty little Anglican Church — the Church of St. James — built on land donated by her husband. Finished with stained glass windows and well laid varnished floor, it was her pride and joy. She saw that the church was shining clean and suitably decorated for the monthly services at which she played the organ. The rich brocade hangings were sent from England; and intricate hand carvings by Churches' daughters, Madge and Elsie, adorned the lectern and altar. Suitably, the first wedding to take place in the chapel was that of their son, Dick, soon after the building was finished in 1931. A large hall adjoined the church and the combination made a valuable contribution to community life. Restored in 1991-92, the building is still in use.

Both Herbert and Gertrude Church believed in taking time for recreation. Even before the hall was built they often held dances in

On the way to spring pasture.

their home, though space was limited. (Dances were held also at
Scallons', Ericksons', Wittes' and Sugar Cane Jacks.) They also
regularly took part in picnics, parties, and outings of all kinds with
their family and the community, and built a tennis court on their
ranch which was enjoyed by the neighbours as well.

The Church family: Elsie, Madge, Dick, Dolly, Irene, Percy, and Marian (who was born at Big Creek) were indispensable in the development of the ranch. They grew, married, and scattered, with the exception of Dick who, but for two years in the navy during World War One, stayed on the ranch to work with his father and finally take over the place. Some years before his father's death in 1933, Dick had assumed full responsibility for the running of the ranch, allowing his dad to spend his latter years writing his memoirs and pursuing his interest in mining. The last days of his life were spent at his mine shaft on Upper Big Creek, happily searching for gold. Dick immediately abandoned the mine after his father died, though in loyalty to her husband his sorrowing widow wished to continue it.

His funeral service was held in the little chapel to which he and his wife had contributed so much. He was buried nearby on land he had staked with intrepid optimism 30 years before. Gertrude Church spent her remaining years at the Coast with daughter, Madge Trethewey. She died there, but her ashes are buried beside her husband on the old homestead at Big Creek.

THE CHURCH FAMILY included PERCY, who was a partner with his father and his brother, Dick, in the Big Creek Ranching Company until 1932 when he married Big Creek school teacher Dorothy Dean and moved to Prince George. Percy and Dorothy did well in logging at Willow River. They had three sons: Albert, Teddy, and Michael.

ELSIE and IRENE went to work in Seattle. Irene drove police car in the city at one time. They both married late in life. Elsie later moved to Vancouver, B.C. After her marriage, Irene lived in California. She died and is buried there.

MADGE married Edgar Trethewey, well known for the Abbotsford Lumber Company and Coniagas Ranch at Maple Ridge. Edgar raised Black Angus cattle and Madge raised and showed Arabian horses. They had four sons: Richard, Allen, Bill, and Joseph Ogle (J.O.); and one daughter, Phyllis Watt.

DOLLY married Ken Moore of Tatlayoko. She left him in the early 1930s and took their children, Isabel and Beverly, to make her own way. Dolly had a varied career, working hard and eventually ranching at Falkland. She remarried in the 1940s to a man named Richards. He died with pneumonia a few years later.

The youngest daughter, MARIAN, married Chummy (George) Gilmer (Rona Church's brother). They ranched at Big

Creek for a few years, and had a daughter and a son, Leslie Anne and Greg, when they moved to Victoria in 1935. Their marriage broke up after the war and Marian and the children returned to the Interior, raising horses near Oliver. Honouring her last request, Marian's ashes were scattered on the hillside above the old Church Ranch at Big Creek.

RICHARD HERBERT CHURCH stood tall in both stature and in character. He was born in Comox in 1899, and was four years old when he came to Big Creek with his parents in 1903. He spent his life on his father's (H. E. Church) original homestead, well respected and well liked.

Dick had blue eyes – which could be merry or cold and hard. He had thick curly hair, prematurely gray. His face, too, aged prematurely but his lean figure, buoyant personality and cheerful sense of humour lent a youthfulness that never changed. For most of his life one leg was bowed and shorter than the other, caused by a broken limb that he walked on too soon. It gave him a limp but never deterred him.

In his youth he scorned hardships to trap, run coyotes, and shoot wild horses for bounty – anything to make a dollar when times were hard. He took over the ranch from his father with progressive new ideas, eventually running about 500 head of cattle. He hired help and put more land under cultivation. Fertilizer was used to increase the hay crop. Both he and his wife were good gardeners and raised a big vegetable and flower garden. For awhile it was irrigated with a water-wheel that Dick built from boards and coal-oil cans.

He began holding his steers over to finish them on grain at home and bought a hammer mill to chop their hay. He bought a truck to haul feed and supplies and experimented with raising pigs. Dick was the first Big Creek rancher to go into guiding. He knew well the mountains and the movement of wild animals and was an excellent tracker, a good shot and had a quick eye. He was at his best on pack trips into the high mountains for grizzly and the elusive California bighorn sheep.

He brought in horses from Alberta and bought a Quarter Horse stallion named Easy Money to raise saddle horses. In 1938 he and Gerald Blenkinsop tried taking steers over the mountains towards Bridge River for summer pasture on the western slope. The steers were driven up Big Creek to Graveyard Valley and over Elbow Pass to lush bunchgrass sidehills around Spruce Lake. A rider stayed with the cattle till fall when the steers were driven to

Dick and Rona Church in 1971 in front of the old house where Dick was raised.

Shalath and shipped on the P.G.E. to Vancouver. Gerald backed out after the second summer but Dick continued with the experiment for about five years. When neighbour Charlie Erickson heard that scientists had suggested there might be grass on the moon he quickly commented: "Don't tell Dick Church. He'll be trying to take his steers up there."

Dick was president of the Big Creek Livestock Association from its inception in the 1930s until shortly before his death. Election of officers was never bothered with. He was instrumental in getting spring turn-outs along the Chilcotin River allotted by the government for Big Creek cattle.

He bought a TD9 cat and when not using it at home hired it out to work on the road or wherever there was a job. Operated by Jack Casselman, Church's cat helped build the Puntzi airstrip. He had a sawmill for ranch use and local sales, built originally on the south side of Big Creek by Dick and his brother, Percy. In the 1950s he expanded his logging operation, setting up a camp away from home to cut and ship lumber commercially. Long time employee, Jim Bonner, was left in charge at the ranch.

In spite of all these ventures, debt plagued him throughout his life.

Cattle drive fording Big Creek at "Scairt Woman Crossing" en route to the Bridge River country in 1938. (The crossing was named by Frank Witte in 1937 when his wife and daughters were afraid of the high water.)

He married Rona Gilmer of Victoria in August 1931 and, after a honeymoon in Likely in the Cariboo, made their home on the ranch. Dick built a big log house with logs squared and lumber cut in their own sawmill. They had two children: Rosalie and Johnnie. Rosalie married John Siebert who was cowboying for her father. They have two daughters. John and Rosalie live in Alberta. Johnnie (Bruce) married Bonnie Wassell, an American girl from Okanogan, Washington, who had recently come to the country with her parents. They have two sons and two daughters. Johnnie went into real estate in Kamloops and became an auctioneer before returning to the ranch at Big Creek in 1963. Johnnie and Bonnie now live in Williams Lake.

In 1949 Dick bought the Brown Place on the Chilcotin River, and in 1957, the Sky Ranch. It was resold a few years later, but the Brown Place across the river from Durrells is still part of the old Church Ranch.

Though he never learned to fly, Dick bought a Stinson aircraft. The hayfield on the far side of Big Creek was used for a landing strip. He traded in the Stinson on a 4-place Taylor craft and built an airstrip on the hill above his home, driving the cat himself to carve a runway out of the jackpines. The Dick Church Airstrip,

In Graveyard Valley climbing the glacier towards Elbow Pass.

enlarged somewhat, is still in use. It has been recognized by the government and shows on aerial maps.

Dick and Rona had moved out of their two-story log home where they lived for 30 years and it was housing hired help when it burned to the ground on September 28, 1962. Living just across the way in the former Bonner house, Dick refused to dwell on their losses even though his prized grizzly bear head and Rona's piano went up in smoke. "Rona and I were through with the house anyway," he said as he cheerfully prepared breakfast after being up all night helping salvage what they could from the blaze. The Big Creek Post Office in a room off the kitchen was Dick's main concern. Nothing there was lost.

Dick loved his Big Creek Ranch and was content with his way of life. He found it hard to leave home. Perhaps his one regret was once turning down an invitation from Tommy Walker to accompany him on a sheep hunt in the Spatsizi of northern B.C.

Dick suffered a stroke in November 1974 and died in Williams Lake hospital in January 1975. He is buried in Williams Lake Cemetery.

Johnnie and Bonnie Church, who had taken over the Church Ranch, sold the old place to John and Betty Weetman of Chimney Valley in 1978 but kept the old brand.

206

Today's ranches in the Big Creek area.

RONA CHRISTIE CHURCH was a tall handsome woman with wavy brown hair, gray eyes and chiseled features. She came from a well-to-do English family in Victoria and found ranch life difficult at first. She was often in ill health and at times away from home under a doctor's care. Often not well, and with hired men to cook for year round, she needed help in the house. Good kitchen help was sometimes hard to come by.

Rona was born in Edmonton but was raised in Victoria and loved the sea. She was a good swimmer and capable with a boat. But gradually the dry Interior became home to her. When she was left alone after Dick's death she stayed in Williams Lake instead of moving back to Victoria.

Rona was Big Creek Postmistress and manned the weather station for most of her married life. She collected for the Red Cross and the Arthritis Society, and was the mover behind the drive that brought the telephone to Big Creek in 1938. She was the one, too, who introduced the game of badminton at Big Creek. Lines were painted on the hall floor and for more than a decade this lively game brought the young people of the community together on Sunday afternoons.

Rona liked to entertain and she and Dick hosted many a merry house party for the entire community. Homemade ice cream was usually among the treats served at these parties. Everyone joined in the well organized games, often ending with a sing-song around the piano. Gospel services were held there, too, as Rona had converted to become a dedicated disciple of Christ. She invited evangelists to Big Creek to hold public meetings in the hall and organized Sunday School for the children. She grew lovely flowers. An armful of sweet peas from Rona's garden graced many a Big Creek table.

Self-effacing, hard working and public spirited, Rona Church was a valued and respected member of the Big Creek community for 43 years. She died from cancer in Victoria on July 11, 1976, and is buried in Williams Lake.

A CANADA GOOSE CALLED SCREWBALL
by Veera Witte

There are two little goslings at Church's Ranch at Big Creek and a proud young lady goose, Screwball, who has never made a nest and never laid an egg, but has become their self-appointed foster mother.

Screwball was only a wee downy gosling herself when she was found just a year ago and brought back to the ranchhouse. She had four little brothers and sisters then, but one rainy night brought disaster upon their little hut and daylight found only Screwball surviving. From then on she depended completely on the two Church kiddies, Rosalie and Johnnie, for company, squawking frantically whenever they left her little box and making sounds of contentment as they drew near again.

Fall came, bringing with it a tang of frost in the air and the clamour of wild geese on their way south but, unheeding, Screwball still followed the children. Full grown now, she was still with Rosalie and Johnnie continually. Wherever they went in their play around the big ranch yard, Screwball waddled along behind them. Only on windy nights would she be restless: sleep would forsake her and she would wander around, honking to the wild gale until daylight brought her human company again.

Through the cold snowy winter months she seemed quite content to live quietly in the chicken house with the hens. But with the coming of spring, Screwball grew restless and discontented, losing interest in the children and becoming cranky and quarrelsome. Then one day she came proudly home with two little goslings toddling behind her. It was discovered that she had stolen them from a pair of Canada geese nesting in the pasture, and when they came looking for their babies an attempt was made to restore them to their rightful parents. At the critical moment, however, the dog took after the wild geese and, in the excitement that followed, the goslings disappeared and hid and the parent geese flew away. After a search, the downy little fellows were found and returned to Screwball who gathered them under her wings.

At first she was a little green about looking after them. She would keep her charges tramping all day as she followed the Church youngsters, and the wee goslings would be so tired by nightfall that they would squat down and doze off anywhere. Screwball didn't seem to notice and sometimes it would be as late as nine o'clock before she would finally settle down with them for the night.

But after a few weeks of practice, she gave them excellent care and would tackle anything of any size that threatened to harm them. It was an interesting sight to see Screwball, the goose who had never made a nest and never laid an egg, marching proudly around the fields with her two little adopted babies toddling behind. That summer we wondered if she would raise unaccustomed wings to follow them south, or if she would persuade them to remain where they were and throw in their lot with the chickens when the nights grew long and cold.

Screwball did go south with her grown babies but returned the next spring, still gentle, and for two years after that.

SCALLONS: At this writing there have been no Scallons living at Big Creek for over 30 years, but the Scallon name is still commonly heard in this community where the family settled in 1906. Their ranch on Lower Big Creek was sold in 1956 but is still known as the Scallon place. High grazing land between Upper Big Creek and Porcupine (Nadila) Creek, which includes wild hay meadows pre-empted by the Scallon boys in the early years, is called Scallon Range and running through it is Scallon Creek. Nearby, rising to 2,294 m (7,524 feet) stands Mt. Tom, named for Tom Scallon.

TOM SCALLON was the eldest son in the family and with his brother Joe was the first of the Scallon clan to discover the

Jim Scallon, Dick Church, Bob Fosbery, and Pat Hutch at Fletcher Lake.

Chilcotin. The two boys set out from Castle Rock, Washington, on horseback in 1901 and worked their way through Kamloops district north, mostly as ranch hands. In Quesnel they drove stage for a change. They were energetic capable boys and had no trouble keeping a job, but their dream was a homestead where the family could make a living together. So in 1905, with cash in their pockets, the young men followed their dream into the Chilcotin, crossing the Fraser River on the Gang Ranch ferry.

Reining their saddle horses west along a well-used wagon road, Tom and Joe met up with Louis Vedan who was located in the canyon on the south bank of the Chilcotin River. When Vedan learned that the boys were searching for land he told them about a likely looking place on the lower end of Big Creek which was right on the wagon road. When the brothers reached the swift, rocky river called Big Creek and crossed on the log bridge, they liked what they saw.

After exploring around the boys agreed that the open country, rich soil and unlimited pure water would make the home ranch they were seeking. They drove in the pre-emption stakes, making out the papers in the name of their father, Felix, an Irish Catholic who was from Quebec but who had settled at Island Pond, Wisconsin, where they stayed for 17 years.

Scallon logged with oxen and had a small farm. Three children – Theresa, Annie, and Jimmy – were born here. Their next permanent home was at Castle Rock, Washington, the birth place of Felix, Sarah and Patrick. Mrs. Scallon died there in 1900 and this tragedy perhaps resulted in their final move. The two eldest boys left home the following year to look for land in Canada. When they returned four years later with good news of their pre-emption in the Chilcotin their father prepared to start on what was to be the final lap of his trek across the continent.

In 1906, Felix Scallon with his family of three boys and a girl – Jim, Felix Jr., Pat, and Sarah – took the train north to Ashcroft. Tom and Joe travelled from the pre-emption at Big Creek to meet them with team and wagon and saddle horses and brought them in to their humble cabin in the wilderness. From this primitive beginning Scallon saw in his lifetime their homestead grow to a profitable ranch, providing a good standard of living.

There was a deserted cabin on the land the Scallon boys had pre-empted, built and abandoned by George MacDonald who moved farther up Big Creek. It was the family's first dwelling place.

Trapping provided part of their living during those first years as Felix Scallon and his sons began developing the land. All the field work and ditching was done by hand. Their first hay crop before the fields were cultivated was cut on the swamp along the road, known as Jimmy's Meadow. A trip was made to Ashcroft twice a year for supplies.

Their holdings were increased as the boys added pre-emptions of their own, including 320 acres on the Chilcotin River and wild hay land in the Porcupine country on Upper Big Creek. In 1926 they first took cattle to this latter area for summer grazing but in later years they gave up this practice, ranging their cows nearer home on the south side of Big Creek. Another meadow was leased on Cooper Creek to add to their hay supply.

In 1910 a spacious two-story log house was started. The huge fir logs were expertly hand-hewn on all four sides by Tom, Joe, and Jim, and the corners meticulously notched in the dove-tail design. When finished it had a dining room, big living room, and two bedrooms, all with hardwood floors, and six bedrooms upstairs. A lumber kitchen and pantry were added. The lumber was cut in their own mill which was powered by water from Big Creek, running from a flume into a penstock and through a turbine. As well as supplying boards for flumes and ranch buildings at the home place and on the Chilcotin River, some of the lumber was sold to neighbours.

The first boards were cut by whipsaw. This primitive method was grueling work: one man stood in a pit and the other on the ground above, while the log was positioned between them. They used a rip saw with a handle at each end and took turns pulling the saw through the length of the log. Working over his head, the sawyer at the bottom had the hardest job and got all the sawdust, so the positions were alternated. In the 1930s, another sawmill was set up across Big Creek from the ranchhouse, mainly to cut bridge timbers and decking. It was powered by a tractor-type steam engine which was borrowed from Arthur Knoll of Chezacut. As the operation of this monster required a qualified steam engineer, Tom Chignell of Kleena Kleene was hired to run it.

The Scallon boys were musical. Joe, Jimmy and Pat were expert violinists, and all the boys, Felix Jr. especially, could blow a rousing tune on the mouth organ. Patrick taught himself to fiddle by ear when he was only eight years old. But he then lost interest in music and 10 years passed before he took it up again. From then on playing the violin became a lifelong joy. Pat had a good voice and sang the old Irish songs with a touch of class. Later, in Kam-

Pat Scallon on his way to start haying at the Far Meadows on Scallon Creek.

loops, he won old-time fiddling contests and when in his eighties was still playing the violin. Jimmy and Pat provided first class violin music at the Big Creek dances for many years, often accompanied by Bill or Pat Huchinson on banjo or guitar.

The Scallon family enjoyed an argument. They were all well informed, loyally Irish, politically Liberal, anti-British and unfailingly hospitable. They lived well and their friends were more than welcome to everything they had. "Have three eggs," old Mr. Scallon would urge his breakfast guests. "These silly hens have got nothing to do but lay eggs." Felix Scallon Sr. died at home in 1929 and is buried on the ranch.

Tom left the Big Creek Ranch in the 1920s to work in the woods at the coast, but he returned to work with his brothers in the late 1930s. Tom died in Kamloops in 1943 of pneumonia when enroute to visit his brother Joe and family at Malakwa.

Joe moved away to work in mills and at logging at Silverdale and various places on Vancouver Island and along the coast. He married Stella Lottus in 1919, and a few years later he and Stella, with baby son Brian, returned to Big Creek to live at the family ranch for awhile. They made their home on the Scallons' River Place. Son Larry was born here with Minnie Robison acting as mid-wife. The Joe Scallon family left the River Place to go back to the coast. They eventually settled at Malakwa. Four more children were born: June, Stella, and twin boys, Joe and Francis. Joe Sr. died in 1970.

Sarah Scallon had an unfortunate romance with a tall dark

cowboy of doubtful reputation named Charlie Morrow and left home at an early age. She later married an Irishman named Mike Sheehan and had a family of five boys and six girls. She died at Kispiox in 1945.

Somewhat late in life, Jim Scallon married Helen Tibbles of Quesnel and for a number of years they lived in the family home on the ranch where three sons and a daughter were born: Kevin, Denis, Mike, and Colleen. During this time Pat and Felix established themselves down the creek from the bridge, putting up a well-built log house on the banks of Big Creek as well as a big log barn and other well-constructed out buildings. Neither Tom, Felix, nor Pat ever married.

Jim sold his share of the ranch to his brothers in 1947 and moved with his wife and family to Notch Hill near Kamloops. He died there in 1976. His widow, Helen, still lives at Notch Hill.

Nine years later Pat and Felix parted with the old homestead, selling everything to John Wade, then owner of Chilco Ranch. Three hundred head of cattle branded with the Scallon N 3 iron went with the land.

Pat and Felix moved first to Clinton and then to Alexis Creek where, in partnership with Joyce Russell, they bought and operated the Chilcotin Hotel. Their next home was at Fairmont Hot Springs where they bought the Meadows Resort. Finally, Joyce retired to the Coast and the two brothers to Kamloops. Felix died there in 1978 and Pat in 1990 – both in their eighties.

The Scallon place is still a valued addition to Chilco Ranch, though many a young couple with a ranching dream has tried to persuade the owners to sell it. The hay land is now used for pasture.

Postscript: The old Scallon house built in 1910 stood empty for 26 years. In 1973 Lynn Bonner, noting the weathered but unmarred beauty of the hand-hewn logs and admiring the skilled workmanship, bought the house from Chilco Ranch. When he first made an offer to Hilda Newsome, then owner of the Chilco, she turned it down, saying the building was not for sale. But Lynn refused to give up and finally a deal was struck. Mrs. Newsome agreed to sell the logs but would keep the floor boards.

The building was taken down, the logs carefully numbered, and moved to the north rim of Farwell Canyon. Here Lynn and his wife, Myrna, assisted by Myrna's brother, Grant Huffman, built a beautiful home with new log beams and high white ceiling contrasting the dark brown of the old hewn timbers. Big windows looked out on a magnificent view of the canyon. Their fireplace was of colourful rocks they gathered themselves, carefully chosen and placed. Old timbers were used to form mantle and base of the fireplace and for the top of the divider between kitchen and living-room.

Ten years later their company, Riske Creek Ranching, bought the Deer Park Ranch above the Fraser where Lynn was needed as manager. Their unique log home was then moved in one piece to the Cotton Ranch (also part of the outfit) to make a dwelling for Grant and Sue Huffman.

Here, overlooking hayfields and scenic pasture land, the logs still solidly stand – monument to an all but forgotten art at which the Scallon brothers were experts.

Dropping down from the Chilcotin Plateau into Farwell Canyon.

215

MIKE (GORDON) FARWELL came to the Chilcotin in 1903 as a mudpup from a well-to-do family in Leicestershire, England. He was bold, spirited and ambitious, and anxious to adopt the ways of the frontier. Being cheerful and carefree and something of a practical joker, it didn't take him long to fit in. He hired on at the River Ranch and worked for Fred Beaumont long enough to become a competent ranch hand. Ten years later he outdid the best of them, winning the coveted Chilcotin Ranchers Cup at the race meet on Becher's Prairie on a horse named Fox. After a few years he went on his own, buying a piece of land on the Chilcotin River in a majestic chasm that was to immortalize his name: Farwell Canyon.

Because the summer sun beat down unmercifully here on the canyon floor and towering cliffs reflected the heat, Farwell began calling his place "The Pothole." He bought the land from Louis Vedan who stayed on to work for Farwell for a few years. Wild-horse chasing in the rugged canyon country was one of their pursuits. Louis was a good worker, competent at any task, but he was mean, sulky and hard to get along with. Farwell stood up to him, called his bluffs and remained cheerful, and serious trouble never came between them. Later, Vedan moved to the Whitewater and took up a wild hay meadow on Tete Angela Creek. Farwell used an LV brand, probably bought from Vedan along with the place.

Farwell began to develop his land. He planted alfalfa in the lit-

The south side of the Chilcotin River at Farwell Canyon in the 1980s.

216

tle field and irrigated it with water dammed in the creek above. It yielded a bountiful crop. In 1912 he formed a partnership with another young Englishman, Gerald Blenkinsop, a man of principle, amiable but determined, and the two became lifelong friends.

GERALD BLENKINSOP came from Warwickshire, England, in 1907 to work on the Chilco Ranch for Claud Wilson. He had known Wilson in the old country where they shared the exciting British sport of riding to the hounds. After five years on Chilco, Gerald joined Mike Farwell in the canyon, a sound move as the two men had an amicable partnership that lasted for 13 years. Although raising horses was their main objective, Gerald also freighted on the Cariboo Road from Ashcroft.

The partners built separate homes when Blenkinsop married the girl Farwell had hired as a housekeeper, Madeline Wheeler, nicknamed Queenie. Small and lively, with a ready answer on the tip of her tongue, Queenie had come to the country on the BX stage about 1910 to work for Mrs. R. C. Cotton. She had left England with an ambition to go around the world, but once settled in the Chilcotin she had lost that desire. She did make a trip back to England with Gerald to meet his family – whom she quickly captivated with her wit and charm.

Queenie was an accomplished pianist, having come from a very musical family, and Gerald was a good singer. Louis Vedan, who was won over by Queenie's bright presence, gave her a Gerhard Heintzman grand piano for a wedding present and brought it down the steep narrow canyon grade and across the old bridge in a wagon. From then on beautiful music brightened their lives. Farwell married an Irish girl named Chris Riley, nicknamed Weenie, and the couples were soon calling their isolated hideaway "Happy Valley." The road leading out of the canyon on both sides of the river was steep and treacherous and the wives seldom left home.

Farwell and Blenkinsop sold the Pothole (the name that stuck) to the Gang Ranch in 1919 and moved to Sugar Cane Jacks, a higher and cooler location in the Big Creek area. They built separate log homes and started over again. Farwell and Blenkinsop were granted the contract to carry the mail between Big Creek and Hanceville in the early 1920s. Gerald took over the job and continued to drive the Big Creek mail stage until 1934.

Needing more hay land, Gerald staked a swamp meadow about 40 miles from their home place and blazed a trail to it. A neighbour took the job of cutting out a narrow, rough road and Farwell put up hay there for two summers. Blenkinsop kept this

Gerald Blenkinsop in 1932 ready to leave the Bell Ranch on his weekly Big Creek to Hanceville mail run in early spring, a two-day trip with horses. Note buggy tied on top for travel at the lower elevation.

At the TH Ranch, Hanceville. Left to right: Rene Hance, Mike Farwell, Joan Farwell-Buckmaster, and Grover Hance.

meadow that he called the Boghole throughout his ranching career. It was sold to Ronnie Thomlinson in the late 1970s and now goes with the Twilight Ranch.

In 1925 Mike Farwell sold his share in the Sugar Cane Jack place to his partner, and with his wife and little children, Joan and

218

Hubert and Winsome Blenkinsop in 1930 with their 1927 Chrysler Coach.

Gerald, left the country and went to live in Victoria. There they spent their lives, Mike returning to the Chilcotin only once to renew old friendships. Daughter Joan, however, with her husband Burgess Buckmaster, regularly visits the Chilcotin in the autumn. Her brother, Gerald Farwell, (named after Gerald Blenkinsop) is also a regular visitor.

Gerald Blenkinsop moved in 1925 to manage the Bell Ranch on Bambrick Creek for owner, Ted Willan, who lived in England. Moving to the center of the Big Creek community was good for the Blenkinsop family, as a school soon opened there with their children, Neville and Fay, in attendance. Gerald's brother, Hubert Blenkinsop, had managed the Bell for a number of years but in 1925 he quit and with wife Winsome and five-year-old son Teddy left for Victoria. They made their home permanently there. When war broke out in September 1939, Teddy Blenkinsop, not yet 19, enlisted in the R.C.A.F.

After serving first as a flying instructor in New Zealand, Teddy became a Flying Officer and Squadron Leader, serving in North Africa and Britain. He was awarded the Distinguished Flying Cross in 1944. Shortly after, his bomber was shot down over Belgium. He was captured and died in the terrible Belsen prison in Germany on January 20, 1945. In the village where he was hidden for a few months, Teddy was highly regarded by the Belgian people. He was posthumously awarded the Croix de Guerre with Palm by the Belgian Government for distinguished

Gerald and Queenie, left, and Fay and Neville Blenkinsop.

Forty below at Hutches' Nighthawk Meadow in 1930. Bell Ranch and other mixed cattle.

service to Belgium during the liberation of its territory.

After a few years, Gerald Blenkinsop bought the place he was managing, including cattle and the Willan Meadow on the south side of Big Creek, and the ranch continued to prosper for over two decades. At one time he looked after Jack McIntire's (foreman at the Gang Ranch) cows as well and ran over 400 head. Gerald's cattle wore the Bell brand and Queenie registered the Mexican Hat.

His summer range was in Paxton Valley and winter range in the swamp country around Dick Meadow. In winter a hired man fed cattle at the meadows. This practice was common in the country. On the big outfits two men fed cattle together, but on the smaller ranches one man alone looked after the cows, living in a low log cabin. The boss would check on him now and then, and when the hay was gone men would ride up on horseback – more often than not on a cold snowy day – and the herd would be driven back to the home ranch where they were fed till spring. Gerald always kept a good supply of hay ahead.

As well as the big fields at the Bell, he took a crop from Willan Meadow and the Nighthawk Meadow which he bought from Bill Hutchinson. Running short of feed in those days was disastrous as there was little, if any, for sale in the country and no way to transport from a distance any quantity of hay or grain. Cattle were always cowboyed to the hay supply, and there is a limit to how far cows can be moved on the hoof in winter.

Gerald set up a wind-charger at the Bell Ranch and was the first on Big Creek to have electricity. Nearly always there was a breeze blowing down the valley brisk enough to spin the windmill and charge the batteries. By 1950 most other ranches had gas or diesel-powered light plants. Blenkinsop had the first one-ton truck on Big Creek and hauled supplies from Williams Lake for his neighbours and for the small store that they ran on the ranch. He soon graduated to bigger rigs and markets, his son Neville doing the trucking when he was old enough. Daughter Fay went to Victoria to work, married there and never returned to live on the ranch.

Blenkinsops sold out in 1948 to Chilco Ranch and Gerald worked on Chilco for John Wade for a short time. Blenkinsops then bought property on the north shore of Williams Lake where they built a nice home for themselves and three rental houses. Gerald died there in 1969, still a handsome man in his eighties. Queenie rented an apartment in Cariboo Park Home for over 10 years. Her 100th birthday was celebrated there in 1990 in her own little place.

She donated her treasured piano to the Home and bought a small Stiegerman console for her apartment. Queenie played the piano regularly until she was moved to Deni House after suffering a cracked hip in a fall in 1990. Fay sold the lakeside property in 1991.

Neville drove truck for Imperial Oil for some time, and also drove taxi in Williams Lake. He married Margaret Fleming and had one daughter, Ray. Neville died in 1985 and his ashes were scattered over the Bell Ranch. Fay (Sage) divided her time between Victoria and Williams Lake for some years but now lives permanently in Victoria, having moved her mother down there as well.

The Bell Ranch was sold by Chilco Ranch to Sky Ranches Ltd. in 1975. Walt Mychaluk and Archie Warren bought it in January 1988. Willan Meadow was sold to Ronnie and Mary Nelson, and is now owned by Randy and Gay Saugstad. Sugar Cane Jacks was sold to the Gang Ranch about 1935 by Chummie (George) Gilmer.

LOUIS VEDAN was born in Empire Valley, worked around the country and finally settled on a flat known as the Pothole on the south side of the Chilcotin River in what became Farwell Canyon. He sold this place to Mike Farwell, lived for awhile at Sugar Cane Jacks and about 1918 moved into the Whitewater country. He cut the 26 miles of original wagon road from Jack Robison's place to his pre-emption in the Whitewater.

Louis Vedan and Jack McIntire of the Gang Ranch went into the Whitewater country together. McIntire pre-empted the place Louis finally took, and Vedan took a piece of wild hay land now known as Whitewater Meadow. McIntire dropped his pre-emption and moved out and Louis acquired the place vacated by his neigh-

Louis Vedan in front of his cabin in the Whitewater. With him are Eve Fosbery and sons, Tony and Tex.

222

Louis Vedan.

bour. Chilco Ranch got the other meadow. Both now belong to Pete Schuler.

Louis could neither read nor write and living as he did in the wilderness had no way of keeping in touch with the outside world. There were few radios then and he seldom went out. Once or twice a year he took team and wagon to Chilco Ranch for supplies. When some cowboy or Indian came by Louis would ask what month it was – not what day! He built up a good ranch but as time meant nothing to him many times winter came and found Louis only about half finished haying. Consequently, he lost many cattle and when he sold out to Chilco Ranch in the late 1930s he had only about half the number he had taken in to the Whitewater. There is a mountain named after him, Mount Vedan, just back of his ranch, and a lake in Nemiah Valley where he at one time ranged his cattle. Louis Vedan was a hard worker and built well but he could be heartless and cruel to his animals. The cabin and solid big log barn he built are still in use. Pete Schuler bought the place in the 1960s and still calls it the Vedan Ranch. Louis branded with $\overline{7}$ (bar seven). Pete uses $\underline{7}$ (seven bar).

Louis was once married and was the father of two children. He died in the Old Men's Home in Kamloops in 1954. He did not know his age but it is believed he was over a century. He used to say he was a man full grown when the railroad went through Ashcroft.

BOB FOSBERY was only 16 when he came to Canada from England in 1911. He had contracted to work for a year at $10 a month for Gertrude Church on an isolated ranch at Big Creek.

Bob no doubt inherited this adventurous spirit from his father, George Vincent Fosbery, who was awarded the Victoria Cross for daring and gallant action in battle in India in 1863. In later years the elder Fosbery came to Canada on various occasions to visit his son at Big Creek. He loved the country, and when he died in England in the late 1920s, Bob erected a tall wooden cross in his memory on a hill overlooking the Fosbery Ranch. Rocks were set there, too, in the shape of a cross. Though the wooden marker rotted and

Bob and Eve Fosbery at their Bar Five Ranch on Big Creek.

fell, the rock cross is still as visible as when, in loving memory, it was placed there nearly 70 years ago.

Bob Fosbery was born in 1895 at Bristol, England, and was given the good old English name of Percy Henry Vincent. But he hated the name and refused to use it, choosing, as soon as he was old enough, to be called "Bob" instead. When his own son was born on the Canadian frontier, Bob resisted the British tradition to pass on the family Christian names and called his first born Texas – a name he considered in keeping with their western lifestyle.

Fosbery was a young man endowed with social graces and an easy charm and he got on well in his adopted land. When his year was up on the Church Ranch at Big Creek, he worked for two years for Jack Temple who was then owner of the Norman Lee Ranch at Hanceville. While there he drove the first car – Temple's high-wheeled Cadillac – over the dangerous Farwell Canyon Hill.

In 1914, Fosbery responded to England's call to arms and returned to his homeland to join the British Army. He served there until after the war and then returned to the Chilcotin to take up a place along Big Creek with the aid of a veteran's plan called Soldiers Settlement. This place had been pre-empted in 1912 and left vacant by a man named Bill Abrams who built a two-story log house on the banks of Big Creek in 1917. Housing the Fosberys and succeeding owners, this picturesque building is still standing. Some 160 acres of swamp meadow on Duck (Abrams) Lake also went with the new Fosbery place. This meadow once belonged to Bill Abrams' brother, Steve, who was killed at the Bell Ranch by a run-away team. He is buried at Duck Lake. The Fosberys always referred to this meadow as the Steve Meadow after Steve Abrams who pre-empted it in 1913 and built a cabin and barn.

Like many of the early settlers, Fosbery was caught up in the gold fever when he first came to the country and staked a claim in the Whitewater adjoining the Taylor Windfall on Iron Creek. Fosbery went in to the Whitewater every year with saddle and pack-horses to do assessment work on his claim, camping for a few weeks in the high alpine country. He helped build some of the mine cabins on the upper level at the Taylor Windfall, snaking out dry spruce logs for the buildings with his saddle horse. Finally, a mining engineer told him the property would never be worth anything and he traded his claim to Herbert Church for a 7-passenger Overland car.

No doubt there was mutual satisfaction in this deal as Church in his memoirs speaks of "getting rid" of a big heavy car that he drove from Vancouver to Big Creek via the Gang Ranch in 1920. "My ignorance of cars combined with the excessively bad roads did a lot of harm to the car; I got rid of it two years later." Getting rid of his mining claim in no way ended Fosbery's involvement in minerals. He had a lively interest and a good measure of success in gold mining throughout his lifetime.

In 1925 Bob married Eve Napier, an attractive tall, blue-eyed English girl who soon learned to drive a team and cowboy with her husband. They had two sons, Tex and Tony.

More holdings were added to Fosbery's Ranch: Cooper Creek flats on Upper Big Creek, the Dolly Meadow on Sky Ranch Road, purchased from Dolly Church and a high swamp on Wales Creek that they named Green Mountain Meadow. Eventually, over 200 head of cattle and 50 head of horses carried the Fosbery Bar-Five brand. They could afford a new car, a fancy little Model A coupe with a built-in vase to hold a bloom or two while the family sped along the narrow dusty roads.

But in 1932 Bob's yen for change and adventure surfaced again and he moved his wife and family (against her wishes) to the Okanagan, leaving the Soldier Settlement property to go back to the government and 40 head of horses running on the Big Creek range. They sold the Dolly Meadow to Dick Church and Green Mountain Meadow to the Gang Ranch.

Fosbery's 200 head of cattle and six horses were driven to Ashcroft by Francis and Charlie Quilt. Gerald Blenkinsop hauled the household goods, machinery, and a flock of chickens that far by truck. There the lot, including the Model A Ford, was loaded onto C.P.R. box cars for the last lap of the journey to Kelowna. Bob, Eve, and their two small sons went along on the freight train loaded with all their worldly goods.

Unhappily, ranching in the Okanagan was a disappointment and that venture soon ended. About 1935 Bob took a job as Canadian consultant for the Dole Pineapple Company of Hawaii, having previously looked after Mr. Dole's mining interests in this country. When World War Two broke out Bob again joined the Forces. This time he served in Canada with the R.C.A.F. as Sergeant in machine gun instruction from Ontario to the West Coast of B.C., making him one of the few men to have served in both world wars.

When Bob was discharged from the Air Force after the war he was hired by a California mining company to go to the Yukon as a consultant and decision-maker looking for dredging grounds near

Dawson City. This meant sinking shafts through frozen ground to bring out placer samples. Fosbery knew he would need help in this venture so in May 1946 he got in touch with his two sons, Tex and Tony, suggesting they go north to work with him in the Yukon.

"I would like you both to come with me," he wrote from Trenton, Ontario, "but I will warn you that the pay is poor, the grub is poor and the mosquitoes are hell." Both boys went – and they loved the north. Tex stayed two years and Tony nine years. The areas they worked in included Cassier Creek and 60 Mile in northwestern Yukon.

The winter of 1947, Fosbery's first in the Yukon, was the coldest in history. During the first week in February the temperature dropped to -80°F in Dawson, -86°F at Snag and -96°F on the Bering Sea. Men had to go out in that extreme cold to cut and bring in fire wood to heat homes and businesses in the city. Some trappers at their isolated cabins froze to death in the terrible, penetrating cold.

Bob and Eve Fosbery found that the action-filled, transient lifestyle of the past few years had taken its toll on their marriage and they were divorced in 1947. Bob remarried a few years later. He and his new wife, Helen, made their home in Lumby where Helen was village clerk and Bob had a profitable placer gold mine at his back door. His last move was to East Kelowna where Helen was again involved in local government. Bob Fosbery died at East Kelowna from pneumonia in 1984 and is buried there. Eve Fosbery died in 1985 in Williams Lake, where she had been living for the past nine years. Her son, Tex, scattered her ashes from his aircraft over the old ranch at Big Creek and placed a headstone for her beside the rock cross on the hill overlooking the old home. Helen Fosbery lives in East Kelowna.

Tex and Tony formed a partnership in the Fosbery Brothers Construction Company and did well with their big machines, both working hard, in the Terrace-Kitimat area of B.C. In 1967 they bought the Hanceville TH Ranch and sold it nine years later. During this time their mother, Eve, was postmistress of the Hanceville Post Office and ran the little store. Tex, a great pilot, learned to fly early and his yellow Cessna float plane has gone with him everywhere. He now lives in Williams Lake, Tony in Sorrento, but both still work with big machines on construction jobs.

The Fosbery place lay idle for two years. In 1934 Chummie Gilmer and wife, Marian (Church) and daughter Leslie Anne, moved there from Sugar Cane Jacks. A son, Greg, was born while they ranched at the Fosbery place. After a few years Gilmers, too, left the place. They sold their cattle and went back where Chummie's heart had always been – to Victoria and the sea. He sold Sugar Cane Jacks to the Gang Ranch. Chummie joined the Navy and after the war continued to make his living with tug boats on the coast.

Cecil and Hazel Henry were the next occupants of the ranch, purchasing the Soldier Settlement property from the government for $1,000. Through the following years, three sons and a daughter were born – Sherwood, twins Truman and Gail, and Larry. Henrys added the Marston place farther up the creek and traded Duck Lake Meadow to Chilco Ranch for the Scallon Pothole on Cooper Creek. They had range on Mud Creek and Groundhog Creek. Their outfit was known as the Pinto Ranch and then the Bighorn.

Bert Russell and sons bought the Marston property on Big Creek and the meadow on Cooper Creek from Cecil in the 1960s, and a man named Penticost bought the home place a few years later. Penticost sold to Guenther and Tilly Achatz. The present owners, Ray and Mary Thomson, bought from Achatz in 1984. It is now named the Bar Cross Ranch. Thomsons had also purchased the Duck Lake Meadow which they sold to Mac and Beth Suter from Switzerland.

Chilcotin winter at Big Creek.

BIG CREEK ALPHABET — SUMMER 1925

by Contie and Evelyn Grey (now Swartz and Smith) who visited the Churches.

A is for Arthur, atop the hayload.	(Bambrick)
Also for Allen, a coy little toad.	(Trethewey).
B is for Billy. He's not Big but he's Bold.	(Hutchinson)
C is for Churches. (May Daddy strike gold.)	(Herbert & Gertrude)
D is for Doris, the Belle of the Ball.	(Bambrick)
D is Dare-Devil Dick, the Dogies Downfall.	(Church)
E is for Emma, so sweet and docile.	(Bambrick)
E is for Eve of the naughty blue eyes.	(Napier-Fosbery)
F is for Fosbery, who captured the prize.	
F is for Frank, of the disarming smile.	(Bambrick)
F for the Farwells, where we lingered awhile.	
G is for Gerald, who drives the Mail Ford.	(Blenkinsop)
G is for Gertie, who'd come home at last.	(Bambrick)
H is for Hubert, Big Creek's noble lord.	(Blenkinsop)
H is for Harold, who works pretty fast.	(Wales)
H is for Hattie, whose good nature's vast.	(Hance-Witte)
I for the Idiots, who come up from town.	(Contie Evie Grey)
J for Old Jack, of good cooking renown.	(Robison)
L is for Lee, the galloping Major.	
K for the Kids; the best ever, we'll wager.	(Tretheweys, Bambricks)
M is for Madge and her never give up.	(Church, Trethewey)
M is for Mie and her steer-riding cup.	(Marion Church)
N is for Nita, a jockey by birth,	
only comes up to her horse's girth.	(Green)
O is for Ornery, a good cowboy word.	
P Pat and Percy, who ride steers backward.	(Hutch & Church)
P is for Pat, whose dancing's divine.	(Hutch)
P is for Percy, whose rope-spinning's fine.	(Church)
Q is for Queenie, at the piano an ace.	(Blenkinsop)

R is for Mrs. Robison, of the sweet-smiling face. (Mother of Pat & Bill)

S is for Slim — he's ridin' 'em wild! (Phil Farmer)

T is for Teddy, an original child. (Blenkinsop)

U is for Us. Big Creek we adore. (Contie & Evie Grey)

V is for Vancouver. Our return we deplore.

W for Winsome, the World's Wonder Cook. (Neuritsos-Blenkinsop)

W Frank Witte; the wild ones he'll hook.

X is for X-ercise we took to reduce.

Y for the Yells, like Bedlam let loose.

Z for the Brand of Percy and Dick

Z that is Lazy for Charlie and Vic. (Erickson)

A. M. Piltz as a young man with his saddle horse.

AUGUST MARTIN PILTZ came to the Chilcotin in 1912. He was a raw-boned, sandy-haired man with deep-set piercing eyes, a healthy weathered complexion, and a trimmed mustache. Though of German birth, Piltz rolled his Rs like a Scotsman and liked to sing Harry Lauder songs. He was cantankerous and unbending at home but was very social when out, thoroughly enjoying company and good conversation.

Piltz at 12 emigrated with an uncle from Russia, where the Piltz family were living, to Winnipeg and went to work, saving his wages to help his widowed mother and younger brothers and sister who came out from Russia to Winnipeg the following year. Through disciplined determination he educated himself in English. As a mature man he was well read, had a keen mind and was at home in any company, but he always regretted his lack of a proper education.

Piltz went to work for Joe Trethewey at Chilco Ranch for a few years and then started a place of his own at Big Creek on what was then known as the "Big Swamp." This big meadow in swamp and jackpine country was 20 miles from the nearest neighbour and for the most part there was no road. He had to cut out timber for miles to bring in his team and wagon and a few supplies. Piltz's Peak, a mountain rising to 2,200 m (7,216 feet) just beyond his preemption, was named for him soon after he settled there. Wild horses were plentiful in the country and Piltz hoped to catch and tame them but it proved too big an undertaking for him and he went into trapping and hunting instead.

By living frugally and working hard he was able to save some of the money from his fur catch and start developing his big swamp into a ranch. In 1918 he bought 30 head of heifers from Erickson brothers on credit – his start in cattle. A hardworking, honest man, he was soon out of debt and eventually ran 300 head of good cows.

August: Cutting a bumper crop of grain hay at the Sky Ranch.

In later years he was a consistent winner in beef shows at the Annual Fall Fair in Williams Lake. Over the years Gus Piltz worked steadily at leveling his rough meadows – inventing and building a machine pulled by four horses to cut off the hummocks, and trying out new things. He planted tame grasses to improve his feed and production but always tailored his cattle herd to fit the hay supply. His brand resembled a flying U.

With his ranch situated at 1,500 m (nearly 5,000 feet) elevation, Piltz saw that spring grazing at a lower elevation was important to his operation and eventually gained a spring turn-out on Churn Creek. He was frequently at war with the neighbouring Gang Ranch and the government over range. "I'll fight them to the last ditch!" was his slogan.

Gus always referred to his ranch as the Big Swamp, but in the 1940s he gave his high meadows at the foot of Piltz's Peak the fitting name of "Sky Ranch." It goes by that name today.

As soon as he could afford it, Gus bought a new Whippet car and regularly went out on Sunday for rest and relaxation, taking his employees with him. He occasionally visited relatives in Portland and they visited him at the Sky Ranch. He had good buildings, neatly laid out, and ran a well-kept, paying operation, never sparing himself, but he was an exacting and overbearing boss and had trouble keeping hired help. His way was the only way and he was never wrong.

His half sister, Olga, and her husband, Gus Fredricks, worked for him in the 1930s and stayed longer than most. Fredricks was a good axeman and did most of the work on Piltz's new house. As Piltz never married, he usually hired a man and wife team and the woman would do the cooking. Many such couples came and went. Other relatives, including nephews Leonard Gildner and Ed, Richard and Roy Piltz, tried their luck as well but in the long term all found him too difficult to get along with. Leonard Gildner, his sister's son, stayed the longest, coming back time and again from Portland to try and ease the load for his hard-working uncle, but he finally gave up and left for good. August Piltz had a live-in relationship in the 1940s with a tall attractive woman named Louise Harris. He got to know her when she lived with her husband and son briefly at the Marston Place on the south side of Big Creek. After Harrises left the country, Louise rode her horse to the Sky Ranch and moved in with Gus. The romance broke up in a year or two when, according to Gus, she wanted to start writing cheques. But according to Louise, he became too hard to get along with.

Gus Piltz and Louise Harris at the Sky Ranch, ready for a vacation.

Piltz's cattle were wild and he was a rough and awkward rider which perhaps accounted for his many broken bones. The first accident had nothing to do with cattle and was probably his worst ordeal. Young then, he was riding home at night on a half-wild horse and galloped under a clothes line, invisible in the dark. The wire caught Gus across the mouth, throwing him unconscious to the ground, his teeth and face broken and bleeding. When he came to, he went into the cabin and tried to put the broken pieces in place and fainted again. When consciousness returned he saddled and got on a gentler horse and rode in great pain through the night the some 50 miles to a doctor at Alexis Creek. He had been feeding cattle for Churches at their meadow and stopped in at their ranch 20 miles down the road to let them know that he would not be on the job in the morning. For the rest of his life, gold teeth showing in his smile were a reminder of that terrible night.

Gus Piltz's last accident was in 1956 and contributed to his decision to part with the Sky Ranch. The *Williams Lake Tribune* tells the story:

"Suffering from a broken leg, A. M. Piltz last week faced the ordeal of crossing two rivers without bridges in the hundred mile journey to reach medical aid at Williams Lake. Gus' leg was broken Tuesday morning when his horse fell on him while cutting out cattle at his ranch. Bill Tymochko, who was working with him, expertly splinted and bandaged the injured limb and then transported Gus by team and wagon over twenty muddy miles to Henry's ranch. Here the swift waters of Big Creek must be crossed and Tymochko soon concluded that their wagon was too low for the undertaking. By dint of much shouting Cecil Henry was summoned with his tractor and wagon in which boards were placed to raise up the bottom. The suffering man was carried over on this and then was moved again to Henry's blue Ford to be driven twenty miles farther where another primitive crossing by cable carriage awaited him at the washed out Chilcotin River Bridge at Hanceville.

"To assist Piltz at the far side of the river, Dan Lee and first-aid man, Chet Leavitt, had been summoned by phone from Big Creek. Upon their arrival Gus was assisted onto the make-shift stretcher by Cecil Henry and Jim Bonner, then into the little metal cable carriage and conveyed through the dusk across the unbridged channel of water. Once over he was moved by Lee and Leavitt into the ambulance. The mercy vehicle then swung swiftly up the long grade from the river, its red light flashing reassuringly through the night as it carried the patient to relief and rest at the hospital in Williams Lake — and we hope to a speedy recovery."

After two months in hospital August returned to Big Creek,

Cable crossing in use in 1956 when the Hanceville Bridge was washed out, Elvina Gildner in the cable carriage.

his leg in a cast, again crossing the Chilcotin River in a cable car. His sister, Elvina Gildner, was with him. She had come up from Portland, Oregon, to keep house for her brother while his leg healed. It was not to be. Mrs. Gildner died on their way to the Sky Ranch. Again the *Williams Lake Tribune* carried the story:

"After suffering a stroke in her sleep, Mrs. Elvina Gildner of Portland, Oregon, sister of A. M. Piltz of Big Creek, passed away while being taken to Williams Lake hospital. Mrs. Gildner was accompanying her brother home from hospital and the two had stayed over with Cecil and Hazel Henry for a few days rest. They were to leave that day for Sky Ranch. When Hazel was unable to awaken Mrs. Gildner Friday morning, the ambulance was summoned after consulting the doctor by telephone. The Red Cross nurse at Alexis Creek was also contacted to come up and accompany the patient to the ambulance at the Chilcotin River cable crossing at Hanceville where a nurse from Williams Lake would take over. On rushing to the cable to meet the nurse, Cecil Henry found that the carriage had been taken to Chilco Ranch for repairs and an hour or two was lost before it could be installed again and the nurse brought over.

Once back at the river with the patient, further delays were endured by the ordeal of getting the unconscious woman across the open channel in the cable car. Again Jim Bonner assisted. A nurse from Williams Lake was with the ambulance. Mrs. Gildner passed away without regaining consciousness just as the ambulance was crossing Williams Lake Creek before entering town. Hazel Henry accompanied the patient throughout the trip and stayed over to be of what help she could to the sorrowing relatives who arrived from Portland early next day. The body was taken to Portland for burial in the family plot. August, with his leg in a cast and just out from a two–month stay in hospital, was unable to attend his sister's funeral."

Some of the heart went out of August Piltz after his sister's death. In the fall of 1957, with his recently broken limb still bothering him, he sold out to Big Creek rancher Dick Church and hung up his saddle for the last time. Piltz moved to Williams Lake and almost immediately set about giving the proceeds of his life's work back to the country that he felt "had been good to him." With the help of Doug and Anne Stevenson, Jack Cade, Judge Henry Castello, Pudge Moon, and Dan Buckley, he decided to make his donation in the field of education.

The biggest part of his life's savings went into the August

Piltz Foundation Fund, established in perpetuity for the advancement of education in the Chilcotin-Cariboo. Interest from this fund is given out in annual grants to young people of the district seeking the education that Gus never had.

August (as he preferred to be called) enjoyed his years in Williams Lake socializing among friends. He stayed first with Buckleys at the Sunny Side Motel and then bought a house on First Avenue North. He also invested in a rental duplex. He spent his last years in a hospital in New Westminster and died in 1967.

August often said he wanted to be buried on "The Peak" – he was proud of his name on the lofty mountain that towered above the little empire he had built below. But there was no provision for this wish in his will and August Martin Piltz was buried in Williams Lake Cemetery.

The Sky Ranch changed hands a number of times over the years and no longer was the progressive cattle ranch it became under its founder. Then in January 1993 it was bought by Ray and Mary Thomson and Hugh Ryder and is once again a going concern.

George Wales at the Bell Ranch.

OTHER SOD BUSTERS IN THIS AREA WERE:

BERT BARROWS, an American whose place was later taken up by GEORGE WALES. Mr. and Mrs. Wales lived in their wilderness home beyond Piltz's Sky Ranch for many years. A creek is named after Wales. They had one son, Harold. Wales was an Englishman and would ride down to Big Creek for the mail dressed in typical English riding habit, step off his lathered horse, riding crop in hand and announce, "We came like the wind!" He later became more Westernized and began wearing western leather chaps. Mr. and Mrs. Wales spent their last years in a cabin at the Gang Ranch.

ADAM CUMMINGS, who trapped in partnership with Gus Piltz. He homesteaded the Green Mountain Meadow which now belongs to the Gang Ranch and is called Fosbery Meadow. Bob Fosbery bought it from Cummings.

COOPER, MILES and BILL, were originally from Kentucky. "She's a grand old state," Bill used to say, "fair women and fast horses." The Cooper brothers came to the Chilcotin by mule team from Edmonton, Alberta, early enough in its history to leave as a memento a creek and a meadow bearing their name. Cooper Creek begins near the Wales place, where they lived for a time, and flows in a northerly direction to empty into Big Creek at the Marston place where they also made their home. Reports are consistent that when food supplies were low they ate coyotes which were numerous. They were nomads and traders, exchanging pre-emptions and horses, usually getting some cash as "boot." The Cooper Meadow is above Alexis Creek where they homesteaded and lived after leaving Big Creek. Bill is buried there. Miles sold out to Tommy Morgan about 1913, lived out his days at Redstone and is buried on a hillside near the Redstone Bridge. The Cooper Meadow is now known as the Morgan Meadow.

ANDERSON – BIGHAM – BRECKENRIDGE: The place later owned by Frank Witte was taken up first by two Americans named Mills Anderson and Ted Wyman, although it had been fenced by Charlie Bambrick for a horse pasture. Anderson, originally from New Mexico, came to B.C. on horseback from Colorado about 1908. Accompanied by Ted Wyman, he brought a bunch of loose horses to the country. Anderson was a civil engineer and worked on roads and bridges around B.C. before pre-empting 160 acres on Big Creek (the Circle A Ranch). Ted Wyman left shortly after to

Mills Anderson.

Ruth Anderson.

return to his family in New York and a career in banking. Anderson built a log cabin under the hill beside Big Creek before sending for his wife, Ruth, who with their two daughters, Jean and Ruth Jr., had stayed behind with his parents in Wisconsin. Heading northwest by train to join her husband, Mrs. Anderson took their baby girl with her but left the oldest, Jean, with his parents.

Mills Anderson met his family at Ashcroft. Travelling down with team and wagon, he lost the dog that had accompanied him throughout his Canadian adventures. Mills was very upset about

Mrs. Ruth Anderson was met at Ashcroft by her husband to begin the over 200-mile wagon trip, which could take up to two weeks, to their Big Creek homestead. Insects were only one of the discomforts. The horses above on the Cariboo Wagon Road have branches over their nostrils to help ward off horseflies, mosquitoes and other insects.

Below: Like Mrs. Anderson, for most Chilcotin housewives their first home was a small log cabin, usually with a dirt roof and even dirt floor. The one below was photographed at Chezacut in the early 1950s.

losing his pet. On the return trip when the animal was found, his wife suspected that her husband was happier to see his dog than he had been to see his baby daughter. Mrs. Anderson came from an easy life in a well-to-do family. She had married an adventurer against their will. The hard work in her husband's dirt-floored log cabin in the Canadian wilderness took a heavy toll on her health.

For this reason, the family gave up the homestead after a few years and went to live in Seattle, Washington. Mills dreamed of returning to his little ranch on Big Creek but he never did. Two sons, Alan and Gordon, were born after the family left B.C. and in 1989 the boys, in their sixties, made the trip from California to see their father's pre-emption.

Next on the Anderson place came Bigham from Tennessee, and after him John Other Breckenridge who brought his family from Mission City in 1914. One of the Breckenridge boys was killed in a horserace accident when he collided with a tree. He is buried on the place. This land, lot 2127, was surveyed in 1914. Frank Witte pre-empted it in 1926, obtaining the Crown Grant two years later.

MAJOR LEE, retired from the British Army, lived in a log cabin below the Circle A in the 1920s and 1930s. Frank Witte leased the property for pasture after Major Lee left and it is still part of the Circle A Ranch.

MARSTON, Bob and Pat, lived on Upper Big Creek, the location bearing their name for many years. It is now owned by the Russell family and named Anvil Mountain Ranch. Marstons both left to join up in World War One and did not return to Big Creek. Pat Marston and his wife came back for a visit in the 1950s.

Englishman SLIM FARMER came to Big Creek in June 1925 to work for Bob Fosbery. He also worked for Hubert Blenkinsop on the Bell Ranch. "They called me a mudpup," he later reminisced. "I didn't like the term then but I don't give a damn now." Farmer's name was Phil but the tall lean Englishman was known only as Slim. With his wife, Violet, he lived most of his life at Kaleden near Penticton. Slim visited Big Creek periodically, once to attend a Big Creek Stampede and the last time in 1981.

Others who worked as steady hands on Big Creek in the 1930s and 1940s included George Stephens, Dick Doidge, Ralph and Lloyd Bowler; Frank, Roy and Earl Brownjohn; Cecil Milliken, Leonard Gildner, Casey Jones, Charlie Mitchell, Bill

Theisen, Bill Fleming, Horace Coffey, Carl Marno, Percy Woolends, Jack Ross, Murray Taylor, Wally Johnson, Jim Bonner, Fred Walker, Brownie Perry, Tom Wilson, Leo Deihl, Jack Casselman; Ed, Richard and Roy Piltz; Charlie and Bill Case; Roy Wilson, Ray Davidson, Shorty Jenson, Andy Westwick, and Alfred George. Many more came and went through the summer months.

SKATING ON BIG CREEK
Veera Witte

There's noise galore near the starlit shore
Where the ice is smooth and strong,
For skating's right on the creek tonight
And the shouting's loud and long.

We're playing tag where the waters lag
To overflow and freeze:
If you listen well you can hear the yell
Adrift on the frosty breeze.

For the hills around throw back the sound,
And spruce nod silently,
While willows doze where the campfire glows
And beckons merrily.

Till stars grow dim o'er the mountain's rim
We laugh and fall and glide;
Then homeward go through the crusted snow
To the warmth and light inside.

With a bit o' chaff and many a laugh
We eat our midnight snack.
We've bruises, yes, but I rather guess
Next Sunday we'll be back

To play at tag where the waters lag
To overflow and freeze,
While echoes bound to the joyous sound
Adrift on the frosty breeze.

**Above: Marker used for cutting irrigation furrows before sprinkler irrigation.
Below: Abandoned steam engine at Chezacut.**

FRANK WITTE was only 5'6" and slight enough as a young man to ride as a jockey, but he was square-shouldered and strong and had a quick temper and steely eye that most men backed away from. He was witty, not only in name, well read, and a capable all-around man. He could also be moody, silent, and selfishly independent.

Frank Grover Witte was an American, born at Davenport, Washington, in April 1890, and was raised on a ranch in the Methow Valley (pronounced Met-how). But he chose to live his life a Canadian in the frontier cattle country of British Columbia. Shortly before his death at 72, he told his wife that if he could live his life over he would do it all again in just the same way.

One of Frank's tasks while growing up on his father's ranch in the Methow was herding beef cattle in the Cascade Mountains. His father took steers into the Slate Creek country for the summers where they were butchered to provide beef for the mines operating in the vicinity. It was young Frank's job to help drive the steers into the mountains and herd them there through the summer and fall.

Later, when Wittes had given up this practice, Frank, in partnership with another young man named Frank Therriault, tried the butcher business himself, leasing a building from his father who owned property in the town of Twisp and who ran a butcher shop there for many years. There wasn't enough business in the little town for two meat shops and trade was slow.

Leaving the Methow Valley for B.C. in 1912. Left to right: George Witte, Frank Witte, Frank Therriault, Sol Madures and Paul Therriault.

During the winter of 1912 advertisements boosting the Peace River district of northern B.C. caught the attention of the two restless young men. The promise of cheap land and unlimited opportunity fired the imagination of others as well, including Frank's father, George Witte, and Therriault's brother, Paul.

In May 1912 the group, joined by Sol Madures, all well-

Frank Witte at Twisp, Washington, before the B.C. adventure.

mounted and leading a packhorse, set off on an adventure that changed the course of Frank Witte's life. The other four men went back to the States in the end, but for Frank Witte the call to Canada was permanent.

Excitement ran high for the adventurers as they packed up, said goodbye and rode off towards the alluring unknown. Left at home on the ranch, George Witte's wife, Elsie, probably didn't share their enthusiasm. She had a younger son and daughter with her and a hired man to work on the ranch. Another daughter was away at college and the eldest, Hazel, was married and living nearby.

When the group reached Princeton in southern B.C. they laid over a day or two and Paul Therriault took a job at a livery stable. He decided to stay and keep working instead of moving on with the others. (Paul Therriault did come on to the Chilcotin the next year and worked at Chilco Ranch before returning to Washington.)

When the rest of the party reached Ashcroft, 150 miles farther on and some 250 miles from home, George Witte found a disappointing cable waiting for him at the telegraph office. It was from his wife and read: "Come home, hired man quit." Next day he and Sol Madures, who was getting tired of the trip, started on the long ride back to the Methow Valley. The two Franks kept on following their rainbow.

While resting their horses in Clinton, Witte and Therriault heard tales of good ranching country in the nearby Chilcotin and decided to have a look at it. Turning west, north of Clinton, they rode on to cross the Fraser River on the scow ferry to the Gang Ranch. At the Gang they went to work in the hayfields helping put up the first crop of alfalfa. When haying was done they moved on. At Norman Lee's, 70 miles into the Chilcotin, they again inquired about a job, telling Lee they were cowboys. "You'd have better luck getting work if you were plough boys," he caustically replied. He gave them a job cutting winter wood. After that they worked for Nellie Hance and her sons harvesting grain at Hanceville.

Frank Witte first became acquainted with Hattie Hance when she, with her brother Percy, friend Fanny Stone and others were making the annual horseback trip into the Tatlayoko Mountains to do assessment work on Mrs. Hance's iron claims. To the young Americans this looked like a good opportunity to see more of the country and they threw in their lot with the party. This light-hearted adventure determined Witte's future. Both Franks fell in love with the modest and beautiful Hattie Hance. She fell for Frank

Witte and this proved to be the one and only love of their lives. They were engaged and married the following year. Five years later Therriault married Witte's sister, Anna.

On October 8, 1913, Frank and Hattie's marriage took place in Bellingham, Washington. Hattie's family did not attend her wedding. Her mother disapproved of Hattie's decision to marry the handsome young cowboy from across the line who had no visible means of support. She favoured the established young Englishmen who were seeking her daughter's hand. (In due time Mrs. Hance and Frank Witte became loyal friends.) The newlyweds spent that fall and winter in Frank's home town where he worked with his father in the butcher business.

In the spring of 1914 Frank and Hattie and Frank Therriault, who had also spent the winter in Twisp, were ready to return to British Columbia. They started out for the Chilcotin, each with team and wagon, when the grass was green. At the border, Therriault was turned back and temporarily delayed as one of his horses failed the required test for glanders, a type of horse disease.

It took the young married couple a month to reach Hanceville with team and heavy wagon. After reaching Hanceville and visiting with Hattie's family, the Wittes began looking for a place of their own. Finding land in the Chilcotin even then was not easy and Frank and Hattie made many moves. In fact, Frank Witte was credited with building more log cabins around the country than any other one man. They lived at Alexis Creek where Frank worked on the first hospital; then at a place called "Cottonwood" on the north side of the Chilcotin River where their first child was born; and, finally, more permanently on a pre-emption on the south side which they called the "River Place," now part of Deer Creek Ranch. The other three children were born in quick succession while they lived here.

The Wittes worked hard on the raw land to get started, building a house, barn, fences, and other ranch buildings. In addition, Frank began with team and scraper to build a big ditch along the river bank to bring water from the Chilcotin with which he hoped to irrigate the river flat. It was never finished. He had ingeniously made and installed a large waterwheel using four-gallon coal-oil cans to lift water from the Chilcotin River to the land above, but its scope was limited.

Hattie found the River Place depressing and was never really happy there. Of necessity Frank worked away from home a good deal, freighting from Ashcroft for two or three weeks at a time, putting up hay by contract, or feeding cattle at some distant meadow. Hattie was isolated and alone, looking after the place by herself, tied down with babies or expecting one. Just across the river was the Anaham Indian Reserve and during flu epidemics she could hear the church bells tolling out the gloomy announcement of each frequent death and in winter see bodies being brought out and left on the river ice.

Coupled with that was a bachelor neighbour named Bob Miller, who, she was sure, was mentally unbalanced and who frequently stopped by when her husband was away. Miller rode a mare with a colt and a yearling following so she knew the tracks and often saw where he had passed by the house during the night. One evening when she was alone with the little children, Bob Miller came in and sat silently, opening and shutting his pocket knife while his eyes followed her about the room. When she suggested it was getting late and was time he went home, he announced that he intended to stay all night. "Oh, you can't do that, Bob." she countered, thinking quickly, "Frank has all the extra bedding with him."

"I don't need blankets," he answered, and went out to stake his horse.

Hattie quickly stashed the spare covers out of sight and, hiding the fear in her heart, offered him the guest room when he came back in. He said he would sleep in the kitchen. In her bedroom which opened off the kitchen, with her little ones sleeping close by, she sat up through the long night with her loaded six-shooter in her hand. There was no way to secure her door. Slowly, the tense dark hours passed and in the early morning she heard him go out the door and leave. Bob Miller did eventually go violently insane and it took three men to bring him in when he was committed to a mental institution.

One particularly bad year, the Wittes were wintering their cattle at the Grover Hance Meadow on Minton Creek and lost nearly everything they had. The hay was of poor quality and, along with deep snow and weeks of -30F weather, weakened their stock and one after another they died. It was a late spring and some of their cows perished after they were turned out – stuck in snow-drifts in May. When spring finally arrived Frank summerized their winter of misfortune with the words, "We've still got the kids."

With little money to work with, developing the dry river flats was slow and discouraging. One day Frank announced that he thought a swamp meadow would make a better poor man's ranch.

He'd decided, he said, that they should move to the Whitewater. Although this change would mean giving up her house to live with four small children in a one-room cabin 30 rocky miles beyond Big Creek with only a morose bachelor for a neighbour, Hattie welcomed the suggestion. So, near the Vedan Ranch in high lonely country Frank built another log cabin and they moved.

While living in this isolated place their only son, Duane, became violently ill. It appeared that he might have eaten snowberries that proved toxic to his system as these were growing near the cabin. Fortunately, Frank was home and he quickly got the horses while Hattie threw together a box of food and packed a suitcase. With the three little girls bundled in the back of the wagon and the sick baby cradled in his mother's arms, they faced a 75-mile journey with team and heavy iron-tired wagon, knowing with an unspeakable dread that, at best, it would be many hours before they reached help.

The first 30 miles of rough mountainous road to Robison's Ranch were the worst. Here they borrowed a lighter rig and, pushing the horses, continued through the night another 27 miles to Hanceville. Frank put his tired team in the barn and the girls were left with their grandmother while Hattie's brother, Judd, drove her and the sick child with a light buggy and fresh horses another 18 miles to the small hospital at Alexis Creek. Often through the long agonizing journey the young mother was frantically afraid that her little boy had died in her arms. But although he was dangerously ill, Dr. Wright performed a near miracle and saved his life. Hattie stayed at the simple little hospital with the doctor and nurse, Miss Goode, and through weeks of anxious attention Duane gradually recovered. He had to learn to walk all over again.

About a year and a half later, while the Wittes were camped in the Whitewater putting up hay on a swamp meadow, Frank's father came up from the States for a visit. He persuaded them to return to Twisp, Washington, and take over his butcher shop. Hattie and the children went back with George Witte in his car while Frank stayed behind to finish haying and make arrangements for the stock. He then went south by train.

Financially, the young couple did well in the Methow but their hearts were in the Chilcotin, especially since Frank had become a Canadian citizen four years earlier at the 150 Mile House. After a year they gave up the security of town life and headed back to the wilderness, although two of their little daughters had started school in Twisp. This time they made the trip in a

Frank and Hattie Witte with Hazel and Irene at Chilco Ranch.

Hattie at the River Place.

Willys Overland touring car and camped the first night on the Canadian side of Osoyoos Lake.

Frank and Hattie settled permanently with their family on the Anderson place in the community of Big Creek in 1925 and named it the Circle A O⊃ after their cattle brand. They were happy there. Hattie's sweet clear voice couldn't carry a tune but she often hummed and sang as she went about the hard and numerous tasks of pioneer living. She appreciated near neighbours and the cheery location with poplar trees where the birds sang and Big Creek rushing by. She was always thankful for the pure cold water brought from a well by a pump in her kitchen. The soft water made scrubbing the board floor and clothes on a washboard a little bit easier.

In November the following year, through Hattie's determined efforts, a school was opened on Big Creek with Blenkinsops, Wittes, and the two youngest Bambricks attending. The fathers had built a log schoolhouse in a central location above Bambrick Creek with a lean-to woodshed at the back. Frank made a table for the teacher's desk, benches, and a tall cupboard for books. Hattie hung curtains made from flour sacks, dyed green, at the windows, and Bambricks papered the inside walls. Blenkinsops did their share as well and the three families involved donated all necessities.

Frank Witte with freight team and wagons, headed home from Redstone after a trip to Ashcroft freighting for Andy Stuart.

**Lowering the Union Jack at Big Creek School, with teacher May Currie.
The flag was raised each morning and taken down after school.**

The Government paid the teacher's salary ($1,800 a year) and supplied the children's desks, canvas-backed blackboards and the Union Jack which was carefully hoisted and taken down each school day. The T. Eaton Company sent free a white wall clock that hung above the side windows to faithfully tick off the hours through the seven years of the school's life. Wound once a week, it was called an eight-day clock. Frank Witte cut out two miles of new road to make a direct link with the new school for his children walking from the Circle A. This route is now officially named Witte Road. Frank and Hattie had one son, Duane, and three daughters: Irene (Bliss), Hazel (Henry-Litterick), and Veera (Bonner). They were all baptized in the Anglican faith and confirmed in the little Anglican Church of St. James at Big Creek, at the time the only Protestant church in the Chilcotin.

Wittes built a roomy log house on the Circle A, as well as barn, loft, and outbuildings, all still in use. A bright pre-fab lumber kitchen was added later, replacing the low log kitchen which had been Anderson's cabin, moved from its original location under the hill. Hattie worked to make the family home cosy and attractive with flowers and bright curtains and cushions, often made from flour sacks and dyed a cheery color. Throughout their lifetime their home was a hospitable place where a warm welcome greeted family, friend and stranger alike. Many a happy sociable evening was spent in their comfortable sitting room, softly lit by an Aladdin lamp. Guests often stayed overnight, a day or two, or longer.

251

Big Creek School in 1929. Left to right: Irene Witte, Evie Bambrick, Hazel Witte, Douglas Kinkead, Veera Witte, Duane Witte, Neville Blenkinsop, Sissie Bambrick and Fay Blenkinsop.

Staying overnight at the Circle A meant sourdough hotcakes for breakfast served with steaming brown sugar syrup and perhaps thin, well-peppered beef steaks. Hattie's sourdough hotcakes were made from genuine Yukon sourdough, started with flour, sugar and water, with no yeast. They were light and delicious and everybody loved them. Hattie kept a "starter" of sourdough going, year in and year out, and made hotcakes every morning. If she put something different on the breakfast table for a change, Frank would look around and ask: "Where are the hotcakes?"

For many years Hattie made sourdough bread as well, but after fast-rising yeast came out she preferred that and baked the best bread in the country. But it was the sourdough hotcakes that everyone remembered. (Carolyn Hotchkiss, Witte's niece in the Methow Valley, and Marianne Drift, of Cariboo and the Yukon, have kept a starter of Hattie Witte's sourdough going for 30 years.)

As well as building up the little ranch, Frank worked away from home at times to enable them to run their small bunch of cows debt free. He hired out with his big team a few summers on government roads, worked at the Sky Ranch helping Gus Piltz build a new hip-roof barn and on Piltz's ongoing project of leveling the big swamp. He and his wife took haying contracts at such places as the Whitewater Meadow for Chilco Ranch, and Green Mountain Meadow for Fosberys.

At their home place the land was broken up with walking plough for dry farming. They pre-empted the Circle A meadow in the Whitewater and later had the Robison place on Bambrick Creek which Hattie inherited after looking after old Jack Robison for many years. Frank's reluctance to go into debt prevented them from expanding further. He had the Bambrick place rented for five years and could have bought it at a low price from former neighbour Lilian Bambrick and her sons, Arthur and Frank. This decision was supported by his wife.

Like most ranchers, Witte raised horses for his own use. He branded them with the dollar sign: $. A new Model A Ford was purchased in 1929, replacing the Willys Overland. Other cars and trucks followed but none was as exciting as that first new Ford.

In winter evenings Frank sometimes made braided rawhide ropes. They required a lot of work but were strong and lasted for years. The process started with soaking a cow hide in the creek to loosen the hair which then had to be scraped off. Cutting the tough hide into even strips was not easy, then the arduous task of braiding the long strands which were usually fastened securely to the ceiling of a meadow cabin. The strips of hide had to be kept damp and supple throughout. One Christmas Hattie found one of these ropes with her name on it tied to the Christmas tree. It led out through the partly opened door and was fastened to the hackamore

Hattie and Frank Witte on Midnight and Taseko in front of their new log house at the Circle A.

Buck fence built by Frank Witte and Phillip Myers in the 1950s at the Circle A and still standing. It was patterned after the fences Witte admired at Anahim Lake.

rope on a snappy little chestnut saddle horse – her Christmas present from her husband.

In 1932 Frank took over the mail contract between Big Creek and Hanceville and 10 years later his son took over from him. Duane ranched in partnership with his dad and they went into guiding American hunters as a sideline. In later times Frank was interested in Brahma cattle and bought a purebred bull and cow from Washington. When the first bull died, he bought a second one. This could not be described as a very successful venture as the cold winters were hard on the short-haired animals. The cross-bred calves were tough. They were small at birth but grew big and strong – and wild! Two half Brahma three-year-old steers from Duane's herd caused a commotion at the Williams Lake Stockyards one year by jumping back and forth over the seven-foot fences in a wild bid for freedom, once landing in a pen of terrified pigs!

Frank Witte suffered a stroke in July 1961 and his wife cared for him in Williams Lake. Though confined to bed, he still longed to be back in the country he loved. He passed away on December 2, 1962, and was buried on the Circle A after a service in the Big Creek Hall. During the graveside ceremony on a hill overlooking his little ranch, a campfire blazed where Indians who had come by team and wagon warmed themselves, horse bells rang in the field below and chickadees sang in the pines. Snow that had held off all fall fell that night, covering the freshly turned earth with a blanket of white and the air turned colder. "It's almost," Hattie said, "as if winter waited."

Respecting Frank's wishes, his grave is unfenced:

"Let cattle rub my headstone round,
Let coyotes wail their kin,
Let horses paw upon the mound -
But do not fence me in."

After her husband's death, Hattie continued to rent an apartment in Williams Lake. She enjoyed living in town and was always busy. She looked after the King Koin Laundromat for five years and then did janitor work in the Johnson Block for her rent until she suffered a stroke in December 1974. She died on March 31, 1975. A woman of faith – gracious, vibrant, and beautiful to the end. She is buried in Williams Lake Cemetery.

The Circle A Ranch was passed on to Duane's son, Franklin, by his grandparents. It now belongs to Franklin's sons, Morgan and Tyler, and their mother, Iris Witte.

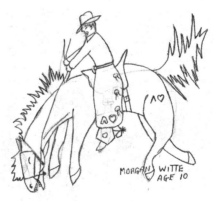

MORGAN WITTE
AGE 10

BORN TO BUCK: A mare called Alamando
by Duane Witte

I had a real pretty mare once long ago that I named Alamando after a famous racehorse in Washington, U.S.A. She had a big round white spot in her forehead, black points, and two white feet behind. When she was about four years old I got her in with the rest of the bunch to break her to lead. She was wild and snorty. When I rode into the horse corral and threw a loop over her head she made a high dive, tripped on a flat rock and smashed all her front bottom teeth out, except one that I had to pull so that she could close her jaws to eat. After she was broke to lead I turned her out on the range again. When I got her back in after a couple of months she was good and fat – she was managing okay without those bottom front teeth.

About this time, Dad and I and a young fellow named Harold Coburn were planning a trip through the mountains to look for hunting territory. I decided to take Alamando along as a spare saddle horse. I had ridden her a few times in the corral and figured the trip would do her good.

I led her for the first few miles to kind of get the kinks out of her back and Dad took the packhorse. Going up the mountain to Dick Meadow we stopped and I switched my rigging onto Alamando and got on her – the first time outside a corral. She bucked a little but not bad. I rode her the rest of that day and off and on during the trip. She seemed to be gentling down and coming along fine. I used a snaffle bit on her to start with but by the time we got back I was using my loose-jawed spade bit. I always wore spurs. Horses like the sound of them and you can "talk" to a horse without using them rough or mean. I always had good spurs and liked two and one-half inch rowels with lots of points on them as they very seldom hurt a horse. Dad and I used tapedaros over our stirrups in those days. They keep your feet dry and protect your boots from brush and sticks. A lot of horses are scared of them though, hanging down below your boots. They make extra weight on your feet so you have to be careful with your spurs.

After we got back from the mountain trip, I turned Alamando in the pasture as I had a good stud at the time and wanted to raise a colt from the two of them. Some time later I needed to make a ride to Siwash Meadow to look for horses. When the mount I was intending to use turned up lame, I took Alamando. After I saddled her up and stepped on in front of the house she lit right into bucking. This bucking surprised me as she had been coming along so well.

She went high and wide, then sunfished so low I could touch the ground with my hand. Pretty soon she bucked me off — and my hand wasn't the only thing touching the ground! Leo Diehl, who was helping me for a few days, was watching. I picked myself up, caught her and led her up to the bronc corral. My knee was bothering me – it sometimes went out of joint – and I was riding a longer stirrup than usual. I shortened my stirrup leathers a hole and got on her in the corral. Encouraged by her success in the yard she went at it again, but this time I stayed with her. When she quit bucking I opened the gate and headed towards Siwash Meadow. Leo mounted and headed out to cross Big Creek and look for some other horses we needed.

For me and Alamando it was a rough day. Alamando bucked with me 17 times on that 15-mile ride. She just wouldn't quit. And that mare could buck! It took me all my time to stay with her. A sun-fishing horse is hard to ride – when they parallel the ground it throws you off balance and gives you the feeling they're going to flop right over on top of you.

When we finally got as far as the meadow I kind of forgot about horse hunting. I was played out and felt too sick to go any farther. My insides were so shook up I was spitting blood and began to wonder how I'd ever make it home. I got off and tied the mare up and lay down under a tree for a half hour or so. The thought of riding her home gnawed at my twisted inards. I took my taps off and cached them behind a log – I thought that might help. Then I climbed on her and turned back the way we'd come. Her mouth was getting sore by now and maybe because we were headed in the right direction she only bucked with me three times.

A few miles from home a young fellow named Hugh Mac-Donald caught up to me in a pick-up and stopped to talk. "That's sure a good looking horse you're riding," he said. "Do you want to sell her?" He didn't ask about her disposition. I'd have been happy to sell her on the spot, but thinking I shouldn't act too anxious I answered kind of slow: "Yeah, I guess so. If you give me $85." That was a good price for a horse then. He said he wanted her, and came up the next day to clinch the deal and take her away.

He came into the house first and paid me. Then we went up to the corral and Hugh threw his saddle on the handsome bay and got on. Her mouth was sore from all that bucking the day before and she walked around the corral quiet enough. Then he rode over to where I was standing and asked if he could borrow my spurs to wake her up a bit. I said "Sure!"

When he mounted her again and touched her with the spurs she threw him so high and so fast she didn't even get to sun-fishing. He came down hard and decided not to get back on. He never did ride her. She went back on the range and one spring, years later, I found her bones. I could tell her skull because of those missing teeth on the lower jaw. I hung that jaw in a little jackpine tree at a

Duane Witte carrying the Big Creek mail from Hanceville with packhorse in winter.

meadow we called Seven Mile. Every time I rode by I thought of Hugh's $85 and a tough little mare called Alamando that was born to buck. She could have earned her living coming out of the rodeo chutes – and I would loved to have seen her – but instead spent her life running free in the Chilcotin hills.

JACK TAGART was born February 3, 1901, in North Battleford, Saskatchewan. Little is known about his early life except that he served overseas in the World War One at what must have been a very young age. In the late 1930s he came to the Chilcotin where he worked for Chilco Ranch on the Deer Creek place long enough to earn him the title of "Deer Creek Jack." He moved on in the 1940s to work for Newton and then to Purjues in Nemiah Valley. Here he took up a small homestead at the mouth of Elkins Creek, but after a few years sold out to Purjues and went back to Chilco Ranch.

258

Jack Tagart tending the Bell Ranch store.

As a loyal employee of John Wade, then owner of the Chilco, Tagart spent a number of years managing the Bell Ranch at Big Creek, which included selling gas and running the little store. Always an outdoor man, Tagart had never had much to do with pen and paper but he tackled the job with good-natured determination and was an unusual and entertaining store keeper. Many Big Creek youngsters were treated to chocolate bars charged up against Jack's wages. Gas was measured out in a gallon can. Customers often had to honk the horn and wait patiently for Jack to come in from irrigating or haying in the big fields.

He accumulated a small bunch of cattle which he ran on shares with the Purjues in Nemiah Valley but finally sold them all.

Deer Creek Jack left the Chilcotin in the late 1950s and moved to Hodgson Road in Williams Lake where he kept a few horses, two dogs and a cat until his death in 1981. He loved animals and always gave them the best of care.

He left no known relatives and made no big waves on the Sands of Time, but all who knew Jack Tagart remember him kindly.

NO WAY OUT BUT HORSEBACK
Ordeal in Hungry Valley

Broken bones, suffering and hardship were common factors in pioneer living. But at a time well past the frontier era in the Chilcotin, Jim Bonner suffered an ordeal perhaps equal to anything in those early years.

Jim was riding for Dick Church gathering cattle in the fall of 1942. He and Jimmy Rosette, who was cowboying for the Gang Ranch, were bringing strays out of Hungry Valley, a remote alpine glen at the foot of the Coast Range not far from the head of Big

Jim Bonner driving cattle in an alpine valley.

Creek. His horse fell with him on a frosty sidehill, shattering Jim's leg between knee and ankle. Rosette quickly rode over. He was able to get Bonner back into the saddle as there was no way out but horseback.

Pain of the unsupported broken limb must have been almost unbearable as the two men rode about 12 miles to the Fosbery Meadow. They stayed all night in an old cabin. Here Rosette fashioned a makeshift splint and bandaged the leg to it as best he could. Next day another grueling 12-mile horseback ride lay ahead for the injured man as they started on their way through jackpine and swamp to Sky Ranch, every movement sending a fresh shock of pain through Jim's body. Next was a 20-mile ride over a rough road in the back of Piltz's pickup truck to Church's Ranch at Big Creek..

But the long painful ordeal wasn't over. It had been raining and snowing and the ungraveled Big Creek Road was almost impassable. Stretched out on the back seat of his car, driven by Cecil Henry, Jim Bonner endured another nine hours suffering to make the last 75 miles into the Williams Lake hospital — and relief after three torturous days and nights. Throughout the ordeal the strong outdoorsman was patient, uncomplaining and quietly courageous.

ROUND-UP TIME
Veera Witte

Cow-horses sleek and shiny,
Saddled up and ready stand,
Waiting for the ring of boot heels
And a cowboy's gentle hand.

Cow-dogs, too, a little restless,
Alert and anxious wait nearby,
Lest the riders leave without them
They must keep a watchful eye.

For it's Autumn, and the round-up
Is beginning once again –
Cowboys young and older riding
In the sunshine and the rain.

Long, hard days out on the ranges
Where the lakes and swamps abound;
Over hillsides, rocks and windfalls,
Where'er cattle may be found.

Starlight nights beside the campfire,
Saddle horses grazing near,
Boots and blankets stiff and frosty
When the morn dawns cold and clear.

Cattle on the move are bawling,
Sunlight gilds the noisy day
As the cowboys crowd behind them
In the old familiar way.

Down the dusty trail to ranches
Where the women watch and wait,
And the old sweet ties of home are found
Inside the pasture gate.

Sketches by Hazel Henry Litterick.

HISTORY OF THE BIG CREEK ROAD

The recorded history of the Big Creek Road that climbs south of Chilco Ranch to the Big Creek country, now sometimes called the Fletcher Lake Road, goes back to 1901 when over six miles of 12-foot right-of-way was cut out by the government and a small portion graded to eight feet. When H. E. Church took his wagon over this route in 1903, taking only half a load at a time, he described it in his memoirs as "an old Indian trail that had been cut out where it went through the timber, just wide enough for a wagon to squeeze through."

A bridge was built across the Chilcotin River at Hanceville in the winter of 1892-93. In those days traffic from the Chilcotin for the rail-head at Ashcroft travelled across that bridge, up through the open country that is now Chilco Ranch pastures, crossing Big Creek on a log bridge built about 1894 at what became the Scallon place and crossing the Fraser at the Gang Ranch where a scow ferry was in operation, thence to Clinton and Ashcroft. This was known as the Ashcroft-Hanceville Road. Those who had settled on the north side of Big Creek were, however, cut off from even this avenue of travel.

The sum of $100 was allotted by the government in 1903 to have a wagon trail made up the north side of Big Creek, probably near the present Lockhart Road, to connect these settlers with the main road near the Big Creek Bridge at the Scallon place. But for this small sum only trees here and there could be cut out, just wide enough for a wagon. H. E. Church took the first conveyance over this make-shift route when he moved his wife and family in to his pre-emption in October 1903. It appears as if this connection was not long in use. A second bridge was built farther up Big Creek at the Erickson place in 1911 to accommodate the growing community of Big Creek. It connected them with the main road to the outside – the Ashcroft-Hanceville Road, via the Gang Ranch.

(Lockhart Road was named for Dave Lockhart of Williams Lake who logged at Riske Creek and Big Creek in the 1950s and 1960s. He was a well-liked, community-minded man and a successful operator. He built this road into his last logging show before retiring about 1983. Art Jackson did the construction work.)

The most direct route from Big Creek to the settlement of Hanceville, to trading posts, police, and Chilcotin neighbours, was via the wagon trail that dropped down from the 1,200 m (4,000 foot) Big Creek Plateau to Chilco Ranch. As settlement grew there must have been some improvements to the "old Indian trail" but it was to be 12 years before any appreciable change took place.

In 1914 high rocks and stumps were removed to allow the first car to come over this road to Big Creek. Jack Temple, of the Beaver Ranch, made several trips over it in his high-wheeled Cadillac that summer. Then, apparently another 12 years went by before the road was improved again.

In 1927 a road crew of seven or eight men under foreman Ross Cullen of Clinton and later his son, Bert, began total reconstruction of the old road past Chilco Ranch up the mountain to Big Creek. They were three summers on the job before the road was completed in 1928. During this time the crew also had their usual maintenance work to take care of at Dog Creek, Alkali Lake, and Canoe Creek.

Many familiar names were among the crew at the "road camp' who pitched their tents alongside the job and moved as the work progressed: Jimmy Scallon, Grover Hance, Tommy Paxton (the cook), and Frank Witte. Right-of-way was cut out and then rocks and stumps blasted out. Frank Witte drove his team of four horses on the road plough and grader. Then came the rock pickers, Grover Hance and others, throwing loose rocks off the road bed. A rocky face beyond Chilco Ranch's West Pasture was tough going as most of it had to be blasted – Cullen and Jimmy Scallon's job. The resulting grade, known as the "Rock Cut" was steep and narrow. Once up the hill the new road followed fairly close to the old one. The road throughout is the route we travel today. Yet another 12 years went by before any of these 20 miles were graveled.

During the spring and summer of 1940-41, when time allowed, local ranchers set up a base camp near the top of the hill and, using teams and wagons and Gerald Blenkinsop's one-ton truck, graveled the narrow, winding Big Creek Hill. The loading and some of the unloading was done by hand with shovels. The wagons were fitted with loose floor boards that were tipped to let the gravel fall though as the team moved along. Wages were paid by the government and in some cases taxes were worked out. Local housewife Annie Hutchinson did most of the cooking.

With the advent of logging and increased traffic in the 1950s, the two miles of blind corners and switchbacks on the hill, in most places too narrow to pass, became dangerous and badly in need of rebuilding. So, once again, improvements took place as Dick Church's TD9 bulldozer went to work widening out the grades and corners. A bad spot near the Chilco known as "Crazy Man's Gulch" was filled in and rebuilt. This sharp corner and steep rise derived its name, so the story goes, when George McDonald, who travelled this route from Chilco Ranch where he was working to his pre-emption on Big Creek, tried to fill the ravine in with logs. The Stoney Indians noted this futile effort and dubbed him "Crazy man" and the name stayed with the gulch. When a fill was put in and the road straightened in the 1970s the name was more or less forgotten.

The old dirt track built for light vehicles, and ungraveled except for the winding Big Creek Hill, couldn't stand up to the wet-weather cycle and the heavier traffic of the 1940s and 1950s. Through those years battling bad roads was a fact of life for the people of Big Creek. On community outings it was common for all the families to meet at a given time and drive the road in a convoy to help each other and be sure everyone got through. Road conditions occasionally made news in the *Williams Lake Tribune*:

"When a truck and two men from the Public Works Dept. at Alexis Creek came up to repair a bridge near Breckness Ranch, they found that we aren't fooling when we sound off now and then about our roads. They were stuck in the mud three times but rescued by Dick Church and his tractor and finally made a safe getaway. But the driver was bare-footed.

"Stepping out of his bogged-down vehicle he sank in the mire to his knees and came up without shoes or socks. Never found 'em either. They were down too deep to be located."

July 10, 1952:

"Mud, sweat and gears wasn't the battle cry of Britain, but it would do for motorists trying to get in or out of Big Creek these days. The lack of effort on the part of the P.W.D. makes us wonder if they are waiting for the low-priced helicopter to solve our road problems. Mr. and Mrs. M. Yule of Spokane driving up to visit Mr. and Mrs. A. C. Henry, and two parties coming to Mons Lake Lodge had to be ferried in by trucks in which they could just barely get through. We like to think of our district as a little paradise but we don't want it as inaccessible as Shangri-la."

Finally in the late 1950s a thin layer of gravel was spread over the main road and residents rejoiced in an all-weather highway. When hydro power came to Big Creek in 1979 nearly 20 years

Two-horse power to the rescue.

later, the road was gazetted by the Department of Highways. Further improvements have continued, widening, cutting back corners, trees and undergrowth, reshaping, straightening and graveling. The old Indian trail that guided the pioneers to Big Creek, up the fir-clad mountain and through the pine forest beyond would be hard to recognize.

When a post office opened at Big Creek in 1907, the mail route to Big Creek was established via Ericksons and Scallons, joining the Ashcroft-Hanceville Road. The telephone line, when it was extended to Big Creek in 1938, also came this long way around to accommodate these ranchers. The line was on poles through the miles of open country but hooked onto trees where it passed through the timber. This line eventually became uneconomical to repair and in 1967 was replaced by an underground wire along the shorter Big Creek-Fletcher Lake Road. Moisture collecting through cracks in the coating of the underground wire caused constant problems and, in 1987, the telephone line was strung on the hydro poles. In December of that same year dial telephones replaced the toll system at Big Creek.

The old wagon road through Farwell Canyon to Big Creek was completely rebuilt in the late 1960s by the Ministry of Forests and the logging companies, giving Big Creek an alternate access to Highway 20.

266

This Forestry Access Road follows fairly close to the old dirt wagon road that ran for many years from Lower Big Creek through Sugar Cane Jacks, Jameson Meadow, and the Gang Ranch summer range country to Farwell Canyon. Here the grade was a narrow, precipitous track sitting on the very edge of the plunging cliffs and balancing precariously on clay ridges with a perpendicular drop on either side. A narrow log bridge, built by the Gang Ranch, was slung between the cliffs at the bottom. This steep grade was built with team and scraper for travel with horses. Beef drives from Big Creek moved this way, and Bob Fosbery took the first car over it in 1913. Numerous other motor vehicles cautiously assaulted its depths and heights over the years. In later times, Bruce Watt regularly drove it in a rickety pickup with faulty brakes; Duane Witte nonchalantly took a renovated school bus down the south side and back out again; and, with a little road work, Hodgson trucks hauled heavy, awkward loads over it, sometimes jacking around the sharp corners, to service the Trethewey-Wells logging camp at the Dry Farm near the mouth of the Chilcotin River. But, in all truth, this incredibly steep, narrow and sinuous track on both sides of the river was better suited to a saddle horse.

In 1965 a huge slide took out the old bridge. The entire hillside

Old bridge over the Chilcotin River in Farwell Canyon built by the Gang Ranch. A Bell Ranch beef drive from Big Creek is crossing en route to the sale ring in Williams Lake in 1935.

Hodgson truck on the narrow canyon hill, servicing the Trethewey-Wells logging camp at the Dry Farm in 1958.

Just across the bridge. One of the drivers, Vernon James, at left.

a few hundred yards below, on the south side of the Chilcotin, tumbled into the river, damming the water completely for about three days. The river backed up over the top of the old bridge and when the pressure of this huge volume of water cut a new channel north of the slide, the force of the receding flood took out the bridge. When work started on the new Farwell Canyon Road, a temporary structure was put in until the new bridge a little farther upstream was completed.

268

Bridge over the Fraser River at the Gang Ranch, one of the few old-style bridges still in use. This bridge replaced the ferry at the mouth of Churn Creek about 1913.

The Chilcotin River in Farwell Canyon.

Now a sweeping 8-mile grade swings down to the Chilcotin River, across the solid new bridge and through long, easy curves up the other side. The Farwell Canyon Road throughout is a wide, well-built and well-maintained scenic route that is a great asset to the country. Many loads of logs from the Big Creek country go over it every year.

The road on to the Gang Ranch is now rerouted, rebuilt and graveled and in the 1990s is an easy ride.

Kathleen Telford with twin sons, Norman at left and Bill.

Below, left to right: Mrs. Perry Martin and friend, Anna Graham, Frances and Duke Martin.

ALEXIS CREEK
by Kathleen Telford

We owe thanks to the late Kathleen Graham Telford for writing the original history of Alexis Creek in 1958. Kathleen was born and raised at Alexis Creek and much of the history she recorded was drawn from her own knowledge of the area. Many of her stories appear here as she wrote them. Thanks to Bill and Jack Bliss, Bayliffs, and Mulvahills, for their help in editing, enlarging and updating this section.

Alexis Creek is the largest village now in the Chilcotin. It is beautifully situated on a bench overlooking the milky blue waters of the Chilcotin River. On the south, across the river, are the extensive Alexis Creek flats and to the north there is a rimrock running along the top of the hills almost the full length of the valley to the west end of Bull Canyon. This canyon is a scenic spot about three miles in length, now reserved as a park, with the river running along the south side and sheer rock cliffs on the north. There are several caves in these cliffs, some ice-bound the year round. In the early 1900s there were grizzly bear skulls found there and many arrowheads and relics and old Indian weapons from earlier Indian skirmishes and wars fought there. Battle Bluff is said to have got its name from a skirmish in the early days between the Chilcotin Indians and the Shuswaps.

The Chilcotins were camped fishing at Siwash Bridge when one young buck set off on foot down the valley to see an Indian maiden at Hance's Canyon. When he reached Bull Canyon he noticed a glow above the canyon wall and, sneaking around to investigate, discovered an encampment of Shuswap warriors. He quickly alerted the Chilcotin tribe. They stole up the mountain to come in behind the enemy, attacked and forced the Shuswaps over the bluff, killing many and driving the survivors from the valley. About 1944 when there was an army camp in the canyon, the soldiers used shale from under Battle Bluff for graveling roads and came upon a human skeleton – presumably from the Indian war

Mr. and Mrs. Alex Graham.

days. About six miles farther up the road a highway construction crew dug up three more skeletons of an early age. One was in a wooden box near the old Hudson's Bay Post site. The discovery was puzzling; none of the local Indians knew anything about a grave there and, in the very early days, where did they get lumber for a coffin?

Bull Canyon got its name from the first ranchers in the district who used it as a bull pasture. It was a natural pasture, all they had to do was put in a fence at each end of the canyon. In those days the main road went along the top of the mountain, bypassing Bull Canyon.

Pioneers of Alexis Creek were ALEXANDER GRAHAM and ARCHIBALD MACAULEY. They were brought up on neighbouring farms in County Antrim, Ireland. They were 18 and 20 respectively when bitten by the pioneering bug and left Ireland in the spring of 1886. They came to work near Tacoma, Washington. The following spring they headed for the Cariboo, coming through Vancouver, B.C. when it was in the logging stage and all stumps. Alex Graham was offered about 60 acres of land in what is now the heart of the city for $40,000. He didn't have the cash.

They arrived at Ashcroft via the C.P.R. in the spring of 1887 and trekked up the Cariboo with packs on their backs, headed for the Chilcotin. At Soda Creek they crossed the Fraser River in a dugout canoe made from a log. Alex Graham worked on the With-row Ranch below Hance's for two years, while Archie Macauley went on to Alexis Creek where he pre-empted property later known as the A1 Ranch.

Anna Scott Harvey, a schoolteacher, left her home in County Down, Ireland, and sailed for Canada on September 9, 1889, to join her childhood sweetheart, Alex Graham. They were married in Clinton at the Clinton Hotel by Reverend Bruce from Barkerville who happened to be passing through on his way to England. Padres were then unknown in the Chilcotin.

Mrs. Graham came across the Fraser River at Soda Creek as a young bride in a flat-bottomed boat, accompanied by a ram that was being brought to the Withrow Ranch. She never went out again to civilization for 21 years until there was a bridge put across the Fraser. She was the first white woman at Alexis Creek, and the only one for many years. Her nearest neighbour was Mrs. O. T. Hance 20 miles to the east down the Chilcotin River at Hanceville.

They came to the Withrow (River) Ranch, then owned by Drummond and Beaumont. Alex Graham worked there for two years, handling cattle, horses, and pigs, and also ground wheat in the Sam Withrow mill and made flour and their own cracked wheat porridge mixture. Two years later they moved in with Archie Macauley as partners in the A1 Ranch. Alex Graham bought 50 head of cattle from the Withrow Ranch and brought them to Alexis Creek. After a few years in partnership with Macauley, Alex Graham took up a homestead near what is now called Graham Mountain and Graham Meadows.

They built their first log cabin there and put up hay for the stock. Later, Bob Graham, Alex's younger brother, took up 160 acres where the village of Alexis Creek is today. He held it for Alex, and they built a home place there and gradually accumulated more land and more stock. They drove the cattle to the Ashcroft Market, sleet overhead and muck underfoot, no holding corrals, no stopping houses, 12 hours a day in the saddle, mowitch (deer) and bannock to eat, a makeshift tent and blanketless bed. No wagon road, no bridges, herding stampeding steers (mostly three- and four-year olds) through the cold waters of the Fraser River down at the Gang Ranch Crossing. There was limitless range, knee-high with bunchgrass which could be mown anywhere in the valley, numerous wild flowers, and abundant game.

Alex Graham spent 47 years building his ranch to 1,000 head of stock by 1927, when Duke Martin took it over. Graham then moved to the Armstrong Ranch three miles west. He was made Justice of the Peace for the district about 1889 and held that office for nearly 50 years.

The Grahams had two daughters, Francis Matilda, born 1891 at Alexis Creek, and Kathleen Alexandra, 10 years later at Hanceville. The girls helped in every way on the ranch, from breaking horses to rounding up cattle. Kathleen married George Telford and they took over the Armstrong Ranch. She became a graduate nurse, and for a time after her husband's death in 1948 managed the Red Cross Hospital at Alexis Creek.

Francis married Duke Martin and lived her life on the ranch where she was born. They had no children. George and Kathleen Telford had five children: Louise, Olive, twins Norman and William, and Robert. The girls married and left the Chilcotin. Bill married Edna Hoare who was teaching at Alexis Creek. They moved to Williams Lake where Bill became a foreman with the Department of Highways. They have five children. Norman married Valerie Jaynes and they continued with the Telford Ranch. The log house built by Armstrong where Telfords made their home was 100 years old in 1992. Norman and Valerie have now built a fine new house. They have three daughters, Beverley, Carol, and Jennifer. Robert (Bobbie) Telford lives at Alexis Creek.

KIN NAUIE from Peking, China, came to Alexis Creek in 1903, crossing the Fraser River in a canoe a few miles from the present Chimney Creek Bridge, and walking in from there. He worked for Alex Graham from 1903 until 1933 before returning to China to visit his wife and family there. When he returned to Alexis Creek in 1935 he found his boss had died, so he started working for Duke Martin on the old Graham Ranch and stayed nearly 20 years. (Alexander Graham died in 1934 and is buried in the Masonic Plot in Williams Lake. His wife, Anna Scott Harvey, died in 1950 and is interred in the same plot beside her husband. Daughter Francis Matilda Martin, who died in 1945, also lies there.)

ARCHIBALD MACAULEY married Elizabeth Hodges from County Antrim, Ireland in 1897. They built up the A1 Ranch just east of Alexis Creek. They had two daughters. Varied were their experiences in those days: Archie traded in furs with the Indians and also collected some live foxes which were shipped out to start fox farms. He built up his ranch to about 500 head, then sold in 1924 to Spencer of the Chilco Ranch. Archie Macauley was generous and trusting, lending money to help others and was liked by his help.

Mr. and Mrs. Macauley both died in Victoria in the 1940s. Their first daughter, Eileen Elizabeth, was born at Alexis Creek in 1902. She married Provincial Policeman Christopher Jacklin in Victoria where they made their home. She died in 1948. Jessie Claire Macauley was born in 1907 at Alexis Creek and married Ray Ditchburn in Victoria in the 1930s.

HUGH PEEL BAYLIFF came from England from a well-to-do aristocratic family. He worked on the Roper Ranch at Cherry Creek near Kamloops, B.C., before coming to Chilcotin. In 1886 he took a string of packhorses to Ulgatcho for Tom Hance to bring back furs from the Indians. He spent the first winter alone in a cabin overlooking the Chilcotin River at a place later known as Hillside.

In the spring of 1887 he was attracted to the present site of the Bayliff Ranch. The Chilcotin River was in flood and the acres of self-irrigating land looked attractive after the dry belt of the Kamloops country. Another enticement was evidence of an earlier C.P.R. survey line right through the property. There were great hopes of a railway going through the Chilcotin, but the difficult terrain and war-like Indians ended that dream.

Bayliff brought his first heifers into the country from the Roper Ranch with the assistance of the Shuswap Indians. All the streams enroute had to be forded and the cowboys had to swim the cattle across the Fraser River at the Gang Ranch. As the Shuswaps were afraid of the Chilcotin Indians and would come no farther, they roped and branded all the heifers there and Bayliff was left to bring the drive on alone. His brand was Bar Eleven, registered in August 1891 and it is still used on the Bayliff ranch.

In 1888, Norman Lee went in partnership with Bayliff on the Chilanko Ranch and started a store to trade with the Indians. After a few years the partnership broke up and Bayliff and Lee flipped a coin to see who would buy the other out. Norman Lee won and made a hasty trip back to England to try to raise the money. He was unsuccessful. In 1891 Bayliff returned to England and brought back not only the necessary funds to buy Lee's share of the holding, but also a bride – Gertrude Tyndle. She was the daughter of the editor of *The London Times*.

Mrs. Bayliff was a great asset to the pioneering community. She had some knowledge of medicine, was a skilled rider and, riding sidesaddle, helped with the cattle roundups. She had her own two racehorses that she entered in the races at Becher's Prairie at Riske Creek and often brought home trophies.

Hugh Bayliff on his favorite saddle horse, Strayshot, in front of their rambling old house. The Bayliff family and the Durrell family of the Wineglass Ranch received Century Ranch Awards from the B.C. Government, given to ranches that have been in operation for a century or longer.

Hugh Bayliff was also an excellent rider. Old-timers said that in his young days he would ride 40 miles to top off a bucking bronc that no one else could master. He was skillful with a rope as well. The Bayliffs kept up their traditional aristocratic lifestyle on the frontier which included playing polo and always dressing for dinner at a table set with silver and fine china.

The Bayliffs' only son, Gabriel Thomas Lane, was born in 1898. At nine he was sent back to England to go to school at Charterhouse. In 1916 he enlisted in the British Army with a commission in the Tank Corp and became a prisoner-of-war in Germany for a year. In 1919 he returned to Canada and home.

After the war the Bayliffs built a big house on the ranch. They had purchased Tom Hance's old sawmill and lumber for their new house was cut with it. (This old sawmill is now on display at the Agricultural Museum in Fort Langley.) The boards were handplaned by Stuart and Gordon Mackay, two young Englishmen from London. In 1923, a beautiful wedding was held in this house when Gabriel (Gay) Bayliff married Dorothy Dyson, only daughter of

Colonel and Mrs. Dyson from Kent, England. Friends and neighbours came from miles around to the wedding. After the festivities the couple left for a honeymoon trip in a 1917 Dodge car, one of the very few in the country.

When Hugh Bayliff died in 1934, Gay inherited the 3,000-acre Chilanko Ranch and continued raising Hereford cattle. Gay carried on the family traditions and was active in beef circles. Dorothy Bayliff was a gracious and lovely lady who was equally at home presiding over a tea table or riding horseback rounding up cattle. She cooked for as many as 16 men in haying time.

Dorothy and Gay had two sons, Timothy and Anthony, (always shortened to Tim and Tony). They kept a Chinese cook, Chew Wy, who also milked the cows and tended the garden. Wy was well loved by the family, especially the Bayliff boys, and humoured by the elders. He was such an honest, hard-working, loyal man that his whims and eccentricities were catered to even when these were an embarrassment to his employers. It was customary for Dorothy to build the fire in the mornings and put water on to heat for tea and baths. Wy would carry the heated water upstairs but the last family member to come down to breakfast was expected to bring the empty buckets back to the kitchen. If this was forgotten there was a rude reminder. From the second floor would come a loud string of profanity, accompanied by a clanging racket as Wy kicked the tin pails down the stairs. A hush followed. Even if company were present, the Bayliffs sat quietly and with characteristic good manners said nothing. Wy usually waited on table in soft shoes, but if someone came to dinner whom Wy did not like he would put on his dirtiest rubber boots to serve the meal.

Wy's devotion to the Bayliff family was exceptional. After World War Two, when Tim was serving in the Canadian Navy doing anti-piracy peace patrol in the South China Sea, Wy instructed his eldest son to go and see him. This young Chinese man walked for three days and crossed over from mainland China to Hong Kong to visit the "Bayliff boy."

When Chew Wy proudly showed Dorothy a photo of his family in China, she was surprised to see so many children. Wy had not returned to the Orient since leaving his wife there many years ago. Wy's explanation was simple: "I have good friend in China."

As was the Chinese custom in those days, Wy wished to die in his homeland and after 20 years or more at Bayliffs he was getting old and returned to China.

Gay Bayliff died in 1977. He was buried beside his parents in

Christmas dinner at the Bayliffs. Left to right: Greta Young, Kathleen Newton, Gertrude and Dorothy Bayliff.

Below: Wedding of Gay Bayliff and Dorothy Dyson. At left are Dorothy's parents, Colonel Dyson and his wife, Florence (seated). Best man Tommy Young is standing behind her. Also standing are the bride and groom, and bridesmaid Francis Graham. At far right are Hugh and Gertrude Bayliff.

the family plot overlooking the ranch. Dorothy now lives in Williams Lake.

In 1954 Tim married Merle Glennie from England, a Red Cross nurse at Alexis Creek. They have two sons and a daughter: the elder son, Hugh, manages the ranch. James is married with two sons of his own and is in the logging business. Elizabeth became a lawyer and practices in Quesnel. Tony inherited the Newton Ranch. In 1962 he married Barrie Boucher from Vancouver. They have a son, Michael, and a daughter Jane.

In 1912 Major Louis Dyson and his wife, Florence, a sister to Reginald Newton, came from England with their young family, James, John, and Dorothy, to visit the Newtons. From the train at Ashcroft they travelled in the first car to arrive in the Chilcotin, driven by a Mr. Cunliff. They crossed the Fraser River on the scow ferry at the Gang Ranch. As the car descended the winding grade to the river, Dorothy Bayliff says she will not forget how frightened she was, looking down at this contraption that was to carry them across the swirling water. The Dysons stayed several years in the Chilcotin before returning to England.

Dorothy returned to Canada to marry Gay Bayliff. John Dyson brought his mother out shortly after and they stayed with Dorothy and Gay at the Chilanko Ranch where Mrs. Dyson died a few years later. John was fascinated with the Canadian landscape and returned to England in the early 1950s to study art. He had already started painting with private tutoring under his uncle Sir Algernon Newton, a renowned artist in the United Kingdom. He returned to B.C. in 1953 and attended the Vancouver School of Art, at the same time working in the summer for the Department of Fisheries at Chilko Lake. With its beautiful setting, Dyson loved that job, photographing and counting young fry as they emerged from the eggs in spring and in the fall counting the salmon coming up the Chilko River to spawn. There were occasional trips up Chilko Lake by boat and miles of walking along its shores. And all the while Dyson was painting, mainly with oils. He became an internationaly known artist and his paintings hang in the Royal Academy in London. He spent his last years in Williams Lake near his sister, Dorothy Bayliff, who was living in Cariboo Lodge. He died in January 1993.

REGINALD FITZ-NIGEL NEWTON came to Chilcotin from England to work on the Bayliff Ranch as a student. In 1901 he bought Fred Copeland's Ranch where the Chilko River joins the Chilcotin, a few miles downstream from Bayliffs. He imported

Arabian horses from England and raised polo ponies, his place becoming known as the Pony Ranch. Later it was named Treglisson after the Newton estate in England. Newton hired a good horseman named William Bliss to bring the first Arabian stallion from England to his Chilcotin ranch. Newton also imported from England an Arabian mare, Gypsy, and a second stallion, Blunderbus, as well as some thoroughbreds. His horse brand reflected his business: the polo stick and ball. Polo was played regularly by the English settlers on the Bayliff fields.

Newton imported Highland cattle that were very hardy but wild and hard to handle. As a result, he eventually went into Herefords. His range extended up the Chilko River beyond Siwash Bridge, and he took up a wild hay meadow on the south side of the river, still known as Newton Meadow. YY was the cattle brand.

Reg Newton married Nora Kathleen Nedwell in England in 1908. They arrived at the ranch in winter with deep snow and cold weather but Mrs. Newton loved it. Extra log rooms were added onto the first log building and, with furniture imported from England and a beautiful lawn and garden, it became a gracious home. Nora Kathleen was an accomplished horsewoman and took an active part in running the cattle ranch.

Reg Newton died in Vancouver in 1922 and his ashes are buried on a hill overlooking the ranch. Mrs. Newton carried on with the ranch and in 1924 a nephew, Edmond Hutton, came from England to help. Unfortunately, Edmond was drowned in a boating accident on Puntzi Lake in 1933. Kathleen Newton died in 1946 and is buried on the hill beside her husband's ashes.

She left the ranch to her nephew, Tony Bayliff, where he and his wife, Barrie, make their home. Their son Michael now works with them on the ranch, their stock still carrying the old YY brand.

WILLIAM HENRY BLISS was born in England on November 16, 1874. When old enough he joined the British Army and served in the Cavalry Division of the Royal Field Artillery, most of the time in Egypt. Bliss was a good horseman and a capable and dependable man. In 1903 he was hired by Reginald Newton to bring a valuable Arabian stallion from England into the Chilcotin. In Ashcroft where the stallion Rebab (pronounced Raybab) was unloaded from the railway, Bliss had a layover while he bought a horse and had a saddle made by the local harness maker. He then rode and led Rebab over 200 miles to Newton's Pony Ranch on the banks of the Chilcotin River.

William Bliss with Newton's Arabian stallion, Rebab.

Bliss stayed to work for Newton who was building up a ranch to raise polo ponies. One of the first jobs Newton and Bliss undertook was to build a bridge across the Little Chilcotin River at Newton's Ranch. Quite a job, using only horse power and saws and axes.

Bliss sent for his wife, Mary Alice, and small daughter, Kathleen. They arrived from England in 1908. Bliss worked for Newton for a year after that, living in the old Copeland house. They then bought a piece of property from Newton to begin ranching on their own. For the next 15 years they rented a large hay meadow known as "The Thicket" from Newton.

Their first son was born at Hanceville on June 9, 1909, with Mrs. Hance as mid-wife. He was named William Maurice. Next came a daughter, Ruth Mary, born at home on August 20, 1912, Dr. Friend from 150 Mile House in attendance. Dr. Wright arrived to set up practice at Alexis Creek later that year. When John Denis came along on October 11, 1915, Bliss was away with the freight wagon on a trip to Ashcroft. Dr. Wright came up from Alexis Creek to attend the birth and Mrs. Jameson was there to look after the other children. Baby John was two weeks old when his father returned.

Twice a year William Bliss, like other pioneers, made a trip to Ashcroft with a wagon and four-horse team for supplies in large quantities that would last for six months.They included flour and sugar by the ton, 25-pound boxes of dried fruit such as prunes, raisins, figs, peaches and apples, 50-pound sacks of coffee beans and a case of tea. For a treat there was usually a case of oranges and a barrel of claret wine. Hardware was needed as well: horse shoes, pitch forks, nails and small tools; sometimes a mowing machine, hay rake or plough. One memorable trip he brought home a gramophone with disk records. Everything came from Wilcox-Hall and Mark Dummond, two big department stores in Ashcroft. Bliss hauled freight for his neighbours, Newton and Bayliff, as well.

The journey to Ashcroft took a week, via the Gang Ranch, and two weeks coming home with loaded wagons, camping out every night. Occasionally Mrs. Bliss went along in the buggy with the children and sometimes to Vancouver by train for a holiday. In 1916 their eldest daughter, Kitty, stayed to go to school at St. Edmonds Catholic Academy.

In 1919 a new log building was erected and Alice Bliss was instrumental in getting a school established on their own property. Gay Bayliff was back from the war and a teacher he had become friends with in England, Vaugn G. S. Pritchard, came to teach. Bliss built an addition on the house for a dormitory and his wife boarded extra children: Eddie and Doug Boyd from Chezacut; Jim and Peter Ross, Alvis and Victor Knoll from Chilanko Forks; Betty Graham from Tatla Lake; and Claire and Eileen Macauley from Alexis Creek. Other teachers were Miss Winnifred Houghs and Mr. Quigley.

Bill Bliss Sr. (his wife called him Will) was an excellent farrier and shod nearly all the horses in the valley. There were many good, well-bred horses in the country since all work was done with horse power: plowing and seeding, haying, logging, feeding cattle, building roads, and transportation from saddle to buggy and wagon.

In September 1916, Bliss got the contract to deliver the mail once a month from Alexis Creek to Tatla Lake. The first day he went to Alexis Creek to collect the mail and back home. Next day he drove to Chilanko Forks and stayed the night. The third day he got to Tatla Lake early and back to Knolls at Chilanko Forks for the night. Next day he went home. One Christmas he travelled some 60 miles from Tatla Lake in one day with his fast team of Arab mares, Abbess and Beauty, arriving home at 3:00 a.m. on Christmas day. About 1926 he turned the mail contract over to his brother Walter.

William Bliss was made road foreman for the Chilcotin Valley about 1925. There was a lot of work to be done on the old wagon road as motor cars and trucks were coming in to the country. Grades needed to be widened, steep hills cut down, and bridges and culverts put in. All the work was done with teams of horses drawing plows and scrapers, and men with picks and shovels. The road grader was pulled by four horses, one man driving the team and one man operating the grader. About 1927 a small Holt tractor was brought in to pull the grader. During this time the road through Hance's Timber was improved and straightened, the road up Anaham Flat was moved over under the hill below the village and a bridge put across Anaham Creek.

Road work was done only from May to November. The roads were never snow-plowed in the winter till the late 1930s. Then, when the snow got too deep, a truck with a blade was sent in from Williams Lake to remove the snow on the main road as far as Redstone. About 1950, a power grader known as the "Maintainer," was stationed at Alexis Creek. Roy Haines was the first operator. All the men employed on road construction lived in a camp of tents near the job, moving as the work progressed.

William Bliss retired in 1949, and in 1954 Mr. and Mrs. Bliss sold their land and cattle to their son, Bill, and his wife, Irene, and moved to Williams Lake.

In 1955 William and Alice Bliss moved to Quesnel to be near their daughter, Kitty Felker. William died on April 7, 1956, and is buried in the Quesnel Cemetery. Alice eventually moved to New Westminster with her daughter, Ruth Mackay. She died there on August 2, 1962, and is buried in the Catholic Cemetery.

WALTER BLISS was born May 30, 1878, in Adstone, Northampton, England. He came to Canada in 1910 and made his home with William and Alice Bliss for a few years. He then bought property at Alexis Lake from Bill McCullough. Walter did a lot of work for Tommy Young through the years and in 1933 he moved down to live in a cabin on Young's Hillside Ranch on the Chilcotin River.

Walter Bliss died February 13, 1937, of a heart attack while out getting a load of firewood. He had loaded the sleigh with big blocks of fir and driven through an opening in the fence onto the main road. He evidently felt unwell as he took off a block of wood to sit on and had filled his pipe. Bill Bliss Jr. went to Williams Lake that morning and on his return at five in the afternoon found his uncle dead, the team of horses still standing in the road. There had been no traffic on the road all day.

Walter is buried on the Bliss Ranch.

THE ALEXIS CREEK HOSPITAL

DR. WILLAM WRIGHT was the first resident doctor in the Chilcotin. He had sailed the China Seas as a ship's doctor for years before coming to Alexis Creek in 1912. He lived in a cabin on Alex Graham's Ranch until a log building was erected for him on land donated by Alex Graham.

Frank Witte and Fred Burdett got out big fir logs for the building and Bob Miller, being a very good axeman, helped in the construction. Dr. Wright and his nurse housekeeper moved into the new hospital in 1915. Bill Graham was the first baby born in the outpost, followed by many more. Often babies were born at home but Dr. Wright was usually in attendance.

The doctor had a large territory and the miles were long – hot and dusty in summer with saddle horse or team and buggy, cold and snowy in winter with team and sleigh. Spring and fall brought mud and ice. Dr. Wright was very well thought of and district residents were saddened when he died in Vancouver, soon after he left Alexis Creek in 1924.

The provincial government paid a stipend of $1,200 a year to the hospital until it was taken over by the Red Cross in 1949.

DR. CHARTER with wife and three sons, Norman, Harold and Cyril came to the Alexis Creek Hospital in 1925. He had been an Anglican Medical Missionary in China. Miss Nelmes, Mrs. Charter's sister, lived with them and acted as nurse.

Dr. Charter had a tough initiation into a frontier life. He was summoned in his first year to accompany police officers, coroner, and jurymen on a rugged trip to attend an inquest into the shooting of Alex Deschamps at the upper end of Chilko Lake. Unaccustomed to the cold and having never been on a horse before, the doctor suffered many hardships on the slow cold trip in sub-zero weather with saddle horse and team and sleigh, then a dangerous voyage up the rough lake in a rowboat. The men left on December 3 and got back just in time for Christmas.

Charters moved to Vancouver in 1930 so that the boys could attend university.

DR. KNIPHEL and nurse, Beatrice Foster, took Charter's place. After him came a succession of young men – Dr. McRae, Dr. Hougen, and Dr. Oliver. None of them stayed long.

An English surgeon, Dr. Hallows, was next. He and his wife came to the hospital about 1938. His nurse was Nan Hopkins who left her position in 1939 to marry a man named Ray Reagan. Dr.

Hallows' next nurse was Ruby Craig. She became Mrs. Frank Shillaker in January 1942.

After Dr. Hallows left Alexis Creek, Mrs. William Anderson took over the hospital and stayed until it became a Red Cross Hospital in 1949. Sophie Smith was the first Red Cross nurse. Her housekeeper was Louisa Ellingsworth who became Mrs. Tommy Lee.

Sophie Smith stayed only a year and was followed by a nurse from England, Miss Lillian Whiteside, who stayed for six years. Her relief nurse, Merle Glennie married Timothy Bayliff in 1954. Mrs Kathleen Telford took over from Miss Whiteside in 1956. Mrs.Swanson filled in for a short time, then Mrs. Humphries, who was the wife of a local policeman stationed at Alexis Creek. Miss Rhoma Walker stayed at the hospital for five years, followed by Mrs. Louise Thompson. Mrs. Dorothy Sanborn came next and stayed for 10 years. When she left a very young nurse, Maureen Duffy, was at the hospital a short time till Ted Christian arrived. Mrs. Mary Engelbert is the present nurse. She is as capable as a doctor and a great favourite of everyone. She had been a Public Health nurse, living next door to the Red Cross in the Federal Building at Alexis Creek staffed by public health nurses since 1961.

In the 1940s a wing was added to the hospital building. The Red Cross put in a basement and installed central heating. There are two wards now, one equipped by Alex Christie in memory of his older brother who died there in 1948. There is also a surgery and comfortable living quarters.

PERRY MARTIN, his wife PRISCELLA and son, DUKE, and Priscella's mother, Mrs. ORMSBY, left their home in Colorado and moved to Alberta by covered wagon to homestead near Calgary. In 1908 they came to the Chilcotin. They bought the store and Gables Ranch, 10 miles east of Alexis Creek, from Phil White and Benny Franklin, also the Nazko Meadows.

Mr. Martin died in 1922 and his mother-in-law, Mrs. Ormsby, a few years later. Both are buried at the Gables. Priscella Martin and son Duke carried on the ranch and store until Duke took over the Graham Ranch (the Cl) in 1927. Duke married Francis Graham in 1928. Priscella Martin lived at the Martin Ranch until her death in 1945. She is buried in Williams Lake.

FRED BURDETT, commonly known as the "Crazy Frenchman," came to Alexis Creek in 1910. He worked for Alex Graham for awhile, then started a blacksmith shop and home near the bridge over the Chilcotin River below Alexis Creek. He married Isabel Annandale, a professor's daughter who had came out from Edinburgh, Scotland. After a few years they sold to Chilco Ranch and their place became part of the Al Ranch. This piece of land is now owned by Slim and Darlene Brecknock.

FRED YELLS and OLIVER HANDY, both from the Midlands, England, were brought to Alexis Creek by Fred Burdett in 1911. They pre-empted the meadows about 30 miles west of Alexis Creek, known as the Handy Meadows (now owned by Walt and Nives Bliss). Yells and Handy started ranching there. When war was declared in 1914 they tossed a coin to see which one would join up because one man had to stay on the ranch. Fred Yells won and went overseas. He married and settled in England after the war. Fred's son, Pete, came out from England when he was grown to work around the country and was road foreman in the Chilcotin during the 1950s, making his home at Alexis Creek. Fred Yells came back to Canada during his later years, living first with son at Alexis Creek and then in Williams Lake.

THOMAS GEORGE HARVEY of County Down, Ireland, came to Alexis Creek in May 1910 to visit his aunt, Mrs. Alex Graham. In 1911 he was mining in Barkerville and walked from there through the Peace River District to Edmonton, Alberta. The following year he returned to Alexis Creek and went to work for Nigel Newton. Harvey went overseas in 1914 and received a commission. He returned in 1919, married Gertrude Chinn, a Vancouver girl, and came back to Alexis Creek. He worked for Newton for a while, then moved down to the place that Fred Burdett had vacated. He later started a place at Alexis Creek and the road leading in to his old homestead now carries his name.

Tommy was a Fish Warden, monitoring the salmon at Chilko Lake throughout his life here. The Harveys had one son, Tommy Jr., who married Loretta Pratt in 1952 and moved to Kamloops, and one daughter, Trudy, who married Ivor Haddleton. They lived in Prince George.

DAVID HUGH FRASER was from New Glasgow, Nova Scotia. He came into the country in 1910 to look after a race horse for Jack Ballock who had a small place on the river where the Chilcotin and Chilko Rivers join. Fraser had come west in 1906 to stay with an uncle, hoping that the climate would help the asthma he had suffered with all his life. Hoodlum Smith, who freighted on the Cariboo Road, was his grandfather. In 1929, Dave Fraser took up a preemption nine miles west of Redstone Store on the Chilanko River. (Now owned by Vernon and Lorraine James.) In 1952, Mr. and Mrs. Morgan of Vancouver bought Fraser's place on the Chilanko for a summer home. Fraser then took up a small place near the Redstone Bridge. He died in 1970.

WALTER ROCK was a young Englishman who also worked for Ballock. When Ballock left him in the fall without provisions or hay for his bay horse named Sharkey, Rock went to work for Bill Bliss for the winter. He helped Mr. Bliss build the cabin that was used for a schoolhouse. Walter Rock left in the spring of 1917, enlisted in the army and was killed in France.

THOMAS CAMPBELL LEE, pioneer merchant, fur trader, and lodgekeeper, came from England in 1897, joined the N.W.M.P at Regina and a few years later came to the Chilcotin to visit his sister, Mrs. Norman Lee, at Hanceville. Generous and neighbourly, he started a small store at Cottonwood near the Anaham Reserve, then in 1913 moved to Alexis Creek to build a store and stopping place. He married Rosamund King Ormsby who had been governess at Alkali Lake for the Wynn Johnsons for a few years.

In 1927 when Mrs. Graham relinquished the Alexis Creek Post Office, Mrs. Lee became post mistress and the office was moved to Tom Lee's store. The Lees had three children: Thomas (Tommy) William Charles, Isobel, and Marjorie. Both daughters died while in their late teens. Tom Lee died in 1946 and his wife in 1955 after a lengthy illness. Both are buried in Williams Lake.

Tommy and his wife, Louisa, and daughters Elaine and Audrey, carried on the family business until 1983 when the store and post office had to be torn down to make room for the widening of Highway 20. The Alexis Creek Post Office had by then been run by the Tom Lee family for 53 years. Tommy and Louisa retired in Williams Lake. Tommy passed away on June 25, 1991. Louisa still owns the old log house at Alexis Creek.

EDWARD PENROSE LEE came out to join his brother, Norman, at the Bayliff Ranch in 1888 and then returned to England. On his return to Canada two years later, he worked for the Hudson's Bay Company in Kamloops. In 1895 he returned to the Chilcotin and established his present ranch at Redstone (now owned by Wilf Anderson), bringing in horses and supplies from Kamloops and taking the rigors of pioneer ranching in his stride. His sister, HELEN LEE, came to visit her brother that same year, but after a short stay went south to San Francisco and worked as a secretary there for 26 years. She was there during the famous San Francisco earthquake. Helen returned to Redstone in 1921 to keep house for her brother. She was there for 33 years, always known throughout the country as "Miss Lee." She died in 1954 and is buried in the family plot at the Norman Lee Ranch, Hanceville.

THOMAS RALEIGH YOUNG, an Englishman, came to Alexis Creek about 1888 and was first in partnership with Hewer and Nightingale on the ranch now owned by Telfords. Hewer and Nightingale started the first store at Alexis Creek about 1888 and traded with the Indians. Young took a place further up Alexis Creek and started a ranch, then sold part of his ranch to the Mackay brothers. Mr. Young also took a keen interest in big-game hunting in the mountains near Klinaklini Valley. He was noted for his many valuable trophies. In 1924 he married Greta Nedwell, sister of Mrs. Newton. He remained at Hillside Ranch, as he called his place, until his death in 1946 and is buried there.

After Tommy died, Greta carried on at the ranch, and in 1950 married Tommy Morgan. In 1952 she sold the Hillside property to Kathleen Telford and retired to Williams Lake. Mrs. Morgan passed away in 1954.

T. A. ARMSTRONG took up some meadows on Alexis Creek and started ranching. In 1890 he bought out R. J. Bidwell and with his brother, Henry, continued ranching. Henry joined up during the Boer War and was killed in 1901. Tommy made a trip to England in 1918 and stayed a year, bringing back an English bride, a big woman named Sybil. In 1927, they sold the ranch to Alex Graham and returned to England. The ranch is now owned by Norman and Valerie Telford.

R. J. BIDWELL, from whom Armstrong bought his ranch, was a remittance man from England, and ex-member of the North-West Mounted Police who served as Justice of the Peace at Alexis Creek. When he sold to Armstrong he moved to what is known as Bidwell Lake and Bidwell Creek. He died in 1921 and was buried on the Armstrong Ranch.

CHARLES CROWHURST came to the Chilcotin during the 1880s or 1890s and did business as a farmer, teamster, and blacksmith. He lived on what he called the River Ranch, later to become

Young's place and named Hillside. He took a Chilcotin Indian girl as a wife. He cut hay with a scythe on a high wild meadow about six miles away and hauled it home for his horses. That meadow is still called Crowhurst Meadow. He returned to the United States, abandoning his wife. She lived the rest of her life with an Indian called Teneese, but was always known as "Mrs. Crowhurst."

WILLIAM CHRISTIE from Scotland, came to Canada in 1907. He later went to Casper, Wyoming, where he took up sheep herding for a few years. He was joined by his youngest brother, Alexander, and William MacLennan. In 1911, they arrived at Alexis Creek and bought the Lambert property across the Chilcotin River from Alexis Creek. There they started ranching and later bought more property from Ed Loomis beyond Alexis Lake.

When war broke out in 1914, Alex Christie and Mac Maclennan both joined up and went overseas. MacLennan was killed and Alex wounded and sent home to Alexis Creek. In 1920 he married Maisie A. Chisholm from Scotland. The wedding took place in William and Alice Bliss's home, with Father Thomas officiating. Later the Christie brothers' partnership dissolved. Alex and his wife continued on the Lambert Ranch, while William Christie started a place at Alexis Lake. He passed away in 1948.

In 1949 Alex Christie and his wife sold their ranch to Gay Bayliff and retired to Victoria due to ill health. Alex Christie died in Victoria in 1953. Mrs. Christie was confined to a nursing home in Victoria for several years before her death.

THOMAS POWELL MORGAN of Wales came to the Chilcotin in 1898 and worked at the Gang Ranch, then known as the Western Canadian Ranching Company. For awhile he was cattle buyer when the Company owned the Swift Packing Plant at Sapperton, New Westminster. As the plant wasn't a paying proposition they sold it and Mr. Morgan then worked for Allan Baker at Loon Lake near Clinton. He went back to the Gang in 1906, and stayed there until he decided to start on his own.

He bought a piece of land on the south side of the Chilcotin River from T. Lambert, some meadows north of Alexis Lake from Miles Cooper and, in 1913, started his own ranch. Cooper Meadow is now known as the Morgan Meadow and is owned by Walt and Nevis Bliss. In 1949 Tommy Morgan sold his property to Bayliffs and a year later married Greta Young and moved to Hillside. In 1952 they sold Hillside to Mrs. K. A. Telford and retired to Williams Lake. Mrs. Morgan died in 1953 and her husband in 1954.

JACK MAINDLY came to Alexis Creek in 1919 and started his ranch about 10 miles north of Alexis Lake. Before that he had worked in Vancouver and had also pre-empted a place at Green Lake, a few miles from the 70 Mile House. He worked on the Armstrong Ranch at Alexis Creek in between building up his own place where he raised Aberdeen Angus cattle. He sold out to Jack Doyle and retired to Victoria where he spent his last years with his sister.

OTHER MEN who lived and worked around the Chilcotin in the early days but of whom little is known were: Walter Barlow, Billy Hind, Ernest Middleton, Bob Ashby, and Willamer.

CLIFTON KINKEAD spent 48 years in the Chilcotin, arriving at Big Creek at 19 with his father, Sam, from Nebraska. Sam Kinkead returned to the States after he had taken up a pre-emption in 1914 on Minton Creek where Cliff and his wife, Maisie, lived with their two little boys, Douglas and Donald. After a few years Maisie left and took the younger boy, Donald, back to the States with her. Douglas remained with his father.

In the late 1920s, Cliff moved to Alexis Creek and built a house and also a harness and saddle shop. Cliff was clever with leather and did a lot of work for local cowboys and ranchers. He also had a second-hand store for awhile, bringing in furniture from Vancouver.

In 1932 Cliff married Nellie Owens and they raised a family of six children: two boys – Stanley and Allan; and four girls – Joan, Janet, Doreen and Marilyn. Nellie Kinkead was in charge of the Telephone Switch Board at Alexis Creek till 1966 when Vera Hance took over.

Cliff drove truck for Andy Stuart's Store at Redstone for a number of years before becoming a lineman for B. C. Telephone. For eight years before he retired he was maintenance man for the United States Air Force at Puntzi Mountain. He died in September, 1965.

ALEX and DOROTHY MARSHALL started a dairy ranch in 1926 on a swamp meadow about 10 miles from the top of Lee's Hill. They had one daughter, Pamela. About 1928 they moved to Alexis Creek and started the first garage there. It was housed in a big log structure built by Jimmy Scallon. Alex had a Chevrolet truck with which he freighted for other people and hauled his own gas for the garage in drums. He was a good mechanic and was doing well until tragedy took his life in 1933. (See page 311.)

The Alexis Creek Hotel in the 1960s.

GUS JAKEL was born in Germany in 1894 and came to Canada as an infant with his parents, one sister and seven brothers. The family settled on a farm in Saskatchewan, then later moved to Montana.

Gus came to the Cariboo in 1919 and worked at Enterprise Cattle Company at 141 Mile, among other jobs. At the early Stampedes in Williams Lake, Gus was one of the pickup men.

Gus and his wife, Doris, moved to Lee's Corner and started a freight line known as "Chilcotin Fast Freight." In 1934 they moved to Alexis Creek and bought a house from Dorothy Marshall. They enlarged the building and started the first Chilcotin Hotel which housed the area's first beer parlour in 1937. Gus remembers renting rooms for $1 a night and serving full-course meals for 50 cents each.

The Jakels established the Chilcotin Garage, later operated by their son, Gordon, for many years. They also built a General Store with a dance hall and movie theatre upstairs, and ran the Post Office for a time.

The store was sold to Frank Pigeon in 1948, and later was bought by Eddie and Suse Pigeon. The hotel was sold to Sam and Irene Barrowman in 1949. In 1980 Gordon Jakel sold the garage to Bob Scott. During all of their busy years, the Jakels grew a good garden and raised chickens, pigs and kept a milk cow.

The MACKAY brothers, STEWART, GORDON, and DONALD, came to the Chilcotin after World War One. They had met Gay Bayliff in England in the British Army. Stewart and Gordon worked for Bayliffs to start with and then began ranching on their own behind Alexis Creek. They sold out to the C 1 Ranch. Donald married Bella Brown and ranched at Four Mile Creek, east of the Chimney Creek Bridge. He also worked for the Department of Highways as engineer assistant for over 20 years. One of his responsibilities was inspecting bridges in the district, including the old Chimney Creek Bridge over the Fraser. "A wonderful piece of engineering," he claimed.

JOHN ROBERT "BOB" FRENCH by Diana French
Bob was one of the many men from eastern Canada who found their way to the Cariboo around the turn of the century. French was born in Ontario in 1879, the third youngest in a family of five girls and three boys. His older sisters, Annie and Maggie, came west first and married brothers, Jim and Anthony Bishop. They settled in the Clinton, Big Bar area, and in 1893 young Bob came to join them. He walked from the railhead at Ashcroft to Clinton.

He worked at various jobs. He drove team on the Cariboo Road, mostly stagecoach, but made some trips out of Barkerville hauling gold and was held up once. He later drove team between Clinton and Alkali Lake, cowboyed for Wynn Johnson at Alkali Lake Ranch; and spent four years at Gang Ranch. He started out as ferryman and ended up as head cowboy. While at the Gang, he married Gertrude Wright, daughter of ferryman Bill Wright. She died in young womanhood. A sister, Mary Wright, married Grover Hance and she also died young.

French must have liked the country west of the Fraser because he stayed in Chilcotin until he died in 1969 at 90. He cowboyed at the Cotton Ranch for a number of years, then in 1923 he went to work at Alexis Creek. In 1925 he moved to Chilanko Forks to work for Arthur Knoll. There he married again, this time to Anna Straube who had come from Germany to work for the Knolls. The

Frenchs ranched at Kleena Kleene and Anahim Lake before moving to Riske Creek in 1934. Bob helped build the Riske Creek School with Wes Jasper, and worked on the road and on ranches for the next few years. In 1937 the family, which included four children – Mary, Bob Jr., Maggie and Hilda – moved to Alexis Creek to stay. Bob and Anna were known for their hospitality, and Anna for her magnificent garden which provided her family and most of Alexis Creek with raspberries and vegetables for years.

Three of the French children stayed in the Cariboo-Chilcotin. Mary married Alvis Knoll of Chezacut; Hilda married Ray Duggan and also lives at Chezacut; and after working for some years on the Knoll ranch, Bob Jr. went to work for the Ministry of Highways and ended up in Williams Lake. Maggie (Endersby) lives at Campbell River.

Bob Jr. married Diana Endersby who was teaching at Chezacut. She later became editor of the *Williams Lake Tribune* and is now curator of the Cariboo-Chilcotin Museum.

KING SPAIN came from Oregon in 1906 with wife and two daughters, Mabel and Maud. They travelled in a covered wagon from Oregon to Alexis Creek with mule team, horses, sheep, chickens, a milk cow and all household equipment. They settled and homesteaded at the present Spain Lake Ranch, six miles west of Alexis Lake. They sold out in 1911 to Ed Loomis and Moses Goering. The Spains had two daughters: Mabel, who married Dick Bauchett and lived in Oregon, and Maud who taught school in San Francisco.

LOOMIS and GOERING got cattle from Alex Graham and started in the stock business in 1911, ranging their animals at Riske Creek. Goering sold his share to Loomis about 1913 and left for Florida. Then in 1928 Loomis sold his cattle to Duke Martin and the property to the MORTON BROTHERS, JESS and BERT.

The Mortons were originally from England. They worked in Vancouver and then at the 70 Mile prior to coming to Alexis Creek. They ranched at Spain Lake until Jess lost his hand in a mowing machine accident. He was cutting hay with a team and mower when the team ran away and he was thrown off into the mower knife. They sold the Spain Lake ranch to DOUG BOYD and retired in Williams Lake. Boyd sold the ranch to ALEX and ANN PAXTON in 1948. That year there was lots of snow and a late spring and Doug Boyd was still feeding cattle with a sleigh on May 24. As well as a cattle ranch, the Paxtons also ran a good guiding business at Spain Lake. They sold to AMADY ISNARDY in the 1970s and bought property in Alexis Creek. The Paxtons lived at Alexis Creek until Ann's death in the 1980s. Alex moved into Cariboo Lodge soon after. A cowboy all his life, Alex was always neatly dressed in cowboy clothes and remains youthful and good looking into his eighties. His wife, Ann (English) was a capable hand, too. She cowboyed, packed and guided along with her husband.

BOB MILLER from Alberta homesteaded across the river opposite Alexis Creek for about 10 years. In 1922 he sold his property to Alex Graham and left the country. He spent his last years in a mental hospital.

HUGH KIRKPATRICK came from the Southern States and was in partnership with Phil White and Sanderson at the Gables. He was part owner of the Archie Flat, a large grassy flat across the river from Alexis Creek, which is now part of the C1 Ranch. He lived in a small cabin near the Chilcotin River. Kirkpatrick suffered a stroke while there and was alone and almost helpless for several days.

He drank his water supply, including what was in the wash basin, then desperately shot off his rifle hoping someone would hear. When no help came, he crawled as far as possible in the direction of the Chilcotin River where workmen were building the Alexis Creek Bridge. He put his hat on a long pole and waved it until someone noticed and came to his assistance. Shortly after he sold his interest in Archie Flat to Alex Graham and left the country.

CLIFF and DOLORES CARLTON drove by car from Minnesota to Quesnel. They pre-empted land on Punchesacut Lake in the early 1930s. Cliff was a carpenter and when they heard of a job building a church at Alexis Creek in 1938, they packed up and moved. Dolores was a school teacher and as there was a shortage of Canadian teachers during the war she got a permit to teach at the Alexis Creek School for three years and also at Tatlyoko. Cliff became postmaster at Alexis Creek and was appointed Stipendiary Magistrate. They were both musicians, Dolores played the accordion and Cliff the banjo, and they often played for dances. They also went into producing honey, keeping their bee hives on Hance's alfalfa fields. They called their honey "Cariboo Gold."

Cliff Carlton died in 1952 and is buried at Alexis Creek.

In 1957 Dolores married Pat (Curley) Swaile. They built a

**Sandy and Margaret Robertson and their family at Alexis Creek in 1935.
Back row, left to right: Sandy, Zander, Phil, Don, and Margaret
with baby Jean.
Front row, left to right: Dorothy, Lorna, Bill, Betty and Audrey. Another
son, Gordon, died in 1927 at three. Joy was born later after leaving Alexis
Creek.**

store and coffee shop at Chilanko Forks which Dolores managed
while Curley worked in the boiler room at Puntzi Mountain Radar
Station. After a few years they sold and moved farther down the
Chilanko River where they built another store. When they sold this
one (Ron Morrow owns it now) they bought a small ranch called
"Hellfire," named after a man named Helfeier who originally took
it up. This was an isolated place 15 miles up the Chilanko River
and they soon sold out to Nick Turner, school teacher at Alexis
Creek, and moved to Quesnel. Curley got the contract to drive the
four-horse team on the stagecoach at Barkerville and Dolores
worked as cashier at the Wake-Up-Jake Cafe and at the Theatre
Royal.

They finally bought property at New Cinema where Curley
made his home. Dolores moved into the newly opened Dunrovin
Apartments in 1975.

In 1886 Ashcroft replaced Yale as portal to the Chilcotin. It retained this position for over 30 years until completion of the Pacific Great Eastern Railway resulted in birth of a new community – Williams Lake.

Below: The Ashcroft Hotel in the 1890s with the last bull team to haul supplies to Cariboo-Chilcotin.

ALEXANDER (SANDY) ROBERTSON came to Canada from Scotland. He went to Tatla Lake in 1911 where he worked for Grahams and other ranchers until war broke out in 1914. He enlisted in the Seaforth Highlanders and went overseas. In Aberdeenshire he met his future wife, Margaret Thomson. Sandy returned to the Chilcotin after the war and Margaret came out to marry him in December 1921.

Sandy brought his bride to the Chilcotin, where he again went to work on various ranches. He also worked with his big team on the road and helped build the Redstone Bridge over the little

Chilcotin River and the bridge over the McClinchy River. On these summer jobs the family lived in a tent near the work site. Their home was on the old Burdett place on the Chilcotin River below the Alexis Creek bridge.

Sandy and Margaret had five boys and six girls. Their second child, Gordon, died in 1927 when he was only three. His grave was the first in the new Alexis Creek Cemetery. Despite the endless hard work of raising a large family in pioneer times, Margaret Robertson always took time to rest and change to a fresh dress before afternoon tea.

The Robertson family moved to McLeese Lake in 1937.

ROY HAINES was born at Hanceville on March 29, 1900. His grandfather, John Haines, came from Idaho and the family lived on what is now the Deer Creek place. Roy's mother died when he was two years old and he was raised at Big Creek by his aunt and uncle, Mr. and Mrs. Charles Bambrick.

Roy started to work at Gang Ranch when he was 14 and worked for several years on ranches in the Chilcotin, including the Chilco, TH, Bell, and the Cotton. He also spent several summers harvesting in Alberta and Saskatchewan but always returned to the Cariboo and Chilcotin.

Roy quit ranch work and hired on with the Public Works. He was shovel operator in 1929 and 1930 and then went to truck driving. He worked for Tommy Hodgson hauling mail and freight into the Chilcotin. In 1948 he started working for the Dept. of Highways and stayed with them until he retired in 1965. He was the first man to operate the power grader, called the "Maintainer," on the Chilcotin Road.

Roy married Dorothy Isnardy in 1930 and they raised a family of eight, four boys and four girls – Bobby, Buck (Arnold), Lawrence, Roland, Daphne, Juanita, Lenora and Karen. Roy and Dorothy moved to Hanceville in 1935 and to Alexis Creek in 1940.

Roy was always a busy man. As well as being a keen fisherman, he had a large collection of arrowheads and rare stones. Soft spoken, pleasant, and well thought of, Roy had many friends.

He died in December 1980 and is buried in the Alexis Creek cemetery. Dorothy still lives at Alexis Creek.

For pioneer Chilcotin ranchers, trees required for their miles of fences were handy and abundant. Among various designs were the Russell, above, along Highway 20 near Riske Creek, and the simpler but sturdy plain log like the one below at Meldrum Creek.

TATLA LAKE

The first man to take up land at Tatla Lake was a LIEUTENANT MARTIN. By the spring of 1890 he had developed a "fine ranch" there, according to the *Victoria Colonist* newspaper. Lieutenant Martin was a volunteer on the Government survey of the Chilcotin, starting at Bute Inlet on May 13, 1890. In April 1891 he took his spring shipment of fur to Victoria, a catch "well up to the average" as reported in the *Vancouver Daily World*. Martin Lake near Tatla, no doubt is named after him. Franklin must have purchased the Tatla Lake Ranch from Lieutenant Martin.

BENJAMIN (BENNY) FRANKLIN started many and varied places in the Chilcotin and cut many roads. He started a dairy ranch across the river from Alexis Creek on the Big Flats in the 1880s. PHIL WHITE, SANDERSON, HUGH KIRKPATRICK and HARRY AITKINSON all took up property and were in partnership on this big flat, later known as the Alexis Creek Flats. By 1892 Benjamin Franklin was settled at Tatla lake.

On March 15, 1892, Franklin, accompanied by two Indian guides, started out from Tatla Lake on an experiment to "prove the feasibility of direct communication with Chilcotin via Knight's Inlet and the water route to Victoria." The trip, "by horse and on foot, by snowshoes and by canoe," a distance they reckoned of about 130 miles, took six days. Franklin was hoping to convince the government that a shorter, more direct road to the Chilcotin from the Coast should be built this way. The *Victoria Colonist* on April 13, 1892, reported that the two Indians who accompanied Franklin to Victoria had never been in a city before," never seen a railway, a steam boat, or a street car," and the Indians were themselves a curiosity to the city folks as they "passed up Government Street with their bundles of furs on their backs and their rifles in hand." A few years later on November 15, 1899, Franklin, who was a J. P., had a run-in with the Chilcotin natives. With his eldest son, he came out to Alexis Creek to report to Constable Robert Pyper that Indians had broken into his place at Tatla Lake with intent to kill him, had chased him out and demolished his house. Pyper was soon on their trail and the outlaws were brought to justice.

Franklin sold his Tatla Lake property to Bob Graham in the early 1900s and in partnership with Phil White started a store and ranch at the place later known as The Gables. In 1908 they sold out to Perry Martin. White left the country and Benny Franklin moved out to what is known as the Franklin Meadows. There he started ranching again. He cut a road all the way from the Hudson's Bay Trail nearly to Nazko, and eventually moved to Nazko. He continued to rove but still spent time in the Chilcotin.

Benjamin Franklin died at Moons Lake (Doc English Lake) of a heart attack. He was found by Dorothy Moon slumped over on the seat of his buggy, the team of horses standing in the water. He had two sons and a daughter: Bertie Franklin, the eldest son, was with the Department of Public Works in Quesnel until he retired. He passed away in 1968 at 84. Daughter Gertrude married Tom Lynd, lived for awhile in the Nazko, then returned to the U.S.A. Major Franklin, the youngest son, was born at Hanceville in 1892. He ranched in the Nazko and died at 78.

ROBERT GRAHAM was born in Ireland in 1871 and came to the Chilcotin in 1891. He took up land where Alexis Creek village is today. Graham followed in the wake of the gold rush to northern B.C. and returned to Chilcotin in 1901. He turned his pre-emption over to his brother, Alex, and in partnership with William Dagg in 1905 purchased the Tatla Lake place from Benny Franklin. In 1909 Bob Graham went back to Scotland, returning in 1911 with his wife, Margaret, baby daughter, Betty, and step-daughter, Alexina. Dagg and Graham dissolved their partnership soon after and Dagg returned to England.

The Graham's son, William Robert, was the first baby born in the new log hospital at Alexis Creek in 1915. Doctor Wright and his nurse, Mary Goode, were in attendance. In 1920 another son, Alexander, was born.

The Grahams built a fine new house in 1930 as well as a new store. That house is now the Graham Inn where good food is served to travelers on the Chilcotin road. Betty, a capable girl who even drove truck at times, managed the store. A post office was established on the Graham Ranch in 1914 with Mrs. Graham post mis-

300

Bob Graham.

tress. Betty later took over this job as well. Mail came in only once a month at first, then every fortnight. The Tatla Lake Post Office now has mail three times a week. Betty married Fred Linder, from Sweden, who continued working on the Graham Ranch. Bob Graham died in 1952 and his wife, Margaret, in 1958. Both are buried on the hill overlooking the ranch.

Bill Graham married Joy Dickinson in 1939 and they had one daughter, Anne. Bill acquired a big bulldozer and other heavy equipment to improve the ranch and also used it to build roads all over the Chilcotin, including helping build the road to Bella Coola. Alex married Ila Holte and they had one son, Roy. It became Alex's job to manage the cattle herd which eventually numbered nearly 1,000. Alex and Ila separated and in 1958 he married Eleanor Butler. They had a son and a daughter. Alex died in March 1973. Bill passed away in 1983 and Betty in October 1980. In April 1980, Betty was special guest at a dinner put on by the Tatla Lake community in honour of her 50 years serving in the store and post office, helping so many over the years. All the Grahams are buried in the Tatla Lake Cemetery on the hill above their ranch.

ANDY AND PETE STUART, whose store on the Chilcotin River at Redstone was started in a cabin by Jack Temple during the time that Temple owned the Norman Lee store and ranch at Hanceville. (Temple also started a small store at Big Creek managed by Elsie Church but it didn't last.) Mr. Willamer, a young Englishman, managed the Redstone store for Temple until it was purchased by Peter Stuart from Vancouver in 1916. Pete Stuart was an excellent axeman and built a good-sized log store building for himself and a high hay shed for his neighbour, E. P. Lee. Unfortunately, his time at Redstone was short. In 1918 Pete was killed in a car accident in Vancouver, along with his friends, Moose Barlow and Jack Spencer. In 1919 Pete's brother, Andrew Lorne Stuart, came to Redstone to take over the merchant business. He made a great success of it. Andy Stuart served in the Great War and married in England. His bride, Henrietta, was from Hythe, Kent.

Stuart hired Johnny Henderson and Fred Hink in 1921 to build a big log house near the store – a permanent home for the Stuarts. Their first son, Harold Andrew, was born in Vancouver in 1921. A daughter, Christine, was born at Alexis Creek in 1924. Harold and Christine went to school in the first log school at Alexis Creek and to Lord Byng High School in Vancouver.

The Redstone Post Office was established at Stuart's store in 1923 and manned by the Stuart family throughout its existence. Harold developed a thriving automotive business. He married Marcella Inscho in 1945 and they raised a family of eight children, five still living.

Andy Stuart died in 1959 and Christine took over the store business and the post office. Mrs. Stuart died on Christmas Day, 1962, in Vancouver. Both are buried in Williams Lake. Christine died in 1977 and is also in the family plot in Williams Lake.

Harold and Marcella carried on with the store, post office, and garage until Harold's death in 1987. Marcella and youngest son, Charlie, closed the business and post office but still own their Redstone home.

RALPH RAYMOND ROSS of Nova Scotia and JOHN HENDER-
SON from England established a ranch on the Chilcotin River in
1902, a few miles up from the Redstone Bridge on the Chezacut
Road. Ross had freighted with teams from Brandon, Manitoba,
west for the C.P.R. when the railroad was being built across the
prairies. Then he worked for the Douglas Lake Ranch before coming to Chilcotin. Ross and Henderson married Chilcotin sisters,
Susan and Emma Charlieboy. After Henderson's wife died he
returned to England before World War One, leaving one son,
Johnny, who was raised by the Ross family. Johnny served overseas in the Canadian Army and returned wounded in 1919.

Johnny Henderson had the name of being a good man: honest, hard working, strong and capable. He worked for various
ranchers in Chezacut and Tatlayoko. Later in life, he married Edith
Purjue and settled on his property at Puntzi Lake, bequeathed to
him by his father who passed away in England in 1940. This was
the first piece of land to be surveyed on Puntzi Lake. Henderson
traded this land to Elmer Purjue for a small place in Tatlayoko Valley where Johnny and Edith lived until his death. Edith then moved
to Williams Lake.

Ralph and Susan Ross had four sons: Thomas, killed in
World War One, James, Eddie, and Peter. Ralph Ross died in 1945
and is buried in Williams Lake, predeceased by Susan in 1918. She
lies in the Redstone Cemetery. Eddie Ross married Emily Henry in
1927 and they had one daughter, Clara. May Richardson taught
Clara for a year and then she was sent away to school in Vancouver. Emily died in 1930. Jim Ross married Mary Ann Turner, took
his share of the ranch and bought George Powers place at Charlotte
Lake, but worked for the Gang Ranch for some years. Latterly,
both Jim and Mary Ann worked for the C 1 Ranch and retired in
Williams Lake. Eddie married again, this time to Jeanie Cooper.
Peter married her sister, Katie, and both raised large families. They
sold the Ross Ranch in 1970 to a group of business men from Vancouver Island. The ranch was sold again in 1975 to a family from
Paris, France – Dr. Lagendre, wife Monique, and three teenage
children. They raised cattle and sheep and had hydro extended to
the place.

Felix Shellenberg and David Altherr from Switzerland bought
the ranch in 1979. Felix and wife, Jasmin, with four small daughters, still run the ranch. When David married Debbie Ross, from
Ashcroft, the partnership divided and Altherr bought a ranch at
Anahim Lake from Mike and Dale Lehman.

JAMES MACKILL, from Scotland, joined the N.W.M.P. and served in the Regina area for eight years before returning to Scotland for his mother's funeral. When he returned to Canada he resigned from the Force and travelled west to Chilcotin. He married Annie Swanson at Riske Creek and then settled at Soda Creek for a few years before moving his family to Kleena Kleene in 1926. He built a lodge on One Eye Lake and became the first big-game guide in the Chilcotin, with clients from many parts of the United States as well as Canada.

Jim Mackill died in 1943. His older son, Clarence and wife, Rocky, carried on with the business. Clarence built a larger lodge on One-Eye Lake, constructed by a master log builder, Sollid, to accommodate the many visiting hunters and fishermen.

About 1952, Clarence and Rocky sold the Kleena Kleene Lodge to move their growing family close to a school. Clarence got a position as driver, transporting Air Force personel for the U.S. Air Force at Puntzi Mountain, and later transferred to Mt. Lolo near Kamloops. Annie Mackill made her home with Clarence and Rocky for many years and is buried in Kamloops.

Hilda Mackill married Leonard Butler and they raised three children at Bluff Lake. Leonard died in 1973 and Hilda in 1982. Lee Butler still lives on the ranch with his grown family near by.

Jack Mackill operated the huge monitor at the Bullion Mine near Likely and then moved to the mines in the Kootenays near Nelson, where he soon joined the Nelson City Police. It was here he married Phoebe Powel and they raised seven children — four boys and three girls.

Jack served in the Canadian Army during the World War Two and on his return rejoined the Nelson Police Force. In 1950 he transferred to the Fish and Wildlife Branch and worked in Invermere, Fort Nelson, Fort St. John and Williams Lake.

In 1978 Jack retired as Regional Protection Officer of the Fish and Wildlife Branch for the Cariboo. He was honored with a dinner along with his wife and 250 guests, colleagues, and friends after 28 years of service. He died in 1982 and is buried in Williams Lake.

CYRUS and PHYLLIS BRYANT with a family of four young children — Jane, Caroline, Alfred, and Florence (Bunch) — came to Canada from Montana in 1919. They settled at Soda Creek but in 1924 moved to a homestead at Tatla Lake in Western Chilcotin.

It was November by the time they had harvested the garden, packed up and were ready to leave. Mr. and Mrs. Bryant and the younger children travelled in two wagons loaded with household goods and the family in a buckboard. Caroline and Jane rode and drove the few head of cattle and horses behind the wagons. They were several days on the road, camping out at night in a tent.

There was a heavy fall of snow the night the family reached Sawmill Creek that made travelling with wagons slow through Hance's Timber and the temperature dropped alarmingly. Mrs. Norman Lee sent a message to them to leave the wagons and come on to Lees' for the night with buggy and livestock, which they were happy to do. They left a kerosene lantern burning under one wagon to keep the vegetables from freezing and, unfortunately, the wagon caught fire during the night and burned to the ground. Phyllis' precious piano was on that wagon and she was terribly distressed about that loss. It was eight years before she got another one. She was a great pianist and through the years played the piano for dances and parties throughout the Chilcotin and Cariboo.

When a school was started at Tatla Lake, Phyllis boarded the teacher and several local children whose homes were too far away. When the Bryant children were ready for high school, Phyllis

Hanceville Post Office in 1965.

moved to Williams Lake while Cyrus went on to Anahim Lake and started a ranch. In a couple of years son Alfred joined him. They packed for Andy Christiansen who had a large cattle ranch and a store at Anahim Lake and had provisions brought in with horses from Bella Coola. There was no road, only a trail to the Bella Coola Valley.

Alfred became a successful big-game guide. Phyllis went back to Anahim Lake in 1937 when the girls were finished school. In 1947 she and Cyrus moved to Alexandria. Cyrus died in Kamloops in 1950. Phyllis later married Levi Kellis. She spent her last years with her daughter, Jane, at Anahim Lake and at Cariboo Park Home in Williams Lake. She died at 94 in 1987 and is buried in Williams Lake. Alfred retired to Bella Coola and died in Kamloops in 1988.

Jane Bryant took training at the Royal Inland Hospital in Kamloops and went to work as a RN with the natives at Anahim Lake. Most of the Indians then lived at Ulkatcho, 50 miles away. Jane was renowned for her medical ability, courage and determination as she worked cheerfully year after year under difficult conditions. She married Bill Lehman in 1941 and even after becoming the mother of twins, Patricia and Michael, she still made many mercy trips on horseback wherever she was called. She often took the twins with her – each in a box on a packhorse. The nearest hospital was in Bella Coola, a 90-mile ride over the mountain. There was no road to the valley until 1954.

Pre-deceased by her husband, Jane Bryant Lehman died in 1983, adamantly refusing throughout her lifetime any recognition for her dedicated work as a nurse in the wilderness. But she was posthumously awarded the Red Cross Florence Nightingale Medal for outstanding service. The medal was accepted by her son, Michael Lehman.

The Lehman place is now owned by David and Debbie Altherr.

FRITZ HANSON arrived in Chilcotin during the depression years after leaving Denmark at 19. He worked on a farm near Montreal for several years, then on cattle ranches in the U.S. before reaching B.C. He did some boxing and prize fighting in the ring and picked up the nickname of "Tex." In Chilcotin he worked on various ranches but was always looking for land to pre-empt. He finally found a beautiful spot on Clearwater Lake near Kleena Kleene.

Tex was good with animals, especially horses, and trained many wild, unbranded horses that he captured from a wild bunch on the range. When he had about 25 head he became a guide and outfitter, taking American trophy hunters into the mountains down the KlinaKlini River. He also raised purebred Shorthorn cattle on his 196 acres.

Tex corresponded for three years with an opera singer in Germany named Ingeborg Holm. In 1955 she came out to Kleena Kleene and they were married. Ingeborg was a good frontier wife, raising chickens and geese and growing a good garden at an elevation of 3,025 feet, preserving much for the long cold winters.

Tex became crippled with arthritis, and in 1980 he and Ingeborg sold the property and moved to Duncan on Vancouver Island.

LILY SKINNER JACK, better known as CHEE WIT (spelled CHIWID in the Chilcotin Indian language), was a legend in her own time. Of mixed blood, she was born Lily Skinner, daughter of Charley Skinner, a white man who came into the country in the early 1900s and settled in the Tatlayoko-Eagle Lake area. Her mother was a Chilcotin Indian woman from Redstone named Luzep who was a deaf mute.

Lily lived most of her life outdoors, camping with only a rude shelter beside a small fire winter and summer. In her latter years she had nothing but a ragged tarp that she covered herself with on rainy and snowy days. In spite of hardships, Lily remained a beautiful woman all her life. She married Alex Jack but was known as Chee-Wit, the Chickadee, throughout the Chilcotin.

Alex and Lily Jack had three daughters: Julianna (Mrs. Willy George Setah), Mary Jane (Mrs. Henry Lulua), and Cecelia. A tragic domestic experience set the stage for her nomadic life. In a drunken rage in their cabin Alex beat his beautiful wife unmercifully with a heavy chain. She could not recover. Her husband, sober and now remorseful, drove a few head of cattle to Chezacut and sold them to Charlie Mulvahill to raise money to send his wife to Vancouver for treatment. But Lily was never the same. She left Alex Jack and refused from then on to stay indoors. Travelling around the entire Chilcotin, she set up her brief primitive camps from Anahim Lake to Riske Creek. She at one time had a few cattle and, riding an old horse with a dog following, moved them about from place to place. Friends or relatives fed them in the wintertime. Many people throughout the Chilcotin tried to help her, bringing her groceries, getting firewood or offering clothes and shelter. Betty Graham cashed her government cheques and offered

Before busing began, several generations of Chilcotin children were educated in small log schools, usually with under a dozen pupils. These two 1965 photos of the schoolhouse and pupils at the Mulvahill Ranch are typical.

Chee Wit, the Chickadee, in her bare camp at Fletcher Lake.

her a cabin at Tatla Lake for winters free of charge, but Chee-Wit chose instead to camp in the snow by a small fire that would freeze out the toughest outdoorsman.

One winter she camped near Willy George and Julianna at Fletcher Lake in the Big Creek country, checking her squirrel traps every day. When the temperature dropped to -20°F Willy went to her camp and persuaded her to move in to the warm house with them. "I don't stay long in her camp," Willy said. "I can't get warm by her little fire." After three days indoors, where she was uneasy and discontented, Chee-Wit went back to her snowy camp, claiming that if she stayed inside any longer she would get sick. By then she had no cattle and was going on foot. Using two sticks as she walked, she would move her meager belongings from one end of the country to the other, tarrying here and there to net fish and trap squirrels and muskrats.

Age, ill health and blindness finally forced Chee-Wit the Chickadee to give up her rugged nomadic life – and her freedom. She spent her last few years in Katie Quilt's home at the Stone Reserve. She died there in 1986.

THE RETURN
Veera Bonner

Consort with the wind
Oh happy heart!
Know the wild embrace of
This land, apart
From the concrete world
Of street and mart.

Respond to the dawn!
And be possessed
By the limitless sweep
Of wilderness.
Released you may soar
Where there's joy and rest!

TRAGEDY AT PUNTZI LAKE

Puntzi is a deep, nine-mile-long lake where a storm, creating dangerous rough water, can blow up in minutes.

Bill Bliss and Pedel Jack once saw this happen when riding for cattle in the fall. The lake was calm and placid as they rode by in the morning but, on their return a few hours later, had changed completely. A violent wind was howling through the twisting trees and the water was wild and menacing. The two young cowboys were both accustomed to braving the elements but this was out of the ordinary. The trail ahead skirted the lake and the men hunched in their saddles, bracing themselves against the tornado-like gale sweeping across the water, sending 12-foot waves smashing on the rocky shore.

Bill Bliss on a mare called Fern that he was breaking in for Mrs. Newton.

One such storm took the lives of two Chilcotin men in a tragic accident on June 25, 1933.

All was quiet at Puntzi Lake on that bright summer Sunday as a group of friends picnicked on the shore. The light wind that sprang up seemed just right for sailing as Alex Marshall of Alexis Creek launched his small craft and hoisted the sail. In the boat with him went his wife, Dorothy, and a friend, 33-year-old Edmond Hutton, a nephew of Kathleen Newton. He had come out from England in 1924 to work on the ranch at Redstone with his aunt after the death of her husband, Reg Newton. On shore, Ed Lee of Redstone – who had a shelter on the south side of Puntzi where he kept a boat – was preparing to take his sister, Helen Lee, and neighbour, Kathleen Newton, out in his small motor boat but was having trouble starting the motor.

The three in the sailboat were well out in the middle when clouds blew in and the light breeze suddenly increased to a gale. As savage winds tore at the sail, Marshall quickly lost control of his small craft and it was bounced around like a toy on the angry waves. The heavy-masted sailboat tipped over, dumping the trio, who had set out so light-heartedly, into the cold, rolling lake. The two men managed to help Dorothy Marshall to the top of the overturned boat while they clung to the sides. But none could survive for long in that frigid water and both men, numbed by the extreme cold and battered by the storm, soon lost their grip and perished. Alex Marshall disappeared first and Mrs. Marshall then tried to hold Hutton up by the hair but in a short time he, too, went under.

Back at the picnic site, Ed Lee tried in vain to start his motor to go to the rescue of his friends. Perhaps it was fortunate that the engine refused to fire as his small craft would have been no match for the wildly plunging waves.

Soaking wet and chilled to the bone, Dorothy Marshall clung to the battered sailboat until it was finally driven ashore near the east end of the lake. She might have perished there but for Little Peter Hunlin, an Indian from the Redstone Reserve, who came riding along the Puntzi trail on horseback and quickly went to her aid. Helping her out of her wet clothing, Hunlin gave her his dry outer garments, built a fire to warm her and dry her clothes and then mounted his horse and galloped away for help.

Although an extensive search was made, the bodies of Alex Marshall and Edmond Hutton were never recovered. On a hill on the southeast side of Puntzi Lake, where their loved ones were last seen, Kathleen Newton and Dorothy Marshall had a cairn with brass name plate erected in their memory. Cliff Kinkead built the cairn.

Soon after this tragedy, Dorothy Marshall sold their Alexis Creek property to Gus Jakel and with daughter Pam, moved to the Okanagan.

Chilcotin visitors should remember that larger lakes are subject to sudden squalls. On big, mountain-ringed ones such as Tatlayoko, below, caution is always advisable.

CHEZACUT

It was the summer of 1900. John Stewart, Ed Sherringham, Norman Lee, E. P. Lee, Fred and Will Copeland all set off with an Indian guide to look over some large natural meadows in the Chezacut country. All staked meadows except Norman Lee. Two years later Fred Copeland, having sold his land at the confluence of the Chilcotin and Chilko Rivers to Reg Newton, moved his family to the big meadow he staked at Chezacut. His wife was the first white woman there. Fred applied for a post office at Chezacut, became the first postmaster and carried the mail from Alexis Creek to Chezacut – once a month by wagon, buggy, or packhorse – a 100-mile round trip. In 1909, Copeland sold his stock and moved to be near a school for his two children. In 1911 he sold the land to E. P. Lee.

ED SHERRINGHAM, a young man from England who had been on the ill-fated Yukon trip with Norman Lee in 1898 attempting to take a cattle drive to Dawson City, settled on his meadow at Chezacut in 1906. His bride, Helen, from Virginia, was the second white woman at Chezacut. They were there for seven years, then in 1913 sold their stock, rented the place to Ernest Middleton and retired at the coast. Sherringham died in 1949, Helen in 1969 in Victoria at 92.

When the war started ERNEST MIDDLETON left for England to join the British Army and was killed in action soon after. His stock was sold to GILBERT AXFORD, another young Englishman who also rented the Sherringham Ranch until it was sold to Chauncy Maxwell in 1916.

CHAUNCY MAXWELL, K. B. MOORE, and a man named SAVAGE in 1912 headed into the country looking for land. Savage was drowned in the Blackwater River, but Moore and Maxwell made their way to Chezacut. Maxwell pre-empted a meadow 20 miles north of Chezacut and Moore moved on to the Tatlayoko Valley. In 1916 Chauncy Maxwell married Susan Hanrohan from New Hampshire and moved to the Sherringham Ranch at Chezacut.

Here they lived until Chauncy's death in 1934. They had three boys: Jack, Philip, and Chauncy Jr. He died in 1936 and is buried beside his father on the ranch. In 1947, Susan sold the Maxwell place to Alvis and Max Knoll and moved with the two boys to the Cherry Creek Ranch near Kamloops. After a few years they sold and moved to Highland Valley. Susan Maxwell died in Kamloops in 1952.

By 1925 there were enough children at Chezacut for a school so a log schoolhouse was built, the government providing $125 for windows and doors. There were 10 pupils the first year. The teacher was Miss Hopwood, from Victoria, who stayed only one year. Then came Miss Ella Ferguson who stayed two years. She and the next two teachers, Mary Cullum and Eve Stoddart, were all from Victoria. Miss Maimie Baron was from Grand Forks and Miss Laine from North Vancouver. The school closed about 1932 for lack of pupils but opened again in 1950 when the next generation was ready for school.

JOHN WILLIAM (CHARLIE) MULVAHILL was born in Illinois where his grandparents emigrated from Ireland. His mother died when he was very young, and his father and stepmother left for Oregon when Charlie was four. They settled on Summit Prairie and established a cattle ranch. There was a school at Summit Prairie where John Williams got his education and the nickname of "Charlie" which he went by all his life.

After a number of years the Mulvahill family sold the ranch and moved to Michel, Oregon, where they planted and established an orchard. There were many wild horses in that country, and young Charlie Mulvahill, and a man named Mundon, went into the business of catching and selling them. The cowboys would run these wild horses into a box canyon, rope and break them to lead and, when they had a big bunch, trail them to Nevada where the horses were sold.

About 1900, Mulvahill and Mundon heard that there was a demand for good horses in Canada and decided to take a drive north. Leaving Oregon with about 50 head of saddle stock, they headed for the border at Osoyoos. Here they had to lay over and gentle the horses enough for the required veterinary examination and tests before entering Canada. At Douglas Lake Ranch, 500 miles from their starting point in Oregon, the men sold or traded their horses as these big saddle horses were just what ranch manager Joe Graves was looking for. The horse traders also dealt with Cameron of the Semlin Ranch. Charlie and Mundon then

J. W. (Charlie) Mulvahill with his freight outfit in 1912 when the family was living at Ashcroft.

went to work on the Cariboo Road where they met Will Copeland.

Copeland told them about his place at Chezacut with its big meadows and great ranching potential. Impressed with what they heard, Mundon and Mulvahill accompanied Copeland to Chezacut and spent the winter, Mundon feeding cattle for Sherringham.

The Americans made two more trips to B.C. with horses, going all the way to Chezacut in 1908, an 800-mile drive from Oregon. Mulvahill got his citizenship papers and pre-empted land at Chezacut Lake in 1909. Mundon went back to the States.

Charlie Mulvahill had intended to save up a grub stake and follow the gold trail to Barkerville, but took the advice of Joe Graves and decided to look for gold other than in gravel. Leaving his pre-emtion in the care of Will Copeland, he rented a house in Ashcroft, bought a good outfit and went into hauling freight from Ashcroft. He made one trip to Barkerville and one to Keithly Creek but hauled mostly to Soda Creek where up-country freight went on from there on sternwheel steamers. He used two heavy wagons with a light wagon hooked on at the back that he called the "Back Action," to carry supplies for himself and his horses. His 10-horse team of Clydes and Shires was purchased from Douglas Lake Ranch. In 1911 he hauled the cables from Ashcroft for the Gang Ranch Bridge. These big cables was so long and heavy they had to be hauled in the winter, coiled onto two sleighs coupled together and pulled by six to eight horses.

316

Martha Mulvahill with her family in 1979 on her 97th birthday. Mrs. Mulvahill lived to be 101. Left to right: Eleanor, Bill, Martha and Randolph.

Charlie married Martha Copeland in 1912 while still living at Ashcroft. A daughter, Eleanor, was born on September 16, 1913. Gas-powered trucks were beginning to take over the freighting business, so in 1914 Mulvahill moved his family to his pre-emption at Chezacut Lake to start ranching.

Martha Secord Copeland was born in Ontario on September 10, 1882. Her first job was with the telephone company where, working night shift for several years, she became run down and developed tonsilitis that wouldn't go away. Her doctor ordered a different lifestyle so Martha packed her trunks and bags and headed west to stay with her brother, Will Copeland, at Chezacut.

Will Copeland came to the Chilcotin in the 1890s and took up land that is now Blisses. He built the original log house which formed part of William Bliss' home and still stands today. Copeland moved to Chezacut and pre-empted land on the Chilcotin River, also taking up the Brush Meadow and Scotty Meadow. He was living at Chezacut when his sister Martha came out to stay with him. He met her at Hanceville with team and

317

wagon in June 1909. At her brother's Chezacut home she met Charlie Mulvahill, the man who would become her husband.

Martha's older brother, Fred Copeland, was also at Chezacut. He took up land at Meldrum Creek where a river bench is still called Copeland Flat. There he married Eunice (Ellen) Meldrum. They moved to the confluence of the Chilko and Chilcotin Rivers, taking up land that Copeland later sold to Reg Newton. Ellen died there on October 6, 1895, and is buried on the ranch. Fred married again and moved to Chezacut, ranching on big meadows along the Chilcotin River that now belong to Ollie Knoll. He left the country later that same year. In 1927, Will Copeland sold his big meadows on the Chilcotin River to Arthur Knoll and the Brush Meadow to Charlie Mulvahill and moved to Kelowna. There he married Etta Downey.

After about a year, the Copelands' mother in Ontario became ill and the family wrote asking Martha to return to care for her. She returned and stayed to work at the telephone office for two more years. But she and Charlie Mulvahill had kept track of each other by mail and in October, 1912, she came west again and they were married at her sister's home in Victoria.

Being acquainted with frontier life by her visit with brother Will in 1909, Martha was undaunted when her husband decided to leave Ashcroft and move to the Chilcotin wilderness at Chezacut. Together, the Mulvahills built a fine ranch, living first at Chezacut Lake then pre-empting the Char Meadow (now the Bill Mulvahill Ranch) and in 1927 buying the Brush Meadow from Will Copeland. Martha took over the post office from Gilbert Axford in 1921 and was postmistress until the office closed in 1933. Her husband, Charlie, hauled the mail in every two weeks from Alexis Creek – a three-day trip with horses, staying overnight at Blisses, then to Alexis Creek and back to Blisses for another overnight stop before continuing on to Chezacut the next day. Later Billy Bliss took over the contract and carried the mail until the post office closed.

Two sons were born to Mulvahills at Chezacut: Will on January 6, 1915; and Randolf on April 14, 1917, brothers for three-year-old Eleanor who was born at Ashcroft. The three Mulvahill children started school at Okanagan Centre, staying with their uncle Sam Copeland. After three years a school opened at Chezacut. Will Copeland sold to Arthur Knoll who had five school-age children. With the three Mulvahills, three Maxwell boys and Bella Brown there were enough youngsters to start a school. Mrs. Mulvahill boarded the teachers through the years. She was an excellent cook and many friends, neighbours and travellers enjoyed good food and hospitality at Charlie and Martha's table.

Charlie Mulvahill raised Hereford and Shorthorn cattle, the favored breed in those days, and branded with the J up and J down, JJ registered in 1915. He was a very successful rancher. He continued to take freight wagons to Ashcroft for his own and his neighbours' supplies. He also raised a lot of good horses and his two sons became topnotch daredevil horse chasers and bronc busters.

Charlie and Martha turned their big ranch over to the boys in 1938. Randolf kept the Brush Meadow home place and the old J up and J down brand. He named his outfit the Spade Ranch. Randolf sold out to Nature's Trust in the 1980s and the big hay meadows are now flooded with water in a Ducks Unlimited project for water fowl. Randolf bought the old Harvey place near Alexis Creek and he and his wife, Cathy, make their home there. Bill took the Char Meadow and branded with the old family iron joined with a slash, creating a flying N. Bill passed away in 1991 but his wife, Mary, and son, Will, still ranch at Char Springs.

Charlie and Martha moved first to Coquitlam and then to North Vancouver. Charlie died in 1950 and is buried there. Martha stayed in North Vancouver with her daughter Eleanor and husband Alf Murphy. When Eleanor's marriage broke up she and her mother went to live in Salmon Arm where they bought and operated a motel. They moved to Williams Lake in the early 1970s. Martha Mulvahill passed away September 19, 1983, at 101 plus nine days. She is buried beside her husband in Vancouver. Eleanor has now moved to Hope to be near her daughter, Cathy Murphy.

MIKE O'BRIAN ran a small store at Chezacut and in 1927 sold it and his land to Frank Shillaker.

FRANK SHILLAKER came to Canada from England after serving in World War One, and to Chezacut in 1920. At Alexis Creek he found work with Tommy and Sybil Armstrong, and later worked for Alex and Bill Christie for several years. In 1927 he purchased the general store and land at Chezacut from Mike O'Brian and was in love with this place for the rest of his life. He had a very successful store business. He married Florence Williams, a widow with two children, Mary and Teddy. Florence died in 1934 and Frank sent the children to England to be educated. Mary Shillaker died in a bombing raid on London during World War Two, but

Teddy returned to Vancouver and married there. He often visited at Chezacut. Teddy Shillaker died from a heart attack in 1963.

In 1942 Frank Shillaker married Ruby Craig, a nurse working with Dr. Hallows at Alexis Creek. They had two children: a son, George, and a daughter, Rae. The children attended elementary school at Chezacut and were great athletes. Tow-headed and long legged, George and Rae were the dread of all the other students at the interschool track meets. The kids knew that if one of the Shillakers was competing in their age group they didn't have a hope. When George and Rae were ready for high school Ruby moved to a house she inherited from her father in New Westminster. Rae graduated from university as a nurse and George became an R.C.M.P. officer.

Frank Shillaker stayed at Chezacut, running the store and trading for furs with the Indians. He hauled his own freight in from Redstone and picked up the mail as well since the Chezacut post office had closed. The 30-mile road from Chezacut to Redstone was still a wagon track through the jackpines and he made many long cold trips with a team and sleigh in winter, hauling mail and freight for himself and for his neighbours. When the snow was melting in the spring, or after a heavy rainfall, there were fearsome mudholes to contend with. Finally, in 1970 Shillaker sold the store to Ollie Knoll but kept the property, and began spending the winters with Ruby in New Westminster. But he hated the city and would return as soon as he could in the spring to his cabin at Chezacut. "So you are going home for the winter," Nives Bliss said to him when he was on his way out one fall.

"No," he answered, "I'm leaving home for the winter." He died in November 1984, and is buried in New Westminster. The Shillaker property at Chezacut is still in the family, owned by Frank's son, George.

EDWIN JAMES BOYD came to Canada in 1906 from the Isle of Man where he had been a champion swimmer and top football player. He worked for Norman Lee, then sent for his wife, Margaret, and moved to Chezacut to work for Copeland before acquiring land for himself. Their first son, Edwin Allen, was born at Hanceville in 1909 and a second son, Douglas Ramsay, in 1911. A daughter, Fanny, arrived in 1918. She married Pete Evjen. Eddy married and lived in the Nazko country. Doug worked at Chezacut, bought and sold the Spain Lake Ranch, bought and sold a ranch near the 150 Mile and a sawmill near Clinton and worked for wages in that country. But Doug Boyd is best remembered as rider for the Cl Ranch on the Eagle Lake Range where he rode through summer and fall for 20 years.

The Ed Boyds left Chezacut in 1938, selling the cattle to R. C. Cotton and the land to Bill Mulvahill. Bill's eldest son, Roy Mulvahill, owns it now. He and his wife, Gwen, raise cattle and horses, along with a very successful big-game guiding business

Ed Boyd bought the Log Cabin Hotel, later named the Ranch, after moving to Williams Lake. He sold it in 1949. Left a widower in 1943, he married again and had a son, Jimmy. Jimmy Boyd was a great athlete, following in his father's footsteps. Ed Boyd died in 1963 in his eighties, refusing to go into a retirement home as he didn't want to associate with "all those old people."

ARTHUR ERNEST KNOLL and wife, ANNA, came to the Chilcotin in 1912 by way of Bella Coola where they met Olie Nygaard who had a ranch on the Chilanko River that he wanted to sell. Knoll bought it, cattle and all, including the old Nygard brand: 15. The Knolls and their baby boy, Victor, travelled to their new place by saddle and packhorse. While at the Chilanko meadow Knoll brought in a steam engine from Ashcroft via the Gang Ranch, travelling on its own power. It was driven by a Mr. Johnson who had the necessary "steam papers." They were accompanied by an Indian, Jack Lulua, with a team and wagon to haul wood along to fire the burner.

By 1926, the Knoll family had grown to five children and were ready for school, so Arthur bought Billy Copeland's place at Chezacut. Here he ranched, building up a cattle herd and making money.

In 1940 he turned the ranch over to his sons and he, Anna, and Victor, moved to Kamloops. Anna Knoll died there in 1951. Arthur and Victor came back to Chilanko for a few years, then to Williams Lake where Arthur died in 1967. Victor moved to Vernon. Max Knoll was killed in a bulldozer accident in 1948. Alfred left Chezacut to live in Toronto. Hilda married and lives in Alberta. Alvis (Ollie) kept the family ranch at Chezacut and married Mary French in 1943. They have four daughters. Ollie has one of the largest ranches in the Chilcotin, mostly natural meadows, and runs about 2,000 head of cattle. He still uses the old 15 brand on his steers and marks his heifers with a V lazy V.

In the mid-fifties, Ollie provided a good water system for the ranch by piping a big spring for two miles – a feat that some said could not successfully be done. The biggest enterprise of his highly successful ranching career was next: a hydro project on Jurgenson

Mulvahill Ranch Meadow at Chezacut, typical of the huge Chilcotin meadows which attracted men interested in ranching.

Creek six miles away to provide electricity for the ranch at a cost of $300,000. In August 1975 power was turned on from a Gilkes turbine, run by water diverted to the gulch from a reservoir above, and has brought ample electricity to the Knoll Ranch ever since. The sophisticated motor requires careful attention and a diesel motor stands by to fill in when the main unit needs servicing.

Ducks Unlimited bought the Chilanko meadows from Ollie and the land is now used as habitat for waterfowl. He and Mary and their family still ranch at Chezacut.

CHEZACUT BEEF DRIVE
from the mountains to the sea

Cattle prices were so low in the 1930s that Arthur Knoll of Chezacut and his son, Ollie, decided in 1939 to take their beef to Bella Coola and on to Vancouver instead of driving them to Williams Lake, hoping that prices at the coast might be higher. It was a tough trip. Ironically, beef prices in Vancouver the day the Knolls' steers went through the sale ring were two cents lower than the buyers were paying in Williams Lake.

The beef drive of 200 head of two-year-old steers and a few dry cows left Chezacut in September 1939. Cowboys Alfred Bryant, Thomas Squinas, Bert Mathews, Wesley Jasper Jr., Ollie Knoll, and cook Gordon McTaggart made up the crew. Earlier in the year Alfred Bryant guided Arthur and Ollie Knoll over the trail from Anahim Lake to the coast to determine if a drive this way was feasible and to map out the route.

Pushing the cattle cross-country to Anahim Lake, the drive took two days to reach Towdystan, camping overnight at Aktaklin Lake. Leaving Engebretsons, they travelled via Holtry Creek and Dean River to Andy Christensen's Clesspocket Ranch at Anahim Lake. From there they took the drive to Capoose Crossing on the Dean River and swung up through the mountains to Tweedsmuir Park. Two men night herded the cattle throughout the trip. Setting up rough camps, sleeping in bedrolls on the ground without shelter at that high altitude in cold autumn weather "...wasn't very comfortable," remembers Ollie in a classic understatement.

It took five days to get through the rugged coast mountains near timberline, following an old trail, with feed scarce. The toughest day was the 1,968 m (6,000-foot) descent down the mountain to Burnt Bridge in the Bella Coola Valley. It took all day. The cattle were strung out single file, 20 in front of each rider. The cowboys moved them slowly and quietly down the steep narrow moun-

Ollie Knoll and his wife, Mary, at their ranch house at Chezacut.

tain track where one false move could have sent an animal plunging to its death over the dangerous dropoff at the edge of the winding trail. But the cowboys never lost a hoof.

At Bella Coola it was a lengthy business loading the 200 head onto a scow for the last lap of the journey to Vancouver. They had to wait for the tide to come in to pull the big scow in to shore with a tug, then wait for the tide to go out in order to load the cattle.

There was another wait for the tide to come in again before the loaded scow could leave. Ollie Knoll and Wesley Jasper accompanied the beef on the 30-hour voyage to Vancouver. The other cowboys and pack outfit went back to the Chilcotin via the Precipice.

Mr. and Mrs. Knoll drove down to Vancouver in their new 1939 Ford to watch the sale and drive Ollie and Wesley home.

The sale at the Vancouver stockyards was a disappointment. The price was only five cents per pound for the best of Knolls' big steers, two cents lower than at the sale held in Williams Lake the same day. And a beef drive from Chezacut to Williams Lake took only 13 days, while the trek to Vancouver took 17.

Looking back, Ollie sums it all up: "A long, hard drive and no money in it. We never marketed our beef that way again."

Ollie's only consolation was that the drive made history.

"Heading for the Ranch."

HEADIN' FOR THE RANCH
Veera Witte Bonner

The cattle on the feed grounds
Will hardly eat their hay;
The sunny, baring hillsides
Are where they want to stray.

They seem to know it's springtime
And want to take a chance
At rustling for a living:
So we're headin' for the ranch.

We've closed the door behind us
And left the little shack;
It's been a home but now, I guess
The mice can have it back.

For chinook winds are sweeping
The winter snow away
And down the waking meadow
We're pulling out today.

We're trading hills and silence
For the noisy haunts o' men,
And we've fed the last durn dogie
Till winter comes again.

326

TSUNIAH LAKE
As told by Johnny Blatchford

I spent 24 years in the Chilcotin and 31 years in the Cariboo, so that makes a total of 55 years in this country. I was born in our farm house at Sumas Prairie on March 15, 1910. In those days doctors and nurses came out to private homes and delivered babies there. I had three sisters and three brothers and we grew up on hard work, learning farming early. My dad was with Canadian Customs at Huntington Port of Entry, so that left the management of the farm in my mother's capable hands. She was also farm-raised. Dad worked on the farm when he got home from his job.

When I was 18, I branched out on my own, working at logging and other odd jobs and starting a small farm. I practiced riding broncs every chance I got and then joined "Strawberry Red's Wild West Show." I rode broncs through Washington, Oregon, California and at the Vancouver Exhibition. We were paid by the head for the horses we rode.

I married Pauline Schallhorn in 1935, and in October 1936

Johnny Blatchford at his Tsuniah Lake home.

joined the B.C. Provincial Police. I trained at the school at Oakalla Prison and we young trainees were locked in at night just like the prisoners. After graduating, and a stint in Vancouver, I served at Oakalla as a police officer for awhile. I was moved around the province as relief Constable, ending up at Golden. In November, 1937, they transferred me to Williams Lake. After three years there I was moved to Alexis Creek. Once we left the Coast my wife and kids were always with me. We had two children, Bobby and Bonnie, and both were a great help to us as they were growing up.

I was acting Game Warden as well as Constable for the entire Chilcotin. It was a big area to cover and I met lots of people while travelling around registering firearms, completing old-age pension applications and looking after trapping areas and licences.

Early in the spring of 1940 I was called to Mountain House Ranch on a complaint from Eagle Lake Henry that someone was poaching on his trapline. I had met Eagle Lake Henry at cattle sale time in Williams Lake in the fall of 1939. He was drinking and got into trouble and I had to throw him in jail for the night. When we met at the Chilko River, he recognized me. "You're Johnny, the man that put me in jail," he said.

"Yes," I answered, "and if you get crazy again I'll throw you back in."

"Oh, alcohol did that," he said, "not Henry." I mounted the saddle horse he had led over for me since there was no bridge, and we rode back across the river to complete the business at his house. I figured I'd found a friend and a man I could trust in Eagle Lake Henry and after more than 20 years as his neighbour I never changed my mind. I asked him if he knew of a place that would make me a ranch and a hunting business. He said he did and on my next trip out he showed me Tsuniah Lake.

Tsuniah Lake meadow had been taken up in 1912 by a Frenchman named Frank Angers (pronounced Awnjay) from Brittany, France. His uncle was a Senator in Quebec and Frank came to Canada to visit him and look for land. He didn't like the East so headed West and ended up at Tsuniah Lake – about as far west as you could get. He hired Indians to cut road from Henry's Ranch to the upper end of Tsuniah Lake where he built a cabin and fenced a small pasture. He had a team and wagon and two saddle horses. When war broke out in 1914 he sold his horses and outfit and joined the army. After he was discharged in 1919 he returned to Tsuniah.

He had been badly gassed and was in poor health, but with a

loan from the Soldier Settlement Board he bought cattle and a few horses and began again to build up a ranch. Tragically, in July 1922, he was drowned when he tried to ford the Chilko River at Henry's Crossing. The water was high and swift and he was swept off his horse and disappeared. His body was never recovered. His brother came out to look for him but gave up. The brother hired two Indians to take Frank Angers' cattle, horses, and equipment out to Alexis Creek where everything was sold to Archie Macauley. Angers' property at Tsuniah Lake was abandoned. As no taxes were ever paid, the land reverted back to the government.

After seeing the Tsuniah country in the spring of 1940 I didn't waste any time. In June I leased all the land that Angers had taken up. Then in 1942, when the Provincial Police wanted to transfer me to Fort St. John, I quit and built a home at Alexis Creek.

I worked at seasonal jobs in the summer – fisheries, highways, and anything I could get the rest of the year. I shipped horses from Alberta and traded some off for cattle and sold others to pay my way. By 1944 I had 27 head of cows and 18 horses. Lashaway Lulua had contracted to build me two drift fences, one on either side of Tsuniah Lake, so in 1944 I was able to move my cows and horses out to Tsuniah that year. Lashaway and Felix also built stackyards for me and put up hay, and that first winter I hired Felix to feed my stock. I had sold my little farm at the Coast and had a few dollars. I bought mowers, rakes, harness, and milk cows down there and had the works shipped to Williams Lake. Tommy Hodgson hauled it all to Alexis Creek. The 84 work horses that I brought in and had unloaded at Ashcroft were too many to haul, so I drove them via Gang Ranch, Scallons, and Alexis Creek all the way to Tsuniah. It took six days from Ashcroft to Alexis Creek.

I made a trip to Alberta and bought two good mares and colts and two broke saddle horses, all American saddle-bred, Kentucky strain. I brought them by train to Ashcroft and Hodgson hauled them to Alexis Creek for me. I drove them the rest of the way. I advertised these horses for sale in the *Vancouver Province* and a man named A. J. (Alex) McPherson bought them for himself and his friends. In the course of the deal he asked me if I knew of a place where he could build a lodge and a dude ranch. I showed him the Tsuniah Lake country beyond my ranch where Tsuniah Lake Lodge now stands and he fell in love with it. So we formed a partnership. He would build a lodge and look after the guests and fishing, I would run the ranch and take out hunters in the fall.

Work started right away on the lodge. McPherson supplied a truck and driver to haul equipment and building supplies from Williams Lake to the Narrows above Dan Weir's place on Chilko Lake. Freight was then rafted across the Narrows, then packed with horses up the mountain to Tsuniah Lake. Alex McPherson and his brother, Norman, worked on the big spruce log lodge, 104 by 48 feet, and oversaw the job which took two years and we worked hard. Pete Mickalson built the huge fireplace. Thomas Elkins contracted to build nine log cabins one winter for $150 each. Maxine Mack, Walter Stobie, Otto Shell, and Jimmy Sammy were on his crew.

When McPherson brought in his son, Claire, a captain just out of the army, to learn the business and take over, our partnership fell apart. I kept the ranch and McPherson kept the lodge. A. J. fired his son and hired another manager but soon got rid of him, sold to Bob Brebner and Art Watson. Tsuniah Lake Lodge is still in the Brebner family. Bob Brebner had a bulldozer and he built a road from my place to the Lodge and improved the wagon road from Tsuniah Lake to Henry's Crossing. My son, Bob, and I built all the culverts, 17 of them, to take care of the creeks and springs that had to be crossed.

Water in the Chilko River is high from the end of May until late August and, as there was no bridge at Henry's Crossing, it wasn't easy getting building material, freight and supplies to my ranch. However, I moved my wife and family in and got a house built. A man named John Jamola helped me build it and copied the Lodge's corner windows the way I wanted them.

I tried to do most of my freighting in the fall when the water was low and I could cross the river with team and wagon or saddle and packhorses.

When the river was high I hauled my stuff to Dan Weir's Lodge on Chilko Lake and he ferried it across the Narrows in his boat. I then packed it from there. A steep trail went up over the mountain to my ranch on the far side. I don't know how many trips I made over the mountain with my packhorses or with team and wagon to Henry's Crossing.

When Jack Casselman, Murray Taylor, and Doc and Willetta Johnson began living on my side of the river, we all started hollering for a bridge at Henry's Crossing. Finally, about 1958 the government started to build one – but the bunch of us had to cut and deliver all the pilings for the bridge free of charge. The road was always rough.

In 1965 I sold out to Brebner and Watson. It had been such a hard tough life that I never really regretted moving out. When I went back after 26 years I hardly knew the place. The whole country which had been fire killed was grown up with trees and brush.

After leaving Tsuniah I worked at part-time jobs and for eight years at Gibraltar Mines. My wife, Polly, was in very poor health for a long time. She died in 1979. I married Gladys Carpenter in 1980. We'd known each other for years. We live on a small farm on land I bought at Marguerite – and both still work too hard sometimes.

BYRON and GLADYS CARPENTER were on vacation when they came with their family to camp at Chaunigan Lake above Nemiah Valley in the summer of 1957. The Carpenters came from a comfortable home in the Upper Chehalis River Valley of Washington. Though they endured every hardship and inconvenience imaginable in the next few months, they were determined to stay in the country. After moving from Chaunigan Lake to Alexis Creek, to Anahim Lake and to Riske Creek, mostly living in a tent, Byron made a deal in early April 1960 with George Terry to develop the Lingfield Creek place near Chilko Lake. The family thought they had made their last move as they settled down (in a tent again) to build a log house on the south side of the Chilko River.

Tragically, just over three weeks later, Byron Carpenter was killed instantly when a tractor turned over on him while pulling out house logs. Gladys was left to deal with her grief, find a place to live and manage alone with her two daughters, Carol and Anne. Her eldest daughter, Joy, and son, Ben, had returned to the U.S. to stay with relatives in Kansas. Bravely, she managed well, even going ahead with plans for Carol's marriage to Sammy Martin of Alexis Creek in August.

On one trip coming out of Lingfield Creek in the snow later that tragic autumn, Gladys came upon a hunter lost and exhausted and helped him back to Felix Lulua's cabin where he was staying. This man was a Catholic priest and a chaplain at Vancouver General Hospital. In a strange turn of fate, Gladys met him again in less than a week in a ward at the Vancouver hospital. Her youngest daughter, Anne, was suddenly stricken with an anuerism and Gladys accompanied her daughter on an emergency flight from Williams Lake to the Vancouver General. The priest was unfailingly kind and helpful, no doubt remembering her kindness to him, all the long time that Anne was in the hospital. Slowly, Anne made a complete recovery.

In August 1963, Gladys and Anne moved from Alexis Creek to Williams Lake where Gladys worked at various jobs for 20 years, ending up as head secretary at Williams Lake Jr. Secondary School. She married John Blatchford in 1980.

For the Dodge City, Kansas farm girl the move to Canada in 1957 was permanent. She became a Canadian citizen and has been a resident of B.C. for over 30 years.

DAN WEIR came from Ontario. Over six feet tall, he joined the North-West Mounted Police in 1919 and was posted to Vancouver. During his two years with the force he was part of the famous Musical Ride. He bought his way out of the police force and headed north to the frontier. Arriving in Williams Lake in 1921, Weir took part in the early stampedes and worked as a cowboy and ranch hand in the Chilcotin. He joined the Provincial Police and served in the Chilcotin as a well respected Constable.

Dan and his wife, Pauline, started the first Chilko Lake Lodge in 1938 and for 20 years catered to fishermen and "that wicked lake" in all its moods. In the late 1950s they sold the lodge to Tom Garner of Vancouver Island but reserved 40 acres. After a brief stint in Prince George, the Weirs returned to the Chilcotin and their 40 acres on Chilko to build a hand-hewn log home and Tullin Lodge on the edge of that deep, dangerous lake that in 1925 had tried Dan's endurance to the limit. (Described in the following personal account.) After being happily in the fishing business again for a number of years they retired to an apartment in Williams Lake. But Dan Weir's heart remained in the mountains beside the big water where the whitecaps roll.

The Weirs had a son, Donny, and a daughter, Paula.

MY MEMORABLE INTRODUCTION TO CHILCOTIN
by Dan Weir

The day I arrived in Chilcotin in 1925 I met Constable Ian McRae of the B.C. Provincial Police at the TH Ranch at Hanceville. He informed me that I was to be a member of an expedition to the Chilko Lake country. McCrae was getting together a posse to investigate a shooting at Chilko Lake. All I knew about that part of the country was that Chilko Lake was the main headwaters of the Chilcotin River – the rest was hearsay.

Apparently two French-Canadian trappers, ALEX DESCHAMPS and FRED CYRE, had a big argument resulting in a gun battle. Fred arrived at the local police office several days later and

At Chilko Lake in June, 1940. Left to right: Constable Johnny Blatchford, Dr. Hallows, Cheta Johnny, Coroner Rene Hance and Dan Weir.

reported the death of his partner. He had phoned the police from Redstone and said: "I am in a big soup." Fred was held at Hanceville under open arrest while headquarters in Victoria made the decision to send in an investigating party under the local coroner.

The official party met at Redstone on December 2, comprised of B.C. Provincial Police Officers Sergeant Dick Bowen and Constable George McKenzie from Ashcroft and Clinton; Coroner and Government Agent Hubert Campbell from Williams Lake; Doctor Charter from Alexis Creek; the prisoner, Fred Cyre; and, for jurymen, rancher Sandy Robertson, cowboys Billy Dagg, Johnny Henderson, Oliver Purjue, Jimmy MacKay, and myself. We cowboys had our own saddle horses and rancher Sandy Robertson had his team of heavy Clydesdales and a sleigh.

Our first difference of opinion was with the police officers who were choosing supplies at Stuart's Store and calculating one week for the round trip. This looked like very short rations to the rest of us. The principal concern of the teamster and cowboys was that there was no grain for our horses. Going into little known country in winter, we knew that finding feed for our horses was uncertain. The upshot was that they allowed us to order the provisions and horse feed. After loading our provisions and bed rolls on Sandy's sleigh, we took off on December 3 into unknown country to most of us. The two police officers, the doctor, and the prisoner rode with Sandy on the sleigh, the rest of us on saddle horses. We mounted members of the party took turns breaking trail ahead of the team through two feet of snow. We camped long after dark at a pothole meadow 15 miles from Redstone. The temperature was between 10 below and zero. After another night camping in the snow we arrived at Eagle Lake Henry's Mountain House Ranch on the east bank of the Chilko River.

During even the first few days, relations among certain segments of the group were anything but good. First, the old country Scots started quarreling over Sandy's team of Clydes. George McKenzie, a World War One veteran and long time member of the B.C. Police, kept ribbing Sandy Robertson, another Scotsman, about the performance of his team, suggesting that we'd have been better off with a team of Indian cayuses – criticism almost amounting to sacrilege to a lover of fine horseflesh like Sandy. Although Sandy did nurse his team, most of us cowboys did not blame him. On the other hand, George, who had been married only two weeks when ordered on this trip, was in a big hurry to get it over with. George was mostly a good-natured, witty Scot, but he was determined to get this trip over with and home as soon as possible. Then two of the cowboys, in rather poor taste, kept ribbing Fred Cyre about getting a rope necktie for a Christmas present! This naturally high-strung French-Canadian, in bad shape mentally already, worried the rest of us – especially at night when we would wake up and see him pacing around the campfire muttering to himself. We finally shamed these two hard-boiled jokers into leaving Fred alone. Sergeant Dick Bowen, a lifetime police officer, was a quiet observant man with very little to say and when he did open his mouth everyone took heed and listened.

We spent the night at Eagle Lake Henry's, some of us sleeping in the hayloft of his barn. We had to leave the team and sleigh here, and the next morning rented horses from Henry. It was snowing heavily and kept it up all day. Most of the men had some riding experience, with the exception of Doctor Charter who had never been on a horse before. He had spent most of his adult life as a missionary doctor in China before coming to this lonely outpost hospital in the Chilcotin. He had been used to an unlimited number of servants who did everything for him. It was pretty tough for a man in his fifties to begin to cope with these extreme conditions and weather. Though he was game enough, he was forever getting into difficulties.

The first night out from Redstone we discovered that the doctor had no winter clothes other than what he had on his back –

about enough for one house call. The most prominent article in his bundle, along with his medical bag, was a dozen stand-up dress collars! Oliver Purjue, a practical joker, elected himself the doctor's batman and proceeded to collect bits and pieces from the rest of us and rigged out the doctor in somewhat warmer attire. Some of it fit only where it touched. Dressed as he was in over-sized clothing and being quite helpless when it came to anything outdoors, the doctor was the butt of many of our jokes, but he good naturedly took part in the laughter at his own expense. After a few episodes around the campfire, like causing a commotion by getting one foot in the fry pan and another in the soup pot, his batman would lead him off to a separate fire and watch that he stayed there till the meal was ready. Johnny Henderson and I did most of the cooking.

The doctor got saddle sore in the first hour and kept dropping back out of sight, making it necessary for one of us to go back to look for him. I once found him wandering in the snowstorm straight up the mountain away from the trail, trying to keep his horse on a moose track in the deep snow.

We made camp that night on Tsuniah Creek. It was still snowing, and after supper we all huddled around two big fires, drinking quantities of coffee, too miserable to turn in. George McKenzie, who had been ladling coffee out of the big kettle on the fire, caused a stir when he, cussing, fished a moccasin out of the bottom of the coffee pot. On finding that it was the doctor's, both he and his batman got hell for putting it to dry so close to the coffee pot and forgetting about it. No one got too upset, but there were funny looks on some faces.

The next morning, after an early start, we arrived at the mouth of the Nemiah River on Chilko Lake about 11 a.m. Here we were to leave the horses in the care of Oliver Purjue and his brother, Elmer, and their partner, Lester Dorsey. The rest of the trip was to be by boat, 32 miles south up Chilko Lake. Oliver refused to have anything to do with the lake, admitting he was scared of it. He said he would be at their little meadow with the horses when we got back — if we did get back. That last remark, coupled with what we could see of this 60-mile lake being whipped into four-foot waves by a stiff north wind, made me and the others want no part of this big water. The lake was five miles wide at this point and white-caps were everywhere.

Fred Cyre, who had made a few trips on it since he first saw

Chilko Lake in September, was really scared and was tearing around among us endeavoring to persuade us all that we should wait till the wind went down. I, for one, did not need any persuading, especially when I looked at the two boats. One was an 18-foot flat bottom scow and the other a 12-foot Clinkerbuilt, the property of the deceased Deschamps. No power, of course, but four oars in one and one pair in the other small skiff. But with that stubborn Scot, George, hammering away at us we just had to tackle it. George had promised his wife he would be back in a week, and a week was already shot and the trip hardly started. After a lot of talk and argument we persuaded ourselves to have a go at it, launched the two boats and loaded our gear. Meanwhile the howling wind seemed to get worse.

We climbed aboard, seven in the river boat, three in the skiff. I was in the larger tub. It was agreed in our boat that four men would row at a time, a man to an oar. We started out in a zig-zag fashion in that four-foot following sea, wallowing all over the place. I never in my life wished for dry land more. I was a pretty worried cowboy as I looked up at the towering waves while awaiting my turn at the oars. I had to do something to settle my nerves so I picked up the homemade Indian paddle that someone had tossed into the boat, not sure what I was going to do with it. But I found that by manipulating it on the stern I could compensate a little for the uneven stroking of the rowers and keep us on a little evener course. Water would come in over four inches of freeboard when we got in a trough and those with free hands made good use of our cooking pots bailing the boat.

We had to quarter from the east side to the west side to a spot named Gold Creek, a distance of 12 miles, to pick up a shovel. The reason was that after we'd been out on the lake for awhile the prisoner said he had broken the only shovel at the scene of the shooting where he had buried the deceased, and that we would have to cross the lake to get a pick and a shovel cached at Gold Creek. This news caused a lot of grumbling. We had to row 12 miles across a storm-aroused lake with the constant threat of being swamped – and all for one shovel.

By the time we reached Gold Creek it was dark and still windy. Though most of us were getting a little more confident that we would make it, we wanted to camp there till daylight. But after some argued that the wind would be worse at dawn, we pushed into the darkness, everyone taking a turn at the oars except the doctor and George. The doctor just could not get the hang of it and kept fouling up the other oarsmen, so we placed him in a very cramped spot in the bow and told him to keep out of the way. George did try to do his share but he had one withered arm, a war injury. We lost track of the small boat after leaving Gold Creek, angling to the east side of the lake. Hubert Campbell, Sergeant Bowen, and Billy Dagg were in the little boat. They never would have made it without Billy and his knowledge of the lake. He knew they were near Bateman's Island so managed to find it, and they landed and waited for daylight.

When we were about in the middle of the four-mile stretch of lake and five miles south of Gold Creek, the wind shifted from the north to the south quite quickly. In the pitch black of night we all knew we were in trouble. We could hardly see well enough to steer properly and quarter that on-coming sea, so it was just row and row some more, bailing and praying. Whoever was on the left facing the stern got soaking wet, and we all experienced a very grim several hours of fear and discomfort from wet and cold.

Finally we could see that we were near the shore so we instructed Jimmy MacKay, who was taking a rest in the bow, to watch for a spot to beach our boat. Jimmy kept directing us first one way, then another, avoiding half submerged rocks, until we bumped against a three-foot shelf of rock. This was the only spot, we found out at daybreak, in a long rock bluff, a mile one way and a half mile the other, where we could have landed. Some of us held the boat off while the others unloaded. After pulling the heavy tub up onto the rock shelf we got a fire going and kept it burning brightly.

This light eventually attracted the three men in the small boat and they came in safely through the boiling waves.

We found that this small shelf was only about 20 feet square, the rest of the immediate vicinity nothing but boulders and shale. Using the pick and shovel we each made a place level in the slide to open out our bedrolls. I heard some cursing then laughter – one of the boys had leveled off a spot for himself and on returning with his blankets found the doctor stretched out on his claim! None of us slept very much but had a chilly rest of sorts, better than the boat anyway. At daybreak the lake was really rolling, whitecaps as far as you could see.

Though all the mountains towered 4-5,000 feet above the water level, which was about 3,900 feet, we were marooned on one of the steepest. We spent the day drying out our clothes, eating, snoozing when we could keep warm, all quietly cursing the lake, especially George.

In the afternoon, answering the call of nature, Sandy went off alone. Spotting a pitchy fir snag he set fire to it, a stunt not uncommon in the country, especially in winter. No one paid much attention when the snag crashed to the ground and started a fire along the ground where there was no snow on the slope. It burned out of sight to the north edge of that particular mountain, but no one worried as we did not think it would go far at that time of year. But we were all awakened about midnight by light and crashing boulders. The wind had changed and the fire had burned around the mountain and was working its way down the south side and above us. As well as the angry water, we now had a forest fire to contend with. Burning logs rolled down the steep slope, some of them ending up in the lake. The worst danger was large rock freed by the burning logs that bounced down all around us. Sandy was in for a lot of trouble while we relayed buckets of water up from the lake to put out spot fires endangering our camp and supplies. Finally, the fire burned itself out enough so we could relax. We were stuck there on that ledge for another day and night while the storm raged around us. But at least we were now safe from being burned or battered by boulders.

The morning of the fourth day after leaving Nemiah Valley we were able to launch our boats and proceed south on the lake. Though it was still rough we made good time by rigging up a bed tarp as a sail. We arrived at Sill River, now known as Edmonds River, about 10:00 a.m. Then Fred told us we had a six-mile walk through slush and ice to where the corpse was buried. After a cold lunch we lined out down the trail. Because the doctor kept slipping and falling down, some of us took turns helping him along, even to packing him over difficult spots. After several hours of tough going we arrived at the scene of the gun battle.

Fred again told us his story. Apparently, he and Deschamps had met in Williams Lake in September and agreed on a partnership for the winter, working Deschamp's trapline which had a large population of marten, as well as other fur. Fred, though a logger, had done some trapping and prospecting and some work on placer diggings around Quesnel Lake. Deschamps warned Fred that he was not to do any prospecting as he did not want an influx of miners in his country. He claimed to own all the Chilko Lake watershed and intended to keep it that way. Fred said Deschamps also told him he had run off at gunpoint several partners before him as well as a number of Indians from the south and west side of the lake. Even mentioned in a vague way about disposing of a previous partner. In spite of these warnings and threats, while out on the trapline Fred kept picking up and bringing into camp likely looking quartz and ore samples. This caused bitter quarrels as time went on.

Fred was not quite sure in his mind just how tough his partner was, nor to what lengths he would go. But he did know, as did some of the rest of us, that the winter before Deschamps had made it out to Alexis Creek Hospital alone – with three broken ribs, a broken collar bone, and some bad bruises. He had had to travel 50 miles on foot as well as the length of Chilko Lake by boat. He had shot a billy goat for meat and it rolled down a steep slope, lodging on a rock shelf below. When he reached the animal it got to its feet and during the scuffle Deschamps got butted over the cliff. Yes, he was a pretty tough customer.

Fred told us that the wrangling went on till this one day on Sill River. Alex Deschamps was in the lead with his mongrel dog when he suddenly turned and fired a shot from his rifle in Fred's direction. The bullet passed over Fred's head and he jumped behind a spruce tree and let go a shot at Deschamps. Deschamps went down on his hands, losing hold of his gun. While Deschamps was on his knees trying to reach his rifle, Fred, ducking from tree to tree, kept firing at him. Though hit three times, Deschamps kept crawling towards his rifle. Fred rushed in and clubbed Deschamps in the face with his gun, laying him out. Then the dog attacked Fred and he shot it.

Fred, while trying to illustrate what had gone on, kept dashing from one spot to another and, going through different antics and postures, picked up Jimmy MacKay's rifle to better demonstrate what had happened. None of us thought it funny as Fred kept jumping from place to place while working that lever-action rifle, pumping shells from the magazine into the ground. We all took cover behind trees and most of us had a look down that gun barrel. It seemed to be pointing in every direction at once. I know I looked down that barrel at least twice. Fred was as active and quick as a cat. Finally, he passed close enough that I was able to grab the rifle.

As soon as he felt me touch the gun he relinquished it and just stood there with a wild look in his eyes, glancing first at the gun and then at his hands. This kind of excitement we hadn't bargained for and could do without. Though Fred probably would not have fired the rifle, anything could have happened in his highly excited state. Everyone was on the alert after that fright and no firearms were left where Fred could get his hands on them. I also noticed that the two wise guys made no further reference to a rope necktie for Christmas. Fred was near strung to the breaking point while he explained why he buried the corpse and dead dog so that wolverines or other animals would not disfigure them. We found, while digging up the body, that Fred had done his best in trying to keep the bodies from hungry beasts. They would have had to dig up layer on layer of rocks and logs, as well as dirt, to get at them.

The doctor performed the autopsy, showing where each bullet had clipped vital organs, and the side of the face smashed in. Death must have been fairly fast. When he was finished and before closing the grave, he read a short burial service. We filled the grave and hurried back to the lake. We spent the night on the bank of Sill River and headed north in the morning down Chilko Lake by boat. The return trip down the mighty Chilko was uneventful, and at Nemiah we found Oliver and Elmer waiting with the horses as they had promised.

Three days later at Eagle Lake Henry's an official inquest was held by the Coroner at which Fred, calmer now, told his story again, mostly for the benefit of Oliver Purjue, the sixth juryman. Also, the doctor told of his findings that Alex Deschamps met his death from bullet wounds inflicted by Fred Cyre and the date and place. It took us three more days to reach Redstone, with a few days to spare before Christmas. Fred Cyre was held in custody till the spring Assizes in Prince George, where the jury acquitted him, calling the act self-defence.

There was such an abundance of marten on that trap line that Jimmy MacKay and I had thoughts of going back to trap there that winter but chickened out when we remembered that wicked lake.

CHETA JOHNNY: Cheta Meadows along Whitewater Lake is named after Cheta Johnny, an Indian born in Bella Coola but who lived his life in Nemiah Valley. He was an incredible boatman. Cheta could cross Chilko Lake in a canoe through a storm that would have been suicide for a lesser man. He trapped on the western slope of the Coast Range and it is likely that the name Cheta was derived from Cedar. Apparently Cheta became Setah. His son was Little George Setah of Nemiah and that is the name the family goes by today.

According to Willy George (Setah), son of Little George, his grandfather, Cheta Johnny, would often take his furs to Seattle by boat instead of coming back over the mountains with his catch. "He look for a big tree then chop out a boat and go down the coast to Seattle. He always come back with new shoes, pants, coat."

Big Creek residents gather at the Fletcher Lake road camp in the 1930s for a picnic. A three-legged race is in progress.

Eagle Lake Henry and his wife, Millie, at Mountain House.

EAGLE LAKE HENRY was born and raised at Mountain House on the south side of the Chilko River, an area occupied for generations by his mother's people who were originally from Bella Coola.

Henry, who took the name "Eagle Lake" from the beautiful mountain lake on the north side of the river, now called Choelquoit, obtained "white man's rights" which gave him privileges and responsibilities denied at that time to the native people. He then purchased the land at Mountain House from the government and leased outlying meadows.

Eagle Lake Henry had no education but he was a proud man, intelligent and progressive, and never asked for government help. He was a good trapper and this fur revenue gave him his start in cattle.

He and his wife, Alyetta, were picking huckleberries on Potato Mountain when they ran across a den of silver foxes – a great find as the price for silver fox furs was high. Henry trapped five of these foxes just after Christmas that year and sold the pelts to Andy Stuart of Redstone for $500 apiece. He saved the $2,500 and in the spring he and his wife rode to Anahim Lake and bought 20 head of yearling heifers from rancher Old Capoose. They drove them home, and a year later he bought a bull from Graham and Dagg at Tatla Lake. He also bought a purebred Percheron stallion and raised top work horses. The price of furs remained high for a few years and Eagle Lake was able to buy mower and rake, harness, tools, and a blacksmith outfit. He eventually ran 160 head of cattle. In later years he bought a thoroughbred stallion and raised good saddle horses.

Henry and his wife had no children but adopted two girls: Mary Jane, and Dona, one of Joe Elkins' daughters. Elkins gave the baby girl to Mrs. Henry as a present as she couldn't have children. Henry paid the Bellamy family and others at Tatlayoko to board Mary Jane and Dona so that the girls could attend school. Both girls went through Grade Eight. Mary Jane married Pete Baptiste and lives on a 160-acre farm on the west side of the Fraser River opposite Marguerite.

Dona married Gabriel (Gabby) Baptiste who was killed in a car accident. Dona now lives in Prince George.

Eagle Lake's wife died in 1961 and he married Millie who pre-deceased him in 1964. Eagle Lake Henry died 1967 and is buried beside his two wives in a solidly fenced plot overlooking the buildings at Mountain House. After his death, Mountain House Ranch was sold to Joe Schuk of Tatlayoko and now belongs to Clifford and Alyson Schuk who, with their three daughters, make their home there. The numerous original log buildings still stand.

MERCY MISSION BECOMES A DUEL WITH DEATH

by Tommy Gordon

The Franklin Arm *was a boat belonging to Bill Bliss, a big-game guide who used the boat in the 1960s and early 1970s to take hunters up Chilko Lake to Franklin Arm, his guiding territory.*

Tommy Gordon an experienced outdoorsman, borrowed Bill's boat for his summer excursions to his mine on Mt. Good Hope at the upper end of Chilko Lake. Of this boat, Gordon writes in the following account:

It is August 21, 1969. I am shipwrecked on the shore of Chilko Lake and, with time on my hands, will endeavor to tell of my ordeal. It may in future help the operator of small craft on Chilko or any other good-sized lake.

This story begins on the morning of August 16, 1969, at my camp at Mt. Good Hope at the head of Chilko Lake. I wakened at 5 a.m. to the groans of a suffering youth who, with another man, had been prospecting in the area. I came to the conclusion that the youngster needed medical attention, so I prepared to take him and his partner (a mature man) to Chilko Lake Lodge at the other end of the lake. Luckily, the lake was fairly calm after a wind-storm that raged for two days. I had the boat ready and we set off at 6 a.m. We arrived at the Lodge at 8:30. The suffering boy and his friend got away immediately on a truck that was just leaving for Williams Lake. I had refueled and started back to my Franklin Arm camp by 10 a.m. Twelve miles from the Lodge the water got a bit rough so I pulled in to Dan Wier's cabin and docked.

The boat I was operating was the *Franklin Arm*, a very sea-worthy craft nearly 19 feet long. But since I was the only occupant, I decided to take along an anchor, an 18-inch-long rock, rather round with a slight depression in the middle that was ideal for rope tying.

I waited until the storm abated and set off again about 12:30, keeping on the west shoreline to what is known as the lagoon. Here the wind picked up again. I anchored and stayed there until 2:30 p.m. The squall died down and no whitecaps could be seen so I proceeded on my journey. After starting the tag-along motor and shifting into forward gear, the shift lever broke. Then, near Gold Creek, I discovered that the steering motor had a gas leak, so I anchored in a small bay to make repairs. The lake was getting rough and it looked to me like it was going to be a real blow. Worse, I couldn't start the motor to get closer to shore. It was getting really rough by this time and I could tell the anchor was slipping along the bottom.

I took off the motors and laid them inside the boat, and then proceeded to make a bulkhead for the transom. I used half-inch plywood from the floor. With this accomplished to my satisfaction, I waited to ride out the storm. It was now 6 p.m. I secured the motors inside the boat as both were out of order and it was too rough to make any immediate repairs. Couldn't anyway, since I was really being tossed about. I moved my suitcase and some foodstuff on top of the cabin and secured them also. By now I was mighty cold, and drifting parallel to shore and about 200 feet out, with darkness descending fast.

By 7:30 the wind had a shrieking sound, like a bunch of banshees – must be 60 miles an hour. I am debating with myself what best to do: stay with the boat and perish from wet and cold, or go ashore while I can still move. I decide on the latter. I sealed my lighter, lighter fluid and matches in a tight plastic bag, then rolled my sleeping bag in a plastic sheet with tea, tea pail, rolled the contents and my axe into a 5 by 7" ground sheet tied securely onto the air mattress. I put a wooden stick to serve as a toggle on the end of the rope so I could hang on.

By now the water was up to the top of the floor and I was played out trying to keep it baled out with a gallon can. I gave up. Next I took off my rain pullover, tied both life jackets on – one in front, one on my back – then put the rain pullover back on which was a job! My teeth were chattering, my hands numb. It must have been the help of the Almighty. I wore my rubber boots with oilskins tied tight around the ankle. I remember pulling my hat tight over my ears, then putting the rain hood up and tying it tight around my throat. I noticed my heart beat was steady, my fingers and hands were no longer numb.

I could just see the shoreline 200 feet away. I grabbed the toggle on the air mattress and stood up, holding on to the steering wheel. With a prayer on my lips for all my friends and loved ones I, being a Roman Catholic, made the sign of the cross, let go of the wheel and found myself in the water. I was quite conscious, always was a good swimmer which helped, but found my legs heavy. I saw mountainous waves coming at me but I seemed like a cork with the two lifejackets. The waves were following the shore line so I had to paddle through them. The air mattress was a hindrance but I had to hold onto it and pull it with me as it meant everything to me.

The waves pulled the mattress back and me along with it, but gradually I was able to make a little more headway towards shore. Finally, a huge wave tossed me onto the big rocks on shore. The backwash on the air mattress was so great I had all I could do to pull it, little by little, but I finally made it. I must have been in the water nearly an hour as it was pitch dark by now. I managed to get up the hill with many stumbles, dragging the mattress, inch by inch. My vision was clear of water by now and, while taking a breather, I made out a big stump and log near me and moved to it.

With trembling hands I took off my rainhood and life jackets. It seemed to take a long time to locate the plastic bag with the matches and lighter. I felt around and found a good lot of pine needles and twigs which I squirted with lighter fluid. My hands were so cold I just couldn't open the match box so I tried the lighter and it worked. I soon had a small blaze going which the wind fanned against the log into a good fire. Gratefully, I stood behind the stump to keep out of the wind till my hands got warm, then I took off my outer garments and boots and put the ground sheet around me. Wrung out my clothes as good as I could and spread them to dry. My sleeping bag was only slightly wet so I wrapped it around me, said a prayer of thanksgiving and passed out.

Came awake at daylight dawning and found my sleeping bag smoldering. Stamped the embers out. The boat was anchored about 800 feet farther down the lake than where I left it, but tossed about as the wind was still blowing a gale. Expected to see the *Franklin Arm* disintegrate any moment as nothing can stand that wind. I took the tea pail to the water's edge to get water for tea but it was mostly sand so I cut a long willow pole to reach out farther for cleaner water. Boiled it up on my fire and, gee, but that cup of tea was sure good! I drank the pot dry. It's Sunday, August 17.

At full daylight I surveyed all my aches and pains. My hands are cut and scratched – bad cut in the palm of the left hand. But when I looked at my landing place I knew that the Almighty Power protected me. Such a jungle of rocks and logs and sticks, and I could see why I had such a struggle to get over the ground. I was fortunate indeed to get away with only minor cuts and bruises.

Old fir logs don't burn so good but give plenty of heat. Catching a cold. Drank a gallon of tea by mid day. The wind velocity must be over 50 miles per hour as the banshees are still howling. Extra heavy waves coming in: first one filled the boat with water, second one swamped it completely. I saw a 10-gallon keg of gas came over the stern so I ran down to the beach where I recovered it. From then on I was exceptionally busy salvaging gas tanks and everything else that came my way. The clouds were very low and roaring whirlwinds picked up water and carried it higher than I could see. Sounds like a tornado.

During this session the rope on the anchor broke and the wind now pounded hell out of the boat on the rocks. I saw the bow end rope floating by, got hold of it and anchored it to a tree. I was wet from head to foot. I kept pulling the slack as the boat was bounced in to shore to where it is now. My fire got away but I was too busy to stop it from spreading. Luckily it was put out by huge waves and a rain and sleet squall. The awful wind roared and screeched all night long as I sat up drying everything by the fire.

Monday, August 18: The wind is down this morning to about 30 miles an hour. I was able to anchor the rear end of the boat and blocked the side near the lake to keep it from rocking. Accomplished this with logs and willow branches. I am proud of this part of the salvage. Still can't get inside the boat to survey the damage. Drying my wet clothes all the rest of the day. Strong winds kept up with intermittent rain squalls, ceiling still at about 200 feet.

Tuesday, August 19: Surveyed damage to the *Franklin Arm* and found it rather extensive. Debating what to do. Put up distress signals; then had a good meal as I had rescued one box of groceries and fashioned a fry pan and hot cake turner from a piece of tin I found still in the boat. Used wood for handles. Got the clock running to pass the time away, then rested till nightfall. A cow and calf moose visited me about midnight, coming to within 10 feet of the boat.

Wednesday, August 20: Still blowing in high intermittent squalls. Able to walk along the beach. Made another survey of the *Franklin Arm* – could be worse. Drew up plans for repairs to make it seaworthy again and decided what materials I would need. Made hotcakes; boy, were they good! I have plenty to eat now and what an appetite I have after the rigors of August 16. Wind down to about 20 miles an hour but snow blowing to timberline across the lake. Clear sky showing in patches. Made repairs to one motor: starts good and sounds good.

Thursday, August 21: My camp is in order, my memory is fresh, and I've time on my hands. This is the day I was supposed to be out to civilization. Wind is down to about 10 miles, occasional squalls. Took a walk along the lakeshore and picked up my

346

parka with hood which was 10 feet above regular water level. Also two oars. Saw a black bear and cub moving along the shore towards Gold Creek. Jets have been flying and breaking the sound barrier every night since I've been marooned here. I've heard no planes, though, since last Sunday when two went over. Don't see how they could fly in such a storm. Seems to be clearing at this time. Wind has changed from east to south but still plenty of white-caps showing along the Nemiah shore.

Friday, August 22: Up at daylight. So quiet! Not a ripple on the water. Brewed a gallon of coffee and started writing again. At 9 a.m. I fired a couple of shots as distress signals as last night I saw a light across the lake on the Nemiah side – maybe a campfire. Just after firing the distress shots I saw a boat on the Nemiah shore. I waved my red-lined parka to attract them. The boat stopped at the rocky point and I fired three more signals but the boat went on. I assumed it was the Fishery boat as it looked like it. Several planes passed overhead at about 9,000 feet – none had pontoons. Then one plane wagged his wings: I repeated my signal. He circled to a low altitude and repeated his wing wag meaning "O.K. I observe." On his second circle he started for a steep climb then dipped down, meaning: "Will report." The boat of the morning passed by at 3 p.m. back to the lower end of the lake, but not a sign from them that they had seen or heard my signal. My hope for the day is gone. Spent the rest of the daylight hours making preparations to try to refloat the *Franklin Arm*. Clouded up at 4 p.m. with wind from the north. At 7:30 a little yellow plane was flying low to the south. I kept waving my red parka but he may not have seen me as the sun was in his eyes, but he did seem to turn towards Tsuniah Lodge or maybe Chilko Lake Lodge. Hope he spotted me.

Saturday, August 23: Calm this morning. Hope it stays calm for the next month. Had a fair night's rest. Three cheers! Bob Brebner arrived at 10:30 by boat with a bunch of fishermen and we made arrangements to transport necessary items to the Forestry Branch at Chilko Lake. It's a full week since I was wrecked here on this desolate shore.

But now rescue is at hand. Thanksgiving fills my soul.

TATLAYOKO

(spelled Tatlahcoh on some of the early maps)

Our thanks to Joe, Katie, and Helen Schuk for willingly providing information about the early history of the Tatlayoko Valley. Thanks also to Gerry Bracewell for her contribution.

In the early 1900s, TOM MORRIS of Vancouver staked a mining claim on a mountain on the south end of Tatlayoko (pronounced Tatlako) Lake. He put in a sawmill and built boats and a camp at the bottom of the valley on Nostetuko Creek. His brother, John, was involved in the work as well. The Morris Mine was hard-rock gold and difficult to extract but ran for quite a number of years. The ore had to be brought down the mountain and then up the lake by boat and shipped to Trail to be smelted. The Feeny mine was operating in the area at that time, too. A man named AL RAFFERTY was there for a short time and then staked a claim on West Branch.

At this time EUGENE MATTHEWS had a place at the end of the lake and a trapline. Sometime before 1912, LOU HUDGINS and CHARLIE JAMESON came to B.C. from Idaho and made their way via Bute Inlet to Tatlayoko Lake. The trip on foot over the old Waddington route through the Coast Mountains took 10 days. These men had worked in mines in Idaho and were hired by Morris to do assessment work on his hematite claim.

Later, Hudgins homesteaded three miles below the foot of the lake. In winter he trapped with Matthews on a circular trapline, staying in small lean-to shelters along the trail, each man travelling one day ahead of the other. They met on Christmas Day at the home cabin. After Christmas, they set out again and trapped until late in February.

Jameson took up land about half way up the lake and ran a trapline on the far side. He had a boat, built by Tom Morris, to cross over to check his line. Frank Therriault, who rode into the Chilcotin on horseback with Frank Witte from Washington in 1912, trapped with Jameson in the fall of 1912 and winter of 1913. Marten and weasels were their main catch. Winter storms made crossing the rough mountain lake to the trapline hazardous and the two men sometimes had to camp overnight in a lean-to on the far side.

In the summer of 1913 Therriault took up a 160-acre pre-emption a mile or so from the upper end of Tatlayoko Lake. He built a cabin with help from Lou Hudgins, whip-sawing lumber for floor and window frames. That fall he went back to the U.S., but in spring he returned to his pre-emption and spent two more years there.

A couple named Wilson, with two children, built a place with house and barn up the hill from the north end of Tatlayoko Lake, and an Englishman named George Laws, noted for his extraordinary memory, lived in a cabin between Wilson and Jameson. When Therriault snowshoed out to Tatla Lake on a regular basis to get his love letters from Anna Witte in Twisp, he picked up mail and tobacco for the other settlers as well, and always Wilson's newspaper which kept them in touch with the outside world.

In 1916 when the U.S. became involved in World War One, Therriault was called back to Washington for the draft. The B.C. government held his land at Tatlayoko until 1918 and when the war was over, he was given 60 days to return to his pre-emption. He decided to relinquish it. He was married to Frank Witte's sister, Anna, by this time and had decided to stay in Washington.

Therriault's place was taken up and improved by George Powers who sold it to Ken Moore. Powers later moved to Charlotte Lake, and Matthews and Hudgins abandoned their places and went to Horsefly. Here Hudgins founded the Woodjam Ranch at Black Creek and spent the rest of his life there. Wilson, Jameson and Laws stayed on longer in Tatlayoko but did not become permanent residents.

CHARLEY SKINNER came to the country in the early 1900s. He took up a meadow at Tatlayoko, still known as Skinner Meadow, which was later purchased by Ken Moore and now belongs to Joe Schuk. He also had a place on the east side of Quitsin Lake, purchased later by Harry McGee. Skinner Mountain at Tatlayoko is named after him. He raised horses, mostly of good stock, and had about 800 of these horses running on the range around Big Eagle Lake when laws came out forbidding horses at large. These horses were so wild Skinner couldn't do anything with them.

Billy Dagg and Eagle Lake Henry tried to round them up but the big strong animals were as wild as deer and they couldn't do it. The range was needed for cattle but was crowded with these useless horses so the government paid cowboys to shoot them. This

was no easy task. Most of the wild-horse hunters were local men, skilled and daring riders with a steady hand and a sure aim. Skinner had by this time abandoned his place and left the animals to their own resources.

Charley Skinner spent his latter days in the Old Men's Home in Kamloops. He died in the 1930s. The legendary Chee Wit (Lily Jack) was his daughter.

FRED CYRE lived in the Tatlayoko Valley for awhile in the 1920s. He built a cabin beside Alsta Creek near Purjues and grew a garden for several years. He also spent quite a bit of time at Lingfield Creek and trapped at the upper end of Chilko Lake.

Other settlers in Tatlayoko before 1923 were the KITCHEN BROTHERS, VAL and DOUG, who lived up the hill across Chicken Creek. They came from Ontario and went to work in the Chilcotin for Reg Newton and W. H. Bliss. Being excellent horsemen, they broke many of the young Arabian saddle horses for Newton. They both joined the Canadian Army in 1914 and went to war where Doug was killed in action. Val returned to the pre-emption in Tatlayoko but didn't stay long.

The HOWE family of whom little is known.

BILL MEGGET and family arrived in 1914 and built a house and barn about 10 miles down Tatlayoko Lake. He only stayed a short time, then left to become a policeman.

DAN PUCKET lived at the south end of the lake. He died there and was buried under the fir trees just south of Harry Haynes' place.

KENNON BEVERLY "K. B." MOORE
by Gerry Bracewell

"When I am but a speck of dust in the Giant Arms of Dust some blood of mine will yet be warm, some heart still echo my old cares and happiness." This passage was a favourite quotation of Kennon Beverly Moore, Tatlayoko Lake pioneer rancher.

K. B. Moore was born in Boston, Massachusetts in 1891 to parents whose lineage dated directly back to one of the *Mayflower's* voyages to the New World. In fact the Boston Commons acquired its name from the "common milk cow pasture" donated to the villagers by Paul Blackstone Moore, a great-great uncle of K. B.'s.

K. B. Moore held true to family type when, at the age of 21, he left Boston for Canada's west, coming directly to the remote Chilcotin. He worked for Norman Lee for awhile before checking out the Chezacut country. An area there is known as Ken Moore Flats. Still searching for a homesite, he rode horseback into Tatlayoko where the spring grass on April 1 was so lush he could picket his saddlehorse overnight on it. Camped under a big fir tree, he saw the potential for a cattle ranch in this unsettled, verdant valley.

When World War One broke out, K. B. joined the Royal Canadian Engineers, as his native land was not yet involved in the war. While laying track for ammunition cars in the front lines in France his entire company was gassed. He alone survived. After spending a period of recuperation in Scotland, he returned to the Chilcotin and the still unsettled Tatlayoko Valley. He immediately applied for a homestead and commenced clearing the jungle growth on a rich river delta bordering the north shore of Tatlayoko Lake. Stumping powder and burning were the tools used in those days.

In June 1920, Ken married Dora Isabel Church (Dolly), third daughter of H. E. and Gertrude Church, pioneer settlers at Big Creek. Moores had a daughter, Isabel, and a son, Beverly. Ken and his wife worked hard at enlarging the "garden patch" to become hayfields that would maintain the eventual herd of Hereford cattle. His first beef drive to Williams Lake, a long twenty-day drive, was good experience but netted only enough cash to buy a sack of flour. When time permitted, he guided grizzly bear hunting parties with Ralph Edwards in the Bella Coola watershed.

Kennon Beverly Moore in the Armed Forces during World War One.

Despite setbacks that would have discouraged lesser men (his wife packed up while he was on a beef drive and left with the two small children), he struggled on, hiring what help he could afford and extending his hospitality and generosity to new settlers following the trail into Tatlayoko. His reputation for honesty and responsibility to his fellow man gained the respect and goodwill of neighbours throughout the Chilcotin.

As the community grew so also did the socializing, and many a dance and picnic were held at K. B.'s Circle X Ranch. His big log ranchhouse, built in two sections shaped like an L, accommodated visitors and eventually the post office. Mail and supplies for the residents of Tatlayoko were brought in bi-monthly by Tommy Hodgson in his two-ton truck. People such as Eagle Lake Henry, riding in from a great distance for their mail, would stay overnight at the ranchhouse, passing the news from that part of the country.

When Isabel and Beverly Moore were in their teens they returned to work with their father, much to his delight. After a few years Isabel married Ben Wilson, a local cowboy and they ranched for awhile on the old Purjue place. Bev married Gerry Lovell of Vancouver, and they joined forces with K. B. to help run the Circle X. Bev joined up in World War Two and Isabel and Ben with their two daughters, Rebecca and Marlene, moved to Heffley Creek near

Ken Moore feeding cattle on his Circle X Ranch at Tatlayoko.

Kamloops to work with Isabel's mother, Dolly Moore. This left Ken and Gerry to run the ranch.

Beverly and Gerry had two sons, Martin and Barry. Beverly returned after the war to ranch with his mother at Heffley Creek. He eventually remarried and he and his wife have five daughters. Gerry and her boys stayed to help K. B. look after the Circle X, which included the long beef drives to Williams Lake. Invariably, K. B.'s yearling steers took a prize or a cup, donated by the Williams Lake business community.

In 1953 K. B. became violently ill and was eventually diagnosed as having incurable cancer. He was given two months to live, but his cheerful outlook stretched that two months to six. During this time he flew to New Mexico to visit his brother, Paul, whom he hadn't seen for 40 years. Upon his return he entered Shaughnessy Hospital in Vancouver. He died there in 1954 but his indomitable spirit lived on to the end. Cremation followed as he had requested and his ashes were returned to the country and ranch that he loved.

Kennon Beverly Moore – a grand pioneer. His favorite quote has come true: numerous grandchildren carry forward his dreams and aspirations.

Gerry Moore married Alf Bracewell and still lives at Tatlayoko. They have two sons, Kevin and Alex. The old ranch has been sold, but Gerry is still a guide-outfitter, taking out hunters each fall, as well as trail rides from their big log lodge on Potato Mountain.

CHARLIE PARKS was one of the first ranchers in Tatlayoko. He drained a small lake situated near Quitsin Lake into the Homathko River and developed a hay field – now known as Park's Meadow. Charlie Parks sold his place to Harry McGhee and spent the winters at Redstone. He was a handy, well-liked man and worked at various odd jobs around the country. Becoming restless in the summertime he decided to drain Whitesands Lake. He was building a cabin to live in and, while working on the roof, a rung in the ladder gave way and he broke his leg in a fall to the ground. He crawled to his bunk and lay there for nearly a week before anyone came by. He blew a shrill whistle every little while and by chance Jim Holt heard it as he was riding by from a cattle drive.

Isabel Moore and Del Haynes were behind with team and

Heading out: Left to right – Dolly Moore, Ben Wilson, Gerry Moore, Ken Moore, and Beverly Moore.

354

wagon and when they arrived the suffering man was loaded into the wagon and taken on a painful journey over a rough road to Tatla Lake. From there he was transported by car to the hospital in Williams Lake. Gangrene had set in and the doctor told him the leg would have to be amputated. Parks couldn't face such an ordeal at his age and just gave up. He died in November of 1941.

His first place now belongs to Terry Jordan, and Ed Schuk owns the Whitesands place.

EMERY and ALICE BELLAMY were from Montana but of English descent. They came to the Tatlayoko Valley in 1924 and ranched on Crazy Creek for 20 years. They had two sons – Cecil and Woodrow – and three daughters – Margaret who married Scotty Shields, and Sylvia who married Tom Stepp. Their eldest daughter, Maud, never lived in the valley. The younger Bellamy girls were educated in Tatlayoko.

Cecil Bellamy met his wife, Gladys, when she came to the valley as the first teacher in the one-room Tatlayoko School. In 1945 Emery Bellamy sold his ranch to Joe Schuk who also bought the Cecil Bellamy pre-emption in 1942 from Tom Stepp. When Cecil died in 1994 his sons, Bill and Stan, scattered their father's ashes at Tatlayoko.

TOM STEPP started the ranch that now belongs to Carol Satre. Stepp spent some of his time at his gold mine on Crazy Creek Mountain, although it failed to develop into a paying proposition. He lost a hand in World War Two but managed well with a hook. Cecil and Woodrow Bellamy did most of the actual mine work, while Tom was busy with hunting and survey parties.

HARRY and HOWARD McGHEE, brothers, came to Tatlayoko from Nebraska about 1924. Harry and his wife, Emelia, and Howard and Cecelia and three daughters made the long journey in two Model T Ford cars. They stayed for awhile at Ken Moore's after reaching Tatlayoko. Howard and his wife and family soon returned to Nebraska, but Harry and Emelia became permanent settlers.

Harry drove his Model T to Big Creek where he traded it for a team of work horses and was soon ranching on his own in Tatlayoko. He bought Parks Meadow and a lower place, growing a big garden, even hardy fruits at the latter. They ran their cattle towards Stikelan Pass until wolves became too costly a problem. McGhees then got range on Potato Mountain.

Harry and Emelia had two daughters, Katie and Helen, who

worked hard along with their parents. Katie was born in Tatlayoko, delivered by Dolly Moore at Moore's Ranch. Helen was born in the little hospital at Alexis Creek. The two girls attended the one-room school at Tatlayoko whenever possible but got most of their education through correspondence courses.

The girls married brothers Joe and Ed Schuk, and both still live at Tatlayoko: Joe and Katie at the old Bellamy place on Crazy Creek; and Ed and Helen at Lunch Lake. Harry McGhee died in 1977 and is buried at Tatla Lake. Emelia spent her last years in a small apartment in Williams Lake, looked after by Mildred Krause and June Draney.

LLOYD McGHEE, a younger brother to Harry and Howard, came to the country later. He started the Peterson Place which was sold several times and now belongs to Joe Schuk, and the ranch that now belongs to Calvin Schuk. In later years he worked as a fire spotter at Puntzi. Lloyd is buried also at Tatla Lake.

IRA PURJUE, elder brother of Elmer and Oliver, with his wife Edith and family of five, followed his brothers to the Chilcotin in 1926, leaving Idaho in their one-ton Dodge truck. Reaching the Chilcotin they camped at Redstone for a time. Then, in order to put the kids to school, they moved to Chezacut and worked on various ranches. In 1929 they moved to Nemiah Valley and stayed with Elmer and Oliver on their Elkins Creek ranch. By the spring of 1930, Ira and Edith were on the move again, headed for Tatlayoko via Tsuniah Lake with a heavily loaded iron-tired wagon and four-horse team. The eldest children rode horseback. They followed saddle-horse trails which meant cutting out trees to widen the track for the wagon and improvising on the steep sidehills. Copying his brothers, Ira plowed furrows for the wagon wheels along the steepest slopes – quite a feat in itself – then anchored a stout 15-foot pole to the reach (a coupling pole joining the hind axle to the forward transverse bar of a wagon) at right angles to the wagon. The far end was slung from a rope lashed to the top of the wagon box so that the pole cleared the ground by two feet or so on the upper side. Then as many youngsters as were able rode the pole to help keep the heavy wagon upright as they navigated the steep hillsides.

Crossing the swift Chilko River was probably the most intimidating part of the difficult journey. There was no bridge, and Tatlayoko lay on the other side so there was no choice but to ford. Electing to seek help from Eagle Lake Henry, who lived nearby at his Mountain House Ranch, was a wise move.

Elmer and Oliver Purjue, twin brothers from Bruneau, Idaho and Mary Baptiste, Elmer's wife. (See also page 370.)

He knew the river well and had forded it many times at this spot, known as Henry's Crossing. He rode his saddle horse into the treacherous river ahead of Ira and his team and wagon and piloted them safely across. Even so, there were anxious moments when the horses were near swimming and the wagon box was often under water as they moved downstream with the swift current and finally to the far bank where the Indians had a safe landing place.

A chore dreaded by pioneers was whip-sawing, or cutting lumber by hand.

From here on their travels took them by Big Eagle Lake (now called Choelquoit). It was beautiful country where grass was lush on the open sidehills, moose and deer were everywhere and wild horses galloped away across the meadows as they approached – like a glimpse of the promised land to the weary travellers.

At Tatlayoko the Purjues picked out a homestead. By fall the children were enrolled in school and Ira and the boys had built a two-room cabin just in time for the birth of Ira and Edith's sixth child on September 21. Neighbour Dolly Moore delivered the little boy and they named him Henry. Edith Purjue worked hard gardening, sewing and keeping a clean, comfortable home for her large family. She was musical and often played the piano at country dances. Her daughter and sons inherited this talent.

The Ira Purjues made their home in the Tatlayoko Valley until their family – Retta, Joe, Willard, Jarrid, Elmer, and Henry were grown. During World War Two, Joe, Willard, and Elmer went back

358

to the States and enlisted in the Armed Forces. Their father went with them. Elmer was killed in action in the war. Willard returned to Canada and the Chilcotin. They all married and raised families. Retta married Hank Law and one of their sons, Milt Law, lives with his wife, Carol, at Chilanko Forks where he has a garage business.

Edith Purjue married Johnny Henderson and they lived in the country until Johnny's death in 1968. Edith died in March 1980 after moving to Williams Lake.

DEL HAYNES came to Tatlayoko in 1930 with her family of four boys – Lou, Laurie, Ray, and Ken – driving up from New Westminster in an old Hudson Essex car. The eldest son, Harry, came to the country the year before to work at Alexis Lake and he joined the family at Tatlayoko a few years later. Del stayed in the valley, working hard to support her family. The younger boys grew up and were educated there, helping peel logs for the schoolhouse that was just being built.

Harry and Lou became big-game guides. Harry's knowledge of the mountains gained him and his first wife, Muriel, the privilege in 1945 of packing Don and Phyllis Munday in to Mt. Reliance, situated 20 miles southwest of Tatlayoko Lake. The Mundays, famous for being the first to explore and climb Mt. Waddington, were the first to scale Reliance.

Mt. Waddington, 4,016 m (13,172 feet), the highest peak totally in B. C., was known as Mystery Mountain until it was conquered in 1936 by the Mundays, who gave the unknown mountain the name of Waddington. A high peak nearby is named Mt. Munday. In 1983 Mrs. Phyllis Munday, then 87, was flown by helicopter as part of a B.C. program, "Thrill of a Lifetime," to the Homathko Icefield and Mt. Waddington. Clad in her old boots and carrying one of her old ice axes, Phyllis realized her dream of walking once more on the beautiful 420-square-mile Homathko Icefield. She was then flown to Waddington to know again the thrill of its lofty grandeur – 47 years after their first ascent.

Harry and his wife, Fran, still live in Tatlayoko. They run the post office and carry the mail from Tatla Lake to Tatlayoko once a week. For many years they had the only phone in the valley until B.C. Tel reached the settlement in 1990.

Lou and wife, Doris, lived at Eagle Lake but are now at Yarrow. Laurie lives at Penticton and Ken in Hope. Ray, who became a Game Warden and was posted for awhile at Alexis Creek, died a few years after serving in World War Two.

CAPTAIN DAVID LLOYD was a dapper Englishman, a remittance man who took up land north of Tom Stepp's place. He lived there as a bachelor. When he was getting on in years he went in the late 1930s to Vancouver Island on a holiday and came back with a young wife named Eva. He moved to Kleena Kleene and then to the Coast. Captain Lloyd's place is now part of Satre's ranch.

JOE and KATIE SCHUK: Joe came to Tatlayoko as a young man in 1936 from the dried-out country around Shipman, Saskatchewan. Because the family farm was isolated, Joe was 10 before he was able to attend school. He came west with his grandparents, Dave Hamm Sr., wife Sarah, and their family – Bert, Dave, Edgar and Wanda.

Joe says that when they reached the Chilanko area he had to get out of the car and scout around to locate the road. At that time the track went from one ranch to the next and Arthur Knoll's road was the plainest. The lush growth and ample rainfall at Tatlayoko must have looked good to the boy from the dust bowl. Things were not easy in this corner of B. C. either, but Joe stuck it out and became a successful rancher. Schuk bought the Bellamy place on Crazy Creek and when his parents, Martin and Sarah, moved to the country they stayed with him for awhile. They then located a half mile from him. Martin and Sarah had nine children. Joe, Eddie, John, Larry and Bob stayed in Tatlayoko. Tommy left the country. The girls, Eleanor (Huston); Doris (Tyrrell); and Francis (McGregor) all married and left Tatlayoko. Joe and Katie run a 500-head ranch operation, ranging their cattle on Crazy Creek Mountain at first. They now use Potato Mountain, and Eagle Lake Henry's range on the south side of the Chilko River.

Temporary residents in the valley in the 1930s were: Cliff and Delores Carlton (Delores taught school); the Frasers, with son Gayland and daughters, Katherine and Nellie, who lived across the Homathko River from Haynes; Percy and Dorothy Church; and Marian Church.

GEORGE POWERS came to the country from Washington in 1914. He was related to the notorious Plummer Gang but had none of their characteristics. A quiet, well-dressed cowboy, Powers fell in love with Jessie, the daughter of a Chilcotin Indian Chief. Jessie returned his affection but her father forbad her to marry a white man. Undeterred, the young lovers plotted secretly. Powers had two good saddle horses and one night the lovers fled on horseback. The Chief and a party of young men pursued the runaways but, realizing the couple were mounted on strong fast horses, soon returned home.

Powers knew the mountain country to the west and headed for the remote Tatlayoko Valley where there was a secluded log cabin. Later, George and Jessie made a permanent home at Charlotte Lake where they ranched and trapped. During their time, there was no road into this isolated lake and no neighbours.

George and Jessie's last years were spent in the old log house at the Gables, owned by Dan Lee. Here, George had a leather shop where he made and sold western gear and repaired saddles, harness and the like. Jessie, who wore long skirts and a kerchief on her head all her life, never lost her shyness but sat quietly in the background when George visited with his friends.

This romantic liaison of frontier days was true love. The American cowboy and his Indian princess lived their lives faithfully together. They had no children.

HANK LAW, in a manuscript titled *Footloose Fool*, has written of his experiences beginning in 1930 when he arrived in Canada from England until he joined the R.C.A.F. in 1939.

With candid humour he tells of his adventures and misadventures, riding the rails across the continent during the great depression, mining at Sooke on Vancouver Island and at Fort St. James, riding a bicycle from Vancouver into the Chilcotin and, finally, of escapades, dilemmas and a few close calls as he rides head-on into life on the frontier. Occasional colorful phrases show his appreciation of the wilderness in his travels: "The heavy timber with its white mantles of snow looked like thousands of giants standing side by side in their nightshirts." "The shadows on the north side were blue. It looked as if the Master Painter had a little color left over and had brushed it on each mountain top with a downward sweep of His brush...."

Hank's Chilcotin lessons in the School of Hard Knocks began with his first job working for Duke Martin on the C1 Ranch at Alexis Creek, and took him to Tatla and Clearwater Lakes, to the Morris Mine at Tatlayoko and a pre-emption on the wild Klinaklini River. He married Retta Purjue at Tatlayoko and built a home there in the wilderness, Retta staunchly at his side. A son and a daughter were born. Both he and his wife were musical and teamed up together with accordion and guitar to play for country dances. The couple and their two small children were at the C1 Ranch again in 1939 when Hank made his decision to join the R.C.A.F and the fight for freedom. Hank and Retta had a family of four boys and a girl.

The following accounts from *Footloose Fool* are used with permission.

THE HORSE WHO CAME TO DINNER

The morning was cold and the fire was out. There were three men in the three bunks, one at each side and one at the end. Each man feigning sleep, each waiting for the other to get cracking. I, being the coldest, fell out of bed and opened the stove door. It was half full of ashes and no kindling.

A large and lone piece of wood lay alongside; this I placed inside the stove. The next item I thought, would be something to make a fast heat. In the little washroom stood a can of gas. It had a hole in it and was a source of worry to me, a potential hazard. Now, I thought, the time had come for me to save others from the same worry. I would eliminate it. Leaving the washroom on a long

As cowboy Hank Law learned, cattle need feeding, Christmas day or not!

trot with the gas in tow, I skidded to a stop in front of the stove. In went the gas on what I had considered cold ashes, but to my terrified gaze there arose a whisp of vapor that grew every second.

The man in the bunk right in front of the stove was by this time sitting on the edge of his bed, his bare and hairy legs hanging down lifelessly like two pieces of thick rope with knots where the feet should be. He was giving me advice on how to get a quick heat. I struck a match and showed him my way. The match sped through the air into the mouth of the stove, an old gas drum laying on its side with the door on the end facing the guy with the gams. There was an ominous silence for a few seconds then I jumped aside as the "WHOOOOOOOOOOPH" and flame came together. It was red and round as the mouth that spat it forth and it reached out 12 feet.

My pal of the legs was only 10 feet away and right under the gun. He therefore had two feet of fast heat all his own. He went over backwards screaming "ALLAH, OOOOOO ALLAH." He shortly appeared on the far side of the bed with just his head showing, eyes sticking out so you could knock 'em off with a stick.

The fire was taking hold – really taking hold. It went up the stove pipe and set the roof afire around the top. Whipping back to the washroom, I filled a wash bowl with water and came around the turn, this time on the dead gallop. One big heave and I hit the roof around the stovepipe with the water. Sad to say, what goes up must come down, right on the man with the red hairless legs the man who smelt like a chicken that had been singed ready for the oven.

The chuckwagon such as the one below that Hank drove was the cowboys' kitchen, dining room and even bedroom since it also carried the bedrolls.

Of course I was sorry for the victim, but his hair was too thick anyway, no doubt he'd feel a lot cooler in the summer.

The next stove mixup came that fall. It was in the old shack at Bidwell Creek. My job was driving the chuckwagon for the C1 outfit whose home ranch was at Alexis Creek. This shack had a dirt floor and no door. It was of logs and probably represented some long forgotten man's dreams. It was a haven nevertheless the night we used it. We had been bucking wet snow all day, snow that finally made up its mind to tighten up. The boys were punching the last of the cows across the creek and having plenty of trouble doing it. The men, horses, cows, calves, and Bowser, the dog, were all bitchy and hungry.

I pulled in to the shack and unhitched the team, leaving them to eat the bale of hay I had lashed to the tailgate. Taking my kindling with me, I started a fire in the old camp stove and in no time the pot I used for coffee was on the boil. That cup of cheer being made and set aside ready for the bitchy boys, I set about making some biscuits. It was dark and I was using a lantern to see by. The shadows were close, about six inches around that lantern. The biscuit dough was coming along fine, the fire was good and hot, the coffee ready, and the boys were on their expectant way to the shack. Then it happened.

First I had a feeling of being watched – but who could watch me in this light? The next feeling was more concrete. The back of my neck was being subjected to a warm intermittent breath of air with now and then a definite tickling as if a few hairs were being drawn across it. I glanced furtively over my shoulder, expecting to see a half crazy, very hungry cowpuncher. It was a half crazy cowpuncher all right, only it had four legs. It was the off-side horse in my wagon team.

Because the place wasn't built for horses as well as skinners, I politely asked him to leave. The idea was to back him out the way he came in, but he wouldn't back. Then I lost control. I had pleaded, pushed, and acted like a gentleman but still he stood there with that hammerhead of his stuck up in the air and one big unshod hoof resting heavily on my foot. I grabbed a stick of fire wood and went after the foot first.

He snorted and swung around, placing one of his hind feet on the top of the large aluminum pot that was full of hot coffee. As his weight came down, the pot collapsed and shot a stream of hot coffee right up his leg. Horses not being used to hot coffee – especially up the inside of the hind leg – he took off.

The first thing to go with him was the stove pipe. It came down across the pan of biscuit dough, breaking where it hit the pan, leaving soot in a little heap on top of the contents. The next thing was the lantern. It slowly laid over on its side and gave up. One hind foot this time was in the grub box and, as it left, slowly tipped everything out on the ground. It was pitch dark now and every man for himself. I still had my club and moving warily with outstretched left hand I hit anything I touched. I longed for a machine gun loaded with dumdums. Something I could spray death and destruction with. But the fit passed with the exit of the horse.

On lighting the lamp I surveyed the damage through the smoke. One overturned stove, one bent and twisted stove pipe, a covering of grub over the floor, a grub box good only for kindling, and a spent cook with his belt buckle kicked right off by a no good, dish-faced, cow-hocked, ewe-necked, spavined up rat that calls himself a horse.

I relit the fire. The boys were outside turning their ponies loose. What excuse to use I didn't know, but I must have the coffee pot going at all costs. Mebbe the pot could be fixed up good enough, I thought, but where is it? A glance outside showed me. My pal, and I use the term loosely, was still wearing it.

We got through the meal somehow. I had retrieved the dough and I think the soot gave it a distinctive flavor all its own.

CATTLE CHRISTMAS

Christmas came up fast after the first frost. On the morning of the 25th I fed everything at the barn, hooked my team to a cutter and headed up to the meadows. The temperature was around 40 below zero. The sun was up and the sky was as clear as a light blue crystal dome. The old vetched biddies I was feeding were cold standing around in their skins on a bunch of hard old feet. They looked like a flock of short legged camels with their backs humped that way, but big hearted me, I would fix everything. Yessir! I'd give 'em the feed of their lives. It's Christmas, ain't it? I drove up to the waiting cattle and stood up and bowed, wishing them all a very happy Christmas. Next thing, instead of loading up three loads of hay and scattering it over hell's half acre, I hooked onto the stackyard fence and pulled it down. That was all I had to do. Them old she cows headed in there like a bunch of women going in to a sale, the only difference being when one fell over the others tried not to walk all over her.

The team were interested in something coming over the meadow towards us. I threw a benevolent look in that direction and what met my eyes changed my whole outlook. Because...so help me, with all the teeming millions in the world...there were just two people that shouldn't be there. But there they were, staring at me over that sea of steaming backs. It was the boss and his wife come to help me with the chores.

The boss' first question gave me my answer. "Wassa matter – they break in on ya? Well," he added, "may as well leave 'em in now, stack's about through anyway. Let's get crackin' at the Christmas turkey." Two hours later we were sitting down to a real feast.

It was great while it lasted but cows have to eat and drink and most of the cowboys attending had a long ride ahead of them. I have often wondered if the people who sit down to a feed of steak ever think of the men who made that steak possible. There have been films on the subject by the thousand. Thousands of books have been written but very, very few tell of the hardships and grief and the eternal battle with the elements that these men of the frontier country endure. At the time these events took place beef was three quarters of a cent a pound on the hoof, perhaps $5 for a prime steer, with a drive across country, up to 200 miles in some cases, before reaching the railroad.

WEST BRANCH

THEODORE VALLEAU (PRONOUNCED VALLOO), BERNAL MULLENS and PAT BRAID were among the first settlers at West Branch. Valleau moved around a lot. He usually had a few goats with him to provide milk which he claimed kept him in good health.

JIM and ADA HOLT came to West Branch in the 1920s. Ada had a son, Leonard Butler, who married Hilda McKill. Butlers had two sons, Lee and Jack, and a daughter, Eleanor. The Holts had two sons, Clay and Dean, who lived at Tatlayoko in 1928-29. They worked at the Morris Mine and at various odd jobs in the valley. Jim and Ada Holt's marriage broke up. Ada married a man named Kurt Heinz and continued to live in the country.

Jim cowboyed for the C1 Ranch looking after cattle at Big Eagle Lake (Choelquoit). The log cabin on the range there, used by cowboys through the years, is known as "Jim Holt's Cabin." Holt shot and trapped wolves for the government when these animals increased to packs and were killing livestock.

About 1932, John Hamm from Saskatchewan came to West Branch. With him were two of his sisters and their husbands and

families: Annie and Bob Nicholson and five children – daughters Ora, Lorna, and Ulah; and sons Don and Terry. Also Tilly and Charlie Godfrey. Tilly died giving birth to a baby boy. Her sister, Annie, looked after the baby, Daryl, and her brother, John Hamm, paid for his care. The baby's father, Charlie Godfrey, went back to England.

Four years later, in 1936, John's parents, Dave Hamm Sr. and wife, Sarah, joined their two sons and two daughters at West Branch, along with another four members of their large family – Bert, Dave, Edgar and Wanda. Another daughter, Lena, with husband Gus Bitner and three children: Rosella, Allan, and Leona joined the clan two or three years later. Other members of the Hamm family were Lizzy Durringer, Mary Switzer and Hugo Hamm.

A school was started in the community for the children of these pioneer settlers. The residents of West Branch made their living trapping, raising cattle and guiding. Bert Hamm had a sawmill and his brother, Hugo, worked with him. Others worked in Al Rafferty's gold mine on Blackhorn Mountain, on ranches, or on the roads for Public Works, anywhere that employment could be found.

NEMIAH VALLEY

The first white man to make his home in Nemiah Valley was an Englishman named EDMUND ELKINS. A lake in the valley and a creek flowing into the Whitewater River bear his name. Elkins, with his Indian wife, ran a trading post in this remote location. He was destined to forsake it all when on the morning of December 30, 1897, his brother LEWIS ELKINS, who had a store at Quitsin Lake in the Tatla Lake area, was murdered by a Nemiah Indian named Samien (also known as Sam'hi'u). There were no witnesses to the deed but it was said that Lewis Elkins refused Samien goods because he had no money to pay for them. Samien, in cold blood, shot and killed the storekeeper and made off with what he wanted from the trading post, taking Elkin's horse as well. Samien bragged to his tillicums about what he had done and the word spread quickly. Ed Elkins rode to Tatla Lake to report the murder of his brother to Benjamin Franklin who was Justice of the Peace. Three men were sworn in as special constables: Charley Skinner, Pat McClinchy and Edmund Elkins, and with Franklin set off on horseback, riding 70 miles to reach the murderer's whereabouts.

With the help of three friendly Indians who knew the country, they surprised Samien and arrested him. By the time the guilty man had been escorted to the 150 Mile jail in Franklin's sleigh and the men had returned home, they had been "on the tramp" for 25 days. The Special Constables were paid $5 a day, including their horses. Out of this they had to pay their own expenses. The three Indians were given $100 each for their part in capturing the murderer. Samien was sentenced to hang but the sentence was later commuted to life imprisonment. In jail he learned to be a shoemaker.

Edmund Elkins had no heart for a trading post in the Chilcotin after this tragedy and, leaving his Indian wife and sons behind, went to live in Bella Coola. The murderer's brother, ALEX HUMM, was a good man and, feeling a family responsibility for the death of Lewis Elkins, he helped Edmund's deserted wife by raising one son, Joe.

Joe grew into an honest, good-looking man and was to raise a family of 12 children at Anaham. Many of them and their children and children's children still reside there. Lawrence Elkins, like his grandfather Joe, is a top-notch bronc rider.

Another settler in Nemiah Valley also came to an untimely end. JIM ROBERTSON was a Scotsman who homesteaded near the mouth of the Nemiah River. He had built up a good bunch of cattle and horses over a period of 10-15 years. Then one day he took his own life with a shot through the brain.

His property went to his brother, Sandy Robertson of Alexis Creek. Lashaway Lulua lived on the deserted ranch and eventually bought it for $4,000 from Mrs. Robertson. Art Watson, of Tsuniah Lake, next acquired the place, but Lashaway kept some of the land where Tommy Lulua lived and this part still belongs to the Luluas. Von Trapps of "Sound of Music" fame bought the Robertson place from Watson. It is now owned by Larry Rudd.

Nemiah Valley gained permanent white settlers in 1923 when two Americans, ELMER and OLIVER PURJUE, twin brothers from Idaho, took up land on Elkins Creek. They made their home in this beautiful valley for many years and were fiercely devoted to it. Early bunchgrass sidehills and verdant meadows provided ideal ranchland. They became friends with the Indians who lived there and got along well with them.

Elmer Purjue was breaking horses for the Canadian Army at Sumas in 1918 when a friend suggested they ride north via Squamish and Lillooet over the mountains into the Chilcotin country to have a look around. They ended up in Nemiah Valley where they were favourably impressed and decided it would be a good place to ranch. Elmer returned to Idaho where he hoped to persuade his twin brother, Oliver, due to be discharged from the Armed Forces, to come to the Chilcotin and start a ranch.

He succeeded, and in 1921 the brothers headed for British Columbia with big dreams and little cash. They got a job at Riske Creek working for Becher and saved their money to buy a wagon, four-horse team and provisions to take them to the isolated valley.

There was only a winter sleigh road beyond Stone Reserve at that time, so taking in a four-horse team and heavy wagon in the summertime meant cutting out trees and stumps and going straight down the steep hills with big logs tied behind for brakes. On the steep sidehills along the Whitewater (Taseko) River they plowed furrows along the bank and lashed the wagon box from tree to tree on the upper side to keep it from tipping over. They forded the river at the foot of Seymour Draw, becoming the first to take a wagon into Nemiah Valley.

They both staked a place on Elkins Creek and began building corrals and cabins. There were hundreds of wild horses in the valley and these capable horsemen enjoyed the thrill of corralling a snorty wild bunch and breaking what they needed for saddle horses. In later years, when there were still many unbranded mustangs in the hills, Purjues entertained their visitors by running wild horses. Bronc busting and horse trading followed for the next few days.

The Purjue brothers were the epitome of the cowboy in their dress, their ability with horses and their love of remote ranch life. The fact that there were no roads or bridges and that they were isolated from stores, doctors and neighbours seemed not to daunt them. Elmer was a very good blacksmith and could make much of the equipment needed for land clearing and other tasks. He also made horseshoes, harness, saddles, and was very talented at making and silver-mounting headstalls, martingales, bits, spurs and silver rings from coins. Oliver did this kind of work, too, but Elmer was the better. They both braided ropes, headstalls, bullwhips and quirts from leather, horsehair, or rawhide and there was always a market for their work. Cowboys throughout the country prized their Purjue-made horse gear.

Oliver and Elmer raised cattle, trapped and dealt in horses. They packed haying equipment into the ranch with horses as there were no bridges during most of their years in the valley. Their beef had to ford the river as they set off each fall at shipping time on the long 125-mile drive in to the sale ring in Williams Lake.

Elmer helped organize the first Williams Lake stampedes, and both brothers were contestants. Oliver did some clowning as well.

Oliver remained a bachelor, but in 1935 Elmer married an Indian girl, Mary Baptiste, daughter of Jakey Jimmy of Nazko. Elmer and Mary had four sons and a daughter while living in the valley: Frank, Voyne, Levi, Grant, and Audrey. It was a great joy to have a little girl in the family but tragedy struck when she was nine months old. She became seriously ill with pneumonia and Elmer went for help on horseback, the fastest way out. Mounted on a big chestnut gelding he made the long ride to Chilco Ranch in eight hours and had a plane sent in, but it got there too late. After that tragedy, Purjues had a radiophone installed and maintained it as long as they lived in Nemiah Valley.

The four boys boarded in Williams Lake to go to school; then Elmer and Mary moved out, too, to a home on the Dog Creek Road. They later moved to property on Hodgson Road. Two more children were born – Wayne and Dora. Again they had a little girl, and Elmer called her "Sweetie." Elmer died in Williams Lake, in 1970, while Oliver stayed in Nemiah, helping his nephews with the ranch until his death in 1959.

Elmer Purjue's eldest son, Frank, married Eleanor Hyde and they raised a family in Nemiah. He became a big-game guide and started Twin Lakes Lodge between Elkins and Vedan Lakes. The resort consisted of a lodge and eight cabins, plus an over 6,000-foot landing strip. He also had a hunting cabin on Mt. Tatlow. But tragedy struck the family again when, at 31, Frank lost his life in Chaunigan Lake in 1967 when on a hunting trip with a party of Americans. He and assistant guide, Billy Sammy, also 31, were ferrying the four sportsmen across the high, two-mile-wide lake early in the morning when the boat capsized. The hunters clung to the side of the boat while Purjue and Sammy attempted to swim to shore. Both guides were strong swimmers but the extra weight of hunting gear and the sub-zero temperature of the cold mountain lake made this an impossible undertaking. The hunters clinging to the boat watched in horror as their guides disappeared. They then paddled the boat to shore with hands and feet and went out to notify the police. The bodies of the two young men were recovered in about 12 feet of water, 100 feet from shore. Both Frank Purjue and Billy Sammy left a wife and a young family.

Voyne finished his education in Spokane, Washington, where he had the opportunity to further his musical talents playing back-up for a band in that city. When he returned home he worked for a time in Williams Lake. He married Grace Brown in 1964. They moved to Nemiah to ranch on some of the original Purjue holdings. They were doing well when Voyne developed a brain aneurysm. He died in 1988.

Levi married Linda Fullerton and lives in Williams Lake. He is a heavy-duty mechanic and welder for Lignums. He has a daughter, Carrie, and son, Oliver, by this marriage. Oliver is named for his great Uncle Oliver. Levi carries on the tradition of working with silver, and is musical like his brothers. The guitar is his specialty but he can produce a one-man orchestra, playing at the same time a guitar and mouth organ, and bells with his feet.

Grant lives in Nemiah at the mouth of Elkins Creek, known locally as "Captain George town." Wayne Purjue also owns 160 acres there. Wayne lives in Williams Lake, as does his sister, Dora Cee.

NIGHT ALONG THE TRAIL
Veera Witte Bonner

Now the eve has flung its shadows
O'er the brightness of the day,
And the gold that crowned the mountains
Fades ... and slowly dies away.
And the vagrant night wind, rising,
Stirs the campfire's ruddy blaze -
Takes the idle smoke and drifts it
To a tangled purple haze.

And the winding trail is silent
Where all day the hills around
Listened to the rhythmic beating
Of shod hoof on rocky ground.
For the riders have dismounted
And their evening meal begun;
Horses freed of pack and saddle
And the autumn day is done.

Soon the murmuring of voices
Fades away, and all is still,
Save the lonely night wind sighing
Through the jackpines on the hill.
And the jangle of the horse-bells
Moving back across the swail,
While in soft star-studded glory
Night comes down along the trail.

OF ROADS, BRIDGES, AND CARS

For a long time there was no way in to Nemiah Valley except by packhorse and saddle horse. Coming from the east, the Chilko River had to be forded, while travelling via the Whitewater Road meant fording the Taseko. Both of these are fast-flowing cold rivers, fed from the glacial mountains.

In 1929, a bridge was built across the Taseko River with government funding under the supervision of Harry Curtis and the wagon road improved as far as Elkins Creek. The bridge was put in at a very narrow place in the river and it was only a short time before high water took it out. Then a cable was strung across the river with a box to sit in and carry gear and provisions. Travellers hauled themselves over with an endless cable running on pulleys. Horses and cows still had to swim. This made do for 20 years until in 1950-51 another government bridge was built, this time under Wendell MacDonald and a crew. But the road leading to Nemiah from both directions, and through the valley itself, remained very rough and twisty.

Old bridge over the Whitewater (Taseko River). The new crossing at this site is called the Davidson Bridge.

Above: Chilcotin River Bridge at Hanceville and, below, Scallon Bridge over Big Creek in the 1980s. It has since been removed.

In January 1953, Sister St. Paul, a nursing sister of Christ the King at Anaham Reserve, took the first motorized vehicle, a Willys Jeep, the length of the valley to Chilko Lake on a mercy trip to bring an Indian woman to the nursing station at Anaham. There was a foot of snow and the road was so rough that the plucky nurse travelled as far as she could on the frozen surface of Konni Lake. Another nun, Sister Mary, went with her and Danny Sammy accompanied them as guide. The round trip from Anaham Reserve took 24 hours.

During the 1970s the army replaced the picturesque old trestle bridge across the Taseko with a plain sturdy span and rebuilt the
Whitewater Road from Chilco Ranch leading to it. The bridge was
named for Davidson, the Army engineer. The Nemiah Valley Road
across the bridge was rebuilt as well.

A bridge was finally built over the Chilko River in 1959 at
Henry's Crossing, about eight miles below Chilko Lake, but the
road remained not much more than a trail for many years. This
rough road was cut out by Duke Martin in 1945, along a route surveyed by Sydney Williams and slashed in 1909.

Twenty-five miles of new road, following fairly close to the
old Jameson Trail up the Chilko River, was built in 1963, mainly
by the resourceful settlers themselves: Bob Brebner supplied the
bulldozer, Jack Casselman ran it and Johnny Blatchford supplied
the grubstake. The Department of Highways had said that one
stretch of bad rock would make it impossible to push a road
through this country, but when officials came out to check on the
road builders they found Casselman was already past the worst of
the rock and snorting his way through the jackpine. The Department of Highways then kicked in $2,000 and the Fisheries Depart-
ment $500. When the cat work was done, Murray Taylor hosted a
"packrat" supper (some food such as wild onions scrounged packrat style from the countryside) at his cabins near Mountain House
on July 3, 1963, to celebrate, and the new road was opened in a
Chilcotin ceremony befitting the occasion. With Bill Bliss Jr. officiating, Joyce Russell, who had been crowned "Queen of the Pack-
rats," cut with a flourishing sweep of a hunting knife the buckskin
ribbon fastened across the end of the bridge and the road was
declared open. In daring tribute to the road builders, Gordon Jakel
dove from the Chilko River Bridge into the swift cold water below
and swam ashore 100 yards downstream.

The road to Chezacut, some 30 miles from Redstone up the
Chilcotin River, was blazed and cut out by the first men to settle
there. They were Edward Sherringham from England, Will
Copeland from Ontario, E. P. Lee from England, Earl and Flint
Niece from the U.S.A., and another Englishman, a Mr. Axford. For
years this road was neglected by the government. In the spring
when the snow was melting, and in the summer and fall when it
rained heavily, the road became very muddy and full of water
holes. Snow removal was unknown till the early 1940s.

After the ranchers acquired tractors, they were used when the
road was bad to get to Redstone to pick up the mail, cutting deep

ruts that lasted for weeks until eventually a road grader was sent to smooth it out. Not till the 1970s was a proper wide road constructed to Chezacut, taking out the twists and turns and putting in culverts where needed. It is now kept free of snow as well. This work was done not so much for the residents as for the logging trucks which go nearly 40 miles beyond Chezacut to Thunder Mountain.

The first car into the Chilcotin Valley was a big seven-passenger vehicle, probably a Cadillac or Overland. It was driven in in 1912 from Ashcroft by Mr. Cunliffe to bring the Dyson family to visit Reginald and Kathleen Newton. They came by the Gang Ranch road, crossing the Fraser River on the ferry. There were bridges over Big Creek and the Chilcotin River at Hanceville at that time but all other streams had to be forded. There was a bridge across the little Chilcotin at the Newton ranch by then, built by Reg Newton and Wm. Bliss Sr. with Indian help.

That same year, Fred Becher brought a Cadillac to Riske Creek, and in 1913 Jack Temple of the Lee Ranch at Hanceville also bought a Cadillac. By 1917 Hugh Bayliff had a Dodge touring car, and in 1920 Herbert Church brought a big seven-passenger Overland in from Vancouver. Soon cars were appearing everywhere throughout the Chilcotin and there were many names and makes: the Church boys had a Viking (made by G.M.), Arthur Knoll had a Hudson; Alex Graham, a Willys Knight; Bob Pyper, a Grey Dart; and there were Studebakers, Chevies, and Model T Fords. Gas was cheap and big cars were quite popular. The biggest problem was tires – lots of flat tires. But the inner tubes could be patched over and over again – and very often were. Cars were put away for the winter after the snow got too deep for them. Tires were taken off and the wheels propped up on blocks, the battery stored in the house until spring. In spring and after a heavy rain there were impossible mudholes, and in the heat of summer the first cars often got stuck in sandy places. The Model T Fords had gravity-fed gas lines and if fuel was low in the tank there was no power to climb the steep hills. Sometimes the only solution was to turn the car around and back up the grade!

Until 1924 the road foreman resided at the 150 Mile House. Road crews worked every summer from May to November fixing mudholes, putting in culverts, and building corduroy (logs placed like railway ties and covered with earth) in swampy areas. Grades along sidehills were first plowed, then scrapers were used to move the dirt, all with horses. The first graders were operated by two men, one to work the grader and the other to drive the four horses. Wm. Bliss Sr. became road foreman for the Chilcotin in 1925, and that year the road through Hance's Timber was straightened. The next year the road up the Anaham Flat was moved over to the base of the hill and a bridge put across Anaham Creek.

About 1927 a small Cletrack tractor was sent down from Quesnel to replace the teams on the road grader, but two men were still needed for the operation. Bliss was the grader man and Elmer Sutton drove the new tractor. In 1948 the first power grader was stationed at Alexis Creek, operated by Roy Haines. The machine was known as the "Maintainer," smoothing the roads in summer and plowing off the snow in winter. By now there were many cars and trucks on the road and you could see a vehicle coming for miles by the cloud of dust springing up behind it. Stan Dowling took the first truck over the Chilcotin Road from Williams Lake to Anahim Lake in 1936 – a long, dusty, rough trip with steep hills and permanent mudholes in the low places.

MY WORST TRIP OVER THE CHILCOTIN ROAD
As told by Stan Dowling

In the early 1930s I started a store at Cahoose Flats, just east of Anahim Lake. In 1938 I bought the old Hudson's Bay property at Anahim Lake and moved the store to the centre of that frontier community. I trucked my freight from Vancouver. Roads were tough, snowplowing unheard of and I had many rough trips through the Chilcotin. But the worst of all was in March 1937.

The Cariboo Road was gravel then and it was a long slow drag from Vancouver, but when I reached Williams Lake I knew I was really in for trouble. The snow was deep and a wind was rising. I had tied a sleigh on top of my load and phoned ahead to have Andy Holte meet me with a sleigh and two teams at Tatla Lake. I reckoned I should be able to make it that far with the truck. The telephone operators would pass on information for me free because they knew I would keep an eye on the phone line and report or repair any damage.

The farther west I went the worse it got, the snow getting deeper and a fierce gale blowing and piling up drifts. Along the Redstone Reserve the fence had acted as a barrier and the road was packed hard with deep drifted snow, impossible to break through. On the other side of the fence the wind had blown a lot of the snow off so I took down the rails and drove through the field, taking the fence down again at the far end to get back on the road.

Shovelling and plugging slowly along, I finally reached Pyper's cabin at Chilanko Forks. Pyper had passed away a year or two before but travellers could still take shelter there and use the phone. I was soon using that phone to call Tatla Lake. I found that Andy was on his way to meet me as planned, and Bill Graham was on the road, too, bringing Ed Collett out. Ed had broken his leg falling a tree at Morrison Meadow and his partner, Tim Draney, had brought him to Tatla Lake, breaking trail as far as Towdystan then changing horses and driving all night to make the 45 miles to Tatla. They were lucky at that – they were just ahead of the big wind at that end. After a long painful trip, changing horses, rigs and drivers again at Chilanko, Collett reached his truck at Dave Fraser's and finally the hospital in Williams Lake.

Heading for Chilanko from Tatla, Holte and Graham found the road badly drifted in with deep snow, so decided to travel over the ice on Tatla Lake as far as they could. It was no better, and when the men reached Chilanko their horses were tired. They said they wouldn't haul anything on the return trip as the going was too tough. So I decided I'd have to do a lot of shovelling and try and make it with the truck. I left next morning but only made 12-1/2 miles. Andy and Bill caught up to me there and we camped in the snow for the night.

Next day we travelled the same distance to Tatla Lake – shovelling, lugging, spinning with the truck; the horses floundering with the sleighs, sweating and frosted up. The going looked a little better here, so next day Andy and I loaded the two sleighs with freight and started out again, my fourth day on the road.

Pan Phillips and Alfred Bryant had joined us at Tatla Lake, coming through from West Branch where Pan bought two horses. They agreed to take over from Bill Graham and drive Tim Draney's sleigh back for him, travelling with us, but wouldn't haul anything except the mail. Draney took a saddle horse home the day before as he had cattle to feed.

A long hard day saw us at the McClinchy Ranch where we got one fresh horse from Nick Cassidy. It felt good to sleep in the house out of the wind but we could still hear it whistling out there. Next day, worn out and cold, we reached Pete McCormick's place on Clearwater Lake. But the worst was still ahead of us.

When we got to the spring on McClinchy Hill the following day, seven miles out at the start of Caribou Flats, the drifts were really bad. The wind hit full force here and had drifted the road high with hard-packed snow. It was swirling the white crystals in merciless clouds across the flat, battering the teams, cutting into our clothing and through the scarves we'd tied around our faces. Pan and Alfred left Tim's sleigh and the mail and took off with the horses into the timber to make camp in the shelter of the trees. Andy and I joined them and we spent the night there – a rough camp with no hay for the horses, only part of a sack of oats, and scant rations for us, too.

Early next morning we hitched four horses to one sleigh and hit the drifts again, leaving one loaded sleigh behind. Even at that, it took all day to make the four miles across Caribou Flats. Andy Holte was a top teamster – we'd have never made it without him. The horse we borrowed off Nick Cassidy was a little lighter than the others and was having trouble in the crusted snow. He was only half broke but that didn't bother Andy. "He needs a little more weight," said Andy, as he walked out on the wagon tongue and climbed on the horse's back to give him that extra weight and make it easier for him to break through the crust. Once across the flats we unhooked and camped to rest awhile but had no water for the horses, just snow. So we pulled out early in the morning for Towdystan, a distance of nine miles. There we were out of the wind at last.

Pan and Alfred left Draney's team and sleigh at Engebretson's Ranch at Towdystan and we borrowed a fresh horse there. We couldn't have gotten along in those days without the Engebretsons, they were the gateway to the whole country.

Next day, the ninth day on the road from Williams Lake, we reached our destination, the last 16 miles mercifully out of the wind on Cahoose Flats. The worst of the long gruelling trip – my toughest ever – was finally over.

Horses and men were tired, underfed, and thirsty but the tough horses were still willing and the tough hombres were still joking. I was grateful to them all.

STANLEY DOWLING grew up in Vancouver and became a top motorcycle rider. One day in 1931 he was at the Motor Cycle Shop and met two men on English motor bikes with round discs on their front wheels which read "Vancouver to Bella Coola." One rider was Tom Chignell and the other A. J. Arnald, who was a partner with Tommy Walker in Stuie Lodge. They were the first men to go by motor vehicle overland to Bella Coola. Dowling's interest in the Bella Coola-Anahim country was kindled.

Stan Dowling established a store and the first post office at Anahim Lake and also organized the first stampede. The photos were taken in the early 1950s.

In 1932 Stan decided to visit his brother in Bella Coola. He hitchhiked to Kleena Kleene, then rode horseback from Towdystan to Bella Coola with Shorty King. He farmed there for awhile, then worked for Christensen's Clesspocket Ranch before starting a store at Cahoose Flats and began trucking freight from Vancouver. At that time he had the only truck in the Anahim Lake area, the wagon road from Tatla Lake mostly used for wagons and pack-horses. Dowling was the first to travel the western end by truck on a regular basis and he literally built a passable road for himself, with little help from the government for the first few years.

In 1938 Dowling bought the Hudson's Bay property in what is now "downtown" Anahim Lake and moved his store there. He also started the first Anahim Lake Post Office.

In addition, Dowling with the help of local ranchers, put on the first stampede in June. Since there were no bucking chutes, the wild horses were snubbed to a cowboy's saddle horn and the contestants handed the halter rope. The bareback horses had to be thrown and the riders got on as the horse got up. At night Bill Woods and Nick Cassidy played their fiddles for the dances in the hall which was only four logs high!

In 1939, Dowling with other stampede enthusiasts, put on another stampede after going "modern" and building corrals and bucking chutes. They ran the horse races down the main street. Local talent provided the music for the dances which were held in Dowling's new garage.

Howard Harris from Quesnel played banjo; Harold Engebretsen the violin; Leona Draney, piano; Thelma McInroy, accordion; her husband, Earl, banjo; and Jimmy Holte, guitar.

Pan Phillips and family and all at the ranch at Batnuni came over the mountain to the stampede, building the road as they came. Anahim Lake Stampede became more and more famous as the years went by.

Dowling married Edna Johnson and had four daughters. He eventually sold his store at Anahim Lake and became a cattle rancher at Kleena Kleene. He now lives in Langley.

MINES

Thanks to Bob Fosbery, Wilf Hodgson, Jack McPhail, George Murphy, and Mary James for their input in this section.

THE TAYLOR WINDFALL MINE on Iron Creek in the Whitewater Mountains has been closed down for nearly 50 years, but the name is still familiar to a lot of people and carries with it a fascinating history.

The rich vein of gold was discovered and staked in 1920 by Herb Taylor of Lillooet, a tall man known as "Long Taylor" by most of his associates. The gold was close to the surface and the Taylor Windfall produced richly for awhile, inspiring its owner to invest heavily in machinery and equipment. Then the gold ran out. The mine was taken over eventually by a group of businessmen in Vancouver who formed a company called the Whitewater Goldfields. It is doubtful if, in the end, the big man called Long Taylor realized very much from his windfall.

When news of the rich strike in the Whitewater spread, a venturesome young man by the name of Tommy Hodgson saw an

Taylor Windfall Mine on Iron Creek in 1936.

opportunity to expand his freighting business. Tommy Hodgson got his start in the Chilcotin in 1914 when the Inland Express Company sub-let their Chilcotin mail and freight contract to him. By 1920 he was on his own and ready to tackle anything.

To investigate the possibilities of doing business with the new gold mine, Hodgson hired Percy Church, who knew the country, to take him on horseback through the mountains via Groundhog Creek and the headwaters of Big Creek to the site of Taylor's Windfall. Hodgson came to an agreement with Long Taylor to deliver goods and machinery to the mine – a colossal undertaking as there was no access through miles of wilderness and rough mountainous terrain. Goods for the mine had so far been flown in by Ginger Coote from Gun Lake on the west side, or packed in with horses from Bridge River over 3.444-m (10,500-foot) Warner Pass. The first heavy machinery and supplies were brought in on pack horses over the rugged mountain trails.

Ginger Coote, who had been a pilot in the infant Canadian Air Force of World War One, freighted for the mine with his six-place Fairchild float plane for $100 a trip. The plane was yellow in color with registration CF-AUX on the wing. A skilled pilot, he landed his aircraft with a 900-pound load at the head of Whitewater (Taseko) Lake where the freight was stowed in a cabin built by Johnny Henderson at the edge of the water. Henderson hauled the freight the nine miles or so on up to the diggings with horses and a narrow gauge wagon, putting in bridges where necessary. Hodgson's first payload headed for the Taylor Windfall in the winter of 1922. He was hired to take a diamond drill in for Joe Trethewey of Chilco Ranch who had an option on the mine.

There was no road beyond the Stoney Reserve, only Indian trails, and Trethewey went ahead in a cutter to site out the best route and start cutting out trees. Tommy Hodgson hauled the heavy machine with a six-horse team and hired 22-year-old Walter Bambrick and Dan Lee, 16, each with a team and sleigh carrying horse feed and supplies, to go ahead to break trail and help widen out the road as they went along. It was a long, slow trip, camping at night in the snow. On the steep grades, holding back Hodgson's heavy load forced his horses to their rumps. They slid straight down to the bottom on their tails while Hodgson braced his feet on the front of the sleigh and grimly held on to the reins, thankful to reach the level without a mishap. Wherever possible, the party travelled on the ice-covered Taseko River to the foot of Whitewater Lake.

It was getting late in the winter and when the weather turned warm the men were fearful an excessive thaw might prevent them getting their sleighs back out again, and decided against continuing on up the lake ice. Instead, they left their cargo at the foot of the lake and came out – a two-day trip even with the lightened load. Joe Trethewey had put together a rough camp outfit and provisions were getting low. To add to their troubles, the piece of potato jammed in the coal-oil can for a cork had come loose and kerosene spilled over most of their camp goods.

Early the following spring, George Myers was attempting to haul the diamond drill up Whitewater Lake for Trethewey when the entire load and four-horse team went through the ice and were lost in the cold waters of the Whitewater. Myers escaped. This was a discouraging set-back for Joe Trethewey and he gave up his option on the Taylor Windfall.

In 1935 the government put in a road, passable for motor vehicles, from Chilco Ranch to the foot of Whitewater Lake. Percy Hance and Louis Vedan were among the local hands employed on the job. Tommy Hodgson and young son, Wilfred, took the first truck over the road. It was the first of many slow, difficult trips to haul in freight for the mine.

From the end of the road the goods were taken up the lake in Hodgson's two 20-foot boats manned by Jack Hodgson, Tommy's eldest son, and Fred Linder, both excellent boatmen. Each boat was powered with two 18-horsepower motors. They made one round trip a day – up in the morning and back at night, 40 miles of sometimes rough and dangerous water. Hodgson kept a team at the lake head and the cargo was stored in Johnny Henderson's cabin and hauled to the mine with team and wagon by Gene Chainey. A five-ton bulldozer, a grader, and a tractor went up the lake on big rafts made by lashing logs together and powered by outboards. When Hodgson bought a 32-horsepower motor with a self starter his boys thought they had the world by the tail!

In 1937 Lyle Mitchell and Wilf Hodgson, who was only a boy, took a steel sharpener weighing 16,000 pounds up to the end of the lake by truck. On Brigham Creek Hill the truck powered out and slid back. The heavy load shifted and tipped, sending the sharpener part way through the truck box. Somehow the boys managed to get the load straightened and tied down and finally made it. This heavy piece of metal can still be seen at the mine ruins.

Taylor's strike went $5 to the pan, but this rich vein was near the surface and the expensive equipment tunneling into the mountain never located anything nearly as valuable.

A staggering amount of work and engineering know-how went in to developing the property on two levels above Iron Creek. A shaft was sunk about 500 feet down, then a tunnel burrowed in to drain it and bring out the slack. This was shoveled by hand into small cars which were then pushed out along sloping tracks and the contents dumped into Iron Creek below. Ten to 15 men were employed there at a time, on double shift. They were housed in log cabins and ate in the bunkhouse. A sawmill to cut lumber for building was run by water power. Oliver and Elmer Purjue of Nemiah Valley had a contract to log for the mill, using horses.

Jack McPhail from Lillooet, now of Williams Lake, worked at the Taylor Windfall from 1937-39. He remembers going in early one year with two other men to help get the mine ready to open. This done, he was assigned the job of snow-shoeing out in April, over Warner Pass to Bridge River, to send word to the miners that the Taylor Windfall was ready to start work. It was not the first time he had crossed the pass on foot, alone.

When Jack was 15 he had helped his father, John Beer McPhail, drive six head of horses from Lillooet up the river trail through Empire Valley and the Gang Ranch to Big Creek, then on by Vedan Meadows and Onion Flat and up the lake to the head of the Whitewater. Here, J. B. McPhail was to pack that summer for a party of topographical surveyors. It was now June, and Jack had to get back to school in Lillooet to write his exams. He walked out alone over Warner Pass, carrying only a loaf of bread, a can of bully beef and a blanket. A huge grizzly track ahead of him in the high peaks made the journey an uneasy one for the 15-year-old boy. He camped at night under a tree at Trigger Lake at the head of Gun Creek, wrapped in his blanket, cold and lonely.

Now he was a grown man and the trip appealed to him. He left early on Sunday morning, April 15, 1939, accompanied by his spaniel dog. The going was good on compact snow over the lofty pass, and McPhail covered the distance to Minto Mines on the other side of the mountains in just under 12 hours. After phoning men in Lillooet and Squamish that the mine was open, McPhail was ready for a good meal and a rest. On Monday morning he started on the return journey. Before he had gone very far it was snowing heavily, making travel difficult, but he had been told by his boss, Elof Mortinson, to be back by Thursday so he kept going. He stayed Monday night at Spruce Lake on the west side of the mountains, sleeping under a tree. The next day he got only as far as Warner Lake where he camped again without food or shelter. By the time he reached the pass two feet of fresh snow had fallen on the lonely summit, making an ever-present danger of slides. By evening of the third day he made it back to the mine camp – both he and his dog exhausted and ravenously hungry. Mortinson's curt greeting was: "Why didn't you wait till the storm was over?"

During those years when miners went out for a holiday, they usually walked the nine miles to the head of Whitewater Lake where the company kept a 14-foot boat with a nine-horse motor. At the lower end of the lake a pick-up truck was parked for the journey to Williams Lake.

The Taylor Windfall had been running at a loss for some time in hopes of yet striking the mother load; but the original find was only a tunnel, or stove-pipe, of gold and when it was gone there was nothing more. In 1939 the Whitewater Goldfield Company in Vancouver, who had bought the mine from Long Taylor for about $25,000 decided to close the operation. The wire was sent to Tommy Hodgson in Williams Lake and Jack Hodgson delivered it. He drove in to the foot of the Whitewater, went up the lake in a boat, and walked the remaining distance, up-hill all the way, to the mine. The boss read the telegram, then turned and moved slowly away to give the word to his men: "Shut 'er down."

The fabled Taylor Windfall had closed its dreams.

But nothing was moved out, and for many years the Taylor Windfall Mine stood ready to re-open at a moment's notice.

THE MOTHER LODE

Many hopeful people staked gold claims in the Whitewater during the 1920s, including a number of struggling Big Creek ranchers, but none made a find. Some later claims did get to the exploratory stage: the Mother Lode on Granite Creek, the Pelaire on Falls Creek, and Vick's Mine at the foot of Whitewater Lake.

The Mother Lode came to a tragic end. Seven or eight men went in to the exploration site in the high, desolate peaks during the fall of 1934. They stayed in all winter, making their camp on the side of a mountain in a snow slide area above Granite Creek. In the spring of 1935, prospector Roly Allaire made a grim discovery.

He found the camp torn up by snow slides and the bones of the men where they had been swept down the ravine, some bodies still buried in the snow. The body of one man was discovered in the root cellar where, escaping from the slide, he had crawled with a broken leg for protection, only to perish from starvation and gangrene. The slide must have struck in the night as the men were in their underwear. There were no survivors. Elmer Purjue of Nemiah Valley was one of the volunteers who went in to dig out the bodies.

VICK'S MINE: Christopher Vick staked a claim at the foot of Taseko Lake in the 1930s, and an exploratory tunnel was driven into the rocky mountain face. Vick returned, after he had sold Chilco Ranch and was living in Vancouver, to oversee work on the claim where he had a fair-sized camp set up at the mouth of Swift (Beece) Creek and a crew working. They crossed the Taseko River by cable car and climbed the steep mountain on foot to go to work. Apparently, the operation showed little promise as in 1939 Vick reduced his crew to two men, Frank and Rex Morgan, who worked for two summers taking samples. He then closed the camp. Though the mine never produced, Vick at least got enough gold to make his wife a ring and the site, Vick's Mountain, stands like a monument to his name.

THE PELAIRE MINE: Roly Allaire and a Frenchman named Pellitier staked a gold claim in the 1930s on Falls Creek and amalgamated their names to call their mine " The Pelaire." A camp was built on the top of a wind-swept mountain above Falls Creek on the north side of the Taseko and extensive exploration done but the mine never really produced.

Tommy Hodgson hauled freight for the Pelaire Mine, taking equipment of all kinds up Taseko Lake by boat to a cabin at the mouth of the Lord River. George Murphy and Vernon James (Mulligan) did most of the freighting by boat and truck at first. Alex and Ann Paxton packed the heavy awkward loads with packhorses up the steep mountain to the mine site, which at over 3,900 m (12,000 feet) was the highest mine in North America. In 1946 a "Cat" road was put in, starting on the north side of the mouth of the Taseko River, and goods were then hauled to the mine by a cat, an Army rig with tracks and an old Army 4x4. Back from the war, Bubs Spencer drove the 4x4 and Jack and Wilfred Hodgson again were at work on boats and trucks.

George Murphy, a daredevil young man who had left his home in Nova Scotia to work his way across Canada, had never run a cat but he thought he'd like to. George was a capable horseman when he reached Chilcotin in 1930 and went to work at Chilco

D8 Cat crossing the Chilcotin River near Stoney on the way to the Pelaire Mine in 1947. Donald Myers, on horseback, is leading the way.

Ranch. In 1931-32, he took the money in saddle bronc competition at the Williams Lake Stampede, then left the cowboy life for other occupations. In 1945 he was hired by Tommy Hodgson to help transport freight to the Pelaire Mine. When the Pelaire operation closed for the winter in the fall of 1945, Murphy told the mine boss he was a cat skinner and applied to go on the dozer when work started in the spring. He hoped to get some experience on a machine in the woods during the winter but the only job he could find was swamping and setting chokers for a D4 in Princeton.

George, looking back, figures it was as well he was slightly inebriated that day in April 1946 when he was asked to unload the big D8 from the flat car at the railway station in Williams Lake. He had never even seen a D8, let alone driven one. Murphy was in the Lakeview Hotel drinking with Jack Hodgson when the boss, Brilinsen, hunted him up and told him that the regular driver was away and if Murphy wanted a cat job to get down to the station. "It was a bit scary, to say the least," Murphy remembers.

But he got the job done, and had walked the D8 out on the Chilcotin Road to the Fraser River and across the Chimney Creek

Bridge before the regular driver showed up. To lighten the load on the bridge the blade and winch were taken off but even so the machine weighed 18,000 pounds. Murphy says that the weight of the D8 took the hump right out of the old suspension bridge and he can't remember breathing at all until he reached the other side. The cat was not allowed on any of the bridges again.

At the Chilcotin River, the D8 had to ford. Above Chilco Ranch, Donald Myers of Stoney went ahead on a saddle horse and guided the driver safely through the swift water. It took two weeks to get the big machine to the Whitewater River crossing at the end of Whitewater Lake. Here the cat road was started and Murphy was second driver on the D8 until, a month later, the regular skinner was fired and Murphy was made head operator. Bulldozing a passable jeep road on the steep mountain face and ploughing snow on the treacherous cliffs was dangerous work and Murphy had a few close calls.

About eight men were employed at the camp, and they stayed in the mountains for six months without a break. Ann Paxton cooked for the crew at the half-way camp on the side of the mountain while the top of the peak was being prepared for permanent tents, but a man held sway in the cook tent on the wind-swept mountain top.

The wind-swept camp, at over 3,900 m (12,000 feet) the highest mine in Canada.

Until a rudimentary road was built up the mountain, supplies for the Pelaire arrived by a horse pack train like that above.

One exception was in July 1947 when Mrs. Leonard James, a war bride just out from Scotland, replaced the cook while he went on holiday for two weeks. There were now two women in camp, the other was Mary Scott, wife of engineer Jack Scott. The wind was howling around the camp the day Mary James arrived, and the talk at supper that evening centered on the wild storm the day before and the two men who had been blown, tent and all, off the mountain in the middle of the night. The men were unhurt, but having to climb back up the cliff to the camp in their underwear made them the butt of their comrades jokes.

The new cook slept little that night as she lay listening to the shrieking wind shaking her canvas tent, expecting any moment to be blown, like the miners, right off the mountain. "There was nothing to worry about," the men assured her next morning. "Your tent is attached to the cook tent and it's anchored by this big heavy cookstove."

When freight was due at the mine a few men went down the mountain to Taseko Lake to meet the loaded scows. Vernon James was one of them. Sometimes a storm and high winds would delay the freight a day or two and the men had no choice but to wait, taking shelter in a small cabin nearby. Vernon would often take on the task of preparing meals and had the habit of mixing canned stuff

Unloading freight for the Pelaire Mine from Hodgson boats near the mouth of the Lord River.

Supplies for the Pelaire Mine at the 40-foot span over the Tchaikazan River.

into a mulligan stew. Bubs Spencer tagged him with "Mulligan" and the nickname stuck.

For two years in a row when the operation closed in the fall, George Murphy walked the D8 some 200 miles from Falls Creek to Quesnel, fording rivers and streams and travelling cross country back of Alexis Creek. He claimed that crossing the many soft swamps on that long miserable journey, sometimes half lost in timber and muskeg, was more frightening than pushing snow drifts off the mountain peaks. He dared not stop one track to steer the cat as breaking the sod would have dropped the heavy machine down into the mire and out of sight, like breaking through ice. All he could do was point the D8 in the right direction and let 'er go, praying that the sod would hold.

The Pelaire Mine closed down in the fall of 1947. In the 1970s a private company called the Lord River Gold Mines Ltd., controlled by Silver Standard Mines, put in a better road to the old Pelaire site and prepared to start working it again. But the bridge over the roaring Tchaikazan River soon washed out, leaving a wide, deep chasm – and the Pelaire Mine to its memories.

Other exploration and promotional work has gone on in the Whitewater over the years, leaving behind catchy names like River City and Scurry Rainbow. And so it goes today as miners and prospectors seek minerals of all kinds among the majestic peaks of the high country.

MAIDEN OF THE SUMMER
Veera Bonner

The leaves are slightly tarnished,
There's a stillness in the air –
As if the maid of summer
Reluctant, waited there,
Knowing well that Lady Autumn
Soon will come to take her place
In a gown of flaming glory,
And rejected she must face

Many weary months of waiting
Till a fresh green gown she'll wear.
Till, with sunlight on her shoulders
And wild flowers in her hair,
She'll be everybody's darling –
Wooed and wanted everywhere.
Lovely Maiden of the Summer!
Wistful now, she's waiting there.

TRAPLINES

Many of the early settlers trapped to help make a living while building up their ranches – or to make a buck when times were tough. Notable among them were brothers DICK and PERCY CHURCH who were renowned as excellent trackers, trappers, and hunters. In the winter of 1927, Dick and Percy made enough money from their fur catch to buy a new Viking sedan. This heavy car had a remarkable V-8 engine that Dick used in the 1950s to run his sawmill at Riske Creek.

The brothers were hard riding, tough, and tenacious. When running coyotes in deep snow, tracking lynx or cougar, or shooting wild horses for the government, they would stay on the trail in any kind of weather, sleeping out under a tree without bedding or provisions. Once when shooting horses in the Fire Creek country Dick slept out in 40 below zero temperatures for three nights with only a tarp and a campfire for warmth. He said he finally froze out and rode across country to warm up at the Nighthawk Meadow where Pat Hutch was feeding cattle. Dick's reputation as a tracker led Queenie Blenkinsop to remark: "When Dick Church sees horse manure on the trail, he can tell if it's the horse he's looking for."

A. M. Piltz, in partnership with Adam Cummings, trapped during his first years at the Sky Ranch. His line ran through the Scallon Creek country and was in good standing 40 years later when he sold out to Dick Church in 1957. This registered trapline was sold with the Sky Ranch again, to Bob Lee, of Oregon, in the early 1960s.

HELGE JOHANSEN, a strong rugged outdoorsman, came to Big Creek in the 1940s and established a trapline up Big Creek into the mountains. Born in Norway in 1902, Helge Afbjorn Johansen ran away to sea at 11 and spent the next eight years on Norwegian ships. After leaving the sea he came to B.C. and worked in the woods at the coast for some time before finding his way to the Cariboo and Chilcotin.

On his Big Creek trapline Helge built two small cabins with axe and Swede saw: one on Upper Big Creek at the foot of the mountains and one higher up near Lorna Lake. At the first cabin he

Helge Johansen at his trapping cabin on Big Creek. Duane Witte packed in his winter supplies.

also built a foot bridge across Big Creek, mainly with materials at hand. Duane Witte packed supplies in with horses for him in the fall, sometimes making a second trip towards spring. Helge at times carried heavy loads in himself. According to Duane, this hardy Norwegian once forded Big Creek on foot in fairly high water with an 80-pound pack on his back.

The chief fur-bearing animals on his line were coyotes, marten, weasels, and squirrels. Johansen travelled mainly on skis in winter and claimed he could make better time than a saddle horse. Once, coming down a steep slope at a fast clip, he sped right between two moose standing dozing in the sun!

When the profit went out of trapping, Helge abandoned his line for ranch work at Quilchena for a few years. He returned to Big Creek in the 1960s, living in a cabin at Churches, Duane Witte's, and Guenther and Tilly's.

After passing 70, Helge was married for the first time, and then divorced. He became friendly with an exotic young dancer whom he met in Williams Lake and within a short time they were

Trapper Dave Munro at Henry's, setting off for the trapline to get ready for winter.

married. His young wife decided immediately to further her education and Helge paid her way at a college in Oregon until she finished her studies. Then, when she refused to come and live with him in the Chilcotin, he divorced her.

Finally Helge moved into the Frontier Village in Quesnel. He did not easily surrender to advancing years and failing health but cancer eventually took its toll. He died in 1983 at 81.

TRAPLINE MEMORIES
by Dave Munro

After arriving in the Cariboo in 1941 I stayed in Williams Lake for a couple of weeks, bought two horses, then headed for Alexis Creek. There I met Walter Bailey who was a Provincial Policeman, in those days also the Game Warden. I told him what I had in mind concerning trapping. We discovered there was a trapline open on the Taseko Lake watershed, also open country on the Big Creek headwaters. I applied for and got a 20-square mile block covering a large area right to the Bridge River, on the Taseko divide.

That first fall I took my horses across country from Alexis Creek to Taseko River on Chilco range. I then followed the road to the north end of Taseko Lake, thence the trail up the lake to where it branched off through Chita Meadows and back to the south end of the lake. There was a vacant cabin at the head of the lake owned by some friends of mine in Bridge River, so I took possession of it for the winter.

I helped Gay Bayliff round up his cattle from the Yohetta Valley range that fall and left my horses with him to winter. Tommy Lee of Alexis Creek Store drove me and my winter's grub back into Whitewater (Taseko) Lake and I took my supplies up the lake in a boat.

That first winter I set out traplines on several creeks and lived in a tent camp on Powell Creek. I built the main central cabin for the whole trapping area that winter. The first winter, while I made a fairly good catch, I discovered that the old original line was very run down and trapped out. Some of the cabins were rat infested and in poor shape, but some had a good supply of traps and snares, also canned food, sugar, flour and other supplies. As well as building the main cabin, I did some exploring, trapping and cutting new lines so I was kept busy all winter.

During my years trapping in the area I had two memorable encounters with bears and one with a cache of dynamite. The first bear encounter was in November 1943.

The early winter trapping season was at hand. The deer all migrate out of the high country in early September, so by the time I had got back into the trapline the deer were all gone to winter on Lower Big Creek, Chilcotin River and along the Fraser River bunchgrass range. I was out of meat and had my eye on a herd of mountain goats on an open bench far up the mountainside across the Whitewater Lake. There was only a skiff of snow and on some open spots it had melted off.

Through the binoculars I could see about a dozen goats, some bedded down, others browsing. So I struck off across the end of the lake to the far side at the foot of the ridge. Keeping down wind and out of sight, I was able to get to within 300 yards of them. I noticed something seemed to disturb them as they all started to move. I fired a few shots but never got one, so I went on up to see if there was any sign of blood, or whether something else had scared them. I came across a bit of fresh blood and noticed what looked like cougar tracks.

Most of the snow was gone on the open flat bench, but I managed to track the animal to a cave at the foot of a small cliff. The cave went down on a slant, then around a bend. I was not able to see what was in there, so I piled large rocks in the entrance to block it off and went home.

The next morning I came back with a .22 rifle, snares and a flashlight. I removed the rocks and pushed the gun and light ahead of me and belly crawled down into the cave – plenty scared, too! All I could see was a ball of fur and one green eye. I still didn't know what it was, so lined the flashlight along the sights and aimed for a spot three inches west of the eye. I squeezed one off and scrambled out, rifle ready. There was a growling and threshing noise so I waited a long time and nothing came out.

I finally got up enough nerve to poke my head down for another shot; but first I had got a springy pole and shoved it around the corner, encountering a soft yielding body, but no movement. So I took two snares and the light down the hole and got the snare around one leg and backed out, tugged and pulled mightily for some time before the body yielded and started to come up. When it got to where I could get a good look I discovered it was a two-year-old cinnamon bear. I skinned it and there was about three-quarters of an inch of fat all over the back of the hide.

With the bear hide rolled up and lashed to the packboard, along with the rest of the gear I had with me, I struggled down the mountainside with a backpack of about 65 pounds.

I stretched the hide on a frame to cool and set to with a sharp knife to carefully peel the fat off in one big sheet. I cut up and rendered it down and it supplied me with the best of bear grease for the next three years – the very best for pies, frying, doughnuts and boot grease.

My next bear encounter occurred one warm spring morning in late May when I decided to survey and cut out a good pack trail up through the Powell Creek Valley to timberline. My main cabin was in Powell Valley. The year before, I had built a drift fence about a half mile above and below the cabin, enclosing an area that provided excellent pasture and water for the horses all summer.

When leaving the cabin that morning I took nothing but a light saddle axe, leaving my rifle leaning against the cabin wall. Within two hours I had finished blazing the trail to timberline and before me lay a big green, grassy valley leading up an easy grade to Powell Pass – truly a beautiful sight. Gently rolling alpine hills, clean, fresh water ponds, and many tiny streams tumbling down the mountainside, glistening in the sun, and the smell of spring in the clean mountain air.

Powell is an easy pass, only a little over 7,000 feet, with grassy open country on the summit. Colonies of big hoary marmots live here, commonly called whistlers because that's what they do best. Coming down from the pass with the sun behind me, I saw what looked like a black bear at the foot of the mountain to the northwest.

At the time I had a useless mongrel pup trailing along whose only ambition was chasing deer, a habit I couldn't cure him of. I tried to sic the mutt onto the bear but he came back, tail between his legs.

I thought no more about it as I slowly wended my way down the trail, blazing the trees on the down side. I noticed a small pine with the top broken off and all the bark chewed off the top end. I thought, "That's the work of an angry bear and he must be going down the trail ahead of me."

About a hundred yards farther on, the trail went through some thick, bushy balsam and pine. Around a bend in the trail, in a little natural opening, stood one of the biggest silvertip grizzly bears I have ever seen. I tried to scare him by shouting, but to no avail. He stood up, huge front legs waving, growling, his teeth snapping and popping – a horrible sound!

The hair on the back of my neck stood straight up. I was never so scared in my life. My horse just stood there like a placid dummy. It was one I had bought from Dan Buckley at the Chimney Creek Ranch where black bears were common and horses paid them no attention. As I quickly broke off a willow switch to whip up the horse and dodge past, the bear dropped down on all fours and came after us. I cut back and forth among the thickets in an attempt to get out of his sight and finally eluded him.

I knew the bear would keep coming down the trail, so leaving the horse at the cabin, I grabbed the loaded rifle and hastened back to the first wide opening. I hid behind a big pine on the edge of the slide. I knew the bear would stop to look around when he came out on the far side. In about five minutes he came shuffling out, stopped to sniff the air and peer around.

At about 100 yards I zeroed in on a light spot below his chin and squeezed off a round. With the crash of the rifle shot he dropped like a sack of lead. Then in about half a minute he lunged up on his hind legs with a blood curdling roar like I'd never heard before. I was so taken aback for a moment I failed to take advantage of the big target he presented. He bawled and beat his chest in a terrible rage, then fell back on all fours. Just as he turned to head for cover in the thick willows I hit him again. He disappeared in the willows. By now twilight was coming on and nobody in his right mind would follow a wounded grizzly into thick bush without a good bear dog.

Next morning I very cautiously took up the bear's trail. There was a little blood to follow. His tracks lead through a maze of scrub willow, ferns and marestail going towards the creek. He had plunged down the steep bank into the creek. He stayed there awhile, walking upstream for a ways. He then left the creek as the water was ice cold, and plowed his way up through the thick brush to higher ground. By this time I was getting a mite skittish, somewhat nervous and edgy. I moved down wind, climbed up onto a rock bluff overlooking the area where he had left the creek. I craned my neck and peered around for a long time before I saw some alder saplings twitching down below and upstream.

I watched and waited patiently and finally he came slowly in sight. I took careful aim, put a shot into his rib cage just behind his shoulder. He threshed around and soon lay still. I never had anymore bear trouble on Powell Creek as long as I was there. But I did have a memorable experience with some over-age dynamite.

The Taylor Windfall gold mine was situated almost in the center of my trapline. By the time I had taken up the trapline in 1941 the mine was shut down and deserted. They just went away and left everything intact. All doors and tunnels had padlocks on them. It had been a very well-equipped mine. They had a powerful six-inch nozzle "pelton wheel" hydro unit for power. This provided electric power for the entire mine and many buildings. It also drove a large compressor to supply air to the drills, stoppers and air hoists and ventilation ducts. They also had a water-driven sawmill out on the open flat below the mine entrance. About 100 yards from the hydro unit was a double wall, insulated powder house with a secure lock on the door.

I realized as the years went by and no sign that the mine would reopen, that the dynamite in the powder house was getting over age and dangerous to use for anyone not familiar with handling it. The glycerine comes out and forms jelly-like beads on the sticks.

On an early fall trip into Williams Lake I went to see the mine inspector and told him about the dangerous over-age blasting powder at the Taylor Windfall mine. I told him I wished to blow it up and get rid of it. Since I had had many years experience handling powder, he gladly gave me permission as it would save him a trip.

Two years previously I had discovered a small hidden "grub cache" cabin on my trapline. It had a stout padlock and no windows. My curiosity eventually overcame the locked door. Inside was a treasure trove of goodies. There were traps of all sizes hung in neat bunches along the walls. There were axes, saws, tools of all kinds, spikes, nails, and other building materials. Also a big grub box with flour, sugar, jam, beans, rice, coffee, salt and much more – enough grub for the entire winter season. Years later I met and talked to the old man who had to leave it behind. While scrounging around in the cabin I discovered four, 50-pound boxes of dynamite packed in dry sawdust, also several boxes of blasting caps and coils of black fuse. As part of my plan to blow up the powder house at the Taylor Windfall, I went to the cabin and got four sticks of dynamite and two 3-foot fuses and took them to the mine. Inside the powder house there were about 20 cases of powder, some had been opened and were only half full. I stacked the boxes all in a pile, placed the four good sticks, caps and fuse in one open box at the bottom of the pile and lit the fuse. Then I ran towards the river – I had three minutes to get in the clear.

After I had got about 100 yards a blast of air hit me in the rear end, followed by a thunderous crashing boom. The echoes reverberated round and round the valley like a giant drumroll. I fell, got up and looked back to see a large column of black dirt and fine lumber debris shooting high in the sky. All the snow was blown off the trees for 100 yards all around and the snow on the hillsides was blackened from the huge cloud of blue smoke. After the echoes had died away I walked back to see the destruction. The ground was bare and black for 50 yards all around and there was now a deep crater where the powder house had stood.

Nobody could now blow himself up with the over-age and unstable dynamite.

Perhaps my most memorable experience was when I almost starved to death. It happened one spring when, after trapping all winter by myself, I was ready to come out of the mountains with my catch. I had made my way down to the head of the lake, bringing with me my furs, rifle, bedroll and what food I figured I would need to get me out to civilization. Upon my arrival at the lake I found the ice was still pretty solid, a month late in going out. However, I decided the best thing was to wait it out rather than walk, carrying all my gear the long trail around.

By now my food supply was nearly gone and I was rationing out the little bit of rice I had left. I began to realize that the situation could become critical and I was becoming weak. I knew there was an old trap cabin in the middle of Chita Meadows about four miles away, so decided to see if I could make it over there and hoped there might be some grub left there. In my weakened condition it was a hard struggle to make the trip as there was still big patches of snow and water to wade through. However, I made it to the cabin, pried the lock off and got in. There were several pounds of rice and beans, a little musty flour and a bit of sugar and jam. I helped myself, then locked the door and started back to my camp. It took me two hours to get back to the cabin on the lake.

Along towards the end of May the weather was sunny and warm, and the thick lake ice was becoming mushy and rotten. I had put the old rowboat into the creek near the cabin to soak up tight for the trip down lake. Next afternoon a strong southwest wind came down the Lord River valley. The ice started to creak and groan and the open water where the rivers flowed into the lake started to widen. My hopes soared like a hawk. I knew with enough wind the ice would soon be gone.

That day I had everything packed and ready to load the boat and start out next morning. After an almost sleepless night I was awakened by the loud honking of Canada geese. Across the bay a large flock of geese had landed to rest where the lake was a mirror of open water. Far down the lake the receding ice was visible, only the bottleneck at the first narrows holding it back.

Within a short time, I had the boat loaded, had boarded up the cabin windows, locked the door and was away. In the four hours it took to row the five miles to the narrows the ice had cleared out of the upper lake. I was very tired by then, so went ashore and made a fire to boil some tea and eat a chunk of bannock, and rested for a couple of hours in the warm sun.

Far down the lake at "Windy Point" the large ice mass was visible from shore to shore. I made fairly good time rowing. By late afternoon the ice had cleared "Windy Point" narrows. Round the bluff in a little cove I camped for the night on a little sandy beach. There was plenty of dry driftwood handy and it was out of the wind. In the middle of the night I was rudely awakened by a very large porcupine chewing on my axe handle. I thought at first it was a bear, scared the hell out of me, he was within three feet of my face. I shouted at him and he rapidly climbed a dead tree nearby. He was gone in the morning.

I was up at sunrise, a nice sunny morning. The ice was still visible about 10 miles down the lake. The lake is very wide from Windy Point on down, so to be safe I skirted the shore line on the east side. By late afternoon I could see the log wharf at the end of the lake, a welcome sight.

On the shore there was a cowboy watering horses. By the time I reached the wharf the sun had gone down behind Mt. Tatlow and the beach was empty. I tied up the boat and walked up the trail through the thick spruce grove to a small meadow. There, a white tent was pitched under a spruce tree and two people cooking supper. It was Alex and Anne Paxton. Boy, was I ever glad to see them. They asked me to stop for supper. I was sure glad to. Anne is a top-notch cook as well as a very good cowgirl and horsewoman. They were Chilco Ranch's top range riders at the time. They had a string of pack horses and a black dog and had just finished putting out block salt on the meadows and near waterholes on the range.

The next morning I packed my fur and gear over to Paxton's camp. Alex was saddling up while Anne was breaking camp. In half an hour we were on our way to Stobie Meadow cabin, about half way to Chilco Ranch. We stopped overnight there. The next day they gave me a ride to Chilco Ranch.

From there I shouldered my pack and walked over to Hanceville where the Hance brothers had a fine ranch, store and post office. I stayed there overnight and next day got a ride into Williams Lake with Rene Hance.

Later in the day I was walking along Main Street and I met an R.C.M.P. officer whom I had never seen before. He stopped me and said, "Oh! I see you made it out from the Whitewater."

He had heard I was a month overdue. I guess he could tell who I was by my long hair and unkempt appearance. He could probably also smell me coming up wind.

I continued on my isolated trapline for a number of years. Then after a very good fur catch in the 1949-50 season, I sold the trapline to Johnny Murdoch and left the Chilcotin to buy a timber farm at Little Fort, 60 miles north of Kamloops.

BILL TYMOCHKO was a trapper in the Big Creek Country. What was unique about Bill when he trapped up Big Creek in the 1950s was that he used a dog team which was unusual in that part of the country. The following account was written by Hazel Henry and appeared in one of the local papers.

"When Bill Tymochko comes out from his trapline to get supplies at the Big Creek Store he harnesses up his dog team, hitches them to the toboggan, jumps on himself and away they race at full speed if the road is smooth and packed. With good going it usually takes 2-1/2 hours to cover the approximate 20 miles from his cabin at Gus Piltz's Sky Ranch to Big Creek. This sounds like the kind of outdoor fun every schoolboy dreams about but is not always so easy.

"Where there is no trail or new or drifted snow, Tymochko has to go ahead on snowshoes to break a trail for the dogs. In steep and sidehill places, the toboggan often tips over, causing considerable confusion and delay.

"This country is not ideal for dog teams, Tymochko says, as his route often takes him along sidehills and across open meadows where drifting snow makes it necessary to be constantly breaking out a new path. By contrast, in flat areas with a trapline running through timbered country, once a trail is broken it remains for most of the winter.

"The three dogs that Tymochko uses are of indefinite breeding. The lead dog is an intelligent looking black and white part Husky, the middle one is a large, rather mean dog and looks as though he may be part Redbone hound, while the third has the appearance of a Collie. They are broke to "gee" and "haw" and "straight ahead." Going downhill in steep places where the snow is packed Tymochko just clings to the toboggan and hopes for the best. When he has to slow down, he

Bill Tymochko's dog team photographed at Henry's Pinto Ranch.

does so by dragging his heels into the snow, using them as brakes.

"Bill has given up his lonely life on the trapline at various times to try other ways of making a living but has always returned to it. Once again, he says he believes he will try for his fortune in some other occupation. But if he does there doubtless will come a day when he'll take his snowshoes and traps off the wall, and with a far-away dream in his eyes begin to plan where he'll try his next trapping venture."

Bruin Makes Good Escape
Big Creek – 1955 by Veera Bonner in the
Williams Lake Tribune

Out bear hunting last week with Al West of the Predator Control Branch, Cecil Henry had the unusual and exciting experience of a panicky bruin going right between his horse's legs. It seems the dogs were crowding Mr. Bear and, as Cecil rushed in to get a shot, the bear ducked back and made his get-away underneath Cecil's mount.

Cecil Henry at the Circle A Meadow. Cecil was known in the cow camp as "Hungry Johnny."

It was good strategy on the part of the bear: how can you shoot a bundle of fur when he's under your plunging bronc? And by the time that terrified cow horse had stopped bucking, bruin had had plenty of time to disappear. Anyway, Cecil was probably so busy staying in the saddle and congratulating himself on it that he'd lost all interest in bear hunting!

In addition to bears and moose which added variety to ranch life, the Church Ranch kept meteorological records. Mrs. Church, above, doing the daily instrument check.

THE MOOSE CAME BACK AGAIN
by Mrs. Hazel Henry
Published in *Wildlife Review* when Bill Ward was editor.

The winter of 1955-56 marked the fifth in succession that a bull moose came back to put in the winter around Churchs' feed yard at Big Creek. It began in 1952 when he brought a cow and two calves along. Adam Wroblewski and Bill Johnson were feeding cattle that year and began giving the moose their breakfast of hay. The animals gradually became more and more tame. They would soon eat hay from the hands of the men and allow themselves to be touched about the head.

When I went to see them we drove down across Big Creek and over the open fields with the feeding team hitched to the sleigh. At the stackyard we could not see a moose anywhere. There was complete silence – not a sign of life. Maybe we wouldn't see the moose after all. Then came two calves which were in a hurry and snapped a twig here and there.

They were slightly alarmed at first to see so many humans (we had brought six children) but they forgot about us when Adam advanced with an armful of hay. The moose were soon fighting among themselves, their front feet slashing viciously with lightning rapidity. Then they would rear up on their hind feet and strike

The moose became tame enough to let us touch them.

Young moose kneeling to eat the forked-out hay at Church's ranch.

at each other. The cow was a scarred-up old girl and looked particularly mean. She would lay back her ears and make a run at the calves, which lost no time in getting out of her way. The bull was the gentlest of them all and, before we left, we all had the thrill of having him eat from our hands and allowing us to touch his head.

As spring approached the moose became restless and lost interest in us. Earlier, Adam and Bill had made name plaques and fastened them around the necks of the animals. They soon took off for the bush. When they returned in 1953 the cow still had her name plate but the bull had lost his. They came again in 1954 but were late and we didn't see them until March. They were as gentle then as they had been the first year.

In the fall of 1954 back they came again, this time being seven strong. The old bull was still the gentlest of all. He watched with keen interest as game biologist Lawson Sugden took pictures, letting him approach within a few feet without showing alarm. When the movie camera whirred, the bull trotted off a short distance and stood stiff-legged for a minute but soon moved back to continue munching on the hay.

The winter of 1955-56 was a tough one. Eleven moose showed up at Church's feed ground and ate with the cattle all winter. The same old bull was there but the cow had disappeared. Actually they became something of a nuisance. They began to think they were the Boss around there and sometimes refused to move for the team and sleigh. It would be interesting to know how far away they roam in summer and by what strange instinct they know when they are safe from man and when they are in danger.

TO SUCH AS SHE
for Hazel

I saw her standing by the fire there
As we drew near,
The soft wind blowing softly through her hair,
As other years
When autumn skies bent blue above this tent
She too has stood
While crisp clear air grew fragrant with the scent
Of burning wood.
And on her cheeks glowed tints of brown and rose
From wind's clean hand,
And in her eyes shone rich content of those
Who love the land.

And that these hills belong to such as she
Full well I knew, who know their loneliness and height to be
A goodness, too.
Who "look unto the hills" for strength and hold
Him near always,
Who are kin to trail and saddle and the gold
September days;
Who love the wind tossed night, and pause to hear
The soft sweet stir
Of blowing pine, for all these are a dear
Deep part of her.

Veera Bonner

Scenes familiar to Chilcotin residents – Bill Woods wonders where the cattle are hiding and, below, author Hazel Litterick boils water for tea at Murray Taylor Lake.

TRAGEDY AND SALVAGE AT LORNA LAKE

Marcel Marcotte and Rudy Johnson kindly gave details for this account.

In October 1960, a tragic accident at the head of Big Creek took the lives of four men when the PWA Beaver they were riding in plunged into the gloomy depths of Lorna Lake.

Lorna Lake lies deep in the Coast Range, south of Graveyard Valley, opposite Sluice Creek, and southwest of Warner Ridge. Three miles long and glacier fed, it is white and cold, deep and dangerous. Sheer rock cliffs rise on the east side of its narrow trench, steep timbered hills on the west. Big Creek flows out of the lake at the north end, taking the lake's milky color.

Pilot Jim Marshall, rated one of the best pilots in Canada and with more hours on a Beaver than any other man in the nation, had flown three oil geologists into the mountainous area, landing on Lorna Lake. The geologists had finished their work and the party

Lorna Lake.

Using a derrick to salvage CF-ICK from the cold waters of Lorna Lake.

was headed home. Marshall lifted the Beaver off the water and was starting to climb when extreme turbulence gusting over Warner Ridge flipped the plane back into the narrow lake. There was no hope for the pilot and his passengers.

When the Beaver was overdue at the Chilcotin Airways float plane base on Williams Lake that October day, Rudy Johnson and

Clarence Moore flew to the western mountains in Johnson's Cessna 180 on floats to make a search. Nothing was visible from the air, but after landing on Lorna Lake the men spotted the tip of the Beaver's tail showing above the water, telling the tragic story.

Moore was ready to dive down into the deep lake in a rescue attempt but after testing the frigid water he admitted that Johnson was right. The water was too cold for survival without proper gear, and the men trapped in the aircraft could not be alive. After securing the tip of the Beaver with rope to an outcropping of rock, Clarence and Rudy taxied up the lake to lift off in the face of the wild wind gusting across the peaks. But takeoff was impossible. Twice they were slapped back onto the water. With no alternative, they tied the Cessna securely at the edge of the storm-tossed lake and spent the windy night under a tree. Next morning they were able to fly out in safety.

Divers recovered the bodies of the four men and the R.C.M.P officer in charge cut the ropes holding the Beaver afloat. "That's the end of that," he said as the plane disappeared. But Rudy Johnson, noted for undertaking difficult ventures, had other ideas.

He bought salvage rights and set about getting the plane out. Dick Church of Big Creek, another man who would try anything, took on the job of bringing overland to Big Creek the tail section, fuselage, and engine. The wings had to be examined for possible defects so these were flown to Vancouver by Air and Sea Rescue. Marcel Marcotte, a competent cat skinner, was working for Dick and agreed to drive Church's TD 9 International on the salvage mission.

They travelled via Sky Ranch and up Big Creek. Beyond the road Dick went ahead on a saddle horse to find a passable route for the cat. They carried two drums of fuel and a scanty camp outfit: rice, Kraft dinner, pots, fry pan, and sleeping bags. Dick shot grouse on the trail for meat. Marcel bulldozed his way with the machine as he went along, but in places on the impossible journey Dick instructed him to drive up the boulder strewn water of Big Creek itself. Here the creek was so narrow between its rocky bluffs that the blade had to be loosened and turned lengthways to get the TD 9 through. It was a tedious, rough trip through the mountains for the two hardy men. They met Rudy Johnson at Lorna Lake.

Rudy had flown in again with Clarence Moore to the scene of the accident. He hired a diver to go down into the water and stash two big deflated truck tubes into the plane. A connected hose was brought to the surface and the inner tubes inflated from a cylinder

CF-ICK on Garibaldi Lake. After the Beaver was rebuilt, Rudy Johnson tested it at the high altitude of this mountain lake in Garibaldi Park north of Squamish.

of air. The buoyant tubes raised the Beaver to the surface. The wreck was then towed by the Cessna across to the timbered north end of the lake and with a derrick pole, blocks and tackle, it was winched with the cat onto a sled made out of spruce logs. The cat was hooked on and Marcel struck off on the trail home. Rudy had extra fuel flown in from Williams Lake. He accompanied Church and Marcotte on the slow, cold trip overland with the aircraft remains.

Half way, the log runners wore out from the rocky ground and had to be replaced. Once on a swamp when the TD 9 was down to the winch and sinking, the men had to tie logs to the cat tracks and lay corduroy as they moved along. The temperature dropped to near 20 below zero before the two-week trip was over but the salvage reached Sky Ranch without damage.

Johnson, with partners Denny McCartney and Johnnie DeVoin, had a shop in Vancouver at the time called Central Aircraft Leasing and Salvage. When the wings were returned to him by the authorities, the Beaver was rebuilt and put back into service. It still flies out of Campbell River.

Central Aircraft Leasing and Salvage was later sold by Rudy and his partners and ended up as ConAir out of Abbotsford.

GOODBYE TO CHILCOTIN-CARIBOO
By Inspector William L. Fernie
B.C. Provincial Police

*When Inspector Fernie retired in 1934 he was in command of C
Division which included the Chilcotin-Cariboo. His attachment to
the region began in the 1890s when he was a Chilcotin cowboy. He
served in both the Boer War and World War One, and during a distinguished 32-year career in the Provincial Police gained fame for
his success in tracking criminals who fled into the wilderness.
Among them was notorious train and stagecoach robber Bill Miner
and several murderers who were later hanged. He was also interested in protecting wildlife and greatly assisted in establishing
Bowron Lake Game Reserve, today Bowron Lake Provincial Park.
His farewell poem appeared in the* Kamloops Sentinal *in 1934.
Inspector Fernie died at Kamloops in 1943 at 73.*

Farewell to far Chilcotin and goodbye to Tatla Lake.
The throughfare that Waddington was not allowed to make
And hunters out at Bowron Lake, who dare the grizzlies' fang,
And trappers at Chilanko Forks, and cowboys at the "The Gang,"
Keep in at dark good people, or, all breathing fire and smoke
You'll see Limpy's sixteen oxen, each coupled with their yoke.
Don't speed around sharp curves at night, or you may meet and spill!
Steve Tingley with his coach and four, tooling to Barkerville;
And the clanging bells you hear are, with ghostly manteaued load
The packtrain of Old Cataline, strung out along the road.

If at Barkerville's old graveyard you cast a friendly glance
You'll see tombs of men from Germany, from England and from France,
From Denmark, Norway, Sweden, and from Alsace and Lorraine
From Austria and Hungary, from Portugal and Spain,
All men of different languages, by God's will once dispersed –
Surely the camp at Barkerville was Babylon reversed.
Here Judge Begbie gave his dictum – "Killers will surely rue,
For those who slay in this northland, there will be hanging too."
If miners covet all the gold, they'll take the people true
For gold is in the hearts of those who toil in Cariboo.

Goodbye! Good folks ... I leave you with a sigh,
My heart aches as I say it, but "Klahowya" and "Goodbye";
Farewell now to the "Mountain" ... I'll never traverse more
And struggle to the "The Hundred Mile," or, south to "Seventy-four,"

Inspector W. L. Fernie and a
B.C. Provincial Policeman.
Although the Force was born
in 1858, until uniforms were
adopted in 1924 officers had
only a badge for identification.

For each of us the time's arrived, to go a different way
I leave you, and I love you – that is all that I can say;
Goodbye! Goodbye! ... Klahowya and Farewell.
Where careless of the winter and comparatively few
The kindest-hearted people dwell – the folks of Chilcotin-Cariboo.

INDEX

RIDIN' THROUGH
Veera Bonner

We don't make permanent camp here,
We're only ridin' through –
The dusty road of earth, one day,
Will end for me and you.

When the going's good and friends are near
And the view around is fine,
We sometimes think that we'd like to camp
And stay for a long, long time.

But there's no use picking a homesite out
Where the grass is green and new
For you can't unsaddle and stake a claim –
We're only ridin' through.

When the way is rough and the hills are bare
And storms shut out the sun,
When we face the awful night alone
As the stars die, one by one;

It helps a bit to remember then
That skies will be bright and blue
In that Other Land where the Master waits –
We're only ridin' through.

We cannot tell how long the trail
Nor what the terrain will be,
But we know through faith there's an open gate
At the end for you and me.